THE LONGEST MILE

THE
LONGEST MILE

Rena Gazaway

DOUBLEDAY & COMPANY, INC., GARDEN CITY, NEW YORK

1969

The author is grateful to
Gladys Pritchard for her help
in preparing this book.

EXTENSION

Library of Congress Catalog Card Number 69–15177
Copyright © 1969 by Rena Gazaway
All Rights Reserved
Printed in the United States of America
First Edition

Contents

THE LONGEST MILE

The Way In

Joanthin was sitting on her rickety porch, passively examining the Appalachian Mountains. I joined her, plopped into a cane-bottomed chair that boasted little cane, and led around slowly to the purpose of my visit. A survey had failed to yield information regarding the exact number of children she had borne—information that was essential. By now my relationship with her was established firmly enough to broach the subject.

"I heard you have nine children, Joanthin," I began.

"Yep."

She resumed her listless inspection of the Kentucky peaks. The long silence that followed her response and the warm sun produced a hypnotic effect on me. My eyelids began to droop.

"Heap 'a 'em's daid," she suddenly announced. "Some 'uz daid afore they 'uz a-breathin'."

I snapped to attention and waited expectantly. Minutes passed.

"W'en Clem 'uz a-livin', 'e could keep th' younguns close by."

Another soporific lull. I tilted my chair against the wall, unable to resist the combination of heat and hush. An energetic fly interrupted my nap and I directed a feeble swat in its vicinity. This sluggish activity galvanized Joanthin into speech.

"Younguns 'at's left out [gone away] hain't th' same 's 'em 'at's stayed."

I almost resented her intrusion on the stillness.

"But they're still your children and part of your family," I responded.

"Reckon."

Refreshed by the pause that attended this brief outburst, I rallied within a few minutes and started to make my departure.

"'Ceptin' w'en you's not eagle-eyin' 'em, you's hain't sure you's claimin' 'em," she called after me.

Days—nay, weeks—later I obtained an idea of the approximate size of her family. I was intent upon my goal, to understand from firsthand contact a depressed Appalachian area and its people. Weeks can become months in the hill country of Kentucky, where time is uncontrollable, and of little consequence. But piece by piece the information and insight I sought emerged out of delays, irrelevancies, and frustration, out of many days with many Joanthins.

My concern was the general sociologic problems of a neighborhood inhabited by families of a lower-strata minority group who lacked the prestige, courage, or personal resources to improve substantially their living pattern. It represented the chance to explore questions that had nagged me for years. Why, for instance, in the richest country on earth were these people so embedded in the muck of privation? How did socioeconomic and cultural factors merge to create the abysmal barrier between them and the Great Society? Many had attempted studies, but they served only to intensify my curiosity. Although they supplied a plethora of statistics, they fell disappointingly short of describing the manner in which the "modern" mountaineer functioned within his home and habitat.

I had always felt a deep interest and concern for the mountaineer, sentiments that were specifically stimulated by two factors. One was his striking similarity to the American Indian. I made my first trip to a reservation in a Model T Ford many years ago. Subsequently, I had observed conditions all over the United States: the Cherokee, the Zuñi, the Navajo, the Hopi—each unique yet indistinguishable in the detached life of enforced deprivation. I lived in pueblos and helped make adobe bricks. I ate their food and slept with them. I was enthralled by their dances and ceremonies. The symbolism and significance of their beautiful sand paintings was awe-inspiring. The sight of the swollen-bellied, barefooted, dirty, scantily clothed, somber children left me desolated.

Although the chief was recognized by members of his tribe as the leader, his influence with the outside world was notably limited. One told me years ago, "The government is going to make a tourist attraction of us." He is dead now, but I am confident that he would not find solace in the knowledge that his prophecy came true.

"It isn't too bad as long as we stay in these hills or on reservations," he conceded, "but we can't progress. We live little better than our ancestors."

The situation remains almost unchanged. Indian reservations and mountain hollows are much the same as they were half a century ago: stagnant, stifled, and shunned.

My second link with the mountaineer is deeper still. The decision to involve myself was a natural one, for I am a product of a similar environment. Were it not for the grim determination of my father that I be educated, I could have been one of the subjects of the investigation in this book instead of the investigator.

This book extends an invitation to enter a world apart from the one which you and I inhabit, where policy is made and politics are played. I can only offer my vision and my experiences, and for that reason it becomes relevant to invite you into the background of my own formative years as well before we travel on.

Measured by twentieth-century standards, I grew up in a deprived setting in Missouri. For many years I was curiously unaware of the stigma attached to this circumstance. Life in our hollow was pretty much the same for everyone—we were all poor. My parents rarely discussed material possessions or riches, but self-sufficiency and the ability to survive were personal traits highly valued by them. I was only three or four years of age when my instruction in resourcefulness was begun. My father had an unending store of hair-raising tales of inadequacy which were calculated to make an indelible impression: a man froze to death because his knife was too dull to cut tree limbs for a fire; another man, whose knife was sharp enough, did not know how to start a fire without matches. We had no money to waste on matches. Consequently, at an early age I became an expert in the use of flint and was never without a bounteous supply of the precious stone, in saddlebag and coat pocket, in the smokehouse and in the kitchen cupboard—everywhere I could anticipate that I might need it.

Happily, Father's tutoring was not restricted to bloodcurdling yarns woven around the theme of survival. He taught me to play tennis, to swim, to run, and to hit and catch a baseball. I could outdistance any of my peers, collect more home runs, and swim for longer periods. Despite his obvious pride in my athletic prowess, I was not encouraged to place emphasis on these activities. The only skill he fully developed and refined was my ability to shoot a rifle with deadly accuracy, a feat I had accomplished before I was five years old. From the first day of school until I became fourteen, a rifle and Maude, one of our plow horses, were my constant companions.

I attended a one-room school located in the mouth of a hollow, a few yards off a "black gumbo" road. It was sparsely furnished and the student body, which seldom exceeded twenty pupils, hung their wraps on nails. Overshoes were arranged in an orderly row just inside the door, but I never owned a pair to add to the collection. My feet were protected by gunny sacks lined with a thick coating of beeswax. Educating a child did not impose a financial burden on my parents. The saddle for Maude was fashioned from quilted gunny sacks and the saddlebags from two more sacks tucked under the "saddle." My lunch bucket was a Prince Albert tobacco can, an ideal receptacle for sausage patties. Each morning I would don my "galoshes," "saddle" Maude, tuck my lunch into the saddlebag, and trot off to school in a blaze of gunny-sack glory.

Two pupils (by gender, not by school grade) shared one desk. A potbellied stove, which occupied a rear corner of the small room, and the teacher's table and chair completed the furnishings. The walls that did not accommodate coats, stocking caps, and mufflers were garnished with the Father of our Country, a dour Abraham Lincoln, a tantalizing map of the world, and several examples of student art which varied in artistic degree and with season. A tree limb, nailed to the floor, served as the pole from which a faded flag hung in weary folds. Although it had lost the vigor of its colors, it retained the power to inspire us with reverence and every morning we would recite the Pledge of Allegiance in emotion-charged voices. This was followed by a less fervent recitation of the Lord's Prayer and the Ten Commandments. After that, the daily chores had to be performed. They were listed on the blackboard, which consisted of a huge piece of brown wrapping paper: sweep out the room; draw a bucket of water; fetch coal; unharness, water, and feed the teacher's horse; carry in kindling. Finally, we were ready for the serious business of learning. The curriculum was limited to reading, writing, arithmetic, and spelling. Everything was written on the blackboard —we had no textbooks. Drawing we looked upon as an entertainment exercise.

School began late in the fall and ended early in the spring because every student had to help during plowing and with the planting and harvesting; our education also came to a halt during slaughtering and canning time. Accordingly, everyone crammed all the learning he could into the brief academic year. Most of our instruction was delivered during the cold winter months and the abdominous stove rarely nudged the inside temperature above fifty degrees. We would gather around its iron sides and when we had thawed enough to bend in the middle we would take our seats, ruthlessly disregarding frosty fingers and icy toes.

I had the same teacher through the first eight grades. She was strict, but the students held her in great esteem and treated her with unwavering respect. We would vie for the honor of unhitching her horse from the buggy, both of which had been donated by the McBath family as their contribution to her salary for teaching their children. At one time there were eight McBaths in school. I rather fancied Lawrence but my parents were stern and would not indulge my youthful passion; there were too many goals ahead, too many more years of indoctrination for my future.

"What you amount to in this life, only you can control. But it is my responsibility to prepare you with a high school and college education," Father rumbled.

At that time I did not even know what the word "college" meant, but I was well grounded in the philosophy of obedience, sacrifice, and discipline. If a pupil were paddled or banished from the classroom for ten minutes, the teacher expected him to notify his parents of his misdeed. I reported the only paddling I ever received and my father promptly favored me with another sampling of the same treatment.

After putting aside the razor strop, he looked at me with disgust.

"What did you do to deserve a whipping?"

"Well, well . . ."

"Get to the point!"

"The teacher said I . . ."

"Don't tell me what the *teacher* said you did. I don't care about that. I want to know what *you* say you did!"

Long before I started to school I had learned that there was no acceptable substitute for truth and that integrity could not be compromised. Once my father gave an account of his expectations, he did not propose to repeat his guidelines for behavior. "Foolishness," as he defined it, would not be tolerated in a child he housed, clothed, and fed.

Rain, snow, mud, flooding of the hollow—none of these was a legitimate reason to entertain the thought of staying home. We had an alarm clock, a devilish mechanism, perpetually set for 4:00 A.M., thus allowing me time to finish my chores and be back in the house by five-thirty. While I thawed out on a homemade stool behind the big cookstove, Father would read the Bible aloud, after which I would have breakfast and go to school. Most of my commuting was done in the dark, mornings as well as evenings. In good weather Maude and I would journey alone. When the weather was threatening and it appeared that I might not make it back home that night, our other horse accompanied us to carry grain and to substitute as a mode of transport should Maude run out of gas somewhere along the eight-mile round trip. In the course of our dark, lonely travels, I would regale my equine friends with original tunes played on a Jew's harp or a harmonica, according to my whim.

One day I left school during a blizzard. The two horses got to within two miles of home before becoming snowbound. After sheltering them I took off on snowshoes my father had made for me, but the petal-soft flakes were coming down so fast and furiously that the landmarks were almost obliterated. I finally made it to a deserted log cabin. In a short while I had a healthy fire blazing in the hearth, but I was lonely and tired and hungry—and most of all I was afraid to lie down; the fire might go out and I would freeze to death in my sleep just as the luckless characters in Father's stories had. I wiped off my rifle and stood it in the corner; it was too dark to shoot anything for supper. I decided to pamper the fire and then began to pace the night away. By the time dawn made its appearance the storm had moved on but the snow it left behind had accumulated to just about a foot from the edge of the roof. After several minutes of struggle, I managed to push the door open wide enough to squeeze through. A rabbit, which had been scurrying along the crusted drifts, made a sudden lunge into the cabin. I was loath to use one of my two shotgun shells on this potential meal, particularly when a piece of firewood was just as effective. With my pocket knife I removed his hide and cut the carcass into six pieces which I roasted. I wolfed down two of the pieces, saved two for my lunch, and kept the other two for my saddlebag as an emergency measure. When I had at last extricated myself from the cabin, I returned to the horses, fed them, and urged them on to school.

I got home the next night just in time to do the chores, and the praise my parents lavished on me for the display of self-sufficiency was intoxicating. I had a fire built in the cookstove, slopped the hogs, fed the chickens, milked the cows, separated the milk, and cleaned the separator before Mother and Father arose the next morning. Wet and shivering, I was taking my place behind the range when they entered the kitchen. Father began his daily routine of Bible reading: "Therefore I say unto you, Take no thought for your life, what ye shall eat, or what ye shall drink; nor yet for your body, what ye shall put on. Is not the life more than meat, and the body more than raiment?" (Matthew 6:25). "For the Lord giveth wisdom: out of His mouth cometh knowledge and understanding" (Proverbs 2:6). "Thou shalt not be afraid for the terror by night; nor for the arrow that flieth by day" (Psalms 91:5). "If ye shall ask any thing in My name, I will do it. If ye love Me, keep My commandments" (John 14:14–15). "I will not leave you comfortless: I will come to you" (John 14:18).

That childhood view of life was threatened the day Father announced that we were going to move in order that I might continue my education beyond the eighth grade. My protestations went unheeded. The small high school was located three miles from our new home and I had to walk both ways—none of the students rode a horse. The complexities of the different environment were staggering; I had no friends, I spoke a language few seemed to understand, I was never able to relate to the efficient, impersonal teachers; every facet of my existence was strange. The students laughed at my cotton stockings, the cold fried egg sandwiches I brought for lunch, the knit petticoats and bloomers I wore. Prior to my high school days I had never seen an inside toilet, lockers, showers. I was submerged in "black gumbo" of a different type. Nothing was familiar in this setting except my home routine. We still lived on a farm, but we had more of everything: more land to be plowed, more canning to be done, more manure to spread, more hay to get into the mow, more corn to shock, more feed to grind by hand—endless hours of labor necessary for our survival.

Not until we moved did I realize that a financial and social structure existed; I had always assumed that everyone lived the way we did. Not until I had completed education in nursing and anthropology did I understand the full extent of the social and financial structure. Not until I began research to investigate the needy hollower did I start to question my insight into poverty. The world of Duddie's Branch opened new avenues of thought, just as the context of a childhood in one hollow lay behind experience of life in another.

Was there a difference between a poor individual and an individual living in poverty? My family was poor and work was essential if we were to live. It was also the one thing that could remove you from the category of "poor." Then there was knowledge. The two kinds of learning, in order of importance, were: (1) school learning and (2) learning to do, to be, and to accomplish. I learned to do everything necessary in daily life. Learning to do resulted in accomplishment. I learned to be worthy of respect: honest, trustworthy, a friend, a good neighbor. I learned to share what I had without expecting payment. I took pride in everything I did and tried to excel. Never once did I feel defective, inadequate; never once did I feel that there were people better than I.

As I grew older the word "poverty" was introduced into my vocabulary. What did "poverty" mean? There were times when I didn't have enough food to fill my stomach, but what is enough? I lacked the necessities of life, but did I mistake comforts for necessities? I endured hardships, but so did the pioneers. Did they live in poverty? My clothing was threadbare and patched, but it was clean. Are these things reflective of poverty or of privation? We didn't have money and our possessions weren't worth much, but we weren't living in poverty—we were just poor.

Today's hollow dweller is a species different from the hollow dweller of my youth. This fact first impressed itself upon me as I came to know the hollow people of urban slums in Kansas City, Chicago, New York, Cincinnati. My long association with hill people who came to Cincinnati to live was especially enriching. The warm feeling they felt for whatever place it was they left behind made me wonder what it was like. Where did they learn the words they used? What did the words mean? If their lives were so satisfying before they came to the city, why did they leave? People ridiculed them. True, they were deficient, but only as measured by the functional yardstick of an urban setting and middle-class standards. Although they worked hard, they failed to get ahead. Things kept happening to them, things over which they had no control. It was as if they were in a small boat, buffeted by the sea of human values. How could they contribute anything? They had no place to anchor. They were constantly bobbing around in a social system that never gave them a voice in their destiny. They didn't want to change; they didn't like the city. They just wanted to get enough money together to rectify their mistake by going back home.

I often visited a relocated hill family that lived in a dark, damp, two-room basement apartment. Their residence had no windows and the only sunlight that ever entered was a golden thread that sneaked in through a two-inch space at the bottom of the door. My calls were celebrated by replacing the 25-watt light bulb with one twice as strong. "Reckon 's long 's we's jist settin', hain't needin' seein'." I was almost blinded upon re-entering the world of sunlight. The mother kept the door closed to prevent the "creepers" (the smaller children) from going out. Two broken concrete steps beyond the scarred door was a busy intercity street.

The "walkers" and I frequently went to the zoo, and sometimes parents, grandparents, and the "totin'" kids would come along. Once I borrowed a station wagon and we all went to the art museum. They weren't exactly sure what that could be, but they were willing to go anywhere with me. We ascended the stairs and entered the striking formal foyer. I had been there many times and knew my way around. As I held out the admission fee, the attendant intimated that we were in the wrong place. I assured the distressed man that we knew where we were but he refused to take my money and quietly suggested that we just look around the foyer and leave. We disregarded his request and walked through every gallery. On the way out, the frustrated man informed me that we owed an admission fee. I reminded him of my offer to pay when we entered and made it clear that I had no intention of paying a dismissal fee. As we left, Larry said, "I likes th' other kind 'a zoo better. The animals were nicer, too."

Several weekends later they included me in a trip they were going to make. The only thing I was asked to contribute was the borrowed station wagon. The generous friend who loaned it was, by this time, beginning to hint broadly that I buy a car of my own. He complained that his was beginning to smell vile and that his family refused to ride in it. He accused me of using it to transport something dead. I had tried to mask the stench of unbathed bodies with air freshener, but the pungent odor had permeated the upholstery.

We started out at 4:00 P.M.

"You's knowin' how t' git t' Kaintuck?" Herman wanted to know.

"Where in Kentucky?" I countered.

"Home," he replied.

"Where is home?"

"Hit's a fur piece."

"What's the name of the town?"

"Thar hain't no town."

"What's the number of the highway that takes us there?"

"Hain't got nary number."

"Well, how do *you* get there?"

"We's jist takin' four [meaning himself with three of the children and his wife with three of the children; each grandparent with one] 'n' bussin' hit."

"When you buy your bus ticket, what do you say?"

"Hain't buyed none."

"Who buys it?"

"A fur cousin."

"Where does he live?"

"Yander."

"Let's drive over and talk to him."

We did. "Hit's closest t' Rousseau, 'ceptin' you's hain't ridin' 'at fur," he directed.

The atmosphere in the car became gayer the closer we got to their beloved eastern Kentucky. The Mountain Parkway and toll gates rendered the children wide-eyed; bewitched, each took his turn tossing money into the hoppers. By the time we got to Jackson it was dark, but my friends wanted to visit relatives before continuing on home. "We's hain't seed 'em fur reckon I's not knowin' w'en." We made our first stop at a house in Lost Creek and by the time I found the shack I thoroughly appreciated the significance of the name. We went from there to Rowdy, then to Dwarf and Mousie. It was well after midnight before we got to Tiptop, just before reaching Rousseau. The end of the trip. Thank God.

The family was up bright and early the next morning, yearning to visit more kin. Our tour this time included Shoulderblade, Index, Relief, Volga, Drift, Kite, Neon, and Jeremiah. Too exhausted to continue, I called Herman aside in a weak voice.

"Herman, all these people just can't be kin of yours."

"Reckon they's bound t' be kin, else I 'udn't be knowin' 'em."

We started out early again Sunday. Our first stop was Hitchins. The next was Rush, unquestionably the slowest-moving hamlet in the world. After that Beauty. Then Ordinary, Means, Judy, and Hooktown. After that it was Berry and Oddville. By the time we staggered into their basement apartment in Cincinnati I was thankful that our visits had not included Bagdad, Pleasureville, Peewee Valley, Wisdom, and New Hope. What an itinerary! What an experience! What a kinship structure! Throughout our trip I was struck with the nothingness of each place we visited and the generosity of our hosts. If such a mob were to descend on me in my suburban retreat, I'd assume another name and stoutly declare, " 'At feller you's lookin' fur hain't livin'."

This family still lives in nearby Cincinnati and I visit them yet. I have watched their children grow up, marry, and start their own families. But have they grown in any way other than chronologically? With heavy heart I must admit that they have not. Why, then, did this family migrate while others stayed behind? Why does the hollow remain "home"? I had to know—I had to seek out the modern mountaineer in his own setting. And thus I began my quest.

A purpose had been made clear. Its achievement, however, became more complex than I could have foreseen. To begin, one had to select a population within distinctive geographic boundaries which typified other communities in the area as well as outlying poverty pockets. I had two years in which to visit other hollows (the grooves channeled between the bases of two adjacent mountains), gain more background, and design a completely self-contained mobile home before encamping at a final site.

I read scores of books and reprints of professional papers and talked with anyone who knew anything about the people in eastern Kentucky. I attended workshops, seminars, and anything else that was remotely related to the mountaineer. Eventually I could identify the counties with the highest illiteracy rate, the lowest income, the youngest population, the highest birth rate, the greatest number of recipients on the various welfare programs. The back seat of my car was covered with maps showing every nook and cranny in dozens of counties. There were places I wanted to see, but no roads led to them. Some of the "dwellings" were simply located on what the legend described as an "intermittent stream." This meant that I would have to do a lot of traveling on foot. Old alarms resounded in my mind: "People aren't safe in those hills, especially women." "Those men won't just be carrying guns—they'll be shooting them." "I've heard that the mountaineers are dangerous people." "None of those people takes to strangers." Would it be the same for me, without the sponsorship of a hollow family?

My thoughts raced back to juvenile fears. I had been terrified of gypsies, but none had kidnaped me. Nor had the Indians demanded my scalp when I visited their reservations. But the memory of the migrant workers I had known was the most reassuring. They had accepted me with unselfishness and had even tolerated my individuality. They didn't credit me with much sense for bathing or brushing my teeth or combing my hair, but when the chips were down they came to my defense. More often than not I would get to the fields late, having stayed behind to give the small children breakfast. When I did join them, my basket would be almost full of beans they had picked for me.

These memories fortified my courage and entering the hollows alone seemed less menacing.

In late 1960 I began my study and for the next two years spent nine out of ten weekends scouting around. My first stop was Wild Cat. I got there early one morning and went into the 4 × 8-foot combination post office and store to ask whether there was a restaurant around where I could get some breakfast. No response. I rephrased the question—was there any place where one could get something to eat? Still no response. Perplexed, I sat down on an upturned Pepsi-Cola case and waited for some indication of friendliness. The men who came into the store gaped at me, but I was resolute. After two hours of penetrating silence the owner relented and gave me pickled sausage and crackers.

A wizened old man had been sizing me up. "You's plannin' stayin' in these parts?"

"No, I'm just visiting," I offered.

"Who?"

I was trapped. The map, I thought. I got it out and pointed to Wild Cat. "Some people up in here."

They had never seen Wild Cat on "paper" and were too distracted to ask for more particulars about the house I purportedly wanted to visit.

It was now early afternoon and the map was still being passed around. More pickled sausage and crackers and little conversation. People came and went, staring in fascination. "Kin 'a your'n?" one would ask another, all the while looking straight at me. "Nope. Hain't seed her afore."

It was almost dark before the interest in the dot that represented Wild Cat began to fade. Felix Wheeler, the owner of the store, was getting ready to lock up. I asked him about a motel.

"Hain't heerd 'a hit," he said. "Reckon hit hain't nothin' close."

My chin dropped.

"You's kin have some grub with me 'n' m' worman."

I held out two dollars.

" 'Em skins hain't worth nothin'," he spurned.

I held out more.

"Grub we's sharin'. We's hain't takin' nothin' fur hit."

After a meal of cold gravy, a piece of salt pork, and corn bread, I made ready to leave.

"Hain't nothin' in hastin' fur somethin' 'at hain't thar," Wheeler observed.

So we engaged in small talk about their cats, their dogs, the beauty of their forest-encased home, the wife's elegant quilts. She didn't know the name of any of the patterns, but they were skillfully assembled. I remarked that my quilting stitches resembled basting, and for the first time they both laughed aloud. We were still going strong at eleven o'clock.

When he learned that I intended to spend the night in my sleeping bag, Wheeler croaked, "Hain't fittin' fur a worman 'thout no man claimin' her bein' yander, even if'n th' moon's hidin'. You's kin bed down hyur 'n' move out at stirrin' time if'n you's want. If'n you's hain't headin' fur nothin', hain't no use hurryin' t' git nowhar."

Mrs. Wheeler wakened me the next morning. "Grub's on," she notified.

Her husband was already sitting at the kitchen table. "Hit's bin a long time sence we's had comp'nies. Not even kin," he shyly confided.

We spent the morning looking at more quilts and pictures of children, the photographs so blurred with age that the youngsters' sex could not be determined. In the afternoon I went with Mrs. Wheeler to a hillside graveyard that held ancestors, children, loved ones, and neighbors with not enough land "fur buryin'." This woman's deeply furrowed face mirrored a lifetime of disappointments, hardships, and compassion. What kind of people are these, I wondered, who are fearful of a stranger yet willing to share their scant provisions with one?

Sunday was fast slipping away and I had to make the long trip back into the "civilized" world in order to be at my job early on Monday morning. I declined their invitation to tarry, but promised that I would return. Mr. Wheeler fixed his eyes on me.

"A promise 's somethin' you's aimin' on."

The next weekend I arrived outside the Wheeler shack at 3:00
A.M. Just as I was about to secure myself inside the sleeping bag,
Felix appeared with a shotgun and knocked on the car window. I
explained that I had not wanted to disturb them at that hour and
was going to sleep outside.

"We's 'spectin' you's. You's beddin' down hyur waitin' fur stirrin'
hain't good. You's kin do yore waitin' in th' lean-to."

The next two days were devoted to my hosts and tracking down
the little squares marked on the map as "dwellings on intermittent
streams." I finally made it to one and knocked on the door. A young
mother appeared.

"You must live here," I said, pointing to the map.

She looked at me with a quizzical expression. "Reckon I hain't.
I's livin' hyur," and she gently stamped her foot on the floor. The
porch vibrated from the light pressure.

People were kind everywhere I went. Where were the hostile
mountaineers I had heard so much about? I made friends with
hundreds of hollowers and was never once intimidated.

As I enlarged my scope of operations, I drew concentric circles on
a map of eastern Kentucky to systematize my intended explorations.
I started with Vortex. It was anything but what the name implied.
The people in this inert, placid setting shared their food with me
and put me up for the night. After Vortex I went to Decoy, Splint,
Viper, Hardshell, Crum, Pomp, Crummies, Ruin, and Mid. "Mid"
what? I wondered. Then on to Martha, Netty, Regina, Virgie, Lou-
isa, Elsie, Sudith, Hilda, Beverly, Mazie. Hollow after hollow, weekend after weekend, the list grew shorter. Millard, Hiram, Denton,
Cordell, Willard, Charley, Harold, Baxter, David, Leon, Preston.
This list, too, was eventually exhausted. My only battle scar was a
troubled mind, and this was not a badge of valor that I could display. I had gained a tremendous amount of insight and formulated
some tentative ideas. Poverty was no myth—I could verify its existence. It was more than just being poor. The plight of the people
could not be imagined—it had to be lived. Only then could one begin to get the idea of deprivation which requires shifting of gears
from high (living) to low (existing). During World War II, I had

crossed the color barrier, but I found that crossing a cultural barrier demanded far more sacrifices. You eat the same kind of food, whether in Decoy, Splint, or Ruin. You wear the same clothes. You walk the same stream beds or lonely briar-strewn mountain paths. You bed down early. You stir at sunup. If you talk, it's always to the same people. You do without the same things—water, fuel, seeds for spring planting, shoes, dental care. The list is endless. No matter the day, the year, the season, your age—the routine is the same.

After having completed the examination of several representative parameters, I decided to converge on a hollow which I here call Duddie's Branch. The place and people of this book exist as I have, to the best of my ability, described them. Indeed it is only to ensure this reality and protect these people and efforts to better their situation that the actual names are changed. The term "Duddie's Brancher" is also a generalization intended to denote persons who are poor and who have made little progress for generations. Those who "qualify" for this category do not even approach the entry point into middle-class society, that group with an average income of $6,000 annually. In fact, they are eligible for the abject-poverty class—far less than $3,000.

Duddie's Branch seemed to offer the potential of fulfillment of my goal. It is located in eastern Kentucky, approximately seven miles southeast of "Shade," the county seat of "Earle." The final selection of the site was influenced by many factors. The neighborhood showed obvious evidence of deprivation and the inhabitants were not significantly different in their degree of social disintegration and isolation from those in comparable hollows in the county. The residents of Shade felt that Duddie's Branch symbolized what they considered to be widespread ill-health, extensive poverty, cultural confusion, broad secularization, limited migration, and a static resistance to social change. It also exemplified a lack of associations, absence of leadership, non-existent recreation facilities. Only a weak and fragmented network of communication operated within Duddie's Branch itself and between it and Shade.

Earle County is sprinkled with mountains and its rugged terrain is consistent with the rugged life-way of its people. It is little more than a hundred and sixty years old, but economic progress has not kept pace with the advancing years. The population of the county was a little over 20,000 in 1960. About three quarters of the people are classified as rural non-farm and the remainder as rural farm. The non-white segment is small (455 individuals). Most of the residents (97.1 per cent) are Kentucky-born. The median school years completed by persons twenty-five years of age and older are seven. Of the teenagers between fourteen and seventeen years, only 65.7 per cent attend school. There are two classes of people in the county— the rich and the poor. The median family income is $1,900. Approximately 75 per cent receive less than $3,000 annually and only 2.4 per cent have annual incomes of $10,000 or more.

I envisioned my effort as a descriptive précis of the neighborhood I had selected—I would chronicle the daily function of the families. Almost from the outset, I discovered that nothing had been published about specific aspects of family life. Census reports concerning population, family size, education, and related information were available, but I soon realized that wide discrepancies existed between the published reports and the actual conditions.

The hollows, apparently, are not centers of attention. I consulted three or four notables in the upper strata of Earle County and discussed in general terms what I planned to do. None seemed too interested in which hollow I chose. After all, there were thirty such hollows in the county, so they were not uncommon. Which hollow had the greatest absenteeism from school? No one was quite sure. Which hollow was the most crowded? No one had any idea. Which hollow had the most unemployed? No one was willing to hazard a guess.

I felt that it would be futile to conform to traditional study approaches to achieve my aims. The only way to conduct a comprehensive assay was to live and interact with the families and become intimately acquainted with their day-to-day activities. This I did for the better part of twenty-four months, ferreting out hitherto unobserved and unknown features of the family system. I had no idea my involvement would grow beyond the bounds of any specific goals but the friendships that developed continue to this day.

I

A Small World

Do you not think it a matter worthy of lamentation
that when there is such a vast multitude of [worlds],
we have not yet conquered one?

Plutarch's Morals:
On the Tranquillity of the Mind

Kentucky, in Indian language, means "river of blood." Although
its early history is replete with gory wars that were waged from hill to
hill, from the frequency with which fortifications occur along water-
courses it appears likely that the bloodiest battles of all were fought
upon the banks of navigable streams.

The vague figures that wandered through its past are known simply as the Mound Builders, a name derived from their multitudinous works. These monumental heaps are ellipsoidal, conelike,
pyramidal, and of remarkable dimensions, but their purpose is a
source of mystery—sepulchers? fortresses? temples? The remains of a
vast and sophisticated system of defenses are conclusive proof that
these prehistoric inhabitants were not a migratory or nomadic people,
and the art they developed, while lacking in aesthetic qualities, often
reveals a rare excellence of finish and an astonishing fidelity to detail
in representing the human form. No definite conclusions have been
established as to their origins, but from the evidence that is available
it is not improbable that they were ethnically related to the ancient
and noble family of Toltecs. An old Delaware tradition alleges that
the aborigines were ultimately destroyed by protracted and fierce
struggles with invading Indians from the North and Far West, a
tradition that is supported by the crumbled ruins of fortifications and
by traces of mortal conflict.

The chronicle of the Kentucky highlander is a crusty chapter in the
history of the United States. The first white men to settle on the
American coast voluntarily left England in search of religious and

political freedom, adventure, and wealth. Most of them were from
the middle class of land people and the climate and soil of New England so closely approximated that of their native country that there
the foundations for a powerful nation were laid. The more adven-
turous among them did not aspire to a life of farming or village living,
but continued on to the Southland coastal regions where they carved
a plantation empire out of tobacco. As the nicotine market expanded,
African slaves were imported to care for the rapidly increasing acres
that were devoted to satisfying the demands of the ever growing
numbers of European addicts. And, when the cotton plant reared
its downy head and began to yield huge profits, more slaves were
required. The planters had imported another breed of servants—the
thieves and cutthroats and harlots who overran the prisons and
the legions of dirty, homeless orphans who timorously crept along the
streets and alleys of Britain. Parliament was eager to wash its hands
of this rabble and decreed that they be indentured to the planters for
seven-year periods. For decades thereafter the flotsam from the Old
World drifted to the shores of the New. Those who were fortunate
enough to escape or to survive indentureship disappeared into the
interior, skulked across the rippling Piedmont, came to rest in the
shadowy Blue Ridge, and spent their seed, which took root and
flourished there. Thus was harvested the first crop of backwoods-
men. By virtue of the rigors of outdoor living, the cynical, invidious,
bondsmen evolved into a species as wild as their surroundings and
as barbaric as the most barbaric of the Indians who plagued their
existence. They multiplied prolifically and gradually spread to the
fringes of the southern Appalachians. Indeed, so prodigious was
their number that their descendants, in search of open land, came to
cover the entire mountain range by the middle of the eighteenth century. By then, however, they were a hybrid strain. Newly arrived English, Scots, and Irish peasants and yeomen had slowly but relentlessly pushed through from the coast to infiltrate the seed stock and
commingle genes. The territory held scant glamor for the less hardy
settlers until the Indians north of the Ohio River were defeated in
the Battle of Tippecanoe in 1811.
    Until the turn of this century the hilly and mountainous region
was a veritable wilderness and the country was blessed with natural

resources worth hundreds of thousands of dollars. But the early mountaineer was ignorant of the treasures in and on his land and occupied himself only with the topsoil he claimed and tilled. The walnut, pine, birch, oak, poplar, beech, and various other trees that fought for footage across the craggy landscape and narrow valleys were a nuisance to him. The necessity of having to clear his land of them clouded his perspective and he was relieved when Eastern and Northern corporations bought timber deeds in abundance and a great number of trees was transferred to "foreign" hands. He could not foresee that he had robbed himself and cheated future generations of his descendants. The timber companies were greedy, the workmen were careless, the methods and equipment were primitive, and the hills were so wantonly stripped that there was little hope that "small stuff" would ever grow again. And the mountaineer had sold his legacy to the marketeer for a mere pittance. Neither did he take an interest in the mineral riches of his land, thereby ensuring his total exploitation. After the wealth of the forest had been depleted, other profiteers from the East and North turned their attention to the great seams of bituminous coal that ran through the country, and the mineral rights to immense expanses of land were sold to them for a few cents an acre. Again, the mountaineer would not look beyond the small patch of earth he managed. Elmo said that his father purchased the land on which he lived for fifty cents an acre and that subsequently coal worth $25,000 or more an acre had been mined from it. The mountaineer's indifference was partially responsible for his fate. What had once been a matted jungle, so dense that the hollows and valleys were concealed behind fluttering layers of green leaves, was now ravaged earth. His land surface was destroyed, his streams were polluted with mining refuse, his crops were devastated by tons of coal grit that spewed from washeries, and his soil was corrupted forever.

Earle County, on the edge of the Cumberland Plateau, was carved out of lush timberland in 1806; in 1798 arrived the first white man known to have entered its boundaries. By 1852 the county was still thinly settled and the markets were too far for the mountain people to sell anything but "walkaways"—cattle, horses, swine, etc. It was difficult to transport crops to market and, aside from the walkaways, there was little incentive for the families to raise more than they could consume. Moreover, their products were not a valuable source of income. Corn sold for seventeen cents a bushel; oats for twelve and one half cents; pork, beef, and venison for two dollars per hundred pounds. Most of the mountaineers kept hogs and cattle for their own use and permitted them to roam through the woods. During "meat years" the forest abounded in nuts and acorns, and the fat, sleek animals displayed evidence of good eating.

Many mountain people could neither read nor write. Of the few who could, their literacy did not extend beyond those two abilities; they knew nothing of politics, history, or geography—not even of other Branches. Unless they lived within a half day's travel of the nearest schoolhouse, their children were reared illiterate too. Unlike the wealthy lowland planters, they could not afford tutors to instruct their offspring. Because of their isolation they were liberated from the stereotype of convention and their behavior, thoughts, manners, and expressions were preordained to retain an originality and ingenuity that would one day be termed "backward."

Shade, the county seat of Earle, is perched atop a mountain overlooking Buck Creek. The rocky, muddy settlement, inhabited by about a hundred people in 1806, was the only town in the county and contained eight mechanics' shops, a seminary, two churches, and a pair each of taverns, general stores, groceries, lawyers, and physicians. Salt was the leading article of export and the area became famous for that product. In the early 1800s a furnace was constructed near Buck Creek; hundreds of wells were drilled and the salt water was funneled to it for long distances through pipelines made of logs fitted end to end. The industry provided a measure of prosperity for the settlers. Some of them worked for the company; others sold every drop of blood from butchered hogs for a good price to the saltworks, where it was used to cleanse the seasoning. Then, during the Civil War, Union forces destroyed the Buck Creek saltworks. Loyal United States citizens were ". . . allowed to remove enough for their own needs on taking oath that none of it would be used to benefit the Confederacy. . . ."[1] Eleven years later, in 1873, President Ulysses S. Grant vetoed a bill Congress had passed to reimburse

[1] L. Collins and R. H. Collins, *Collins' Historical Sketches of Kentucky,* in *History of Kentucky* (Frankfort, Kentucky: Kentucky Historical Society, 1966), Vol. 2, p. 142.

the families owning the saltworks. He defended his action on the principle that its destruction ". . . was a military necessity and he cannot consent to the doctrine that the U.S. are liable for all claims for property destroyed by the Union armies during the war. . . ."[2] The boon created by the salt-mining industry gradually declined and thereafter Shade was slow in advancing. Paved highways and railroads came late. There was no rail line until 1917 and then, as now, it was only a dead-end run, greatly impairing its value to the economy. Some of the roads into Shade were paved in 1925, but even yet many are narrow, poorly constructed, and expensive to maintain. Winter weather and floods make them useless a good part of the time and low-water bridges are common; it is frequently necessary to cross a stream in order to continue on a road. Today Shade is served by a paved highway that runs past the mouth of Duddie's Branch, seven miles southward.

I had viewed the hollows of this area by plane and jeep and on foot and had interviewed a number of prominent people in Earle County. None of those with whom I talked could understand why I wanted to live among the Branchers—they were concerned for my safety, for my health. My explanations only intensified their concern.

Part of my plan was to live for a short while with a family from a different hollow, preferably in a home near the center of the county but distant enough from Duddie's Branch so that the mistakes I made would not be transmitted there.

My first introduction to the Boones came through a horticulturist who knew of my interest in grafting fruit trees. He was going to see a man who had done some remarkable work with apple trees and asked me to come along.

Mr. and Mrs. Boone, their eight children, and Mrs. Boone, Sr., lived in a one-room log cabin with a lean-to. It had housed four generations of Boones and the only change over the decades had been one of progressive deterioration. The furnishings were meager—two double iron beds, a large scuffed trunk, an ancient, battered sewing machine, a badly worn divan, and three homemade kitchen chairs.

    [2] L. Collins and R. H. Collins, *Collins' Historical Sketches of Kentucky,* Vol. 1, p. 241.

Coal-oil lamps with sparkling chimneys flickered in the room. Part of the cabin had been papered with colored pages torn from a mail-order catalogue. The paper had been applied with an adhesive made from flour and water. Everything about the place shrieked of poverty, but it was spotless and the occupants were cheerful.

I visited the family several times after that first meeting. One day I arrived at lunchtime and was invited to eat with them. A long home-made table stood at one end of the room that served as the kitchen area. It was set with an odd assortment of chipped and broken plates and a lone piece of silver—a mutilated tin fork—that they had exhumed for my use. The wind drove the stinging rain through a paneless window and it was cold enough in the cabin to vaporize breath.

The Boones' only cash income was the forty-five dollars a month which Mrs. Boone, Sr., received from public assistance and about twenty-five dollars a month that Enon earned for occasionally "mechanicin'"; he did not have a regular job and had been unemployed for many years. I was told that they were on commodities (surplus foods) and that the grandmother gave her check every month toward their grocery account.

This first luncheon consisted of commodity peanut butter, canned commodity meat, and fried apples. To supplement this, Tressie had prepared a huge bowl of pale blue gravy. The children, she said, were inveterate gravy eaters and they proceeded to corroborate her claim without delay. Never had I seen youngsters eat so much gravy with so much enthusiasm. Each would pinch off a bit of bread, eagerly dip it into the gravy, and pop it into his mouth. Since most of the gravy adhered to his fingers, these too disappeared behind greasy lips. This process was repeated until the azure sauce was consumed. The thought occurred to me that the children would be an instant success at a poi party.

Eventually it was time to implement my plans, and I approached Enon.

"How much would it cost me to stay with you for a few days?"

"Reckon nothin'. We's got rough grub 'n' you's hain't gonna starve but you's hain't gonna be eatin' fancy, neither."

At my insistence he agreed to accept a dollar a day for my keep.

I thought it would be prudent to have someone drive me to the cabin when the day arrived. Enon did not have an automobile, and if I were without a car it would be strong proof of my intentions.

"You's cain't git outta hyur 'thout hoofin' if'n you's hankerin' t' take off," he noted.

My presence did not disrupt their sleeping arrangements. The grandmother slept in one bed with some of the children and the parents slept in the other with some; I was to sleep in the barn loft with the two oldest boys. The children did not keep regular sleeping hours—they just went to bed when they were so inclined. Not one member of the family wore night clothes or, indeed, even undressed before retiring. This procedure did not vary and no one changed apparel at any time I was there.

Personal hygiene, for the most part, was dispensed with and I did not feel that I should deviate from established routine. In the morning, everyone washed his face and hands with the same cloth and that constituted the extent of the daily ablutions. The few times I groomed my hair I used the family comb, an implement whose wide gaps were interrupted by an occasional tooth. In accordance with their custom, I did not change my dress or brush my teeth all the while I was there.

Meals were plain and followed no regular time pattern. Some of the children ate standing at the table because there were not enough seating possibilities. Mealtime was usually a disorderly and frantic period. Once the cat jumped through the window and landed in the middle of my inevitable gravy.

" 'At cat's a-walkin' off with you's dippin'," Enon dryly observed.

Should I or should I not reclaim my lunch from the cat? I hesitated only for a moment before grappling for the gravy. During my exploratory visits, subtle testing sessions had been artfully conducted by me, Enon, and Tressie—I had examined them and they had examined me. These exercises had mentally conditioned me to respond in the proper manner now. My muscular responses were not as worthy—it required several seconds to defeat the tenacious beast.

The family laundry was washed once a week in creek water heated in a large kettle outside. The tub was the body of an old washing machine and Tressie would scrub each piece on a badly worn washboard. Considering the size of the family, the laundry was not large: one pair of jeans for each boy, one dish towel, six bath towels, three washcloths, a few pairs of raggedy panties, no petticoats, and no sheets. If one of the children wet the bed, the grandmother would wash just the area of the sheet that had been soiled.

There were no toilet facilities; it was necessary to relieve oneself behind the barn. None of the Boones used toilet paper, but I kept a supply of tissues tucked in my pocket. Whenever the site behind the barn was in use, someone would venture that a member "had gone to hockey" and no one else went out until he returned. Disposal of waste matter did not pose a special problem—the chickens consumed the feces immediately.

The conditions were outrageously primitive, but I had become genuinely attached to the Boones and extended my visit another week. Enon and Tressie wanted me to stay even longer and I would have, had not the time arrived to commence my next job—that of sharing the small world of the Duddie's Brancher.

This time my hours were consumed in a store at which many of the Duddie's Branchers traded. It was nearby that I wanted to park my mobile home. The vehicle was complete with everything I would need for one year: paper sheets, paper pillowcases, disposable cooking utensils and dishes—an impressive inventory. It contained a complete kitchen, a bath with shower, and a toilet that did not require a holding tank. I would eventually have a jeep for transportation into otherwise inaccessible places. There was plenty of space by the store and I hoped I could hook up to the electricity once I had become friends with the owners. Establishing this kind of relationship took time, but I was successful. From my new vantage point I could watch the mouth of Duddie's Branch; with binoculars I was able to see how many went in and out of the hollow, thereby obtaining a rough idea of daylight activity. Finally I began planting myself in the Hiram store at five o'clock every morning. Some miners from the Branch bought lunch to take to work, others waited for a driver to pick them up there. After the miners left, the children drifted in to await the school bus. Then the unemployed men shuffled in.

I listened to their talk but never asked questions or engaged in conversation myself. Soon I learned who came from Duddie's Branch, the latest gossip reports, and who was ailing and the improvement or deterioration of his state of health. After some time I was better able to understand them and to mimic their talk. From the bits and pieces of what was said, I gathered that the man who was the sickest was the patriarch of possibly the biggest kinship group in the hollow. His name was Farmer; he was fifty-six years old, had lung trouble, was bloated, and had trouble walking. His family had been on welfare for generations.

I had decided to acquire all the information I could without asking questions. The next step was to install myself in the hollow and work my way into the families. I had to remember everything I learned until I was able to get to a dictating machine; I would not be equipped with pencil or paper and would do no writing in front of the mountaineers.

On a bleak winter morning I started walking towards the hollow. By the time I got to the mouth I was numb with cold. A man was heading out and I managed to bid him a good morning through chill-stiffened lips. No acknowledgment, not even a glance. I continued on, my spirits as depressed as the temperature.

The only approach into Duddie's Branch is by way of the creek bed, a serpentine ribbon which stretches for one mile from the mouth of the Branch to the head. It is just wide enough to admit one car and tricky maneuvering is involved when two vehicles meet; one must go in the reverse direction until it comes to a gradual slope in the bank where it can pull in and permit the other automobile to proceed. Only a four-wheel-drive jeep with a chassis high enough to surmount the boulders and hurdle the bottomless holes can hope to meet the challenge of the rock-infested "road" and survive the journey. The driver and his passengers may not be so fortunate; it is a wild, spine-jolting, tooth-rattling ride.

To compound the abuse, it is not unusual to have debris rained upon you. There is no garbage collection service here and, because of the peril of forest fires and the proximity of the shacks, the residents are forbidden to burn their refuse; neither can it be buried— solid rock is too close to ground surface. And so the yards become their dump and the creek their disposal system. When the water runs high, accumulated junk is pushed over the banks and slowly floats down the turgid stream until it snags on low projecting tree limbs or spiny stones. During especially heavy rains the creek cannot be used as any sort of roadway. Offal and rubbish: a significant first sight and the symbol of Branch life. Bottles, boxes, papers, tin cans, clothing, tires, ashes—all are bequeathed to the Branch and the outer world wrinkles its nose at the "trashy hollowers," overlooking its own wanton dumping practices.

On that rainy day of my first visit I fatuously believed that I had the choice of following a path that led up a sheer hill or accomplishing my purpose by walking down the stream bed. Out of consideration for personal comfort, I selected the path; it also had the incidental advantage of permitting a better view of the dwellings. I joined issue with the hill and after considerable effort conquered it, only to discover that the path abruptly ended a few feet from a fence that served as a reminder against trespassing. There was no alternative but to continue by way of the stream bed and I managed, with trepidation, to slide down a high bank and into the creek, abandoning all hope of keeping warm. The water was almost knee-deep and sloshed into my boots, and the portion of my hands that protruded beyond the sleeves of my raincoat were blue with cold. I was unable to give much thought to discomfort, though, because each precarious step increased my concern to stay mobile.

I was stunned at the sight of the neighborhood. Shanties, a few yards apart, are time-marked by decay, and you feel a ghostly sense of desertion as you enter. About halfway into the hollow, I saw a group of naked youngsters busy at play in front of one of the small shacks, scarcely larger than playhouses, which stud the banks of the Branch. The children, of spindly shanks and protruding bellies, were inured to the icy, driving rain and their endurance wrung my heart. They and the tumbled-down houses formed a tableau of unrelieved poverty which completed my wretchedness. It was, I think, the most depressing and perilous expedition I had ever undertaken. Suppressing my dismay and shock, I walked in for a third of a mile to "case" Farmer's house. Several people passed me, but not one returned my "good morning" greeting. The cold weather and colder reception convinced me that I had gone far enough for the first time.

Each day thereafter I would walk in a little farther and stay a little longer, but I was always given the silent treatment. Then one morning, on my way in, a hoary-maned man came out of the house that stood before the entrance to the hollow. He called to me.

"Reckon you's lost," the wily oldster prompted. "Hit's chillin'. Come in 'n' set a spell."

I accepted his invitation with alacrity. Over a cup of coffee, he told me that his name was Seafle and introduced me to Flossie, his wife. He tried to discover my motives for visiting the Branch, but my explanations were less than satisfying. Nonetheless, he insisted that I stop in for coffee every morning and before long I found myself looking forward to the kaffeeklatsches.

"Reckon you's think th' Branch is a tacky place," he would begin. "Ever see sech sorry people?"

I would evade his questions by telling him stories of the people who lived in city slums. It did not take him long to learn that I wasn't "free talkin' 'bout holler folk," even though his technique to elicit information was honed to a razor sharpness. He and Flossie were secretly pleased that I did no "mouthin' 'bout nothin'," and in time he stopped playing the inquisitor.

Little by little I made my way to the head of the hollow. Seafle had told me that "Howdy" was the only greeting which would evoke a response and, sure enough, the Branchers began to mumble a subdued "Howdy" in return. A few weeks after I had begun my daily visits, a man Seafle had pointed out as Amon was walking in the hollow just ahead of me.

I saluted him in the accepted manner. "Mind if I walk out with you?"

"Reckon." That ambiguous word could mean that he did mind, but it could also mean that he did not. I followed along behind him, as is proper for a hollow woman.

"If'n hit's storin' you's headin' fur, I's hain't goin' thar."

I told him that I was just heading out and that it was nice to have someone to walk with.

"Reckon," he repeated.

The big day arrived six weeks later, at which time a thin, doe-eyed woman hesitantly addressed me.

"Seed you's headin' fur Seafle's. You's hain't never bin t' my place."

"Well, if you don't mind I'll come in now and warm up a bit," I said, as casually as I could, my heart thumping with the excitement of this breakthrough. Children were strung out all over the house and a slender finger of flame wavered in the fireplace. It somehow seemed warmer outside. We did not talk much, but soon the hostess said that they would be pleasured if I "et" with them. I began to eat the corn bread and pinto beans with my fingers, until one of the children demonstrated the proper manner in which beans are eaten: holding the saucer up to the chin, one scoops off a mouthful of beans with corn bread.

Other Branchers kept popping in and out all the time I was there, it being their first opportunity to "hawk-eye" me at close range. I did not contribute much in the way of conversation, but I was much wiser by the end of the day. For one thing, I learned gestures were a part of the communication pattern. Two specific kinds, shoulder shrugging and a kind of nodding of the head, were especially significant, but I was unable to interpret these movements. As a result, I was cautious in the use or translation of the signals. Their speech, too, was cryptic. Although I heeded every word, I repeatedly had to reshape my original understanding as its meaning gradually became clear. It was equally difficult for them. Their follow-through clearly demonstrated that they failed to comprehend most of what I said.

I had seen Farmer's house and I called on him the next day. He was indeed a sick man and the weather aggravated his asthmatic condition. I spent all day with him, each of us having taken to the other at once.

Before long, I was going into the Branch at dawn and coming out later and later. Sometimes I did not come out at all but would spend the night with one of the families. Then I began staying there for several days at a time. The Branchers learned that I did not talk about them, that I did not reveal the things I observed, that infractions of the law never got "mouthed" by me—and I was "in." How thankful I became for the word "reckon."

"You's seed this 'n' you's seed that."

"Reckon."

That was an acceptable answer for anything and can be loosely translated as "yes," "no," "perhaps," "don't bother me," "mind your own business," etc. I had almost forgotten how to say "yes" and "no," but this was just as well. Both words are highly dangerous as they have positive meaning for the hollow folk. As long as I was "reckonin'," I was neutral.

Their mistrust and ambivalence made my effort a series of ups and downs at the beginning. During the time I was trying to convince them of my sincerity, whatever progress I had made was negated when I absented myself from the hollow for a few days. From the moment I left until I returned they would ascribe every unlikely circumstance to my credit and the reasons for my interest in them had villainous connotations. The first time I was away, Rover Smuts underwent a vasectomy and I was incriminated as an undercover agent for a birth control organization. On other occasions I was a revenue functionary, a special investigator sent by the army to expose ineligible bonus recipients, a deputy policeman, a school truant officer, and a federal spy. It took many months to persuade them that I was innocent of their charges.

As all strangers must, I gingerly felt my way around and learned to guard against questioning until I was accepted as one of them. Their hatred of interrogation borders on the pathologic. "Cain't 'em fellers out yander talk 'thout questionin'? Seemin' like questions 's 'bout all they's knowin'." They also resent cameras in the hands of strangers. "We's hain't hankerin' t' have 'em outsiders pitcherin' us."

After I was a full-fledged Brancher, a reporter asked me to get the others to agree to being televised and photographed for national magazines and newspapers. He was a free-lance operator and said that Appalachia was a great "money-maker." I suggested that he enlist the aid of someone more willing to lend assistance, and after several meetings I sent him to talk to the county judge. He came back and said that if I gave my permission it was agreeable with the judge. I still would not concede to his request and went to see the judge myself. He was not at all in favor of picture taking and told me that he had made this clear to the reporter. I thought that the incident was closed, but on a day when I was not in the Branch the journalist returned with loaded camera equipment. Until I became a resident, few strangers had entered the area. After my arrival, however, the hollow was regularly invaded by my "alien" friends who asked the first person they saw for directions to my place.* If a stranger was not looking for me, he was given short shrift. The persistent reporter did not get beyond the first house.

"If'n you's a-lookin' fur 'at worman, she hain't hyur," Seafle advised him.

"I'm . . ."

"If'n you's hain't a-lookin' fur 'at worman, you's hain't goin' no furer."

The man was incensed. "This is public property!"

"Hain't knowin' 'bout public nothin', 'ceptin' I's knowin' this holler's our'n. Mostes fellers leaves out quiet-like w'en we's axin' 'em t' git."

The man was not easily dissuaded, so Seafle stepped inside his door and reappeared with a shotgun.

"Reckon you's aimin' on leavin' out now," he invited.

"I'm not afraid of any gun," the newsman defied.

"Reckon hain't nary feller fearin' guns. Hit's 'em firin's [shells] they's hain't hankerin' t' stop."

The intruder hesitated and Seafle fired one shell at his feet.

He concluded the story. "I figgered on missin' 'is hoofers fur from hyur t' yander, 'n' I did. Onc't that dust 'uz a-settlin' 'e 'uz headin' out. Reckon 'e warn't no friend 'a your'n."

I paid him for the shell he had wasted. "No, he was not my friend. He was a stranger to me."

A stranger does not necessarily describe someone you have never met or do not know; it can also mean someone you do not like. Seafle understood what I meant.

"Figgered if'n you's 'spectin' 'im, you's 'ud 'a mouthed hit 'r gived 'im some writin' [a note]."

Yet they extend all courtesies to people they know to be my friends. In one of Melda's letters, she wrote: "I had compiny today one of the Guys had Came up with you about three years ago. He give me his name and what he is doing so you would know who he was. a girl,

---

* After two years I fixed up a house at the head of the hollow, which I live in as much as I can. The mobile home is still parked in its usual place.

and a Boy was with him." In this way I am still able to keep abreast of what goes on in the Branch. Many of the hollowers who can't write ask the visitor to put his name and place of employment on a scrap of paper. Some make an effort to remember these details, but they usually are not too successful.

Within three months I knew everyone in the hollow and felt comfortable among them. They, in turn, were interested in me, not in my reasons for being there, and liked having me around. I accepted frequent chaws of tobacco and learned to sit and spit with the best of them. Day after day, I wore one of four identical dresses and the same pair of shoes. I stopped having my hair done, never wore jewelry, and quit wearing my watch. What difference did time make? If I missed coming into the hollow every day, they would comment, "You's warn't 'round 'bout." I helped them plant their gardens and went with them in search of greens for salad. Then I discovered that many families stayed around their houses in the mornings waiting to see if I would come in that day and hoping that I would stop by their place. Often it was late afternoon before I could make it to the head of the hollow, if I made it at all. Sometimes I would catch a ride in and start at the head, working my way from house to house down to the mouth of the Branch. Regardless of when I came or which route I followed, the reception I received was worthy of royalty.

I became increasingly reluctant to leave the Branch and the people would invent all kinds of reasons to keep me there. Layuna was going to have her baby any minute for two months before it was due. "You's leave out 'n' I's sure t' drop 'at youngun." A climate of affection surrounded me. I could supply no cure for the ills and wrongs the Branchers had suffered, but they molded a whole new way of life for me.

For geneticists, the hollow is a treasure house. On the one hand, there seems to have been virtually no new blood introduced to create genetic confusion; on the other, children born out of wedlock are more common than one would expect (the old-timers say that they were plentiful in the early years, too). Muscular dystrophy, a combination of hereditary disorders in which muscle fibers are damaged and eventually destroyed, is found in only one family unit. The father is not from the local area.

There are no purely ethnic groups represented in Duddie's Branch. Their origins are almost as obscure as are those of the Mound Builders—these twentieth-century anomalies cannot establish a common heritage. Having neither Bibles and in most instances no ability to write nor the desire to keep genealogical records, they did not preserve their past. Few can verify that their forefathers migrated from the Virginias and Carolinas, a hypothesis which I found to be popular in literature and genealogic surveys. History books suggest that the long rifles and folkways of those in the general area of Duddie's Branch identify the early settlers as having predominantly English, Scots, and Irish forebears, with only a few Germans, Jews, Poles, French, Swiss, Greeks, Syrians, and Lebanese among their numbers. Yet no one in the Branch claims ancestry to the French, the English, or any other nationality. In my attempts to make such connections, their responses revealed that they had not the slightest knowledge of lineage. "Hain't kin t' none 'a 'em," "never heerd 'em named by my paw; must not be kin 'a our'n," "we's jist al'ays lived hyur; most 'a us holler fellers come from Earle County." There is a peculiar lack of distinguishing mountain characteristics, the customs and crafts that are usually associated with the highland people. They do not know what a dulcimer is, much less how to strum one. They are not the storytellers that the ancients were and those who first inhabited these mountains and hollows did not hand down tales to their children.

Some allude to parents or grandparents who might "recollect kin," but none manifests a curiosity in his ancestral descent. This lack of interest makes it totally impossible for any of the people to take pride in their heritage. The ultimate destiny of most families appears to have been determined by a stem which is not now evident or perhaps one with which no domestic circle wants to be associated. The intimacy of blood grouping is based on the acceptance or rejection of kin.

"You must be kin, Sam. You two had the same grandmother."

"C'd be," he snorted, "but I hain't claimin' kin t' sech a sorry outfit."

Dill said, "Heap 'a Browns 'round 'bout, 'ceptin' hain't nary one 'a 'em my kin."

"You have to be kin to Herman. He was your father's half brother."

"C'd be, 'ceptin' we's hain't kin. If'n hit's lookin' t' be fur sure, I's still hain't claimin' 'im."

"Claimin' " often depends on immediate situations. If a law official is looking for a Brancher, no one—not even his own children—is kin to the pursued.

I wondered what effect kinship—concealed or admitted—had on family behavior, but how could I trace and record ancestry of families now living in the hollow when older individuals did not know with certainty who their grandparents were or from where they came? One Brancher said that his name was Shifter but that his father's name was Wheeler and that his father's father was named Smuts. Obviously, the training I had in genealogy would be of little help. They had to have ancestors, they had to come from somewhere, but the tools available in the outer world, such as baptismal records, did not exist here. I was told that there was plenty of " 'em knowin', not sayin'." Actually, there was much less "knowin' " than I had been led to believe. Conversation disclosed that Troy went to school in a neighboring county, but there were many Troy Shifters. Some enrolled in school under the nickname attached to a family and the real name never appeared on the register. "We's started out hollerin' fur 'im Juds-Judfer, 'ceptin' 'e's s'pose' t' be Judfer 'cordin' t' birthin' writin' [birth certificate]." Everything needed to trace ancestry is missing in the hollow. There are no family Bibles in which significant events were documented. There are no old letters because their ancestors could not write. Few have the space in which to store keepsakes, if there were any. Churches were not a source of information; in the early days, as in many instances now, church meetings were held in homes, and births, deaths, marriages, etc., were not registered. Courthouse records are incomplete. Proving kinship is, as the hollower might say, "fur 'em 'at's knowin'." At first it all seemed so simple, but coming across certificates of two or more marriages with twenty-one children in the first, fifteen in the second, and five in a third is a bewildering experience.

The people in Duddie's Branch, typical of their difference from others in the "outside world," couldn't care less about their ancestors —who they were, where they came from, and, most important of all, how much their forebears passed down to them in terms of personal characteristics. To them the past is a dead issue, one that they are not about to revive. The possibility of uncovering something which might reflect on their image is a hazard none wishes to risk. There may have been a "shooter" [murderer] in their family tree that they "hain't hankerin' fur knowin'." My efforts to point out to Meander that his ancestors had some influence on what he is were futile.

"Hain't fur lookin' fur knowin' 'bout daid fellers."

"But you must be interested in knowing who your great-grandfather was?"

This was too far back for him. He doesn't even know who his grandfather was and wouldn't bother to find out if he could.

"Maybe he was a famous man."

"Hain't likely."

"Maybe some of your ancestors left you land or money."

"Hain't likely. They's hain't leavin' w'at they's hain't got."

"But if you don't know who they were, how can you be so sure?"

He scanned the mountainsides and then his home, a small weather-beaten shack which he erected a couple of marriages ago. Then he wiggled the worn toe of his laceless shoe in the dirt and contemplated. He looked from me into space and back to me again.

"If'n you's hankerin' t' know kin 'a your'n, reckon hit's . . ." He faltered.

"Maybe worth knowing?" I supplied.

"Reckon so," he agreed. "But daid, they's daid. Hain't hankerin' fur 'em I's hain't knowin'."

I explained to him that eastern Kentucky families were pioneer settlers and that many of them were of English, Irish, and Scots descent. He started to drift away.

"Meander, these early settlers—these brave, courageous people— came to America to set up a new life and make a new country."

"Hain't reckonin'," meaning that he knew nothing about that and if he did he would still hesitate to attach himself to such a nebulous past.

"Many of the early settlers were Revolutionary War heroes."

"C'd be."

"That's something to be proud of."

"Hain't fur claimin' 'at I's hain't seein'."

The only family history they want to know is that which is before them and that which they are willing to admit. I finally had to recognize that family trees, if there were to be any, would have to be traced since I could expect no help from the Branchers. Yet how can ancestry be attractive to them when they are unable to recall their own life history? Even the young adults have great difficulty in remembering their early years—where they lived, for how long, what they did before they started to school, or even the size of their own families. Letcher, when asked by a visitor how many children he had, replied, "Don't rightly know. Never bothered t' count 'em." It is useless to ask them to start with the oldest child and name their offspring in chronological order. They can remember "we got six daid," but are unable to fit them into a birth pattern or cite the age at which they died. Miscarriages are included as births by some. Others say, "I dropped hit early, three months, maybe, 'r more likely four. Hain't sure. No way 'a tellin'."

Their detached attitude toward heritage may be related to the fact that the hollow in which they live is not an old, long-settled community. Even though Kentucky became the fifteenth state in 1792, it was a hundred and two years before anyone lived in what would one day be called Duddie's Branch.

Kentucky is a land of picturesque name places. Whether Indian legends were built around the names of some streams and settlements or whether the names resulted from Indian lore is not known, but the sagas of the Cherokee—a tribe alternately friendly and savage—are colorful. Legend has it that their chief, War Eagle, was killed beneath a rock cliff he had carved with turkey tracks and that his body was thrown into the fork of the Kentucky River bearing his name. Memorials of the Mound Builders can still be seen in this vicinity. The humble mountaineer, though, did not bother to dignify his valleys and hollows and mountains and creeks with formal names. Instead, he distinguished his regions through descriptive terms. Dead Injun Valley was discovered by an early settler who came across the remains of an Indian brave. That area then became known as "th' low spot 'twixt 'em hills all humped t'gether whar Ephraim found 'at daid Injun a-rottin' 'n' a-stinkin' in a patch 'a birch trees." Over the generations, its distinctive qualities were leisurely abbreviated and it came to be referred to simply as Dead Injun Valley. So it is with hundreds of other quaint name places associated with the Kentucky highlander.

Conflicting tales confuse the issue of the original Duddie's Branch family. Ho-Babe Wheeler, who has the most descendants in the hollow, is thought to have built the first shack there in 1894. When the timber rights became the possession of the Transylvania Company, the supervisor of the operation moved in with his family in 1922. As soon as the once beautiful mountains framing the hollow had been plundered, though, they left. Ewell Wheeler, probably kin to the "original" settler, also established a residence there in 1922 with his second wife and large family. Flossie and Seafle Yancy built their home at the mouth of Duddie's Branch in 1923, as verified by the records, and both affirm that no one else lived there at that time. This allegation is hotly contested, particularly since a commanding number of kin to Ewell Wheeler still reside there. A certain prestige is attached to the oldest resident. Awarding status to the first, second, third, and fourth families would have required much fence mending had I said the improper thing to the "rightful" holder of the title.

Seafle diffidently admits that both he and Ewell settled in Duddie's Branch the same year, but adds, "If'n I'd 'a knowed 'e 'uz stuck back thar in th' holler I'd 'a moved on." He disdains to fraternize with other contenders for the title of "first," and only one woman and her descendants remain to offer a threat to his claim, a charge he airily dismisses. "I's bin knowin' 'at gal from early 'n' she's allus bin short on memorin'; hain't gethered none durin' livin', neither." Detta, however, insists that her family arrived in 1903 or 1904—"one yar 'r t'other, hain't no matter." She says that her parents put up a small cabin and "b'gun raisin' their younguns 'n' we's bin hyur ever sence. I's kin t' jist 'bout ever' one in th' Branch—close kin t' some 'n' fur kin t' a heap 'a 'em." But at seventy years of age it is hard for her to remember just how she is kin to all but her brothers and sisters.

The status that Seafle feels belongs to him is neither recognized nor

accorded by those living in Duddie's Branch and the battle of
"who's on first" is still being fought. He scorns all other suits and told
me that he wanted "t' straighten th' kinks out. Hain't wantin' you's
fallin' fur lyin'."

He was born and reared near Snake's Creek and first saw the hollow where he now lives seventy years ago. He liked to reminisce
about his trips over the mountains and through the wilderness to
Duddie's Branch to have his hair cut by an uncle. "Onc't I's a-walkin'
yon mount'in 'n' somethin' big come straight outta th' bushes. I's so
close I cun't miss hittin' hit with m' shotgun, but hit jist keeped
a-movin'. I's scart 'most near t' dyin'. My hairs stood up so straight
they heisted my hat plum off'n m' years. I warn't figgerin' on chasin'
hit if'n lead hain't slowin' hit down none ner stoppin' hit. Pryin' kin
d'stroy a feller."

After he and Flossie married they moved to the Branch and their
nearest neighbors were the Hustons, who had more than a dozen
children. "Reckon th' number don't 'specially matter sence they plum
cleared out." Seafle reasons that even if you were the first family in
the hollow you would lose this status, or place once you left the hollow. This is especially true if you leave no kin behind. None of the
Hustons nor any of their descendants—or kin however distant—
remain, so the competition is reduced to Ewell and Seafle. "But daid
fellers hain't talkin'," says Seafle, "so I's still first."

The house in which Seafle and Flossie live is situated close to the
main highway that runs through the county, but in 1922 there were
no roads. "We had a pore way t' git in 'n' out. In wintertime hit 'uz
too hard t' go nowhar." Not even in earlier days was there a church
on the Branch. Meetings would take place in houses or at buryings,
he reminisced. "But thar' 'uz lots 'a comin' 'n' goin' in ol' times,"
and feuds were common in Earle County. "'Em ol'-timers, they's
somethin'. 'Thout knowin' hit, you's stirrin' 'em up. First thing a feller
knowed, 'e's prickin' 'em deep. Blood warn't thar, 'ceptin' hit's plum
ready fur seepin'. Walkin' through briars, you's jist gits skin-deep
scratchin'; facin' firin' 'at's done left a shootin' iron, 'at hain't no briar
scratch."

The first "drivin' road," a gravel highway, was built to pass by the
Branch but it did not incommode the Yancys. "Hit din't take none

'a my land, so mostly I jist watched. 'Em fellers with bottoms did th' cussin' fur they's givin' up thar'n. Atter they's all done, my house right out front 'a 'em in th' holler." Since Seafle's house stands at the entrance to the Branch, there is no need to clarify the matter of who came first as far as he is concerned. Seafle paid only a dollar an acre for his land but the hard work of clearing fell on the purchaser, if he was so inclined. Some cleared it themselves, and some let time clear it for them. " 'Ceptin' fur mine," he remarks, "cain't rec'llect nothin' 'bout most 'a 'em clearin' nothin'."

Seafle worked for the timber concern, rafting logs down the river to Ottisville. He earned eight dollars a week for working on the front end of the raft, while experienced men got ten dollars a week for working on the back part where the steering mechanism, a kind of paddle, was located. It took two days to raft down to Ottisville and another two days to walk back. He also worked at the sawmill to augment his income, to "make support" for his family. "I cleared 'n' fenced on my rough hillside 'twixt times. But even with hard work I din't bring up my family th' way I wanted to, but I did set up a shed 'n' moved in. I worked 'n' added t' hit 'n' later built some more on hit." He paused. "Warter 'uz th' hardest thing. M' brother 'uz stayin' with us 'n' we digged a well t' git warter from. We started drillin' th' well in my yard, but run into a vein 'a gas. We finally got hit down t'whar we got warter, but I thought th' gas might interrupt [contaminate] th' warter, so's I sent hit away fur testin' t' see if'n hit 'uz pure 'n' hit come back plum pure. 'At gas 'at 'uz in 'at well, I bin foolin' with hit 'n' tamperin' with hit 'n' like t' burned m' eyes out. I larned my lesson 'n' quit messin' with hit. Reckon 'at gas's still thar."

Flossie, too, earned an income by hoeing corn for fifty cents a day. After the timber was completely cut down, leaving nothing but stumps, there was but one way to use the land, she said. "We had t' grub corn in 'round th' stumps. In plantin' season I'd take a grubbin' hoe 'n' a big bag 'a corn 'n' jist walk up 'n' down th' hillside, diggin' little holes 'n' puttin' in th' corn 'n' then trompin' hit down with th' hoe. I hoed th' same way—grubbin' 'n' trompin'." The tree stumps eventually decayed, but as soon as this occurred the farmers plowed the hillsides and before long the topsoil had washed away. Now,

Seafle says bitterly, even fertilizer cannot help the tired soil. "Nothin'll grow in sorry subsoil mostly hidin' 'twixt rocks."

Flossie continued narrating their early years. All but one of their children had been born when they moved to the Branch. She and Seafle cleared the ground, planted corn, tended two cows, reared their offspring, and lived off the land. Flossie did the milking and also canned in the summer and autumn. And because it was difficult to buy clothes for children at that time, she made most of their clothing herself. The hollow life being depicted sounded in so many respects like that I had known. And less and less like the place that was still their home.

The two doctors who ministered to the people had horses and made house calls at that time because the hollowers had no way of getting to them. When the Yancys moved to Duddie's Branch there were no hospitals and not even a drugstore nearby. Seafle went on to say that Shade had grown considerably since they came to the Branch but gives no credit to the railroad for its growth. "'At thar railroad—they made a mistake; they din't build hit t'go nowhar."

A few years after Seafle and Flossie settled in the Branch, Monk Razorback and his wife moved in; they were followed by Leander Shifter and his family. Another couple, the Lonnie Gilberts, set up housekeeping early too. No one is certain of the order in which the families arrived, and no two accounts agree.

"Thar's lots 'a people livin' on th' bank, now," Seafle added. "Then in '47 a flood come along 'at 'bout d'stroyed us 'n' th' warter got almost in t' my floor 'n' warshed away homes in this section 'a th' country. Hit costes me 'bout three yars' work atter 'at. Life hain't bin too bad, though."

The past that Seafle speaks of, bygone days that were marked by hard work, was far more prosperous than the present. The difference seems to have been primarily based on the mountaineers' willingness to work harder and to avail themselves of every opportunity to earn money. But such opportunities were never plentiful; the remoteness of the area, and of the county itself, is an inescapable handicap. In those days 60 per cent of the Branchers kept cows and had milk, even enough sometimes to make butter and cheese. "Back then thar 'uz grass," Seafle recalled. "Hain't 'nuf grass now t' feed

out a goat, 'n' they'll even eat weeds." The early settlers raised their
own meat and fowl; in addition to owning cows, every family had
hogs, ducks, chickens, and geese. Now, there are only two cows and
four pigs in the Branch. There is not enough potable water for human consumption, much less for livestock. Seven of the present
families own range chickens but they do not pen them and the fowl
go to the timber to lay and hatch their eggs, which the half-starved
dogs and 'possums consume. The chickens themselves often fall prey
to the marauding animals. Farming was never conducted on a large
scale because there are too many mountains and too few bottoms
to grow much of anything except table crops. Even that is harder now
because the topsoil has washed away from the bare hills, but in the
early days there was surplus enough to feed hogs. And after butcher-
ing there was grease enough to make soap and the people kept
their bodies and clothing cleaner.

While time was virtually standing still, the mountaineers' way of
life was not dissimilar to that of the people who lived in Shade and
there were no restrictive influences to prevent a free and easy exchange between the two communities. But the Industrial Revolution
that was felt by Shade failed to penetrate the hollows and the hazy
mountains, both of which were beyond the reach of automobiles
and all but the most determined humans. And so the mountaineer
was not wrenched from his old ways. Hence, a gradual difference
began to make itself seen in the clothing he wore, the way he spoke,
his level of education and experience, his hygiene—his very way of
life. As the disparities became more and more pronounced, the back-
woodsman withdrew more and more from community interchange
and no one protested his self-imposed isolation. The rift broadened
to such proportions that today no social or political integration
exists between the two communities.

One important truth emerges: Duddie's Branch was and still is
an unplanned neighborhood. According to present-day standards,
the twentieth-century primitives who inhabit it live in a 3-D world:
darkness, destitution, and deprivation. Their plight seems to be a
combination of social and economic conditions that have deepened
their poverty, while the same combination of forces has brought
affluence to others in our society. Their problems are so fundamental

that they inhibit analysis and remedial measures. What appears to the outsider as irrational conduct and behavior becomes intelligible only when viewed from within because the values peculiar to those in poverty cannot be explained or interpreted apart from their culture.

When one describes the people in this hollow as typical many are eager to challenge the term. For me typical is that which identifies people who share a way of life. True, typical has many meanings. Here the use of the word typical is intended to create a frame of reference within which to describe the life pattern of a social entity, hollows.

They feel that their homes and small pieces of land belong to them in a way that removes any need to participate in the outer world's senseless tension-laden pace. Their world belongs to them in the way that nothing else in society does or can. More than anything else, they belong to the Branch. They do not belong to Shade, or Hardstone, or Earle County—they belong to the closed society of the hollow and it is beloved by them. The adhesive that holds this populace together is the environmental setting and the atmosphere of security that transcends any economy of dire scarcity, and that pulls them back when they go forth to better their plight.

The outside world takes on a different hue when examined from the Branchers' frame of reference. And that frame of reference is paradoxical: in terms of length, only a mile; in terms of width, only about fifty feet; in terms of misery, limitless. The long period of isolation has been devastatingly effective in creating and perpetuating the small world, a world that must represent a rung on the "ladder infinite-stepped."[3]

[3] Sir Richard Burton, *The Kasidah of Haji Abdu El-Yazdi,* I, 7.

II

Deprivation: A Way of Life

The three problems of the age—the degradation of
man by poverty, the ruin of woman by starvation,
and the dwarfing of childhood by physical and spiritual night.

Victor Hugo
Les Misérables

Press a handkerchief to your nose and plunge into the slick, muddy
necropolis of the living dead—Duddie's Branch. The narrow artery
that dissects the ripe community is a fetid, honeycombed, mile-long
creek bed of slime stippled by debris-draped rocks. A miasma of
malodorous mortals and garbage slams into your stomach the deeper
you penetrate and even the packs of limp-tailed ravening dogs slink
about with compressed nostrils. On wintry mornings, pungent waves
of wood smoke scald your throat and when the sun burns off the
pearl from the dense atmosphere, a microcosm of poverty is exposed between gloomy canyon walls. Tarpaper shanties, tilting
drunkenly on rock stilts, huddle along the scabrous banks of the
creek and trash is strewn about with riotous imagination: under the
dwellings, on the porches, in the yards, on the banks, in the stream.
Shells of abandoned automobiles, silhouetted against the opaque
horizon like squat sepulchers, are left to corrode and crumble in the
Valley of the Poor.

The substandard houses rival the trash for space. Two thirds
(65.5 per cent) of the fifty-five dingy shacks cling to the very edge
of the Branch; 70 per cent are separated from one another by fewer
than two yards and 16 per cent are removed from their neighbors
by an additional yard or two. A coal storage shed and a chicken
coop also serve as dwellings, but these structures are not included
in the total number of residences. All of the shelters are constructed
of random combinations of old, weathered boards (some have a

clapboard lean-to attached to the back or side), but none is insulated. Only 12 per cent have the benefit of exterior finish, while the rest are partially protected with flapping sheets of tar-treated canvas. When dry twigs are not available to start a fire on cold mornings, the inhabitants rip off chunks of the tarpaper for fuel and spasmodic wisps of blue-gray smoke soon begin to writhe from clay pipes that protrude from the huts like Penrose drains. Little by little, the exterior reverts to rough lumber and even houses that are painted fall prey to the uncompromising weather that claws away enamel and denudes wood.

No surfaced paths lead to or around any of the hutches. A few flat stones have been dropped in the black pool the hollowers euphemistically call a yard, but these are glazed over with a slippery film of wet clay. Charybdis and Scylla await you. "Better take t' th' mud," Jabe counseled. "Footin' hain't fur sure on 'em thar rocks." But I tried. After two or three hard falls, a laceration or two, and soiled clothing, I sensed the wisdom of his recommendation. "Hit's better t' git mud on jist 'em shoes than t' spread hit all over," he reasoned.

In the dwellings that have windows, the general tendency is to install the type that do not open because they are cheaper and easier to cobble in. Except for letting in light, they say, there is no need for windows—the flies will just have to come in through the door. Ventilation is no problem; construction defects are so extensive that air, snow, rain, dust, and small creatures circulate freely through every part of the house.

The adequacy of the shelter is proportionate to the degree of discomfort. If a leak from the roof trickles into the room, measures are taken to keep the bed dry. If the leak is not above the bed, it is left to drip and find a hole in the floor boards to escape through. "Hain't no use hurryin' hit by sweepin'; hain't got nothin' to sweep with nohow." What about a mop? "'Em things costes money 'n' I hain't never had a hankerin' fur fancy things. Hain't no need wastin' stren'th t' do somethin' nature's plannin' on doin' anyways. Th' warter'll creep yander through 'em cracks.

"You's gotta keep movin' if'n you's wanta keep outta th' way 'a 'em drippin's. I knows whar they is 'n' if'n hit's measly rain I sits in 'at thar place, but if'n hit's a hard rain I runs outta places t' sit. Sometimes I cain't git th' younguns off t' larnin' 'cause they's duds gits froze on 'em while they's sleepin'. But if'n we stirs early we kin git th' ice thawed out 'n' they kin wiggle in 'em. 'Course if'n hit's bad cold, they's plum froze agin w'en they gits t' school."

The houses all lean backward or forward and you soon become accustomed to walking uphill or downhill in them. Since well-being is not immediately threatened, floor joists are not repaired.

"Somethin's bound t' give 'way 'neath thar one 'a these days," Al perceptively noted.

"Shouldn't you take a look and fix it now?"

"Nope. Cain't be sure w'at's gonna need fixin' first. Hain't plannin' nothin' till I's sure."

Al's equilibrium has to operate on a full-time schedule too. He notes his shack is "leanin' right smart." But as long as it is still standing, he figures he won't bother it.

The first and only step to Meander's door is three feet in height. If you are wearing a tight skirt, you can ascend it best by being launched from a pogo stick.

"Why in the world did you build your step so high?" I demanded.

"'At way I only needs one t' git t' m' door. 'Sides, I 'uzn't plannin' on nobody comin' in but me 'n' I's got long laigs."

My head collides with the ceiling in Willis' house. I have the choice of a possible spine curvature from standing in a stooped position throughout the visit or being rendered anemic by the legions of aggressive bedbugs which engage a vicious assault the moment I sit down until I leave. A considerable number of suicide squadrons embed themselves in the seams of my clothing and carry the battle to my camp.

"We's all built low t' th' ground, 'n' figgered thar warn't no point in buildin' a tall roof," Willis apologized. "Hit heats easier low down 'n' you's cain't live near th' roof nohow."

The broken-down stoves cannot compete with the wind that whistles through the shacks and the inhabitants stay cold all winter. You don't expect to thaw out until summer, I am told, so you just heat the spot that is coldest. At first, this was impossible for me because I was literally cold all over. I took to wearing thermal underwear and socks, lined boots, and wool suits in order to be reasonably warm. I even slept fully clothed and kept shifting position during the night to distribute the reflective heat of my body to different areas. My early reluctance to sleep in boots was shattered the first morning I tried hobbling about on two functionless appendages at ten degrees below zero.

Fuel represents such a large financial investment that the coal pile is a status symbol in the Branch. The few families that can afford to purchase a ton at a time would not think of storing it; it is left in the open for their neighbors to envy. If the coal reserve is modest, it is concealed. Letcher kept his two or three bushels in an old car body whose interior accessories were all missing.

"What happened to the insides?" I asked.

"We burnt w'at we could 'n' junked th' rest," he answered.

One of the doors had also vanished. Letcher explained that since none of the doors could be tightly shut, it made no difference if one was altogether removed, and why bother opening it each time coal was needed?

Most of the families have no fuel supply at all, but collect the small pieces of coal that fall from trucks as they round curves on the highway. They go out daily and search the highways for enough pieces to fill half a gunny sack, which is about all they can carry on their backs. In severe weather they must go foraging two or three times a day.

I was walking toward my jeep, having just watched a late, late movie on television with one of the families, when I caught sight of Willis walking down the Branch.

"Are you heading out?" I shouted to him.

"Reckon. Jerry's croupin' so we's gotta have a fire. I's borryin' some snake oil, too, if'n I gits up inta th' next Branch."

"At two o'clock in the morning?"

"They's prob'ly not sleepin' no how. Mostly huddlin' in this cold."

I drove him to his sister-in-law's shack in the next Branch. He opened the door without knocking.

"It might be better to knock," I advised.

"Nope. They's hain't got no gun. Anyways, they's slow t' stir w'en hit's cold."

It was as frigid inside the house as it was outside and I stood shivering while Willis conformed to prescribed protocol before making his request. On the return drive, I expressed concern that he would be unable to find coal in the dark.

"Reckon I won't look fur litterin's now; hit's too cold. I'll jist borry a picce hyur 'n' thar on my way in. Won't need much till sunup w'en I kin scour th' highway. Don't never need much nohow, 'cause we's only got one room and they's seven 'a us fur huddlin'."

Willis' story is typical of the hollow. The shapes and sizes of the dwellings vary, but the majority are overcrowded. In 67.7 per cent of the families, three or more persons sleep in one room and in 20 per cent anywhere from five to ten or more people share the same quarters. The houses cannot be classified in terms of rooms because one chamber usually serves multiple purposes—sleeping, eating, living, cooking, bathing; the homes must be classified in terms of space. The living area considered minimal for human requirements is 102 square feet per person, but statisticians seldom poll the Duddie's Branchers. Jude and his wife always have twelve children at home, and when their married daughter, her husband, and child stay with them—which is most of the time—the minimum space requirement is 1,794 square feet for seventeen persons. There are only 343 square feet of space in Jude's house, or an 81 per cent deficit of the minimum need.

Privacy, a retreat from noise and confusion, and a place for the children to play are not available. Youngsters are sent out even in raw weather to allow mothers and fathers a brief respite from the din and overcrowding. The unwholesome sleeping arrangements cannot be modified so easily, and parents and children of different sex sleep in the same room and frequently in the same bed. Many times I have bedded down in the middle of a urine-soggy mattress with three children on either side of me and two or three at my feet. We all slept in the fetal position, not through choice but through necessity. If by "stirrin' time" we were one degree removed from paralysis, we had the rest of the day in which to coax our numbed limbs to respond to mental commands.

The living deficiencies are not confined to comfort and space. Water is a scarce and, for the most part, impure resource in the

Branch. All but one of the twenty-three sources supplying the area have been tested for bacteriologic quality. Three contained potable water, three were questionably potable, and sixteen were contaminated. Five of the former are sufficient in quantity and serve eighteen per cent of the population. The remaining 82 per cent make do with polluted and/or insufficient water. The least brackish must be used for human consumption and parceled out frugally; miners and students attending one-room rural schools must furnish their own daily water requirements, which they carry in a jar. Many of the families use the contents of the creek several times over, even when it looks and smells like sewage: first, for washing hands, then for washing dishes; next, fruit jars are washed in it, after which it is used to wash the laundry; finally, it waters the livestock or a bite-sized garden plot.

During the time I lived in the Branch the creek was very low for a few weeks and what little water remained was as thick and dark as chocolate milk. Despite its appearance, the residents continued to avail themselves of it by siphoning off the top with a Coca-Cola bottle. I asked one boy how long it took to fill a tub in this manner. "If'n I gits hit filled afore you's drive up th' Branch, hit don't take more'n two hours," he solemnly replied. "But if'n you's stirs up th' mud, hit takes a heap longer."

The expense of drilling and the uncertainty of finding water are significant factors in discouraging the Branchers from sinking wells. Beyond that, they have adjusted to their desertlike existence and the need for an abundance of water rates low on their priority list; anything in excess of drinking and cooking requirements is not considered essential. No one can divine whether their sanitation would be improved if water were plentiful, but as the situation stands now, they bathe remarkably infrequently. " 'Udn't be much reasonin' t' usin' a bucket 'a warter jist fur warshin' up with. We'uns hain't much fur takin' off our duds nohow," declared Dana. "Scourin' younguns is a waste 'a time too. They's dirty filthy agin afore you's gits 'em clean th' first time. I jist scours up th' ones 'at's goin' schoolin'."

Although four of the dwellings have kitchen sinks, only two have running water (the quantity of which varies with the weather). Three of the sinks drain directly under the houses, and one drains into the

Branch. I mentioned the virtues of a drainage system to Claude, who does not endorse extravagant expenditure of energy. "If'n th' warter gits t' crowdin' me 'r m' shack, reckon I'd stir 'n' send hit headin' out."

"But what if it ran across Tiny's yard?"

"'At 'ud be his problem. If'n I's rid 'a hit, hain't my worry."

None of the fifty-five households has an inside toilet and only one has a privy that can be described as "good," and one other as "fair." Twenty-one of the families use toilets that are unfit for waste disposal and thirty-two families have no privy. The rocky nature of the soil partially accounts for the absence of suitable pit toilets; the other reason is that most of the hollowers fail to see the advantage of building a facility to satisfy their simplest needs. "Hain't no use buildin' fur somethin' nature's s'posed t' take care of. 'Sides, thar hain't no sense in pilin' shit in one place; hit'll stink if'n you's do."

On the basis of this simple philosophy, the somewhat seasonally related use of the toilets is easily understood. They are occasionally utilized in the summer, but outhouse traffic is light in cold weather or rain—particularly to those conveniences without roofs. Human excreta is consumed by the dogs which, in the words of a Brancher, "gotta eat somethin'." But the dogs do not dispose of it quickly enough; it is very much in evidence in the houses, on the porches, and in the yards.

To ascertain the value dimension of an inside toilet, I asked Shelly what he thought one would cost.

He scratched his head. "Heap 'a skin, I reckon."

"If someone gave you one, what would you do with it?"

Shelly was baffled. "Hain't 'xactly sure. Figger I'd not be a-needin' hit, so I'd prob'ly swap hit fur somethin'."

"Who would want it in the Branch?"

"Reckon nobody," he admitted.

"Then with whom would you swap?"

"Jist anyone."

"Anyone, Shelly?"

He deliberated. "Nope. Jist th' feller w'at's got somethin' I wants."

"Like what?"

"Hain't knowin' till I sees w'at th' feller's swappin'," he concluded.

Swapping personal, household, and food items is a general pattern of behavior for most of the men, many of the children, and some of the women. Commodity foods are the most prevalent items of barter, but the frequency with which other articles show up for interchange gives rise to suspicion. Gid Shifter suddenly began displaying a Winchester rifle in the Branch and said he paid ten dollars for it. During the next few days the weapon was swapped back and forth among almost all the families in the neighborhood, with a swap value of eight to ten dollars, until it ultimately became the property of Judey Shifter. Another time, a new television set (acquired for twenty-five dollars) went the rounds for several weeks before it found a permanent home. Although the men never specifically say that most of the barter articles are stolen, the admission is implicit in their general talk and in the low rate of exchange placed on them. Stolen goods are prized as a medium of interchange because they are cheap and can be traded back and forth for small sums of money that can be used to purchase clothing and essentials otherwise unobtainable.

Television sets are popular trade merchandise; it is not unusual to go up the Branch in the morning and see a television set in one home and find the same set in another house on the way down in the evening. The precise number of utilitarian appliances is extremely difficult to determine. Most of the families have radios and television sets, but the majority do not operate—in fact, the cabinet is generally all that remains of the original product. The same situation is true for the cars that stand idle in the hollow. Not only are they not in running condition, they have not enjoyed that distinction for some time. Washing machines constitute another perplexing statistic; almost every porch supports one, but only a few are operative. On one of my visits I asked Marshall why Alice did the laundry by hand when they had a washing machine. Hearing that it had not worked properly for quite some time, I was then curious why it was kept on the porch.

"Reckon hit jist 's well set thar 's somewhar else. Leastaways, hit's ketchin' a heap 'a things thar hain't room fur otherwise."

Alice washed a few pieces of clothing, emptied the tub into the yard, and sank down on the porch. I referred to the mound of dirty laundry relaxing against the washing machine.

"We's plannin' on warshin' 'em if'n we needs 'em 'n' if'n we has th' warsher a-runnin' 'n' if'n we has soap 'n' if'n we has warter."

"And if you don't get all those things?"

"Cain't rightly tell w'at'll be, then," she calmly responded.

The amount of water available for laundry purposes is the most portentous determinant of how much and how frequently it is done. When the Branch is high there is no problem, but when it is running low this activity is sharply restricted and it is not unusual for the family wash to be done only once every five or six weeks. There is no staggering accumulation of laundry because none of the families has much to accumulate—no tablecloths or napkins, rarely sheets and pillowcases, only a few towels and washcloths, scarcely any underwear, not one sleeping garment, and not more than one change of apparel per person. The most obvious effects of the infrequent washdays are seen in the grimy clothing the people wear and in the two or three towels that serve all family members until they are rigid with use. Notwithstanding the small laundry, this chore is still oppressive. Every wife in the Branch does the washing in the yard all year round because there is not enough space to do it inside or a stove capable of heating a tub of water. The women build a fire close to the creek where the water is most accessible and keep filling and heating their tubs as they need them. The entire wash is done by hand and spread over bushes or on fences to dry.

Most of the work in the hollow descends upon the females who, in addition to the laundry, do the housekeeping, yard duties, and gardening. They are also responsible for collecting coal, getting food supplies, cooking and serving the meals, carrying water from the well or creek, building and tending the fire, and caring for the children. The older daughters are of little assistance, spending most of their time in play activities. Because of the primitive manner in which the tasks are performed, the most routine housekeeping chore is difficult. Few households have more than one pan or a skillet in which to cook food or a bowl or a place in which to prepare it. In the summer the women peel potatoes and string beans on the porches, but in cold weather they must do everything inside. Eating utensils are likewise sparse; when I ate meals with a family I was the only one who sometimes ate from a plate or pie tin and had either a fork or spoon. Everyone else dipped into the pot of beans or gravy with his hands or used the bare breastbone of a chicken as a scoop. I talked to Elsie about applying for a job in Shade as a waitress, and explained the duties. The idea of furnishing each customer with a set of silverware was intimidating. "I sure hain't knowin' w'at outside fellers eats with; I hain't never used nothin' 'ceptin' fingers fur eatin'. Bestes I's findin' a feller fur marryin' 'n' hankerin' fur holler livin'." A few chipped cups without handles are owned by some of the families, but never did I see a saucer. Tin cans are often substituted for cups. The dearth of cooking and eating implements is not of much concern since few homes have kitchen cabinets or other storage places in which to keep them when they are not in use. Dishwashing, therefore, is not a time-consuming task, but it is done in such a perfunctory fashion that even the little time spent in this effort is wasted. In lieu of a sink, dishes are washed in a pan of cold or tepid water. No soap is used to make the job easier, nor are the utensils ever scalded or rinsed to make them more sanitary. As a result, they usually carry stubbornly encrusted remnants of one meal over to the next. The skillet in which corn bread is mixed and cooked is never washed or even wiped out and one generation could well be digesting grains of an adherent layer that fed a previous generation.

The rewards for being a hollow wife must be more spiritual than material. Even the tension-releasing exercise of gossiping conveniently is denied her; there is not one telephone in the neighborhood and all communication is entirely by word of mouth.

Electric lines were run through Duddie's Branch in 1952 and some of the families do pay for this service. Others benefit by having "borried from th' light line. Figgered 's long 's hit's passin', might jist 's well take some 'a hit." The ingenuity of the functional illiterate to tap a power feed line for electric current without the protection of insulated gloves or tools, knowledge of electric power, and understanding of distribution patterns is mystifying. A number of the families, however, neither pay for electricity nor borrow it—they still depend on coal-oil lamps for illumination. "We beds down

early so thar hain't no need fur dark-seein'. Hain't got nothin' much
t' see in hyur nohow."

The truth is grossly understated. With few exceptions, the housekeeping is shocking and the filth defies description. The air is foul
with the stifling odor of dried urine, stale cooking, unwashed bodies,
dirty clothing. The incomprehensible chatter of children at play
drifts through boards and breathing is further endangered as the
dust they stir up seeps through the crevices. A wide variety of bugs
and rodents, which claim squatter's rights to every corner and loose
board, leisurely emerge from their territories and trek to the generous hunting ground—the floor. Food particles are so bounteous that
all species grow and multiply in harmony, and even the bedbugs are
defiantly secure. Their hosts bear the badges of battle but have
neither the means nor the knowledge to exterminate the night-
marauding armies. Because they are unequipped to counterattack,
the Branchers regard all insects as immortal foes—especially the
flying kind that "kin make a hole in you's faster'n a woodpecker
kin bore out a livin' tree. Thar hain't no leaves t' fall off w'en we's
dyin', but we's dyin' jist as daid."

The floors of the shacks are made of roughly sawed boards between which fissures have been created by the natural aging of the
wood. Some of the surfaces are concealed with well-worn linoleums
that have molded themselves to the contours of the "humpin'
timbers." Cracks also develop in the walls and ceiling and the cold
air comes whipping through those that are not invested with
cardboard, newspaper, or pages from magazines. Decorating paper
is seldom employed; when it is, several different patterns and colors
are often seen in one room. Other coverings are used as well. Since
none of the houses has closets, anything that is not being worn or
that can be hung is suspended from nails. Family portraits also
often adorn the walls; pictures of deceased relatives are most often
displayed, and those of dead children apparently have more emotional
significance than photographs of adults consigned to coffins.

Coal- or wood-burning stoves are used for both cooking and heating purposes. Two families have electric ranges and upon delivery
were told that special electrical wiring was required. It took several
months for them to save enough money to have the appliances

properly installed. A number of the homes have electric refrigerators, but there are many which do not even have iceboxes.

Crude, hand-made tables and benches are found in many homes. They are made of scrap lumber and are neither painted nor stained. Some families own a backless chair or two, but lard cans substitute as a seating facility with astonishing regularity. Dwellings contain filthy, decrepit couches and a few have old, banged-up dressers tucked away in a corner. The most common piece of furniture is a bed, and no other appointments are seen in any of the homes beyond the insufficient, well-worn pieces mentioned.

Personal possessions are as skimpy and shabby as the furnishings. In answer to her teacher's question as to why she was absent from school for two days, Kizzie replied that her dress was being washed and it took one day for the washing, a second for drying. Her shoes were so broken down and shapeless, it was little short of miraculous that she could keep them on her feet. Most clothing is purchased from secondhand stores and, even though it is less expensive than new merchandise, the prices often exceed the value of the item. Faded dresses with missing buttons and belts cost from ten cents to a dollar and none of the clothing is cleaned or washed before it is put up for sale. Children's used shoes are in such poor condition that they are generally rejected, but new shoes that cost two dollars cannot withstand the daily punishment of mud and water for any length of time either. Most children, and some adults, walk about barefooted or in raggedy, soiled tennis shoes several times too large or a size or so too small. Only one man in Duddie's Branch has a wool suit and overcoat, both old but serviceable.

Such grooming articles as nailfiles, hairbrushes, deodorants, and razor blades are seldom acquired. "Rags, dirt, whiskers—we lives like this. You know how much shavin' costes?" Most of the Branchers will spend a lifetime without ever having brushed their teeth and the snags they might retain at the time of their demise will give the grim reaper little cause to wonder where the yellow went. The consequences, however, will be slight: they rarely have an opportunity to bite into anything more solid than blue gravy. It made such a regular appearance at meals that I became one of the most expert finger gravy eaters in the Branch. I learned to eat the thick type in short order and after a brief training period I mastered the technique of eating the thin, watery variety without losing a drop in transit. In the beginning, the blue gravy on three of my fingers provided an interesting contrast with my dirt-blackened hands; after eating several meals of very thin gravy, the trio of digits began to regain a normal appearance, after which the contrast was dramatic indeed. Much to my chagrin, I was unable to match the Branchers' skill in bread-sopping; I could never accurately estimate how much gravy the bread would support or where it was most apt to buckle when overburdened.

When pinto beans make the menu, nothing else does. Sometimes a microscopic piece of pork is available to add flavor to the unwashed pintos. Potatoes, green beans, tomatoes, and sweet corn furnish a refreshing change in the summer. Most commodity foods are staples, and the canned meat is far from a favorite among the recipients. Nonetheless, their very survival depends on the surplus foods and they have no alternative but to overcome their aversion to them. As Herb delphically submitted, "If'n a poke's got nothin' in hit, hit cain't stand up." Those who are ashamed of being on welfare hide the commodities in the hills and return for what remains of them after it is dark. If another resident discovers the cache he is not above helping himself to the most desirable goods and converting them into cash. One day I saw Winn, a ten-year-old, in a clump of trees guarding the family supply of surplus food. I asked him why he was not in school and he told me that he had accompanied his mother for their allotment but that she had to walk six miles farther on to care for an ailing parent. He was waiting for her to help him carry the groceries home.

"What if someone were to come along and take some of your commodities, Winn?" I asked.

"Reckon I'd not be doin' nothin' if'n th' feller 'uz bigger'n me; I'd jist be seein' him takin' 'em. But Paw 'ud hide me fur losin' our grub."

The miners are addicted to a high-glucose diet. Mr. Hiram is of the opinion that sweets are digested easier than anything else in the poorly ventilated shafts. I was in the store a few times and took note of what the men bought for lunch—a pie, an apple turnover, a jelly roll, and nothing more. One man who always took a Pepsi-Cola to work had to stop drinking them when he was transferred to a low coal vein; the combined height of his head and the tilted bottle amounted to more than the sixteen inches from the bottom of the tunnel to the top.

Filth, overcrowding, discomfort, hunger, thirst, rags—these are the ingredients of deprivation; the Duddie's Brancher is its product and a one-way journey to the human slag heap is his destination.

Reva was only six years old when I first saw her, but even at that age she had reached the point of no return. Enormous, deep-set eyes seemed to occupy her entire face and she had not started to school yet because of her small stature; chronic malnutrition had delayed her growth to half of what is considered normal. She lives in a 10 × 10-foot shack with her parents and eleven brothers and sisters.

Reva was always the first to sight me on my way up the Branch and she would run barefooted through the snow or frozen mud to clasp my hand. Jude, her father, told me that he worked in the mines for thirty years (employment records indicate eight or fewer years for short periods) before his poor lungs forced him to quit. He is emaciated and haggard and appears to be fifteen years older than his actual age of forty-three. The army rejected him in 1940 and he considers this unfair. "They's ejected me fur nothin'. Hit warn't 'cause 'a m' shootin', neither—I's right good gunnin'."

"They must have said why they wouldn't accept you."

"They jist mouthed 'at I warn't physical."

The only time he has been away from Earle County was shortly after the army turned him down; he and some other men went to Baltimore to find work but no one would hire them. On his way back to the Branch he stopped in Indiana and tried unsuccessfully to get a job on the railroad. He attended school for three years and thinks that he finished the third grade. Layuna, his wife, has no education.

For a long time this family lived on commodities amounting to thirty-nine dollars a month. The supplies never lasted more than two weeks and Layuna would have to secure an emergency order. Much of the food was thrown out because they either did not know how to prepare it or they did not like it.

The only water available to them is a bucket a day they get from neighbors—when all is well. When the donors are temperamental, they go without water. "If'n they's a mite friendly, we gits drinkin'."

The children are covered with big sores and are often sent home from school because of them. Layuna could not treat the youngsters properly because she never had enough medicine. Although the salve is free, it is only distributed in two-ounce tubes and the amount was not enough to cover the sores of even one child. In addition, each round trip to pick up the ointment cost a dollar and a half. Every time I went into town I would stop for the medicine and once I asked the workers why Layuna was not given an adequate supply.

"If she were, she'd sell it instead of using it on the kids."

I knew that this would not be the case, but kept silent.

I was able to talk a physician friend out of a one-pound jar of the medication and told Layuna that he had sent it to her. All the scabs had to be removed before the ointment was applied, so I had Jude cut the children's hair close to their scalps. It took me one day to remove the crusts from four heads and the next day I tackled four more. The neighbors were not cooperative at this time, so I made compresses from Branch water to soak off the incrustations. Much to my surprise, their scalps remained intact and the scabs finally loosened. When the medication was used up, Layuna asked me to "'preciate 'at feller fur hit."

If these people are not low family on the Branch totem pole, they are but a millimeter away. Their regular welfare applications have not been approved in ten years. "'Em fellers jist hain't took no likin' fur us'ns." One physician reports that Jude is physically sound, while another says that he is unable to work. Jude volunteered to enter a tuberculosis sanatorium so that he could qualify as "disabled," but chest X rays disclosed no evidence of tuberculosis and a test of his "spittin'" was negative.

He returned to the mine long enough to earn "rockin' chair" money, at which time he would quit. When the money gave out, he would work again for a while and this was his schedule for some time. But for many years now the mine operators will not hire him because of his erratic work pattern.

He "borrows" electricity from the REA line and the children scavenge coal along the highway. The fuel is so precious to them that they use it only when Layuna cooks and the children must stay in bed most of the time in order to keep warm.

Most of their children have been delivered at home by the local midwife. The babies come often and are thin and frail and prone to long periods of diarrhea. Layuna does not take them to the clinic because she cannot pay "fur haulin'." When Keith was a year old he weighed only sixteen pounds and could not stand even when holding onto something. He was extremely anemic and malnourished from the daily doses of Castoria his mother gave him to get rid of worms. The Health Department provided Layuna with Duofoam birth control cream, but she refused to use it because she did not think that anyone should "stick somethin' in you's body. I hain't usin' hit; I hain't aimin' hit up me."

Layuna keeps hoping that someday they will live better and she often wonders if anything would improve the children's health. "One 'a 'em nursin' wormans sayed vitins [vitamins] lackin'. If'n I's knowin' 'em, reckon Jude 'ud dig 'em up in 'em fur hills. Hain't costes nothin' then."

One day I asked her what she would most like to have if she were granted one wish. In a home where there was so little, I was curious to hear what she would want.

"Hain't big."

"I don't think I can guess, so you had better tell me."

"Hit 'ud be a picher 'a you."

I tried to bury my emotion. "Oh, Layuna, what good would that do you?"

"If'n you's headin' out fur long, I's still got you's hyur, in a way."

Her wish was granted.

I have sent several people to the hollow and always request that they check on Layuna for me. She never fails to point to my picture on the wall and tell them that I have a house in the head of the hollow, " 'ceptin' her hain't hyur 'nuf fur suitin' us'ns." My place is the only one referred to as a "house"; all the others are called "shacks."

"Right nice fixin's in hit, 'ceptin' no picher maker [television].

But I's glad. 'At way we's gits her fur watchin'. Mouths she's from th' 'versity, but she hain't never claimin' high-like. Her's our'n. Hain't nary one afore her took no likin' fur holler folkses. We's prayin' fur her's stayin', 'ceptin' she's claimin' job workin' some-whars. We's hain't th' missin' kind 'a folkses, 'ceptin' we's missin' a heap fur her."

And I miss them and I ache for them. I can hold out my hand for Reva to clasp, but I cannot hold her back from the inevitable journey she has already begun.

III

The Meaning of Isolation

> Life, misfortunes, isolation, abandonment, poverty,
> are battlefields which have their heroes; obscure
> heroes, sometimes greater than the illustrious heroes.
>
> Victor Hugo
> *Les Misérables*

The components of isolation depend on the frame of reference used by the one defining it. For some they are physical; for others they are intellectual, or geographic, or traditional. The meaning depends on the circumstances in which it is identified and described. If it recalls the cloistered nun, you visualize one who is isolated from outside life. But those who prefer a monastic environment may look upon outside life as a form of withdrawal. The penitentiary inmate who is detained in solitary confinement is more isolated than his fellow prisoners who are merely kept behind bars. The patient in a hospital quarantine ward has daily encounters with health personnel, holds telephone conversations with family and friends, is supplied with newspapers and other reading material and watches television programs without restriction. Yet his medical attendants, his loved ones, and he himself will say that he is isolated.

Isolation is a complicated assemblage of particulars. It is relative. It is chosen or imposed. It varies in degree.

Isolation is an all-encompassing way of life to the Duddie's Brancher. The dictionary does not define the kind of separation that is absolute, the kind that is spatial and temporal. It begins with "stirrin'," and continues until it is time to "bed down." The hollow man understands this form of exile as a never-ending condition. His principal motivation is daily existence and there is no novelty in any day's experience. Of this perpetual time sequence, Meander says, "Wa'al, you's stirrin' 'thout knowin' hit hain't th' same 's w'en th' sun left out."

The days of the week are meaningless to them. They do not measure time, because they have no concept of time—the notion that there is something to be measured.

After an absence of one month, I returned to the Branch.

"You's left out 'n' you's gone a heap more'n Paw's bin daid," Frank reproached.

His father had been dead for eight years.

They are capable of only the crudest calibration and use nature, not events, as their time yardstick.

"What day is this?" I ask.

"Reckon hit's gonna be a waterin' day. See 'em rain makers [clouds] yander?"

"Gonna be a hungerin' day way 'em hawlers [wolves] 'uz rarin' 'n' tearin' durin' sleepin'."

"Reckon hit's aimin' on bein' a right perty day."

"Hain't gonna be a heatin' day long 's 'em leaves is hurryin'."

If it is a Saturday or Sunday, the inevitable response is, "Hit hain't a schoolin' day."

They do not use clocks to enable them to keep count of passing hours or to plan their day. "Clocks 's one 'a 'em things 'at goes broke all th' time. We got shed 'a our'n—traded hit off fur coal. Now we don't have nothin' t' worry 'bout."

They do not use calendars to enable them to keep count of passing days or to plan their future. They covet them for their "perty pichers" and their prestige value. A calendar advertising the bank is deemed more valuable than one advertising a small store; that distributed by the funeral home or "th' undertakin' man" ranks next to the bank's offering. " 'Em buryin' fellers 's might' nigh th' pertiest." Calendars with only one picture are less desirable than those with a different illustration for each month.

The hollower is oriented to the past, not to the future, and time lends a grim continuity and shape to his life. Today is like yesterday and tomorrow will be like today. His life has been deadened by sameness. Ovid might have been portraying Duddie's Branch when he wrote, "One would think that time stood still, so slowly does it move."

Isolation is a girdle of mountains.

"'Em thar hills 'r' liken shack walls holdin' up roofin'; keeps outer a heap. 'N' th' sky's right perty roofin'."

It is "home" in the hollow and it has been so for generations.

"I growed up 'twixt 'em mount'ins. Paw too. Paw's younguns, my younguns, reckon right smart 'a m' kin growed up hyur 'twixt 'em. Thar'll be a heap more younguns 'at hain't bin dropped 'at'll grow 'twixt 'em."

The prospect of living and dying in this hollow is not viewed as an assault upon human dignity—it is all that they have ever known.

I asked Meander how he felt about living in Duddie's Branch.

"I's jist liken a rabbit in high weeds."

"How does a rabbit get out of high weeds, Meander?"

His astonishment that a rabbit would embark on such a reckless course was plainly evident.

"'S long 's you's 's in high weeds, you's hain't gonna be starvin', thar hain't gonna be no outsiders, 'n' you's 's gonna be livin' 'cause they cain't see t' shoot you's daid."

Every Brancher embraces this philosophy with a quiet resignation; he is not disposed to make confessions of hardship because he knows that outer society is firmly closed to him. He wordlessly accepts his lot and is able to live with pride in a social complex that is deplorable simply because "deplorable" is the outer community's word, not his. His standards have been forged in a setting of isolation, and they are as old as the stone walls that helped fashion them.

He is resistant to change because he believes that his way of life is just as good as anyone else's and will vigorously defend what he considers to be his rights. He is, perhaps, more practical than we are. He does not feel that his situation can be changed. "Hain't a feller livin' 'at kin make somethin' outta a junk heap." With automation condemning all humans to physical uselessness, how realistic are we when we try to make the unwanted misfit feel that he is needed? "If'n they's not knowin' we's hyur, how kin they be missin' us fellers?"

The mountains are to the hollower what the weeds are to the rabbit and what redwood basket-weave fences are to the suburbanite—a shield from the outside world. The towering parapets flank the sides of the hollow, making it appear even more submerged. Nature has adorned the austere cliffs with shimmering trees, gay wild flowers, colorful birds, and countless kinds of animals and "creepers" or insects. These embellishments contribute to a feeling of security and pride, and favor the hollower with something to survey while he's "sittin' spittin'." Secluded and serene, he is at liberty to meditate on his possessions: the birds, the animals, even the creepers. "If'n they's usin' my land, they's mine."

The mountains are his sanctuary and his curse; they protect him from a foreign world—a world made foreign by virtue of their presence.

Isolation is a one-way road to desolation.

To some urban dwellers the ideal location for a home is on a dead-end street. The hollower is spared the agonizing decision of which street to select as a site for his home. There are no streets in Duddie's Branch.

The absence of a roadway plays a vital role in his exile. A pitted stream bed filled with slick boulders and bordered by high rock ledges affords the only approach—a one-way, single-lane passage from the mouth of the hollow to its head. The channel cannot be described as a dead-end street because the stream bed goes nowhere; it is a "dead-beginning" street. There is no through traffic and any form of transit is limited. "Hain't nary none 'ceptin' you's hankerin' t' rock fur headin' in," Seafle heeds. "If'n 'e does 'n' 'e's a stranger, we jist rolls a car in th' Branch, stoppin' 'im movin' till we's seein' if'n 'e's a pizen stranger we's hain't keepin'. If'n 'e's a quar stranger, we hain't keepin' th' likes 'a 'im, neither. Sech quar stranger be leavin' out liken lightnin'. Hain't 'lowin' tarryin' 'r us fellers 'ud band up agin 'im."

If he appears to be "aimin' on snoopin'," or to be too "knowin'," he is soon "stretchin' 'is legs, headin' out" toward the mouth of the hollow. If his goal is to find a specific person, his first attempts will be repelled. " 'E daid shore hain't gonna find 'im." The hollow's responses are discouraging.

"Never sot eyes on 'im."

"Reckon 'im hain't livin'."

If the venturesome stranger persists, he will eventually be advised that "thar hain't nary a feller hyur you's aimin' t' see."

"Thought I saw a man heading in a while ago?" I wondered aloud.

"Reckon," Meander agreed.

"What did he want?"

"Warn't 'at w'at 'e's mouthin'."

"He wasn't easy to give up, was he?"

"Nope. One 'a 'em strangers 'at's hard dyin'."

The rare straggler who does challenge the stream bed does not penetrate the hollow very deeply before someone is hawk-eying him. The hollowers are obliged to build their dwellings on the bank of the Branch, but they are rewarded with strategic position. "We's kin look down 'n' see a heap more faster'n 'em fellers tryin' t' look skyway."

Their privacy is not often imperiled, however; the almost impenetrable terrain precludes mass invasion. Having to immerse himself in the continuous task of seeking a foothold in the thick, slimy mud, the pedestrian is too occupied to engage in extensive reconnaissance. Pedestrian activity is as scarce as automobile traffic, and after much painful experience I concluded that walking, being more down than up, is surely the most hazardous form of travel. "You's gotta be a sure-footed rock hopper t' keep you's shoes dry," Nancy cautioned. "If'n thar warn't fillin's 'a busted glass and 'em cans, I'd be wearin' m' bare feets. They's most 'a th' time rusty [dirty] anyway, 'n' they's a heap easier t' scour 'n shoes. Feets lastes longer'n shoes, too. 'Sides, thar hain't money t' buy 'em back [replace worn-out shoes]."

The lack of a thoroughfare is a two-edged sword; it keeps the outsiders out and the insiders in.

Isolation is living in obscurity a few miles from a thriving community.

The world whizzes past the turnoff into the hollow and does not even know that it is there. Coming in from the direction of town, a precipitous right turn plunges your car nose-first down a steep grade and onto a narrow dirt road with a "sprinklin' 'a mite rock." Your side view is completely obscured by the tall, healthy weeds that surround the car. Farther in, a junked automobile relaxes at an odd angle, critically balanced on the narrow edge of the bank. Its glass is shattered; tires, wheels, all removable parts are long since missing. The orange-pink hue of its battered, weathered exterior offers a bright spot of color against the drab background. The car's life ended right where it stopped; the hollower's life stopped right where it began. They are seldom needed, never wanted, and rarely noticed by the outside world.

"You's ever walked in wet smoke [fog]?" Westley wanted to know. "W'en you's in thar, any fellers seein' you's?"

An eloquent way of telling me that no one in the outer society ever sees a Brancher. And if they are acknowledged, it might take a long time. Anton was cited for the Bronze Star on March 26, 1945, after heroic ground combat in Germany. Twenty-one years later he received the medal. "Hit jist goes t' show 'at th' gover'munt hain't never furgot me," the hero said with a proud smile.

"Don't go out much," confided Bert. "Hain't no use. Oh, I mosey out t' th' post office, but hain't 'spectin' no mail 'n' don't git none. Most times w'en I sez 'howdy,' outside fellers jist looks away less'n they's knowin' me. They might speak if'n they's knowin' my paw, but reckon they hain't fur mixin' less'n hit's with their own kind. We hain't used t' people likin' us jist fur visitin' with."

He is perceptive enough to know that his presence makes the people in the outside world uncomfortable—that they are ashamed of him, anxious to avoid him, reluctant to admit him into their society, unable to understand him. The only attention he receives, if indeed he receives any, is contempt. Some of the outsiders frankly admit that the Branchers' smell nauseates them. Others disdain to talk to the Brancher. "It's all one-sided talk, anyway; they can't even answer a simple question."

"It's better they stay up in the hollow. They can keep out of trouble there."

"If they earned fifty dollars a day they'd still be hungry and stink."

It is impossible to find a single instance of an attempt to draw a hollow dweller into any activity in the community.

"Where are you heading, Bert?"

"Jist a-walkin'."

So I walk along. Bert knows me well; we have sat together for many long hours, the rocks "punchin' our sittin' bones." When he is "hankerin' fur mouthin'" we talk but, like all Branchers, he abominates interrogation. I have had to resist that temptation more times than I can remember, but I had rather forgo questions than reap a harvest of silence.

"'Ceptin' fur you's, hain't many fellers talkin' back sense."

He seldom raises his eyes when he talks. As we walk along, I chide his habit of looking down. He lifts his head just enough to "squar-eye" me.

"I's watchin' these feets movin'."

Bert knows that I am not deceived. He has acquired the custom from a lifetime of avoiding the puzzled mien of the outsider. He knows that he is not articulate, that he employs a special language unfamiliar to the more fortunate.

How do we listen to the language of the deprived? How do we respond to incomprehensible speech? One of the hollowers visited Washington during a poverty march in an effort to apprise the welfare officials of the needs of the poor.

"What did you say to the committee, Seafle?"

"Them fellers is funny listeners," he replied. "They's talkin' at th' same time I's tellin'."

The Branchers are inhibited by the limitations imposed on them by their past and hampered by a meager vocabulary. They are keenly aware of their difference, and their loneliness is profound.

"Thar's fellers you's takes a likin' to 'n' fellers 'at takes a likin' t' you's. Most 'a us holler fellers took a likin' t' you's atter we's knowin' you's warn't aimin' on pryin'. Nary stranger 'fore you's took no likin' fur holler fellers. Most 'a us fellers wantin' you's 'round 'bout even if'n you's left out."

"I wish I didn't have to make a living, Bert. I'd just hole up in this hollow."

"Hain't no need you's leavin' out. Grub's rough, but 'nuther mouth fur feedin' hain't starvin' none. Hain't bin nary none stayed hyur 'ceptin' kin afore you's got holler in you's blood."

The hollower knows that he belongs only to the Branch. His isolation, which began as a physical restriction from living in the upland area, has become a mental shell he has no desire to pip. In the Branch he is among his own kind; he has authority and he is respected.

Isolation is a total ignorance of events at all levels.

The Brancher does not subscribe to local or other newspapers. He could not read them if he did. I went to see Seafle, the Brancher I considered to know the most about the outside world. I had a paper under my arm.

"You's aimin' on readin'?" he wondered.

"I brought the paper to show you some pictures of people you might know."

"Reckon I hain't knowin' 'em less'n they's from 'round hyur close."

The pictures were of twenty-four famous people who had died in 1965: Albert Schweitzer, Winston Churchill, Lady Astor, Bernard Baruch, Cardinal Meyer, Linda Darnell, Edward R. Murrow, Adlai Stevenson, T. S. Eliot, Constance Bennett, H. V. Kaltenborn, Marie McDonald, King Farouk, Jeanette MacDonald, David O. Selznick, Nat King Cole, Spike Jones, Felix Frankfurter, Quentin Reynolds, Dorothy Kilgallen, Helena Rubenstein, Stan Laurel, W. Somerset Maugham, and Henry Wallace.

He studied the likenesses for a long time. "Glad t' see they's on'y five wormen. Men's bounden t' be wu'th most." Because of the short, straight, severe hair style of one of the females he mistook her for a man.

"Three 'a 'em feller's 's got hats on. Never c'd git a good look at fellers hidin' under hats."

I made the names visible to him. "Now do you know any of them?"

You learn to wait a long time while they are in the process of "reckonin'."

Finally, "See they's two kings 'mong 'em." [King Farouk and Nat King Cole].

"What is a king?"

"We's on'y had one king—Kennedy. But reckon most 'a 'em's rich liken our'n."

"How rich is rich?"

"I's heerd hit's havin' so much money you's cain't count hit. Th' wormens 'r' right perty."

"Do any of the people look like farmers?"

"Don't reckon in 'em duds. Reckon they's done somethin', but hain't knowin' w'at."

The Brancher does not file a federal income tax return or pay state personal taxes because his income is not sufficient for either one. The census takers don't even include him in their reports! This is supreme isolation. They know he is there, but getting up the Branch requires more effort than the pollers apparently care to invest.

Most of the boys are rejected for the armed forces for mental or physical reasons and not one has full insight into the significance of his absolute uselessness—that he is fated to become a burden on society. Clifford, one of the few who has even a glimmering of the war in Vietnam, tried unsuccessfully to join the army. I asked him if he knew why he was turned down.

"Yep. I's a dropout. I's handied [handicapped]. M' ol' man's on relief 'n' I hain't never worked. I din't pass th' mind text. 'At thar worman sayed m' schoolin' 'uzn't nothin' sence I cun't read 'r write none. I tol' 'er I 'uzn't aimin' on joinin' so's I c'd be readin'. I c'd shoot, 'n' 'at's why I 'uz goin' t' join 'em. But if'n 'em fellers 's choosy, not wantin' me as I is, then I hain't wantin' 'em none."

It is not surprising that they are prevented from performing as citizens of their country; they must first be regarded as citizens of their county.

The Brancher is not a member of the county group that buys $125,428 worth of Series E and H savings bonds and notes each year. He does not even know what they are. The only bond he understands is the kind that requires money to get out of jail.

The Brancher does not know that there are opening and closing dates for hunting seasons. When he wants a squirrel, and if he has shells, he shoots. There is no need for him to buy a hunting license; he is too isolated to participate in this law.

He does not know that there is a Saddle Club in his county. I de-

scribe the horse show: classes for lead line, pleasure, open rack-
ing, three-gaited walking horses. I might as well be explaining the
intricacies of a space ship to a herd of cattle.

"Hain't hankerin' t' wastes talkin' 'r sittin' fur th' likes 'a 'at."

I hold court and expound on matters they do not understand or
have little interest in and am distressed to see my formerly intent audience disappear one by one. Their message is conveyed. I change
the subject and recapture their attention by discussing an increase in
welfare payments, a topic of great consequence to them. Not only
does my assemblage return, newcomers swell its ranks.

They do not know that construction of the Ford Creek Dam is
necessary for the growth of Earle County. Beyond the recreational
potential, the primary purpose of the lake is to ensure a source of
water for the city of Shade. They couldn't care less. *Their* water
supply won't be increased.

They do not know that a plan has been proposed to extend the
sewage plant in the county seat at a cost of $366,000. They *do* know
that no one will run sewer lines up to the hollow.

They do not know that Kentucky is barren ground for million-
dollar-a-year men; not one resides there. I tried to explain to Meander
that the poorest 20 per cent of the United States population earned
about 5 per cent of the income in 1960. He was genuinely touched.

"Right pitiful fur 'em rich fellers. Reckon they's havin' t' eat biscuit
bread? They's a heap better off drawin' [welfare]. If'n they lights
hyur, I's tellin' 'em 'bout drawin'."

They rarely, if ever, come in contact with the currents of modern
thought, with changing reality, with the twentieth century. A few
outsiders may profess concern for them, but the hollowers do not
become excited. They indulge the benevolist and patiently listen to
his schemes to modernize their hollows, to eliminate their dialects,
to prohibit them from sitting on their porches, and to render them
functional in society.

"'Em fellers 's dreamin' big. We's jist figgerin' shoulderin' our guns
fur huntin' if'n we's struck by a notion 'n' if'n we's got firin',"
shrugged Ben.

Nobody hears the Brancher as he urgently insists in his non-verbal
means of communication that he wants to be himself. In isolation he

can escape the pressures on the individual to conform and adjust to our democratic autocracy. Agony for him is the outer world, not the hollow. In the Branch he is not subjected to exploitation and rejection, and he had rather be a have-not in a have-not world than a have-not in a have world. There is no rebellion in his sphere because his neighbors' circumstances are the same as his. The last thing a fish would be conscious of would be the water in which he lives. So it is with the Brancher—an embedded man lives just as innocently in the culture of his neighborhood. It provides for him an insulation from all other cultures and protects him from having to accept values that he feels are contrary to his best interests.

Isolation is not selective; it attacks the young as well as the old.

For the first six or more years of life the child is utterly dependent on those who care for him. During that time he acquires deeply rooted social habits in terms of communication, self-awareness, and other characteristics that are passed on to him through the social order and biological nature of his being. Since each Brancher interacts only with others of the same kind, the child is doomed to become a carbon copy of the products of his community. He is accustomed to the intensely personal transactions of his immediate family and associates and is incapable of analyzing and developing his attributes. He speaks and walks later than other children, has far less curiosity and imagination, and learns more slowly. The only thing he grasps quickly is the routine of crisis. The result of these experiences tends to glue him to his tradition and to his family. He is passive and shy, and regards the outside world and school as sinister places. Estranged from the outer community, he is committed to a lifetime of nothingness in a mile-long hollow of emptiness.

Childhood is not a special time of life in Duddie's Branch. The circus comes to town, but hollow children are not impressed. The vivid posters extolling the fabulous monsters, the ferocious felines, the dangerous stunts of the performers either go unnoticed or are misunderstood. An elephant is hard to visualize in its massiveness, even though some of the youngsters recall having seen a picture of one in a school book.

"Where do elephants live?" I asked Winn.

"If'n they's one hyur, he's livin' hyur."

Mary remembered a picture of an elephant with a "licker [tongue] touchin' dirt ground."

I shrink from the opportunity to explain an elephant's trunk. But to be a child without having known any of the joys of childhood is tragic, so I endeavor to illustrate a performing elephant. Their incredulous expressions inform me that the representation has been a failure and insinuate that my gyrations more nearly characterize a psychotic in a manic phase.

The willingness to share my knowledge not only has little meaning, it serves no worth-while purpose. Sharing sometimes hinders my relationship with those so removed from the world about them. They are unable to understand and I am unable to impart meaning to strange experiences.

Branch children are deprived of cultural enrichment. There are no museums or symphony halls near the hollow. One transplanted Duddie's Brancher, aged fourteen years, was taken by bus to an art gallery and I wondered whether he had found the experience stimulating.

"We's toted in a big car."

"What did you see?"

"Reckon nothin'."

"But it was a big building, wasn't it?"

"Reckon 'twas."

"And what did you do?"

"Reckon nothin'."

"Did the big car drive right into the building?"

"Reckon thar warn't no door big 's 'at."

"Well, what did you do?"

"Jist walkin' mostly. They's hangin' things [paintings] atter you's 's walkin' straight up [ascended the stairs]."

"And then what happened?"

"Warter 'uz goin' up 'n' we's drinkin', if'n we's ketched hit."

"Why couldn't you catch it?"

"Hit left out."

"You could have put your foot on the pedal and kept it going."

"Reckon, but I hain't cravin' warter 'at's 'at hard t' come by."

"But you must have seen something?"

"Nope. Hit 'udn't be livin' fur fellers liken me. They's no beds, no grub, 'n' th' winders, they's whoppin' [huge]. They's not ownin' nary a stove. 'Em fellers 'ud shake a heap harder'n us'n's if'n snow's stickin'."

Not many of the young people aspire to any kind of achievement that would permit them to become part of the outer society. They cannot read, they cannot write, they cannot draw. In fact, they are unfamiliar with most educational materials because they receive little in the way of education. The state law requires school attendance through sixteen years of age, but there is scarcely any enforcement in the rural areas. The attendance officer is pompous and the teachers and principals are nonchalant.

"Any kids up that hollow that ought to be in school?" the attendance officer asked.

"Yes, many. Can't something be done to get them to attend?" I pleaded.

"I'm not going to run after them, haul them, and tissie them around to get them in school. If they don't want to come, that's their problem," he retorted.

"But there's a law," I protested.

"Sure," he snorted, "there's a law. There are lots of laws on the books. But I'm not paid to run ignorant kids over these hills."

Parents, too, are responsible for creating an attitude of indifference among the children. They have not had the advantage of education and they question its value. The youngsters are not encouraged to make a serious effort because their mothers and fathers cannot appreciate the applicability of what is taught.

"Is you's knowin' who C'lumbus 'uz?" the child asks his father.

"Reckon I hain't knowin' 'im. 'E hain't never lived 'round hyur."

Life has not been dynamic for the Brancher child. Isolation does not inspire high motivation.

The portrait of a community in isolation is a portrait of despair. The residents do not share in our great country's prosperity. They have fewer jobs, earn less money, receive less education, suffer more from illness and disability. They have poorer roads, fewer public services, more floods. They are on the draw. They are stagnant. They are disjoined from the outside world by almost every standard measure —economic, geographic, educational, cultural—and vegetate instead in Duddie's Branch.

Isolation assures an existence in which there is no future, and the people imprisoned within its confines are unable to escape the continuum of perpetuation. Their sentence is life; their pardon is death.

Isolation is to tread backward in time.

Isolation is also selflessness, and ingenuity, and devotion.

I was heading out of the hollow at 2:00 A.M. when suddenly I lost control of the jeep station wagon; it somehow turned over in a space scarcely wide enough to admit an automobile. I was stunned. When I regained consciousness I was aware that my hollow friends had come to my assistance. I tried to look about, but as Bert would say, I's lookin' 't one 'n' seein' all 'a m' kin. The double vision finally disappeared and in a short while I could even distinguish words from that which had previously been a verbal rumble.

The Branch was so narrow that the jeep doors could not be opened. Sie lost no time in figuring how to get the back window open and came "sneakin'" through to help me. Water was running six inches deep, and I was cold and wet and sore.

"If'n you's not bad hurt, you's bound t' live," he comforted. "Hit's better fur you's if'n you's kin worm out. If'n I 's t' pull on you's, I might break off'n somethin' if'n hit 'ud be jist a-hangin' by skin."

I worked my way out, but could not stand. My skinny, undernourished friends were undaunted.

"Sittin's hard anywhar in this branch, but we's plannin' sittin' you's outta warter."

With all the ease and skill of a trained first-aid crew, they placed me on a board and moved it "jist fur 'nuf so's you's feets hain't warshin' in 'em warters." The women hovered about and covered me with their threadbare coats that provided little warmth. They made me lean against their scrawny, shivering frames. "You's gonna be feelin' bones, but they's not 's hard 's rocks a-pushin' through you's meat."

I fearfully reviewed the potential of my injuries and could, at least temporarily, rule out a broken neck since I could hold my head up, after a fashion. As partial feeling returned to my extremities, I tentatively ruled out a fractured spine.

The next project was to get me dry.

"Hit 'udn't be fittin' t' take off'n you's wet clotheses exposed t' seein' men," Jemima whispered, so the women kept changing the various articles of clothing with which they had covered me.

"We's plannin' t' soak you's duds mostly dry by seepin' 'em out int' our'n."

It worked.

Meander appeared with a partially filled bottle of snake oil. I had never expected to see the day, or night for that matter, when I would be willing to accept an offer of their favorite panacea for any and all ailments, but I was grateful for it then.

"I's decidin' you's not got stren'th 'nuf fur moonshine. This hyur hain't 's good curin', but hit's better'n nothin'." He unscrewed the cap and rubbed the mouth of the bottle on his filthy overalls. "Hain't hankerin' fur you's t' ketch ailin's from us'n's. Swaller hit all," he recommended. "Hain't never knowed 'a hit killin' a feller."

Three ounces of any remedy containing 78 per cent alcohol can, under special circumstances, induce miracles—to this I can attest. Aware of my improvement, Meander solicited additional medication from the others.

"Hain't you's willin' t' share?" he rebuked.

The men sheepishly departed and soon reappeared with more snake oil.

Maybe it was the snake oil or maybe it was just the passage of time; in any case, I had reached the stage of upright posture and was alert enough to worry about getting the jeep out of the Branch. Four miners had to leave for work at 4:00 A.M., and it was blocking their exit.

"Wastin' a day's pay hain't nothin' if'n hit means death 'a our friend," Letcher soothed.

But the jeep had to be removed; I had to get a wrecker. Even though I had consumed some eight ounces of snake oil by then, I managed to worry how the jeep would fare, dragged half a mile on its top.

Sie, stoutly declaring that a wrecker would not be needed, began to direct the men to fetch "poles 'at hain't bendin' sorry-like," and after much expenditure of muscle—little of which most of the participants could spare—they slid the jeep up the hill. After anchoring it upside down at a site where it could be rolled over, they withdrew the support of the poles. To my utter amazement it slid down and landed upright in the stream bed.

Clem then proceeded to examine the undercarriage of the vehicle. "Th' tie rod's plum busted," he diagnosed. "Hain't fittin' fur drivin'."

"Why?" I wanted to know.

"Wa'al, you's be pointin' one way 'n' you's be goin' t'other way."

"How am I going to get it out of the Branch?"

"'At hain't nothin'." Between fresh applications of external garments, I watched the hollowers work. Clem attached himself to the front bumper and guided the jeep out as the mass of human energy, male and female, pushed from the rear. Leaving the vehicle on high ground at the mouth of the stream bed, they once again concentrated their attention on me.

"You's 's allus sayin' we'uns sh'd go t' a doct'r; reckon you's oughtta make tracks gittin' thar now."

It was decided that I should be taken to a hospital located twenty miles away on the Drop Hole route. In a short while a pickup truck came bumping out of the Branch. Dirty, lumpy cushions, confiscated from the few sofas that graced the hollow, were scattered in the back.

"Figgered you's hain't up t' sittin' fur sech fur ridin'. We's figgerin' t' help you's bumpin'."

Having traveled by way of Drop Hole many times, I shuddered at the thoughts of the soft shoulders and the chug holes. The mutated pickup belonged to Coffee. I had some degree of familiarity with its state of roadworthiness and was apprehensive about my ultimate arrival, but before I could protest I was gently lifted onto the pillows by the men who were supervised by the eight women.

We pulled out onto the highway and I could see headlights of several cars making their exit from the hollow.

"Who's leaving the Branch at this hour?" I was puzzled.

"My man borried a couple 'a batt'ries 'n' some tires w'en 'e headed out, but jist t' be sure we's gittin' you's t' 'em medicine men we's got cars 'at's fittin' if'n this hyur truck gits sorry," Coffee's wife explained.

During the trip the people following behind would hot-rod ahead of us and stop the pickup for the sole purpose of inquiring whether I was still alive. Satisfied that "she hain't quit breath yet," they would resume their places in the cortege.

We approached the 45-plus-degree angle of descent into Drop Hole and two of the cars pulled around the pickup and screeched to a halt. One of the drivers informed us that he was going to "feel out th' bottom"; the other was "aimin' t' go backwards," for what purpose I never did learn. The water was up "might' nigh over th' tires, but thar hain't no need fur worryin'. We'uns hain't hankerin' t' let you's swaller warter 'nuf fur drowndin'."

It was determined that the water had not reached the level of "drowndin' high," so we continued on our journey and eventually arrived at our destination. We made a strange parade as the raggedy hollowers assisted me through the impressive hospital lobby and into the examining room. Meander confronted the physician.

"We's hain't aimin' t' pack our bestest friend all this way 'n' leave her. Hain't respectin' t' leave her alone with you's. I's sendin' th' wormen in."

The ladies were stationed in various positions of vigilance even before he could get through the door.

Dr. Nute, a personal friend, made a cursory examination through my clothing and told my guardians that he must take X rays. The women huddled together and quietly conferred for some time before granting their permission. I had to remain on the X-ray table until the films had been developed. The hollowers were unable to understand why I was behind closed doors with a man for such a long time. He had to come out of the darkroom several times to reassure them that I was not being compromised.

After reading the films and concluding that there were no broken bones, Dr. Nute administered a tetanus booster and medication for discomfort. He suggested that I remain in the hospital for observation and while I concurred that it probably would be wise, it would be entirely unacceptable to my friends. I vowed that I would return if I felt the necessity for further attention.

Somewhat dubious of my judgment, Dr. Nute instructed my friends to take good care of me.

"We's aimin' on takin' care 'a her jist 's if'n we'd birthed her."

Twenty miles and two and a half hours later, we arrived at the mouth of the Branch and the procession slowly wound its way up the hill to Melda's house where it had been decided I would recuperate. I was cared for with a tenderness that is indescribable. All of my "crawlin'" friends, the under-two-year age group, were brought to see me. At times the bed held a dozen of my "hain't yet talkin'" friends, who were completely oblivious to the events that had led to my bedridden state but who, nonetheless, were "aimin' fur you's t' live."

I had no difficulty in following the doctor's instructions to force fluids; I was made to drink gallons of unidentifiable potions concocted to combat specific possible ailments. Effie brought a nostrum that she claimed would cure anything "'ceptin' death." It had to be drunk "hot off'n th' dipper," and I was hard-pressed to avoid a second-degree burn on my tongue while meeting this requirement. My mettle was sorely tested when she informed me, "Hit's never failed 'ceptin' twic't when hit stopped th' breathin' 'a Emily's maw 'n' Kurt's paw."

During the convalescence period, every resident came to visit me and each brought an identical gift. The most worth-while contribution they felt that they could make to my recovery was coal, a precious mineral to them. They would walk along the highway for miles to collect choice chunks that had fallen from the trucks and presented their offering with love.

These are the isolated, the "undesirables," the primitives. These are the ones who are destined to a life of poverty. These are the ones who are excluded from the good things of life, but who do not complain. These are the ones who cannot speak a language that we can understand because it is an idiom that originates from the heart and not in the mind. These are my friends.

IV

The Duddie's Branch Family

The sunless pleasures of weary people, whose care
for external things is slackening.

Walter Pater
The Renaissance. Michelangelo

The shapeless, disorganized, unstructured social complex known
as Duddie's Branch embraces, or, more correctly, clutches two hundred thirty-eight people. Most of her captives are young, an overwhelming proportion are hopelessly destitute, a few are mentally ill,
and all are social outcasts. Their countenances reflect the inexorably
and everlastingly dreary conditions of the hollow; there is no fun
here, no glamor, not even excitement in violence and sin. Worse,
there is no escape. The outside world is unsympathetic and aloof.

The hollowers' lives have been defined by their surroundings, and
the effect is withering. Few appear to know where they are going,
and even fewer seem to care. The drudgery of mere survival has discouraged orientation toward a higher standard of living. They are
concerned only with gratifying immediate needs and all actions are
based on a "here and now" philosophy. There is a marked tendency
to surrender to their environment rather than strive for ascendancy,
and no time is devoted to assessing their motives. Long-range planning and insight into the future do not obsess them. The women will
bear children as long as they are generative, and will cook, wash,
tend fires, and fetch water as long as they are able to plod about.
And the men will persevere in their idle pastimes, their aimless roam-
ings up and down the Branch, their good-natured gossiping, and
their inconsistent and careless management of small, resistant garden
plots. Generation after generation will persist in frittering away the
daylight hours and will disappear at dusk to wrest their cramped and
sordid quarters from the vermin which prowl the night. But an unde-
manding existence is dearly purchased: wraithlike, apathetic women

silently steal through a lifetime of bondage. The men, too, have been scarred in the bargain. Dehydrated, crusty, deeply furrowed skin, grizzled beards, and dull, cavernous eyes are the disfigurements of monotony. Nor are the children immune to the sterile climate. They listlessly play amid the eternal litter of automobile carcasses, broken glass, garbage, bedsprings, tin cans, and eviscerated bowels of long-deceased sofas. Scant affection or attention is shown them once they have been weaned. These wan, emaciated, spiritless, wee creatures are a poignant study in neglect. Their pants are always full and wet and they are clothed in a minimum of soiled, worn, grotesque garments. Little feet are seldom acquainted with the luxury of shoes. Indeed, "rough winds do shake the darling buds of May"; their petals wilt almost before they unfold.

This gross disregard for reality also infects the young adults, who are in a majority in Duddie's Branch. Although the average age of the population is twenty-two years, there is no manifestation of the ebullience, the joie de vivre, the curiosity of youth. Almost all lose themselves in the rudderless world of their families with a resultant feeling of frustration and futility. Unlike their parents, they do have some awareness of the intricate social order which surrounds them and of their ineptitude to contend with its variety of features. Yet they had rather endure privations than work or attain an education. Boredom and restlessness are their shibboleths and they are unwilling to combat these evils. The girls are careless about their appearance; they seldom bathe, their tangled hair throbs with lice. Small clumps of sullen-visaged lads congregate for the sole purpose of deciding how best to dissipate their day. They are not eager to seek adventure beyond the hollow. "I hain't never bin fur" typifies the young Brancher, but his definition of "fur" is hazy.

"Reckon I's seed most 'a th' world," crowed an unusual twenty-five-year-old sophisticate.

Hoping I succeeded in concealing my astonishment at this startling revelation, I asked him to tell me more.

"I's bin t' London [thirty miles away]. Figgered on goin' t' 'at town acrosst th' river [Cincinnati] 'n' maybe git me a job. But we runned outta gas afore we neared Lexin'ton. Never knowed hit took so much gas. Put in a skin's worth [a dollar] afore we left out. Must 'a leaked right smart, else we's bin a-goin' furer. Had t' push 'at ol' car off'n th' road 'n' jist left hit set 'n' thumbed on home. Heerd thar warn't much work thar nohow. Passed lots 'a big towns, though. Went back fur th' car, but hit warn't thar. Figgered someun junked hit."

"Did you call the police and report your car stolen?"

"Nope. Only gived thirty dollars fur hit. 'Sides, th' rubbers [tires] 'uzn't mine 'n' I borried th' batt'ry, too."

"Won't you have to pay for the tires and battery?" I questioned.

"Don't reckon. I din't thieve 'em. I jist borried 'em. If'n th' fellers 'at we's borried 'em from wants t' fit over 'em, we's fittin' fellers too."

The ability to assume a responsible role in society is beyond them. Leadership?

"W'at's 'at?" Dill screeched. "You's meanin' bossin'? Hain't none 'a us'ns a-hankerin' t' tell nobody w'at t' do. Got a right t' do yore own decidin'. Leastaways 'at's how I figgers hit."

Janice Wheeler, a mother of two living children at the age of nineteen, is far from representative of the young adults. Her husband's periods of employment are short and infrequent and the family is bogged down by debts. She wanted more from life than the Branch could offer and secretly began putting aside small change from their welfare checks. After several months her treasury contained three dollars. A few weeks later her husband acquired a small amount of cash from some unspecified source and gave her part of it to apply on a finance company account. She withheld two dollars of the money, added it to her savings, and mailed the five dollars to a secretarial correspondence school. Such unprecedented action was sensational—Branch wives always consult their men before making a decision, however minor. Furthermore, they are economically dependent on their husbands and are expected to remain that way.

Toley found the first lesson soon after it arrived; furious, he threw it into the stove. "'E called me ever' kind 'a name," Janice divulged. "No wife 'a his'n 'uz gonna do somethin' like 'at, 'e sayed. 'E sayed all kinds 'a things."

Toley did more than talk—he beat her thoroughly. She was lacerated and bruised. " 'E promised t' kill me if'n I tried hit agin," she quavered, " 'n' I think 'e 'ud. 'E tol' me 'at 's long 's I lived with 'im, I had t' do w'at 'e sayed 'n' if'n I left home I c'dn't take th' younguns with me."

And now Janice is filling the only role her husband considers appropriate: she is pregnant again. She regrets having married at such a young age, admitting that five pregnancies in four years are too many. "I hain't hankerin' on bein' pregnant th' rest 'a my life. But w'at kind 'a job c'd I git with only a eighth-grade ejucation?" Scrawny, her teeth badly decayed, her body covered with nothing but a dress that was stiff with grime, her blond hair unwashed and uncombed, she dejectedly stood in the door of her bare, one-room house and reflected, "Wa'al, guess I sh'u'n't complain. I's got hit better'n some."

Has she? Without exception, young adults in Duddie's Branch live half-lives and are not equipped to assume their personal and social obligations. The defects in their communal organization have made them insecure, incomplete, and inconsequential; the high price of their circumscribed intercourse with the outside world manifests itself in distorted physical, mental, emotional, and spiritual growth. Owing to this, it is hard to equate maturity and personal confidence in terms of chronological age or to expect the young Brancher to be able to express himself categorically. A positive or negative attitude is elicited through inference, certainly not through direct admission. No matter how trivial the issue, the response is evasive. I attempted to find out whether they thought that chopping down weeds and dead trees along highways would make a substantial contribution to beauty.

One young man said, " 'Em 'at's got cars t' drive on this hyur road goes so fast 'at th' trees looks liken weeds t' 'em. None 'a 'em'll never know they's bin cut."

Another responded, "Trees looks better standin' than layin'. Standin', they looks right; layin', they don't."

The background of young people from poor and isolated families does not provide them with middle-class values, concepts, and information. The homes from which they come are breeding grounds for poverty and progeny. There is not one single-person household in the hollow. The birth rate is 44 per cent per 1,000 plus, as compared with approximately 31 per cent for Earle County, and 23.4 per cent for the state. A recent five-year fertility ratio for Duddie's Branch was 1,130; for Earle County, 750; for the state, 576. The average family consists of seven persons. In four, there are seven living children; in five, there are six; and in one, there are eleven. Unemployment, shortage of constructive activity, and inability to use "leisure" time effectively cause the people to concentrate on the basic animal drive of sex. Although their physical stamina and nutritional status do not compare with that of the average American, they are not handicapped in their ability to reproduce and, in fact, lead the nation in numbers of births. Wilmore Gilbert, father-in-law to Delphia Halt Gilbert, had twenty-two children. Interestingly, the less able the father is to support children, the more he sires. In the whole fifty-five families there is only one man and his wife who remain childless. Although longevity is not uncommon (seventy or more years), the child death rate is high. One man and his first wife had twelve children, all of whom died as babies.

While the incidence of illegitimacy appears to be low, it is difficult to be certain about parentage when couples are married. Branch gossip leads one to believe that sexual promiscuity is commonplace.

The Branchers are unconcerned about soaring birth rates, population growth, and life expectancy. Birth control by a bold, realistic attack would scarcely make an appreciable dent in the continuing high birth rate in the hollow. Resistance is strong and deep. It is fraught with religious connotations, even for the non-churchgoer. "If'n God starts 'em 'n' grows 'em till they's droppin', hit hain't fur us t' feud none with 'Im."

Three or four years ago a birth control program was begun in Earle County. The Branchers were resentful that it focused on low-income families, reasoning that welfare had no business to meddle in their affairs in the hollow, in their living conditions, and especially in the "birthin' 'a younguns." Spacing or limiting the size of their families "hain't nothin' fur 'em fellers reckonin' with." Sterilization, from the male point of view, is sinful for himself and his wife. The men have a strong feeling that continued production of children is a symbol of virility and this feeling takes precedence over logic.

Jude warns, "W'en you's cain't plant, you's no longer a full man." Spawning large families is an economic liability for parents who can least afford it and underscores their "get-by" philosophy. Cultural heritage, healthful conditions, and financial security are cast aside in the decision not to interfere with God's will.

It requires more than a little imagination to analyze the problem and understand why a birth control program may never be successful in the hollow. Dana was told after the birth of her ninth child that she should take precautions not to become pregnant again for reasons of health—she has hypertension and eclampsia and is endangered and uncomfortable throughout the entire pregnancy periods. Her husband refused to accept the doctor's advice for a number of years, but finally agreed that it would be better to restrict the size of his family than to risk losing his wife through pregnancy. Nonetheless, he refused to permit any form of birth control except the oral pills.

I gave Dana a big wall calendar and a pencil and told her to cross out the date each day that she took a pill. We practiced by marking the previous month and she seemed to understand what she was to do. Because she was unable to rotate the dispenser which enabled one tablet at a time to drop out, we put all of the pills into a big, open-mouthed bottle. Four days later I checked on her. She said that she had taken a pill every day but could not mark the calendar because the children had lost the pencil. Twenty-eight of the thirty pills were still in the bottle, even though she professed to have taken four. I gave her another pencil which we tied to a string and hung around her neck. Two or three days after that she told me that she needed another "writin'." I thought that she meant another pencil, but she was talking about a calendar. She had crossed off the entire month and still had most of the pills.

"Why did you cross off the whole page, Dana?" I was baffled.

"I 'uz scaret th' pencil might be losted agin 'n' I marked th' time paper afore th' younguns got aholt 'a hit," she confessed.

I gave her another calendar and at the end of the week returned to see how she was progressing. Not one date had been crossed off. Did she lose the pencil again? No. Then why no marks? She didn't make marks because she hadn't taken the pills. Why? Her husband had a backache and he took them. I explained to Letcher that they were not for a backache. He insisted that they were the only medication that had ever helped him.

The next day I took more pills to Dana and was confident that everything would be all right now. She knew how to cross off the 2 × 2-inch squares on the calendar, her pencil was protected, Letcher's backache was cured, and I was relieved. When next I saw her she told me that she now had trouble remembering whether or not she had taken a pill! The count would have been an accurate record of how many days she had missed except that on some days she would take more than one. Several months later Dana became pregnant again. She was certain that the pills were responsible for her condition. Letcher was convinced that the pills were a cure for backaches. I was satisfied that the pills were misused.

Pansy was given a big box of triangular vaginal suppositories as a birth control measure and was told to use one each night at bedtime. A few days later I saw a group of children playing with something in a large tin can of Branch water. I strolled over to the discarded auto top on which they were sitting. Sure enough, they were using the little triangles "fur funnin'." They would let the water drip off the end of a finger, drop by drop, and the triangles would belch forth a glob of foam. From the looks of the mess on the old car top, they had foamed away most of the supply and rendered the vehicle permanently sterile. Pansy was not disturbed; she wasn't sure she was going to use them anyway because her husband's objections were too strong to overcome. "I hain't one fur hagglin' if'n I hain't never winnin'."

Most of the babies are delivered without the aid of a physician. Layuna has had eighteen children and none of the births was attended by a doctor. She delivers one day and is up and about the next. "Too many younguns 'round fur layin' abed," she explains as she resumes her responsibility for the brood of children who are always underfoot. When the midwife is inside, the children huddle outside with the father or roam the hills of the hollow. The father is troubled, but he is not quite sure how to express the extent of his anxiety. Without his "worman" he would not know what to do. Many times I have sat out in the hills with a father and his children.

Usually he does not talk much. When he does speak, it is about his wife—how she has been faithful over the years; with a baby coming every ten months or so she has little opportunity to be otherwise. Sometimes I have felt that the father-to-be would like to kick over the traces, defy custom, and be at the bedside of his woman; his presence would undoubtedly boost her morale, particularly during long hard labors.

Iva has delivered hundreds of babies in her long career as the favorite midwife for the hollows. She hasn't received much pay for her services, but says that in previous decades she was more generously compensated for her time and effort. "Holler fellers 's gittin' worser," she condemns. Her methods are unsanitary beyond belief, but then most homes do not lend themselves to sanitary conditions. Draped in a voluminous apron with a bath towel tucked inside the band and two pockets full of supplies, she goes about her work. Not once have I seen her without the bag approved by the Health Department, but neither have I ever seen her open it. When I displayed interest in it she said, "If'n I's botherin' 'em things in hit, they's not givin' me birthin' rights. I's not knowin' how t' use 'em." Every month she takes in her bag and she is approved. Everything inside is in perfect order, as if it had never been touched—and it has not.

Upwards of fifteen conceptions by the age of forty is par for the course in Duddie's Branch and birth control is a "licked afore you's startin'" program. Most women feel that it is their obligation to keep their husbands satisfied—and that means having lots of children. Beve has eleven and every one was born in the same month of successive years. More fundamental than her obligation to her spouse, a Branch woman feels that she will deliver the number of babies she is destined to have. Interventive procedures are useless because it is inconceivable to her that anything can alter "th' Lord's will." She feels helpless to change the predetermined number of children, but earnestly hopes it will not be eighteen, twenty, or more.

To describe even the smallest families as independent or self-reliant is inaccurate and deceiving. It is factually true that all of the families are at the lowest end of the economic scale and that their status has remained materially unimproved for at least two generations. The median family income is $1,900; half earn between

$500 and $750; about one quarter earn less than $250. No family has an accumulated savings of any kind and their debts are so extensive that they will live their lives without ever having experienced solvency. Scarcely one can function with economic independence, but must rely on some financial assistance from the outer community. When I first came to Duddie's Branch, 62 per cent of the families received surplus food commodities. Later, all families were reevaluated in compliance with a new ruling and only 37 per cent qualified as eligible. At one point in time 81 Branchers received Old Age Assistance, 3 families received Aid to Dependent Children, 4 residents were on Aid to the Permanently and Totally Disabled, and 17 were on Blind Assistance. The number of families and individuals receiving aid from some program has increased markedly.

Time and circumstances have mellowed the fervor of the early mountaineer. Problems of a wide variety are never far from him: illness, job layoffs, unemployment, alcoholism, grave financial crises. The nature of these catastrophes is so crushing that he takes refuge in apathy; in mind and body he is out of phase with his surroundings. Nonetheless, there is not the breakdown in family life which is so prevalent in the outside world. The father symbol is around most of the time because he does not work. Those who die are replaced when the mother remarries. The mother in no way wears the pants. She does not earn any money and even her welfare allowance is turned over to her husband. The father does not take to responsibility, but he does take whatever there is to be taken. A young couple moved to Indianapolis and found employment in a factory where each made fifty dollars a week. When they returned to stay in the Branch, the man proudly told everyone that he "got" a hundred dollars a week. Never once did he say that he "earned" that amount.

As a parent, the Brancher is inflexible and not pragmatic, but he exerts the first and perhaps the most diffuse influence on his children. Each youngster develops his opinions of neighbors and outsiders within his family group. The meaning he attaches to all persons and events is a duplicate of parental beliefs and attitudes, a bias which colors his perceptions and establishes a permanent base upon which he will form habits and interpret future experiences.

Many of the hollow children have begun to chew tobacco by the time they are four or five years old. Girls and boys smoke by the time they are ten, and many before they are six. Even though they roll their own cigarettes, this increases the amount of money families spend for non-food items. But the parents accept this and feel that if they smoke their children should be allowed the same privilege. The school once tried to find out how many of the Branch children smoked. Each time a child was asked, he would say, "Smoke hyur?" "Yes. Do you smoke?" "Nope." Had they asked the child whether he smoked in the hollow, the responses would have been quite different—silence. This is like many things hollowers do; as long as it takes place in the Branch it is nobody's business. As I walked up the hollow with children after school, they began to light up. "Those cigarettes could cause you to die." Herman looked up. "You's daid if'n a rattler bites you's, too." Most of them patronizingly say that when "we's growed" they will smoke only "store-bought 'un's."

Expectations and obligations, if not home-defined, are fashioned within the broader kinship framework. These concepts are exceedingly vague, however, and the lack of adult control at the adolescent level is clearly evident. Cliques and friendship groups among young children often intersect lines of animosity existing between some families. The children are expressly forbidden to associate with the "enemy," but unless they are closely watched the liberty to select friends takes priority over parental objection. At the other extreme, the parents are unrealistically permissive and often do not know where their descendants spend the night. If one is missing in the morning, panic does not ensue. "'E must 'a bedded down with someun." The young of various family units are frequently absent for as many as three or four days without inspiring consternation or apprehension among their begetters. Most of the time they are not questioned about their disappearance, but upon request will furnish a frail excuse. One or two from Jude's litter are chronically missing. "Wa'al, I's got 'nuf with 'em 'at stays home, so one 'r two missin' don't make no diff'r'nce."

The child acquires the habit of wandering from his father—it is routine for all men in the Branch to disappear for short periods without any explanation.

Winn, a ten-year-old Brancher, overheard someone in town say that he was going to Hamilton. He asked the man if he could ride with him—his grandmother lived there and he wanted to visit her. Winn's stay stretched to two weeks. When he was ready to leave he thumbed a ride back to Duddie's Branch. His absence was only casually noted.

"Whar you's bin, Winn? We's thinkin' we's hain't bin seein' you's 'round fur a spell."

"Visitin'," he laconically supplied.

No further account of his absence was sought or forthcoming.

Yet the parents harbor a peculiar kind of warmth and affection for their broods and the fathers try to compensate for their apparent indifference by assuming an authoritative manner. Usually the results are contrary to the intent; while he is saying, "I's hain't wantin' fur you's t' go outta th' holler t'night," the boy is slowly wending his way down the Branch.

Such overt disobedience does not culminate in punishment. In fact the parents never resort to punitive measures. And except for running an occasional errand and watching out for the baby now and again, the youngsters are not required to fulfill obligations consistent with their abilities and age. Under these relaxed conditions they feel secure in a family setting where they are able to measure up to the low expectations of their clan. Parental and sibling approval is based on them as they are, not on their behavior or their contributions. Thus each generation becomes more subordinate, more conditioned to be receivers than donors, more unprepared, and more likely to exhibit subnormal biologic and social maturity.

In terms of physical appearance and mentality, the most important single factor responsible for the young Branchers' massive underachievement is environmental deprivation. It seriously restricts entire development of full intellectual aptitude because they are never faced with a new set of problems and never have the opportunity to participate in a new situation. Branch parents, however, are not distressed over a child's failure to develop in physical size, increasing skills, and complexity of function if indeed they assess his progress at all. If undersized upon attaining school age, his introduction into formal education is delayed until he has "growed more." Behavioral patterns are likewise ignored, with no thought given to

the many factors responsible for deviation. The youngsters, particularly the infants, are strikingly inadequate in motor coordination such as grasping and manipulating objects; language and speech development closely parallels that of parents and siblings; responsiveness and power to concentrate are conspicuously absent. Deafness and poor vision go unnoticed. For the most part, the child must fend for himself as best he can.

I observed the unsupervised children every morning for a week. At about 7:00 A.M. they would straggle into the Hiram store (the closest shelter to the Branch) to await the school bus. They usually came in pairs, and all were attired in worn and inadequate clothing. During the period of observation it rained every day and on two mornings it was decidedly cold. Only one youngster was protected from the rain; she used a tattered plastic laundry garment cover as a rain cape. It had obviously served its original purpose long ago, but the little girl shook off the water, folded it into a small square, and carefully put it into her coat pocket. Just a handful of children wore socks and all had on soggy shoes that oozed Branch water at every step. Not one child was clean, and from the ponderous accumulation of mud on their clothes I suspected that they just slid down the creek bed on their way out. Their dirty faces harmonized with their attire, and many had huge sores resembling ringworm on their faces, especially around the mouth area. Most of them suffered from colds and the store reverberated with the rasping sound of sniffles and coughs. There was other evidence of poor general health: malnutrition, eye edema, lethargy, pallor.

It struck me as being inappropriate to their appearance and health, yet all had spending money and their buying sprees were fascinating to behold. One morning every child bought a five-cent balloon. Another morning their whimsy turned to what they called a "surprise package"—a little envelope containing a plastic toy and one piece of candy. On yet another day they all converted their silver into pennies and made a run on the gumball machine. Boys between the ages of eight and eleven often bought cigarettes. Not one day passed that they did not purchase soft drinks, ice cream cups, and divers kinds of candies and cookies. The untold varieties of food they ate

lent the impression that they had left home without eating and that whatever they consumed in the store constituted breakfast.

I counted the students each morning, and their numbers ranged from eighteen to thirty. The latter represented two thirds of the forty-five Branch children of school age, but this tally was reached only once. Stimulus to obtain an education is not forthcoming from the homes, and inducements often emanate from the most preposterous sources. One boy proudly displayed a new ballpoint pen and declared that he was so eager to use it he had decided to go to school that day. Previously he had not caught the school bus for two weeks.

The low income of the household heads reflects their educational level; the median academic training is two years. None has progressed beyond elementary school and such slight value is placed on knowledge that I have rarely seen even a newspaper or a magazine in a single Branch home. Few speak English like those in the outside world. Neighbors know each other, but they don't talk much. Their limited vocabulary and anything worth the effort of talking about make verbal communication in the truest sense unnecessary. The awesome result—they are not acceptable to any but their own kind, who understand, at least partially, whether communication is verbal or non-verbal. Have you ever been around a family all day and all night when not half a dozen words have been exchanged? For months I thought that most of the people were mute. Communication between parents and children is poor. Before I began to spend time there, any outsider who came in always brought paper and pencil and took notes relative to his purpose. I had to figure out what they meant when they kept asking me, "Hain't you's got no writin's?" Melda, who is probably the most literate inhabitant, wrote me the following letter:

"feb.2.
"Dear Rena an all
    "Will ans your litter was much Pleased ta hear from you.
    "I can say we are having bad weather. the temp goes doun at night 10 below xero This branch is a mess. Lester sold 5½ pounds of sane. at 21 dollers a pound

".he sold one hundard eight dollars Rena Lester will try ta git all the half dallers he can git All the stores are trying to git each one They can if we knowed sooner.

"I am some better I will go take a exray when they come ta taun from London.

"All the family said a Big hela

"Rena be creful driving weathr like This. Lester give me a list of the greens ta pick in the spring. Isaiah has ta go be examine again the 16th

"I will be pleased ta see spring come.

"I will give you a List of the greens

"1 Suckie. 2 crows foot 3 Pake. 4 wild lettice. 6 dangle line. 6 Shaney. 7 Speckle john 6 siscles. 9 Rack salat. 10 wild mustard. 11 wagan wheel. 12 ground hay salat. 13 creses. 14 cat lau 15 Sweet pake 16 drum salat. 17 dack.

"Hope you can read this from Melda an family with so much love."

Most of the Branchers are unable to count change and unscrupulous merchants find them easy marks. "Things costes diff'r'nt. Sometimes I comes in hyur with a couple 'a skins [two dollars] 'n' leaves out with lard, flour, 'baccer 'n' candy on a stick fur th' younguns, 'n' th' next time I on'y gits one can 'a 'baccer 'n' cain't git th' younguns nothin'."

"What do you suppose is the reason for that?" I prodded.

"Don't reckon I kin figger 'ese fellers."

Some of the adults are ashamed to acknowledge illiteracy publicly and are demoralized when, by virtue of an X, they admit that they cannot write their names. When requested to sign a document, they will ask, "Will a cross do?" The diagonal lines of an X are a cross to them. "Hain't no point takin' time t' write m' name w'en a cross'll do," they sheepishly add.

Loyd approached me with a request for help in writing a business letter. The communication was to the government, justifying his eligibility for a war-service-connected disability payment. He instructed me as to content and I composed a letter for him to copy. The time-consuming task of duplicating my words caused huge globules of perspiration to gather on his forehead, descend in dirty rivulets down his nose, and splash onto the paper. In the course of his labors he omitted one or more letters from almost every word. When he came to the ending, instead of copying the "Yours truly" I had written, he wrote "yers enso forth" in lower case letters and signed his name—under which he affixed an X.

Any reference to their illiteracy is met with hostility and their resentment is incubated for some time. I was in the post office when Jake came in to buy a stamp for Jabe. He put six cents on the counter top and the clerk pushed the postage toward him.

"Figured it would be for someone else; I know you can't write," he snidely laughed.

Jake was mortified.

"Howdy, Jake," I greeted.

"Howdy."

"Mind if I walk back to the Branch with you?"

"Don't reckon."

At the mouth of the hollow we rested on a big rock whose surface had been polished to a high luster from long hours of sitting. Not one word was exchanged. Finally, Jake fumbled around in his jacket and produced a crumpled and soiled envelope. I knew that all but one of his children still lived in the Branch.

"Bet Preshia will be glad to get that letter."

"Reckon."

He cautiously probed for the stamp he had carefully committed to a dark recess of his coat pocket, licked it, and surrendered it to the envelope.

"Had one 'a th' younguns write hit 'n' Melda backed [addressed] hit fur me."

Having contributed long hours to burnishing rock tops while observing the comings and goings of the Branchers, I anticipated his next move.

"Guess I'll go down to the Hiram store."

He fell for the bait. "I's goin' yander m'se'f."

I walked behind him on the shoulder of the highway. The coal trucks barreled past, taking their half of the road from the middle. I shuddered. "Those trucks are dangerous."

"Long 's 'em guys stays in th' middle, you's not gonna be hurtin'."

I crossed the highway when we got to the Hirams' and Jake continued on to the mailbox. After posting the letter he shuffled into the store.

"How about a Pepsi, Jake?" I offered.

"Druther have some papers."

I instructed the clerk to give him five packages of cigarette papers.

He sat down on a box, rolled a cigarette, and handed it to me; then he rolled one for himself. Neither of us had a match, so he "borried" a light from someone. I lighted my cigarette from his. After we had finished smoking, Jake spoke up.

"Guess I'll take a colored stick. Pepsi costes a dime 'n' 'em papers 'uz on'y a nickel. Guess you's 'ud not be carin' if'n I's t' spend m' other nickel?"

I nodded my approval and he selected a popsicle.

Days later, while sitting on his porch, I brought up the subject of the letter.

"Preshia probably has your note by now."

"Reckon."

We sat for another fifteen minutes before he spoke again.

"Hit's a quar thing 'bout 'em stamps," he mused. "They seems t' think you's oughtta be th' writin' kind t' buy one. I's really helpin' keep 'em gover'munt fellers a-workin' by buyin' one now 'n' agin."

In order to avoid the tensions brought on by derisive allusions to his illiteracy, the Brancher sometimes resorts to elaborate stratagems. Jude was getting ready to go to the store on the highway and asked one of his older children who could write to fetch a scrap of paper. She returned with a small, dog-eared, dirty tablet on which she wrote the list of groceries he dictated. Not one of the five items was correctly spelled. I decided to see what Jude was going to do with the list he could not read, so I made plans to be at the store when he got there. I was the only one in the place when he arrived two hours later and without ever referring to the list he told the grocer what he wanted. I drove him back to the Branch, hoping to discover the purpose of the unused grocery slip.

"Did you lose your list?" I quizzed.

"Nope. I jist took hit casin' thar's fun-makin' fellers thar. If'n they 'uz, I'd 'a got m' things from th' paper."

Although Duddie's Branchers are organized into family units, the larger kinship clan to which they belong accounts for their function or dysfunction. This circle prescribes how members will react toward people, things, or institutions. Assumption of tasks and utilization of services are likewise patterned in conformity with the larger kinship family. Very often an individual's capacity to make a decision or assume some responsibility depends on the advice of the closest relative. A simple problem often requires days of consultation, discussion, and debate before a solution is found. Initiative is not often displayed because it places the aspirant in the category of trying to get ahead, thereby lowering his status not only within the neighborhood but within his kindred structure, which is of immense importance in the Branch. In some families these ties are their only firm, sustained relationship. Furthermore, there is a tendency to intermarry and the reasons for this are obvious: there is a paucity of information concerning who is kin to whom; propinquity; a limited opportunity to enlarge social activities and circles because of enforced isolation and because of restricted travel relating to economic conditions; few attend school long enough to establish lasting associations; church membership consists of the same local people or of residents from neighboring Branches, which are also inbred. Extending clan membership by birth reflects the stable composition of the hollow over the past decade. Even social prestige is difficult to determine by last name, so many possess the same.

Most of the inhabitants of Duddie's Branch represent three generations of a family group, although there are fourteen children who are fourth-generation in their families and fifteen younger children who are fifth-generation. Four children of one of the first pairs of parents still live in the hollow. Detta, who is now seventy-four, was about ten when her family settled (her reckoning has them moving in about 1904) and her brother Dill was five. Her sister Delphia was born five years after the move to the Branch, and Diza was born three years later.

Their grandmother was not married at the time their father was born, so she gave him her own surname. Delphia says, "My grand-maw 'uzn't married, so my paw took my grandmaw's name. But my grandpaw 'uz a famous man. 'E 'uz a gin'ral in th' war—they writ 'bout 'im in th' hist'ry books. People 'uzn't so p'tic'lar 'bout marrin' in 'em days." Dill says that their grandparents planned to marry but wanted to wait until later. "I on'y married onc't," he added, "so's I hain't kin t' 's many 's m' sister. She married seven times."

Delphia's heritage and relationships, which are tangled and com-plex, are similar to those of many Branchers and of persons in other hollows in the county. In order to appreciate the full significance of the involved nature of family ties and to see who the Duddie's Brancher is when placed in his kinship structure, it is helpful—albeit confusing—to examine Delphia's kinship structure in detail.

Delphia's maiden name, Halt, was the maiden name of her grand-mother, who was also the grandmother of Delphia's first husband. When this grandmother married Delphia's first husband's grand-father, her name became Gilbert. On the maternal side of her family, Delphia's grandmother and her first husband's father were siblings. In other words, Delphia's grandfather was her first husband's uncle; hence Delphia and her husband were blood second cousins. Their blood relationship results from their having the same paternal grand-mother and because Delphia's natural grandmother was sister to her first husband's father.

Delphia was married seven times. (The role of successive hus-bands can be curious; each is the husband of his wife but rarely the father of all of her children.) Following her first marriage, she lived with a man by whom she conceived her youngest son. She gave the child the last name of her first husband. On two other occasions she lived with a man without benefit of marriage. She then married and divorced another man—not once but three times. Her fifth husband, from whom she was divorced twice, is the man to whom she is now married. Her sixth husband died. Her present husband (number 5 and 7) is ten years her junior.

Of the fifty-five families in the hollow, Delphia is related to thirty-six, or 65.45 per cent. She has relationships to persons representing sixteen different family names. There are sixteen families of Shifters; she is related to twelve of them. One of the Shifter families has three children to whom she bears a marriage relationship, although she is not related to the head of the family.

Of the 238 persons in the Branch, Delphia is related by blood or marriage to 141, or 59.24 per cent. Fifty-one of the 141 are blood relatives; hence, 21.43 per cent of all the persons in the Branch are related to Delphia by blood. To several of her relatives she bears more than one relationship. There are 364 different relationships.

To 56 persons she bears 4 or more different relationships.

To 25 persons she bears 5 or more different relationships.

To 6 persons she bears 6 or more different relationships.

Through the marriage relationship and relationship through marriage, she is wife, second cousin, and half first cousin to her present husband. Both Delphia and her first husband had the same paternal grandmother but different grandfathers, thus making them half first blood cousins on their paternal sides.

Delphia, through marriage to her first husband, became niece to her maternal grandmother. Her first husband became grandson to his paternal aunt. Delphia's children's maternal grandfather was half brother to their paternal grandfather.

Delphia's relationship to her first husband was:

Wife through marriage relationship.

Half first cousin through paternal blood tie.

Second cousin through maternal blood tie.

Second cousin through relationship through marriage.

Since Delphia's first husband was her blood kin, one might go so far as to develop a relationship that exists between Delphia and herself. Anyone marrying Delphia's half first blood cousin would, through marriage, be Delphia's half first cousin through the paternal marriage relationship. In this case, however, it was she who married her own half first blood cousin; therefore, genealogically speaking, she is to herself half first cousin through paternal marriage relationship. Developing this further, Delphia is to herself:

Half first cousin through paternal marriage relationship.

Half first cousin through marriage relationship.

Second cousin through maternal marriage relationship.

Second cousin through marriage relationship.

Second cousin through maternal blood tie.

In view of this extensive intermarriage, one can readily see that the relationships of the progeny of Delphia and her first husband are double. For example, their children are siblings and double half second cousins and double third cousins to one another. Inter-marriage between other of her kin further compounds the crossover of relationships.

To one daughter, Delphia is:

Double half second cousin through paternal blood ties.
Double second cousin through maternal blood ties.
Double half second cousin through marriage relationship.
Mother through marriage relationship.
Second cousin through maternal marriage relationship.
Double third cousin through marriage relationship.

To her four other children, Delphia is:

Double half second cousin through paternal blood ties.
Double second cousin through maternal blood ties.
Double half second cousin through marriage relationship.
Mother through marriage relationship.
Double third cousin through marriage relationship.

To her grandchildren, Delphia is:

Half third cousin through paternal blood tie.
Double half third cousin through marriage relationship.
Double third cousin through maternal blood ties.
Double fourth cousin through marriage relationship.
Grandmother through marriage relationship.

In addition to the above relationships, Delphia is great-aunt through marriage relationship to two of her grandchildren.

One of Delphia's daughters married her own second cousin. Their children will be to each other double third cousins.

One of Delphia's sisters-in-law married her own half second cousin.

Two children to whom Delphia is great-great-aunt through maternal blood tie, great-great-aunt through paternal blood tie, half fourth cousin through marriage relationship, and fifth cousin through marriage relationship, are double first cousins to another child who bears the same relationship to Delphia as they do.

To one son-in-law, Delphia is:

Double half second cousin through paternal marriage relationship.

Double second cousin through maternal blood ties.

Double half second cousin through relationship through marriage.

Second cousin through maternal blood ties.

Double third cousin through marriage relationship.

One first cousin to Delphia married Delphia's son's wife's second cousin. Delphia's son's children are therefore double third cousins to the child of this first cousin to Delphia.

One of Delphia's sons married the aunt of his brother's wife—that is, son married aunt and niece. Therefore, through marriage one of Delphia's sons is uncle to his own brother. The children of these marriages are double related in that those of one family are both double first cousins and double second cousins to those in the other family.

There are other interesting relationships:

Two step-first cousins to Delphia married, making them second cousins. These second cousins' children are siblings and double third cousins.

Two of the step-second cousins are brothers, two are sisters—they are married. Their children will be double first cousins.

A sister-in-law through the marriage relationship married a man who had the same grandfather as she. They were half first cousins.

Two of Delphia's nieces married brothers. Their children are double cousins.

Delphia's sister's husband is father by second wife to the wife of one of Delphia's sons.

Thus, Delphia's brother-in-law is her son's uncle and father-in-law.

To her own brother, Delphia is:

Sister through paternal blood ties.

Step-first cousin through maternal relationship.

Half first cousin through marriage relationship.

Second cousin through marriage relationship.

To her own sister, Delphia is:

Sister through paternal blood tie.

Sister through maternal blood tie.
Half first cousin through marriage relationship.
Second cousin through marriage relationship.
Delphia is, to two of her blood kin:
Great-aunt through paternal blood tie.
Great-aunt through maternal blood tie.
Half third cousin through marriage relationship.
Fourth cousin through marriage relationship.
To her first husband's brother, Delphia is:
Half first cousin through paternal blood tie.
Second cousin through maternal blood tie.
Sister-in-law through marriage relationship.
Half second cousin through relationship through marriage.

A half second female cousin to Delphia through the marriage relationship bore a girl out of wedlock to her own second cousin.

Bewilderingly complex as Delphia's relationships are, her kinship pattern is not unique in the hollow. Jake Shifter, one of the first settlers, is sixty-five years of age and has 168 living relatives in Duddie's Branch. This is 70.59 per cent of the total Branch population. Jake bears 199 various relationships to persons representing 16 different family names. By blood he is related to 103 individuals, or 43.28 per cent of all the inhabitants. Of his 168 relatives, 61.31 per cent are blood kin. Of the 55 Branch families, he is related to 34, or 61.82 per cent.

In Jake's genealogy, as in all those traced in Duddie's Branch, there is evidence of intermarriage. Two of Jake's fourth cousins are to themselves first cousins, are married, and have thus far begot four children. These children are to each other double first cousins.

To one relative, Jake is:
Half first cousin through paternal blood tie.
Brother-in-law through paternal marriage relationship.
Fourth cousin through maternal marriage relationship.
To another relative, he is:
Half first cousin through paternal blood tie.
Father-in-law through relationship through marriage.
Brother-in-law through marriage relationship.
Jake's wife's sister married a man who later became the husband

of Jake's son's wife. In other words, Jake's brother-in-law married Jake's daughter-in-law.

To three younger children Jake is great-uncle through his paternal blood tie and fifth cousin through his maternal blood tie. To two other children to whom he bears the relationship of great-uncle through his paternal blood tie, he is sixth cousin through the maternal blood tie. To one woman Jake is uncle through his paternal blood tie and fifth cousin through his maternal blood tie. By the same token, through marriage Jake is uncle and fifth cousin to this woman's husband.

Jake is half second cousin through his paternal blood tie as well as fifth cousin through his maternal blood tie to two individuals. The spouses of these two bear the same relationship through marriage.

One of Jake's third cousins through the maternal blood tie is a deaf mute; he married his mother's sister, that is, his aunt, who is also a deaf mute. This man is therefore his own uncle and his own nephew. He is both father and first cousin to his own children. To each other, his children are siblings as well as second cousins. Jake's brother married his half first cousin. Jake's son married his half second cousin.

Jake Shifter's descendants living in Duddie's Branch fall into five generations of individuals from a few days old to seventy-two years of age. Most of the persons, however, fall within three generations—there are fifteen youngsters in the fifth generation and only one older person representing the first generation. Representation in several generations can be explained by the tendency of the men to marry several times, the wide age differences between spouses, the production of large families over many years, and the marriage of persons in their teens. The husband and wife age difference generally is not great at the time of the first marriage and the wife is usually the younger. There are three notable exceptions to this generalization: one wife is five years older than her husband, another is six years older, and a third is twelve years older. The total age difference of twenty-four husbands in Duddie's Branch is 178 years. In other words, the twenty-four husbands represent 178 total years' more living than wives as a group. Six of the twenty-four men are 126 years older than their wives. Subsequent marriages of the males tend to increase the age difference markedly. A man can thereby considerably extend his years of fecundity and beget large families with a wide age difference among the children. There are now fathers in the Branch who have sired babies at the ages of 57, 51, 46 and 44 years.

The close-knit relationship of the Duddie's Brancher is apparent through four persons who bear direct relationship to 229 individuals of a total population of 238, or 96.22 per cent. That even the nine escaping direct relationships have many of their own relationships further attests to the closeness of kinship ties in the Branch. There is not one single person or a single family which is not connected in some way to another family.

Although I found discrepancies while collecting kinship data, accuracy was eventually determined by checking and rechecking many sources. Conceivably there are some errors since the Brancher finds it difficult and even impossible to remember the relationships of earlier persons who are by now deceased. If it were possible to trace back a generation or two further, even more relationships would probably emerge. It is quite likely, in such a close kinship structure, that all of the Owens and Flynn families could be traced back to one original Owens and one original Flynn.

It struck me as peculiar that there were seventeen Shifter families in this mile-long hollow. My first thought was that they were all related to one another, and this may well be the case, but after five years of intensive research effort I could come up with only five separate clans. I felt convinced that if records existed I could go back far enough to identify a stem family—a mother and a father who emigrated from Virginia, thus the Shifter. When this information was finally forthcoming after months and months of daily intimate contact in the hollow, I said, "Jabe, you must be kin to all the Shifters in the hollow."

"Hain't likely."

"But then why are there so many families with the name Shifter?"

"Hain't knowin'." He could have added that he wasn't caring, either.

"Your wife's name was Shifter. Perhaps her 'fur kin' were kin to your parents."

He turned his back and slowly walked away. I overtook him. "Jabe, your wife's sister married Willis."

"Yep."

"So their children and your children are cousins."

"They's hain't even fur kin," he muttered.

Individuals and families who feel they are beyond the "sorryness" of their relation simply develop a mind set against anything which links them as products of a common ancestry.

Lizzie Shifter married Leander Shifter, but their last name is sheer coincidence, I am told. Nole Shifter married Malvie Shifter; Rhoda Shifter married Ulysses Shifter; Vick Shifter married Mittie Shifter; Lola Shifter married Oren Shifter. First cousins marry first cousins. First cousins marry sisters. Four brothers marry four sisters. As Meander says, " 'Twixt all th' firin' 'n' back-firin', hain't no knowin' kin." "Firin' " means legitimate children; "back-firin' " describes children born outside marriage. The results add up to "her'n 'r his'n's younguns." Since it is common for two individuals to live together for a period and then marry, the "her'n" and "his'n's" blends into "their'n" without any semblance of stigma. Dana said that her mother and father were married, " 'ceptin' they's slow gittin' provin' [marriage license]."

The circumstances of conception do not diminish a fervent sense of loyalty to the family organization, which tends to be founded on a kinship rather than a marital relationship, with the dominant role going to the eldest clansman. His home serves as the gathering place for succeeding generations and it is there that extended family is brought together from time to time. The kinship circle is bound by joint property or by ownership of adjacent pieces of land by family members and its unity is awesome when the clan is rallied in support of or in opposition to some proposal. Even a marriage partner is decided upon within the kinship system. It is this extended structure which blurs the identity of nuclear units. These are patrilinear, the culture being that of the husband's father or kinship group. If the father is "sorry," his children and his children's children will be "sorry" too. The smaller patriarchal families are stable; disruption is uncommon because the roles of father, mother, husband, and wife are clearly defined and accepted. In the two instances of divorce over a seven-year period, both men remarried their former wives. They each brought back children of the intervening marriage whom the first wife thinks of as "us'n's" younguns. The term "stepchild" is never used and efforts to explain the true meaning of the relationship fail because the hollowers have no frame of reference for the prefix *step*. Likewise, "mother-in-law" has no meaning and therefore is not subjected to the barbs so frequently tossed in the civilized world. I could never get beyond "hit's m' man's maw" or "hit's m' worman's maw." The same can be said for aunt, uncle, nephew, niece, etc.

The dynamics of change have exerted no pressure in Duddie's Branch and peptic ulcers are unheard of there. Children have a fierce allegiance to their mother and father, particularly the latter. The authority of the patriarch is supreme and he is respected and obeyed without question. Offspring rarely escape from the category of "children," even though they marry and become parents themselves. Farmer proudly said that all of his children were "seein' close," meaning that he could see all eight of their places from the porch of his shack. When a marriage partner dies, one of the children moves into the core domicile to care for the survivor. The reverse is never true. The question of which of the brood will assume the responsibility is decided peaceably among the siblings. Brothers and sisters have a close attachment and cling together, mutually dependent upon one another in their state of deprivation. Garnett said, "Hain't sharin' w'at you's hain't got, 'ceptin' we's all sharin' nothin'."

Although the kindred relationship is strong, it does not preclude conflicts within the structure and the bonds of blood are especially fragile when money is involved. Seafle Yancy charges his relatives ten dollars to drive them to Lexington and back. Melda complained about the cost and Flossie, Seafle's wife, concurred. "Hit do seem 'at 'e sh'd carry you's fur nothin', 'r leastaways fur less 'n' 'e does 'em 'at hain't kin."

In general, however, the kinship structure is far more important than any friendship or neighborly bond.

Duddie's Branch is not a community of families or groups of people who are united in some formal way; in fact the closest the hollowers come to directing a consolidated effort toward satisfying common needs is "borryin'." The Branch is an area of incoherent disunity. But this very "strangeness" that sets them apart from other people helps weld them together in a resolve to thwart invasion by outsiders. Anyone who does not reside in Duddie's Branch is labeled a trespasser, a cognomen that I bore for several months. The door of the first home I called on was opened to me in silence— Harry simply stood there and stared. When I asked permission to enter, I feared his eyes would leap from their sockets. After he had recovered from the catatonia my request had induced, he moved aside just far enough to permit me to wriggle through. No one in the house appeared to be uneasy about the untidy room in which a shabby table supported the variegated crumbs of remote meals. The walls were covered with newspapers, soot, photographs of coffins bearing their dead burdens, artificial flowers, and biblical reproductions. As I covertly appraised the residents, they brazenly inspected me. They asked no concessions and gave none; it was plainly evident that if the social distance that separated us was to be bridged I would have to be the engineer.

Authority figures also find the going rough in Duddie's Branch, but in their case it is hard to distinguish between suspicion and distrust. The Branchers are not ignorant of the power systems in the political arena, but they are fatalistic about the chances of improving their lot. "They hain't got nothin' t' help us with, but they moved 'at highway a quarter of a mile jist t' straighten out a curve." Except for the county judge, they are certain that the community leaders are indifferent to their situation. Even when they try to buy advice or representation, the inability to communicate hampers the transaction and they usually come out on the short end of the stick. Never do they attribute this to their defect, but bitterly declare that they have been exploited.

They make a great show of courage, but fear underlies their every action and they rarely emerge from the Branch alone. The miner who starts at the head of the hollow will be met midway by another miner and near the mouth of the Branch by still another; they will then all walk out together. They do not even go to the store unattended. One resident was ill and had to be taken to a hospital in London. Before his friends sought means of transportation, they canvassed the neighborhood and organized an escort party, body-guards actually.

The harshness of their lives, however much of it they overlook, undoubtedly adds to their distrust of and contempt for strangers.

While watching a late movie on television at the Nuratt home, we saw the married couple in the drama prepare for bed.

"They's took off they's duds 'n' put a diff'r'nt kind on," marveled Lester.

The next scene showed the husband in one twin bed and his wife in the other. Lester attacked the man with vigor.

" 'E's quar. Looks t' me liken 'e hain't plannin' on beddin' down with 'is woman. 'At hain't nach'ral." He was obviously revolted at what he considered to be an aberration. "But you's kin never trust nary a stranger fur nothin'. They's all quar in some way."

Coffee told me about a man from Detroit who had a flat tire at the mouth of the Branch.

"I's headin' out w'en 'e named helpin' 'im."

The man had the tools needed to change the tire, but Coffee did not know how to use any of them. He went back into the Branch and returned in a little while with four men. They hoisted the car on rocks and changed the tire with only the aid of a wrench. When they were ready to push it off the rocks, one of the men kept kicking the right front tire, "keepin' hit headin' fur th' road."

Later that same day I met the stranger in the Hiram store. He told me that he had offered the men a five-dollar bill but that they would not take it. The next day Coffee spoke of the man's offer of money.

"I'd 'a took one skin, but 'em big'uns mought bring in th' law."

"The law wouldn't care if he paid you."

"Reckon not, but 'at feller could 'a had a homemade 'un. Home-made 'uns brings in 'em law fellers."

Counterfeit money has been passed off onto the Branchers before by strangers and they place more faith in a single dollar than they do in bills of higher denomination. Had Coffee been articulate, he could have asked for one dollar.

It requires no special skill to take advantage of people handi-capped by cultural accumulation. The natural protection they all cherish attenuates the process of assimilation, thus assuring a kind of segregation. Their profound differences in values clash with those of middle-class society. Fundamental to their way of life is the custom of "borrowing" for keeps, a tradition that no one calls thievery. "Thievin's stealin'; I jist borries. 'Course, I hain't 'tendin' t' pay back w'at I gits, but if'n they's got some t' spare, they don't need none back." They most often do their "borryin'" at night and are unconscionable about taking vegetables raised by others. Instead of picking the plants, they pull them out by the roots, with the result that the entire crop is destroyed.

Fundamental, too, is moonshine. The Branchers do not look upon alcoholic habits of other residents as offensive, but the alcoholics themselves might regret their vice. I attended a church meeting and heard a chronic alcoholic pleading at the prayer rail for his thirteen-year-old son to be spared the evils of imbibing. "I hain't a-wantin' 'im t' be drinkin' liken I 'uz. You's pertec' m' boy 'n' I won't even smell a jar."

We rode back to the Branch together; he told me en route that he was introduced to alcohol at the age of ten while delivering moonshine for his father. He would sip the contents of the quart or half-gallon fruit jar and then replace the amount he had drunk with water or even with gasoline he siphoned from parked cars. Now, at forty years of age, he consumes 200-proof alcohol without batting an eye; there is a good possibility, however, that he will set himself aflame with his fiery breath.

Branch immorality also causes the outer world to catch its pious breath. If a young girl consents to sexual intercourse, her legal age does not hinder its consummation. Sexual appetites develop as prematurely as the sixth year of life in some of the precocious females. Young boys and girls both are "full 'a sexin'," but this is to be expected in light of their crowded living quarters. They share sleeping space with parents and older married brothers and sisters and intercourse is very much a part of their everyday life. The girls develop earlier than the boys and attract men much older than themselves. They frequently copulate with married men whose status protects them when the girl finds that she is pregnant. The idea of commercial abortion is never conceived. The rare girl who does try to bring about a miscarriage or an abortion uses slippery elm or more brutal methods. As a rule, though, the mother-to-be is not anxious about her condition because she knows that she will eventually marry and that her future husband will accept her child as his own. One would have considerable difficulty in identifying children born out of wedlock because they are not treated differently from the other children. There is no prejudice, they are not abused, they are never abandoned, and none ever ends up in an orphanage. They are given the same food, shelter, and schooling as the others and I have never heard a single child referred to as illegitimate by the Branchers. The child himself is not ashamed of his origin. "Hain't 'xactly sure 'bout my paw, but reckon I's got one somewhar." Nor is he curious about his parent. "Hain't worth knowin'."

Non-support, physical abuse, neglect, and promiscuity among males exist in the Branch cultural pattern. Perhaps unorthodox behavior is the hollower's only means of emotional release. Typically, there is no group-oriented or collective frame of recreation; no societies, no meetings, no sewing circles, no clubs, no rituals such as showers or charivaris—not even heritage traditions because the Branch is not ethnically homogeneous. No family belongs to a school or community or fraternal group. Church activities do not exist; formal religion is an irrelevancy to them.

The Branchers are a people following their own simple, unenlightened self-interest. They are not immersed in the time demands of existence; their habit of squandering time is not disrupted by regular hours of work. They need spend only a minimum period on tasks essential for the continuation of life and the remainder of their day is unrequisitioned by nature or society—it is theirs to waste in idleness or to spend profitably. A relationship between the individual and some larger system of ideas or values involves obligations as well as rewards, and the residents are unwilling to accept any role which exacts a price. Status is never earned by anything so prosaic as being a good provider or a good worker. There is a significant scarcity of candidates for either of these categories, so the inhabitants use criteria that every person can fulfill at one time or another.

Probably not more than four men qualify as semi-skilled workers.

Most cannot even do simple carpentry work around their homes. Some of the younger men do tinker with old cars and trucks, but their repairs and modifications are so inadequate that it is a rare vehicle that will go a mile without a relapse. Whether they work on cars for pleasure or as a source of dependable transportation is debatable. Wilford labored for several days on an old junk heap and the moment the motor turned over he took off. I saw him on foot about a mile from the hollow thirty minutes later.

"I thought you had that car fixed?"

"I 'uz jist aimin' on fixin' hit t' go down t' th' store 'n' back, but hit din't quite make hit. Hit's good in a way; if'n yer car hain't runnin' nobody axes you's t' pack 'em nowhar."

Few exhibit a serious interest in work. The general feeling is that nothing will be gained by it and therefore it should be avoided if possible. On my way out of the Branch I saw Meander occupying a rock.

"Come set a spell," he coaxed.

I arranged myself on an adjacent rock. "I guess you're all caught up with your work?"

"Nope. Hain't never bin behint."

"I'm always behind."

"Wa'al, if'n you's startin' whar you's stoppin', reckon you's hain't laggin' none."

The idea of adhering to an employer's schedule fills them with loathing and the desire to do things at their own pace accounts for their aversion to "bosses." If they must work, they would rather mine coal than anything else because no one supervises them in the tunnels. "Hit hain't too safe workin' in th' mines, but thar hain't no bosses standin' 'round tellin' you's w'at t' do."

When Ned returned from Indianapolis, the Branch buzzed for days about the deleterious effects two months' work had had on him. Sie was shaken. " 'At pore Ned had t' do a heap 'a sittin' 'n' reckonin' w'en he come back from 'Napolis. Hit most d'stroyed 'im bein' so fur yander fur sech a long time 'n' havin' so many bosses. Hain't knowin' if'n 'e'll ever be right agin."

Preferable to working for someone else is living off the land if it is at all productive. This pursuit removes them from the malignant influence of "bosses" and enables them to relax during the winter months when their only occupation is to scavenge along the road for coal that falls off the trucks going to the tipple.[1] In the growing season, though, they spend hours of backbreaking work tilling the soil to compensate for their lack of machinery, fertilizer, pesticides, and good seed. Research, experimentation, and development programs appear to be designed for those who hold huge acreages and deal in mass production rather than for those who spend heavily in human resources to eke out food for sustenance. The Branchers derisively claim that most of the help goes to the prosperous farmers in the county. This is undeniably the case when it comes to the distribution of free fertilizer. To my knowledge, not one single family in the Branch has ever had the benefit of free fertilizer even though they apply for it every year. Yet down Puvella way, rich tobacco farmers get it by the carload. Even though they are not eligible according to application requirements, the fertilizer is reserved for their use and when the small farmer makes application he is told that there is not enough to go around.

The poor quality of the land contributes to the widespread malnutrition in Duddie's Branch. The lack of money with which to buy essential foods they cannot raise on their land is another factor. Milk and oranges are rarities and fresh meat, fish, or poultry is almost never eaten. The inadequate diets of pregnant mothers lead to toxemia, premature births, and weak infants. Undernourished children develop anemia and low resistance to infection. Malnutrition is not the only health problem in the area, however. There is not one resident who does not suffer from some kind of disease and/or illness. The number of diagnosed tuberculosis patients, who are sup-

[1] "In the tipples near the 'head houses' the output of the mines was cleaned and loaded for shipment. In the best tipples the coal was washed, but in most of them this phase of preparation was omitted. Powerful 'shaker screens' vibrated the coal as it moved along conveyors. These agitated screens separated the coal into various sizes—'nut and slack,' 'egg,' and 'block.' The slate and 'bone' that had escaped the miners was picked out and cast aside by sharp-eyed 'slate pickers.' Much coal was broken in the process, and clouds of the pulverized stuff rose from the screens and 'loading booms' which lowered it into the railroad cars." Harry M. Caudill, *Night Comes to the Cumberlands* (Boston: Little, Brown and Company, 1962), pp. 144–45.

posedly quiescent and non-infectious, indicates that these people are in real need of constant medical attention.

The residents view the high incidence of disease without alarm and consider illness as inevitable. Shelly spoke about Tiny's physical condition, and volunteered information about his own in the process.

" 'E's got a pecul'ar stomick 'n' cain't eat reg'lar grub. It 'ud cost a fortune jist t' feed 'isself. They put 'im in th' hospital jist so's they c'd have 'is turds fur studyin'.

"I ruint my stomick in the army. Hain't memorin' w'at they sayed I had, but I used t' c'd pernounce hit. 'Em fellers din't look out fur me very good. They jist left me layin' 'round so I hain't thinkin' much 'bout doct'rin'."

Are these people then thinking much about migrating? I have asked some of the Branchers in which of the states they would most like to live. None was able to answer my question because he could not imagine life outside the Branch. "You's meanin' some fur country?"

Most of the inhabitants of this area have a strong attachment to it and many of the people who tried to relocate have come back to the Branch with discouraging accounts of their experiences. Projects intended to stimulate industry and employment offer little hope to most of them because they do not have the skills to compete for jobs or the cultural background that would enable them to conform to contemporary practices, which are far too routine and demanding for them to be good workers. They complain about the treatment they receive, the high cost of living, and their low status in an urban population. The competitive aspects of society in general are beyond their capabilities and they quickly acquire a sense of failure and inferiority which is difficult to tolerate and which ultimately forces them to seek the security of the hollow from which they had fled. It is not solely the conditions in the outer world which keep them in the hollow, though. Close kinship involvements, the security of an isolated environment, and a pride in home ownership are some of the other factors which we want to view in greater detail.

Not more than three or four families have successfully relocated; in Branch terms, "relocation" means to leave the county. The out-migrants who move from the hollow to some other area in Earle County are thought of as being too good for the Branch and "gittin' 'bove their raisin'." Jude's daughter married and moved to a small town a few miles away. "She took a hankerin' fur bed sheets and turned plum agin flies," he lamented. "She's plum furgot who Duddie's Branchers are."

Who, indeed, are they? Generalizations are unkind and unfair, and to classify the residents of Duddie's Branch as "briar hoppers" or "hillbillies" is to strip them of the innate qualities every human possesses.

No matter how hungry they are or how long it has been since their children have eaten, they will tell you, "We's makin' out." They possess pride.

None would admit that he lives in poverty, no matter how expert a frame of reference is used to picture life in an impoverished setting. They possess self-esteem.

"I's a right good cook, if'n they's somethin' t' cook." They possess dignity.

The relief check arrives and the Branchers go for their surplus food commodities. "We waits till last t' line up 'n' then goes in w'en they's not so many seein' us." They feel embarrassed and ashamed. They possess humility.

They are resigned to a lifetime of poverty and hardship and have learned within their miseries to find some degree of happiness. They possess courage.

The area in which they live is isolated, but they neither struggle for liberation nor patronize emancipators. They possess independence.

Society has not afforded them an opportunity to grow, but there is no resentment. They possess charity.

Pride, self-esteem, dignity, humility, courage, independence, charity—an impressive number of credits to be balanced against the debits:

They live in a lonely hollow of poverty in the midst of an explosively prosperous society. They are impoverished.

All are inarticulate and most can neither read nor write. They are illiterate.

The daily routine of living is fraught with crises. They are burdened.

Stunted physical growth is characterized by their pale, thin, undernourished appearance. They are neglected.

Each vital characteristic—mental, emotional, social—is dwarfed. They are ineffectual.

They are accused of being genetically inferior. They are maligned.

The cultural complex of their setting does not stimulate gentleness, kindliness, or generosity. They are emotional dropouts.

The extent to which they are deliberately conscious of their behavior and motives is exceedingly narrow. They are unaware.

These debits could not have accrued without considerable assistance from the organized world.

We smell their stench, scorn their sloth, shrink from their squalor, and silently hope that they will stay in the hills.

We utterly disregard the real limitations that surround their every action.

They must rely on some kind of welfare aid because they cannot meet the requirements of a labor market that passed them by generations ago. The Brancher says, "We hain't has-bins; we's jist never-bins," and he voices our sentiments.

Malicious insinuations unite brother with sister, father with daughter, uncle with niece, and we listen avidly, not caring that their genetic inferiority has yet to be proved by those who equate everything in terms of statistics. We accept the stories as fact, but it is and will remain theory until all the crippling environmental conditions are ruled out.

We deride their inability to read and write and laugh at the way they speak. We call them stupid while at the same time we view them through a prismatic middle-class orientation and try to fit square pegs into round holes. Even the dullest Brancher can distinguish between a square and a hole.

Are Duddie's Branchers, then, the persons whom we put in the plus column of the ledger? They are not. Duddie's Branchers are the persons whom, consciously or unconsciously, we keep in the minus column, in a world apart. But the complex society of these primitive people cannot be understood by gross examination, as we shall see.

V

People to People

This world is a difficult world, indeed,
And people are hard to suit,
And the man who plays on the violin
Is a bore to the man with the flute.

Walter Learned
Consolation

The family is the basic unit which perpetuates the narrow world of Duddie's Branch. For many of the inhabitants, their very survival depends on the abler members of the kinship circle. Because of the strong familial orientation, friendship alliances are casual, and only when a problem cannot be solved within the family group will an attempt be made to secure assistance from neighbors. If, for example, a certain kindred unit is without transportation, they might ask someone who has a car to drive one of theirs to a hospital in an emergency. Their hesitation to ask for aid is apparent and refusal of help is always anticipated.

In the impersonal atmosphere of the Branch, problems and imperfections are viewed as public property and human failure is the subject of casual conversation by all. Howbeit, this climate does not reinforce respect and little value is placed on the need for friends. "Our land borders, but we hain't 'xactly friendin'."

Neighborliness, as we know it, does not exist; tolerance or indifference typifies the usual relationship. Interactional paradigms have no framework but hinge on the satisfaction of bare necessities—requesting a light for a hand-rolled cigarette, seeking the loan of a knife, borrowing a speck of salt to season an otherwise tasteless pot of squash or beans. A hatchet may be "borried" by as many as seven families to chop wood for the morning fire. But the unions that issue from the crowded conditions are not based on the sheer enjoyment of human interchange. They are marked by lack of depth or intimacy, and mutual respect and genuine friendship are rare. The residents do not engage in small talk among themselves and articulation is not common among those who are not related. Horizontal communication revolves around essentials of daily life; vertical communication simply does not exist.

Strangely enough, an act is not judged on the basis of merit but on the cleverness of the perpetrator. Jerry regards his moonshining as "jist slantin' th' law," yet someone else who sets up a still or peddles alcohol is "breakin' th' law, pure 'n' simple." When I suggested that the guilt was equal, he was affronted.

"If'n hit's legal 'r not 'pends on whose eyes you's lookin' with. Hain't all 'a us kin live outside th' law legal."

"But what makes it different?" I asked. "Seems to me it's either legal or illegal."

"W'en you's livin' outside th' law, you's jist hain't got no need fur hit. Hain't w'at 'at makes th' diff'r'nce, liken you's says, but who. You's jist larns how. But you's hain't likely t' know, 'cause hit takes a heap 'a knowin'."

Predictability of behavior is impossible; their reaction to me was the only consistent example I could detect. Families who were speaking one day were alienated the next. In each instance the hostility originated from something that was or was not said, or from something that was or was not done. Their erratic demeanor frequently degenerated into ruthlessness.

I was living in Duddie's Branch when an epidemic of dog killing erupted. The excessive number of canines had been criticized by all of the inhabitants at one time or another, but feelings ran high during the extermination period. Everyone was held suspect by everyone else, and the community was almost sundered.

I was sitting on the porch with Onzie, a twenty-four-year-old unemployed man. We had not been visiting very long before he got out his rifle and began to clean it. Upon completing the task, he expressed a desire for a target; I recommended a tree that stood on the other side of the hollow.

"'At 'ud be wastin' a shell," he sneered.

Just then a dog appeared in the Branch. Onzie was well acquainted with its owner but he sighted his gun anyway.

I was electrified. "You're not going to shoot that dog, are you?"

"Wa'al, I's gotta shoot at somethin'," he whined.

With this he fired, and the dog fell dead.

"Don't you like dogs, Onzie?"

"I likes dogs perty good, but then I likes some better'n I does others. If'n I hain't likin' a dog thar hain't much point in lettin' 'im live."

"Why didn't you shoot at the tree?" I was bewildered.

"You's jist don't wastes shells shootin' at trees; you's shoots at somethin' t' kill."

"Why not shoot a human then?"

He pondered this for a moment. "Reckon I 'udn't shoot a youngun 'r a man 'r a worman." Once more he deliberated. "But then agin, I jist mought."

Onzie is not unique—many of the men kill animals just for the sake of killing. It was impossible for me to reconcile their urge to destroy another's pet with the deep affection they felt for their own. If someone were only to throw a rock at their animal, the dog owners would viciously attack the rock throwers.

The quality of interchange is so tenuous that it may be temporarily suspended by any act of aggression, and the first attempts at restoring harmonious relations may be preceded by combat. Most of the individuals are ill equipped by education, training, or background to settle personal disputes on a verbal level and physical contests frequently become the vehicle for resolving conflicts. Unstable reactions keep the hollow in an almost constant state of flux. After one or two unsuccessful engagements, some residents employ ingenious methods to avoid further collisions.

Layuna was hoeing out potatoes and I climbed the steep mountainside to survey her plot. One of the plants looked wilted and I called it to her attention.

"They's some 'at gits like 'at. Jist tired 'a growin', I reckon."

She hoed on and I unobtrusively dug my fingers into the ground for a more complete examination of the plant. The root base had been cut off; someone obviously had been "borryin'." I quickly replaced the top in its weary stance and walked back to where she was working.

"How big would potatoes be now?"

She scratched away the soil with a stick to show me one about the size of a golf ball.

"When will they be ready to eat?"

"Reckon afore long."

She scrupulously shunned inspection of the violated vine. Had she looked at the plant in my presence, she would have been forced to acknowledge that a thief had visited her garden. Upon acknowledging the thievery, she would have had to attempt to identify the intruder; to omit this from protocol would have been tantamount to cowardice. The next step would have been to confront the accused. In order not to activate this cycle, her only recourse (at least her only safe recourse) was to feign ignorance of the theft—which she did.

Sometimes neighborly disapproval is so stern that a family might move. Addie was resented by her first husband's family for many reasons. Her mother-in-law disapproved of the marriage so energetically and so unremittingly that Curt went into the army to get away. When he found out that he would have to give Addie an allotment each month and make her the beneficiary of his insurance, his mother talked him into seeking a release. The army records were adjusted and carried the names of Curt Shifter (mother, Heddie Shifter) and Curtis Shifter (mother, Heddie Shifter).

Curt soon re-enlisted because of the assurance of a regular income, but this time he used the name of Jess E. Shifter and served until the end of World War II. When he changed his name to Jess E. his mother changed her name to Hed E. Heddie got one check for a son Curt and, under the name of Hed E., got another check for the same son who served in the army under the false name of Jess E.

The check to Heddie Shifter from Curt Shifter came to the Hardstone post office and the check for Hed E. Shifter (Heddie) from Jess E. Shifter (Curt) came to the Beeville post office. Curt's father, Jabe, disapproved of the fraudulent practice and in a strident voice nightly applied to the Lord to deliver him from the irregularities in which his wife and son had become involved.

In 1963 Kentucky passed a 3 per cent sales tax for the specific purpose of paying veterans' bonuses. The one and only Heddie Shifter, according to those who know of the incident, got three bonuses when the money was divided in the state—one for Curt, one for Curtis, and one for Jess E. This was a $1,500 windfall "fur nothin'." The other Branchers became so churlish about the bonus money that the family finally moved off the hollow—"wanted t' git close t' kin," so they said.

About the only thing that draws neighbors and kin together in a group is a church meeting. The hollowers have, for generations, been fundamentalists and church membership as outsiders practice it does not exist. Participation in spiritual affairs has never been essential, nor does it enhance social status. In fact, hollow folks are repelled by religion as an institution. They mistrust the organized church which makes some attempt to collect money, encourage participation in a variety of activities, and keeps record of attendance. This "Big Brother" attitude is interpreted as interfering with their individual right to structure their lives as they see fit, particularly as related to money.

I can recall my father's consternation when the biggest "blow-gut" in our church loudly pledged $2,000 before the entire congregation. This was back in 1920. Father, church treasurer at the time, turned white and then red. As he listened to the oration about the obligation of the parishioners to give, he twiddled his thumbs. This habit, I had learned, was an indication of extreme annoyance or agitation.

We never had much time together, but driving home from church on Sunday afforded the opportunity to reflect on the preceding week and talk of the future. Father had his own way of explaining things, which more often than not varied considerably from the printed word in the "Good Book." But he always made it quite clear to me "that if you get, you give until it hurts." I have seen the time, all too frequently, when we would have one roasting hen or fryer left and the preacher would get it. "Money isn't the only thing in the world. There are many other things you can give, including yourself. You pay in kind, not necessarily money."

Safely away from the church, Father exploded with oaths which I am sure the Lord would not have approved. "That s.o.b. has given less than I have for the past five years." And then he added the

famous unfinished threat which he applied to many situations: "If
I ever catch that guy in the dark . . ."

In the Branch and elsewhere in the county I have become involved in discussions about an individual's sense of responsibility
toward support of the church. Employing my "never give up"
philosophy, in spite of the supportive points of view to the contrary,
I persisted. "After all, one's health, money, worldly goods, etc.,
come from God."

Ace was not convinced. "You's claimin' now 'at God's runnin'
welfare?"

Over the years one learns that elaboration only complicates the
conversation with the result that the point which initiated the
original discussion is soon buried "under a mount'in." This is about
as deep, according to the Duddie's Branchers, as you can get.

"But shouldn't we give back to Him a portion of that which He
has given to us?"

"Measly 's hit is, hit's comin' from welfare 'n' I hain't plannin' on
sharin' hit, not even with 'Im."

In the outer world, religious contributions are a necessity. In the
hollows, financial support is neither expected nor provided, and
the church fits very adequately into the get-by philosophy of the
worshipers.

There is no organization and no communication between the different religions. Each group of worshipers patterns its services to
suit itself and there is no central authority. The Holiness Church
believes that war, class discrimination, and economic disparity are
flagrantly contrary to God's plan and Jesus' teachings. The church
embraces the Bible, but at the same time everyone is free to interpret
the Scriptures as he chooses. The members disapprove of smoking,
drinking, and dancing and frown upon political liberalism; the
ecumenical movement is violently disapproved, even though they
know little about it; they plan to stay with the Bible and avoid any
affiliation with any other group; they welcome members who are
disillusioned with programs and pledges of progress; they reject the
value of life's material rewards. In heaven all worldly possessions
have been left behind and everyone is equal. This gives them inner
peace.

Perhaps, as some say, the hollowers are unable to come to grips with modern problems because of these primitive and fundamental beliefs. A point of presumed weakness is the Holiness Church's insistence on a kind of spiritual isolation—a separation from the sinful world where everything material is evil and a concentration on a world centered on God. Faultfinders agree that it is easier to turn your back on problems than to solve them. They call Holiness a folk religion and insist that it is not a standard by which the members pattern their daily lives.

Preachers are expected to support themselves by working, forever remaining non-salaried because this is considered too much of a symbol of the material world. Local preachers are short on education and their sermons take on the dimensions of hell-fire and brimstone warnings; they are dominated by evangelistic conceptions rather than by doctrinal distinctions. Even today churches splinter because of discord. They divide into groups and one moves out to start anew in another building at another location. In some cases the same pastor is welcomed in both church houses.

The simplicity and emotionalism of the Holiness churches appeal to the hollowers. In the 9 × 9-foot church house, which is little more than a shed, the preacher calls upon his faithful flock to "git with God." Services begin around 7:00 P.M. and continue until 11:00 P.M., at least. During revival, it is long past midnight before the members surrender to exhaustion. The congregation sits on benches facing a platform, the men on one side and the women on the other. Child care is an exclusively female occupation, whether in the church or in the hollow. The loud, fiery preacher rekindles the faith in backsliding brethren and bolsters the faith of the loyal. When man-made laws conflict with church dogma, the latter always applies.

Everyone prays aloud simultaneously and the chanting of familiar hymns becomes more and more clamorous as the worshipers voice their praise of the Lord. The musicians sit on a bench near the back of the platform and face the congregation. Cymbals, tambourines, and guitars provide the rhythm for the faithful. Foot-stamping and hand-clapping are the signals that the emotions have reached a fever pitch and the congregation sings the lusty hymns with unin-

hibited spirit. Some of the members rise and cry out that the Lord
has moved them, and little by little a deafening noise of incoherent
shouting and hair-raising shrieks provides a cacophonous background for the minister. The shouting grows louder and more difficult
to understand. The tempo is heightened and built-up tensions culminate in overt behavior—the worshipers wave their hands toward
heaven and babble in unknown tongues. This communication between themselves and the Lord is a means by which He manifests
Himself to them. Speaking in "tongues" is done in a rapid, staccato,
unintelligible monotone. "It was this gift of speaking in tongues
which the Apostles were supposed to have received at Pentecost by
the Grace of the Holy Ghost. . . ."[1] This traditional type of religion helps pattern their belief that they should not expect to find
satisfaction and security in the material world. They feel that they
are truly God's chosen people and the fact that so many look upon
them with contempt has little impact. They deny any similarity to
what they call "Holy Roller" religion and regard their hyperemo-
tional behavior as special gifts from the Holy Spirit. Visitors are
branded as the Devil's workers if they are in any way suspected of
ridiculing the worshipers' conduct. One of my friends was ejected
just because he smiled. "Th' Devil's sent someone t' test us'n's—
cast 'im out!" And out he was cast!

Now it is time for the sick to be made whole. The healers begin
to lay hands on the ill and the afflicted, all the while adjuring divine
miracles. A grateful member arises to testify. "I wants t' thank God
fur healin' my lungs 's they 'uz marks 'r spots on 'em. I went back t'
th' Health D'partment 'n' took 'nother X ray 'n' they 'uz all right.
God kin heal you's if'n you's pray 'n' looks t' Him 'n' b'lieves. We's
lettin' th' Lord do our doct'rin'."

The Bible furnishes the guidelines of the church; it advises members to avail themselves of herbs for use in healing, it reminds them
that the man is the head of the house and so on. In being saved, the
individual is reborn through accepting the Holy Spirit. Lem's bap-
tism by the Holy Spirit had instantaneous effects. Cleansed from all
sin, he believed that he had been endowed with powers to accomplish any task. Receiving the Holy Ghost was the most significant

[1] S. Reinach, *Orpheus* (London: F. Simmonds, 1909), p. 251.

event in his seventy years of living. The Holy Spirit dwells inside the physical body and is present in every temporal experience; nothing keeps alive the sense of unworthiness more than the fear of God's watchful eye. The meaning and value of salvation are based on the belief that faith alone is enough. Salvation is not related to worldly behavior, as attested by their failure to observe the commandment, "Thou shalt not steal."

The strongest group relationship exists among the churchgoers. The lay preacher constantly brings them together as children of God, and each shares his trials, tribulations, troubles, and tortures with the others. The group is unified around the passionate desire for salvation and their joint effort descends on those whom they wish to save. Many place a high value upon their religious power and individuals join forces to focus on the wavering, undecided sheep who has lost his way and cannot find his flock.

Revivals, once called "camp meetings," are vital activities because they place emphasis on the importance of salvation. Being saved is how you reserve your place in the hereafter. Once saved, it is important to continue attending revivals. The straight and narrow path is often trod with faltering footsteps and assistance is usually required. Lem says that revivals ensure that a slip does not degenerate into a slide.

The first Branch church meeting I attended was held in a small vacant house and most of the hollow population was present. A few families, however, stayed away; they were outraged that Jeems Smuts was in "charge" of it in view of his daily conduct. The main preacher, Roma Hayseed and her assistant, Isom Fish, were from London. During the sermon, Mr. Fish and Miss Hayseed told the congregation that they had spent all of their money for gas to drive in from London and had no way of returning. A collection was taken up for them and amounted to a grand total of $1.40. Hymns were sung to the accompaniment of two guitars. There were no hymnals and the members made up words as they went along. Most of the adults sat in what might be called the living room of the house and the teenagers and younger children who could be left without supervision stayed in the kitchen. A number of families observed but did not participate in the service. Some vacillated between participation and passiveness, while yet a good many others were uncontrollably responsive during the entire meeting.

Some of the Branchers practice what they describe as "my kind" of religion. Others profess no religious belief at all. The majority, however, regard religion as something apart from the principles which guide their daily behavior. Praying, testifying, and laying on of hands never influence their consciences. The active participants emphasize eternal salvation rather than earthly rewards and the most deprived look upon their lot in life as a virtue, justifying its acceptance as God's will. A more formalized pattern of worship is wholly unacceptable to them—religion provides the opportunity to see other people and furnishes an emotional release. They have no other substitute for disburdening themselves and would feel out of place if they were to express such behavior outside the place where meetings are held. Some of the Branchers profess to believe every word of the Bible, even though they cannot read.

I went to a prayer meeting in Hack Bottom, which is some distance from Shade, with Ace and Beve Ross. We arrived at the mountain shack at about seven o'clock only to learn that the services would not begin until dark. This seems to be the usual custom. The owner of the cabin had cleared off an area beyond his house for parking and three or four cars were already ensconced there. A few people were sitting on the porch and a few more were inside. During the next hour the faithful trooped in on foot and in cars and trucks. As they came onto the porch they went from person to person, shaking hands. This greeting consists of slightly elevating the hand in a single, somewhat firm, short movement and then releasing it abruptly. Voices buzzed ceaselessly. A bucket of water stood on the porch and everyone drank freely from the rusted dipper which floated on its surface. At dusk we went inside, carrying our benches with us. The music and singing became progressively louder as the emotional atmosphere sharpened. Suddenly an elderly woman arose. The entire length of her slight frame was quivering violently. She shouted praises to the Lord and rhythmically swayed back and forth. At the height of her passion she agilely hopped up and down. An overalled man stood and worshiped in a hoarse voice. The two guitarists laid aside their instruments and flapped their perspiration-soaked shirts against bony chests. Other members rose and joined in the swaying motion of the ecstatic old lady. The man in overalls continued to talk swiftly and indistinctly. I could occasionally understand a few words referring to his salvation and a commentary on current religious practices. Midway through the proceedings we were asked to relinquish our bench, which was carried up front and used as a prayer rail. Several people knelt before it and bedlam broke loose in the form of supplications. The music resumed. Two men stood and offered their testimonials in such loud voices that they became red in the face and then blue from lack of oxygen. As they were recovering, the prayers for the sick appropriately began. A chair was placed in the center of the altar and the debilitated would sit in it briefly while the healers touched him and the congregation worshiped. As soon as a cure was effected, the indisposed would leap from the chair, raise his arms, and frantically jump around.

The meeting ended at ten o'clock. As we left I noticed that the young people had either stayed in the kitchen or remained outside.

The local newspaper often prints items related to the church:

"We prayed the old year out and the new year in so they had real good supper about 10 o'clock, cake, coffee and pop so they had lots of women who brought cake. We want to thank everyone who brought cake and everyone who stayed till after midnight."

"Bonnia and Gennete are selling Christmas cards to help raise money for new shutch [sic] seats in our church."

"We went to the tent meeting a Sunday they were a preacher doing the preaching he had a mirkle formed to him his arm that has got no bone in it, he can use it to pick up big things with God give his strength back in his arm. Come to the tent meeting."

"They will be a broadcase [sic] for Rev. Denner and Rev. Einn a Sunday 20 minutes past twelve please come out and be in the broadcast."

"Christian people don't get old becaus [sic] 'Everlasting Life' is springing up within them."

"People are encouraged to go to a city about 200 miles away for a tent revival holding for 2 wks. If you want to be healed and see the blined [sic] eye open and the deaf can hear, the lame can walk. You will be glad you did."

"Well, people is passing away every day I went to London Saturday and Sunday to the Funeral Home they said that they were 7 people in the Funeral Home dead so I am telling everbody [sic] they better be studying about their soul before it to [sic] late God is calling people out and we don't know when our time will be next."

"They had a large crowd of people at Horntoad Church Saturday night. They had a good meeting. Pray that God will help get the people back together."

"Revival: All the Christian people come out and get renewed up and lets us all help get lost souls saved."

Funeral services, in contrast to revival meetings, are simple if maudlin affairs. The demise of a family member stimulates exaggerated grief, even among those who previously expressed little affection for the deceased. Upon learning of a death, some of the relatives and neighbors go to the home of the bereaved family and stay there until after the burial.

Since embalming laws are now enforced, as soon as a homemade casket is assembled, it and the body are taken to an undertaker (whose modified fee is very seldom paid). Some caskets are plain and somewhat mummy-shaped, padded with cotton and lined with a shimmering, white, satinlike material. The lid is set aside until time for burial. It is usually nailed or screwed on; some are hinged, depending upon how much time the craftsman has to make the container. Handles are fashioned from a small, straight tree.

If the family does not have its own burial ground, the members look over the countryside before selecting a site. "We's aimin' on buryin' 'im in 'at thar hill," and thus a new graveyard is born. The only cemetery in Duddie's Branch is back of Sap Shifter's house, but it holds only his family. The ownership of this cemetery and the restriction of burials was made plain the day the baby born to Dob and Preshia Halt died. They were firmly told that it was a family plot and that outsiders could not, under any circumstances, be buried there. Having land enough for use as a graveyard is a Branch status symbol. •

Most babies and young children are buried soon after death, but not always within the twenty-four-hour limit. Weather and location are always determinant factors; the rockier the soil and the more inclement the weather, the longer the body is kept.

Most funerals are held at the Pentecostal Church of God (also a Holiness Church). This denomination does not deem it mandatory that a member of the clergy be present when death is imminent or sudden, nor does it have rules, opinions, or rituals regarding the removal, embalming, dressing, or encasketing of the remains. Earth burial is preferred, but there is no objection to a full mausoleum crypt interment. Cremation is definitely forbidden. There are no rituals prior to the regular funeral service and no special equipment is needed on or about the encasketed body. The family selects the burial site, casket bearers, etc., without qualification or counsel.

The Pentecostal Church rests atop a high hill about two and a half miles from Duddie's Branch. A narrow, winding dirt road, heavily laced with low-water bridges, snakes its way up the side. When the water is high, you hope that the bridge has not been washed away and plunge your car nose-first into the swirling, foamy stream. An old rattletrap usually rides point. If he stalls, the hearse and procession pause long enough to push him aside before cautiously continuing on its way. Jude says, "Hit 'ud be shamin' fur 'at daid feller t' git wet on top 'a dyin'."

The open casket is placed in front of the altar. As usual, the sexes are segregated and the children generally sit in the back. The immediate family occupies the first few rows. The service is punctuated by loud wails, weeping, and moaning. After the eulogy has been delivered the choir sings either religious or purely sentimental songs. The casket is then moved by the attendants to the back of the church for final viewing of the deceased. The mourners file past it and mill about in the churchyard until the family joins them. After all are assembled outside, the minister leads the procession to the casket coach and the body is taken to the grave where it is laid to rest. Ministers may use flowers in place of sand or dirt in the committal.

After the burial, the family of the deceased expresses elaborate thanks through the newspaper to everyone involved: to visitors, to those who sent flowers or cards, the flower shop, the undertaker, the choir, the attendants, etc. "To those that dug the grave and helped in anyway we want to say thank you and may God bless you."

Most graveyard reunions are held over the "crackin' day" (July 4) holiday. Independence Day has deeper significance than anyone in the outer world can comprehend. Most of those who come home to celebrate can't tell you what the day means or why it came into existence in the first place, but they know and value the word "independence." For those who are now in the care of their Maker, this is independence in its purest sense—no more worldly troubles, no grinding poverty in heaven. The rich can take nothing with them to the hereafter, nor can the Brancher, and all are equal. "If'n you's hain't got nothin', you's hain't leavin' out sorryin'."

The hereafter is about the only place most Branchers will "leave out fur" without firm resistance. Their low desire to migrate is lowered even further by the tales related by the ones who have experienced urban living.

Wives are the least satisfied members of migrant families. They must, for the first time in their lives, devote more attention to their children and they are required to make more radical changes in the pattern of daily existence than their husbands. Men who work spend little time at home when they are not on the job. They generally find some of their own kind and congregate much as they did in the hollow. The nearest hole-in-the-wall tavern is a favorite spot, or they might walk to a nearby busy street and lean against a building, observing the passers-by.

Because of limited income, migrant families live in conditions worse than those in the hollow. People, even their neighbors, are unfriendly. They can no longer spend much time out of doors and this increases the crowding inside their already cramped living quarters. Small children can't negotiate second-, third-, and fourth-floor walkups over creaking stairs. In the Branch they can crawl out the ever open door without exposure to danger, but in the city there is no place for them to play. The physical size of the buildings cuts off the sky and the sun and pens them in. Two-way streets constitute a nightmare for them—they have difficulty remembering that speeding cars approach from two directions at once.

In the hollow they never thought of themselves as disadvantaged, but in an urban area they feel "put upon." They are uneasily conscious of the loss of their individualism and this comes as a deep shock. The emotional impact of urban living is soon felt, but they no longer have the Branch to go into for escape from the problems of adjustment. In an effort to combat a feeling of inadequacy, they cluster in areas inhabited by their own kind and form little cultural islands (no one goes to a city where he is unknown). Integrated neighborhoods further complicate their lives and add to the pressures of daily existence. Most of the places they can afford are run down or condemned and they are continuously thinking about or trying to find new hovels. They cannot afford to pay out more dollars for rent, though, and most important, nobody renting slum apartments asks them how many children they have or how many other than family members will be living with them.

They are removed from all the things that are meaningful and worth while—kinship ties, peer groups, familiar places. No matter where they relocate, home always remains in the Branch. They live in the urban area between trips back home. Their one goal is to live until the next time they can visit their hollow and the happy day when they can go back there forever.

What impels them to leave, then? One family left because they wanted to be near their children, who attend a state school for the deaf. Another family left out of desperation when they were unable to qualify for welfare funds after the father and older boys were unable to find work. Regardless of their privation in the hollow, however, few are willing to leave their beloved hills for the canyons of the city tenements. For the first time many families recognize how ill prepared they are to adjust to urban living, and nostalgia for their birthplace motivates their frequent return trips to the hollow even though they cannot afford the economic and physical cost. Their pilgrimages hasten the time when they will give up and go back forever. Ben says, "Bein' away, hit's one thing; missin', hit's hurtin'. 'At'll plum d'stroy a feller." One must be impressed by the limited perception these people have of society outside the hollow neighborhoods.

Edell and Kash Marse and their seven children lived in a two-room tarpaper shack in Duddie's Branch before moving to Cincinnati. It had withstood almost twenty-five years of punishment and the roof had been patched so many times and with so many different materials that it looked like a crazy-patch quilt. "Jist 'nuf fur coverin' big drippers." But they had lived among their kin and were unmolested by the harsh unfriendly people who plagued them in the slums—the landlords, the attendance officers, the visiting teachers, the social workers—all "question axin'." After months in a Cincinnati tenement, Edell said, "Livin' in this place with all 'ese people hain't nice's home [an 8 × 8-foot shack with a lean-to, the interior dilapidated]. You's jist animal-like hyur. Fellers fittin' 'bout nothin', hollerin' 'n' mouthin' cussin'." Their apartment has no hot water and no sink, but their house in the Branch didn't have them either. There are many similarities to the hollow: trash and filth everywhere, leaking roofs, sagging floors, rotten porches, broken windows, a mudhole for a yard. "We's got mud in th' holler, 'ceptin' younguns gits fur off in 'em hills. Mud, onc't hit's dry, you's kin push hit out afore comin' back in later addin' more." The slums are inconvenient. The door on the oven, which is their only source of heat, is propped closed with a stick and the plates on the top are broken, forcing Edell to cook over an open hole. The pipe leading out is riddled with holes and is closed with a tintype portrait of Prince Albert and wire.

"Your husband at least has a job."

"'At hain't meanin' nothin' if'n fellers gotta live in sech 's this. 'Em winders 'at hain't busted you's cain't see through. I's peepin' through a busted winder ever' sunup. Dudes in fancy duds be footin' 'twixt me 'n' th' road."

Edell is now an expert on substandard housing and she feels insecure and degraded because she is forced to live in such a dangerous, unsanitary building: filth, rats, roaches; plumbing that does not work; walking down five flights of rickety stairs for water at a faucet in the "courtyard"; falling plaster and no heat. Complaints are ignored. "If you don't like it, move out. We'd like to rid ourselves of the likes of you hillbillies." The Marses pay forty-five dollars a month for their slum apartment, two small furnished rooms. Why is the rent so cheap? Simply because they are willing to walk five flights up. The landlord grosses seven hundred dollars per month on people like them. The taxpayer picks up the welfare family's tab to subsidize the landlord's profit. Edell's toilet does not flush and has no seat. The landlord told her he would have to raise the rent one dollar a month to put on a seat. "If'n hit hain't workin', 'at seat hain't worth nothin'." For ten months she lived in a building where the toilet (which again did not flush) was next to the stove without an enclosure of any kind.

One day I made an appointment to meet the landlord, who lives in the most exclusive residential district. I did not tell him that I was interested in Edell's family because of possible repercussions. We went to his club for lunch, riding over in his Cadillac. He righteously said that he spent twenty dollars a month on that building and even bought as much as ten dollars' worth of rat bait a year. In the luxurious surroundings of his club he confessed to me that his aim was to make as much money as he could before his tenement buildings were condemned (the building code was adopted approximately thirty-three years ago). He was not happy about his tenants. "Just as fast as I fix up something, they tear it down." He did not exaggerate. Someone threw a beer bottle through the glass in the Marses' one door and the landlord replaced it. "Hit warn't no time till Herman busted hit out. I's licked 'im 'n' 'is paw licked 'im. We's back t' hard paper [cardboard]. Younguns gotta git in mount'ins fur roughin'."

One family planned to migrate to Cincinnati and I expected that they were taking all of their possessions. "Nope. Jist takin' a couple 'a pokes." Sure enough, they took less than when they leave for a few hours' visit. Two weeks after they moved, one of the Branch children told me, "Gid 'n' 'em is in." That, I thought, was a short trip and went down to their place. They were eating breakfast. "We's back fur 'taters. 'Em 'taters costes 'n' tastes garbage-like in Cincinnati." It was expensive to drive a round trip of more than four hundred miles just to eat and take back potatoes. Coming back, they had started with just a dollar's worth of gas, they said.

"You're kidding me; you didn't get down here on that little bit of gas?"

"Nope. But they 'uz plenty 'a cars settin', so we borried if'n they's any left. I 'uz al'ays fair, though, 'n' never did take ever' drop a feller had. My tires 'uz sorta slicken, too. One feller left 'is lid up [either hood or trunk] so I borried one 'a 'is tires. But I din't steal hit. I changed hit onto my car 'n' put mine back on his'n. Jist tradin'."

For a year or more I had been weighing the idea of undertaking the rehabilitation of a young teenage hollow child. Rehabilitating a girl was out of the question; her level of sexual maturity and affinity for older men meant that I would be limited to one aged six or seven years. Therefore I concentrated my efforts on the boys.

My first choice was Herman, who seemed to want to go with me. His aunt lived about a hundred miles from my home and he had far kin in a small town about thirty miles away. I discussed the idea with his father and grandfather, who expressed no enthusiasm. He was needed for chores at home (but he never did any work about the house). When this obstacle was hurdled, he was too "porely"—he suffered from headaches and sick stomachs. I knew that he was infested with a variety of intestinal parasites, but a physical examination revealed that aside from malnutrition he was otherwise sound. A chest X ray was negative. Once out of the environment the intestinal parasites would disappear with proper treatment. One obstacle after another was eliminated and the talk had advanced to the planning stage. When the time came to set a date, the father was willing to let Herman go providing he could return home every weekend. This request was impossible—I could never meet it. Then the father supplied a way out. Brother Backerjuice came down from the city every Friday night to preach at a nearby church. He was willing to bring Herman with him. "Fur kin" came to the Branch with a truckload of used furniture almost every week and Herman could ride back with them. Others came down a couple of times a month. Under these conditions, I agreed to take Herman. Saturday and Sunday were my only days off and it was to be then that I would have the most time to spend with the child; even so, I was willing to make the sacrifice. I set the date and outlined activities for the first couple of months. All seemed to be going well. A week before departure I went into the hollow. Herman's father was lying out on the bank of the Branch, waiting for me. He had ingested too much moonshine to be his usual reticent self. He demanded a monthly payment of thirty dollars for letting Herman come live with me. After all, he reckoned, he should be worth that much. We sat on that bank until sunset while I matched wits with the continuous inward flow of moonshine. I knew that I was fighting a losing battle but somehow just could not bring myself to the point of admitting defeat. Finally moonshine won. All the possible alternatives fell on deaf ears. Loyd agreed to inform Herman that the arrangement had been canceled and I thanked him for his time and effort. He stumbled to the mouth of the hollow without speaking. I did not mistake his escort for courtesy. He did it to give me an opportunity to tell him that I had changed my mind. Hollowers feel that a walk in quiet meditation weakens one to the point of surrender.

After I left Loyd I was miserable. How could he, who had so little, defeat me, who had so much? I reasoned that brain, brawn, and education are not necessarily assets when you interact with hollow folks. Nonetheless, I was bitterly disappointed. There would be some face-saving and some fence-mending ahead. I would have to admit defeat to those in the outer world who had said I could never get a child, no matter who, out of that Branch. Somehow they bothered me a great deal more than the hollowers, with whom I felt secure. As my Branch friends had so often said, "If'n you's in front 'a th' gun w'en hit's firin' fur blood, you's gonna git shot. Bein' daid hain't nothin' t' fear. Th' mis'ry 's dyin' slow-like." This gives one time for reflection and contemplation.

I purposefully stayed away from the hollow for a couple of days. I needed time to think and to plan. I needed time to restore my ego. When next I ventured there, dawn was just beginning to break. Loyd was waiting for me—same place, same liquid companion. I decided to take no notice of him.

"You's hain't highin' [ignoring me], air you's?"

I reluctantly padded over to the "set-a-spell" spot. Two hours passed without verbal exchange. Finally Loyd said that he was willing to decrease the monetary requirement but that Herman could only go on a week-to-week basis. My explanations why this was not desirable and how it would handicap Herman were received with good humor and rejected. He assured me that it was not for lack of faith and trust in me, but those were his final conditions. I told him that I harbored no malice toward him and asked whether he had told Herman. Nope. Should I tell him? Nope. Wouldn't he be expecting to go with me? Nope. That's good. I continued up the Branch. I saw Herman almost daily thereafter. Some time later he expressed his feelings. He had wanted to go with me even though he could not visualize a life outside the hollow. He wasn't sure why he had wanted to go. He had a strong allegiance to his father, but he might be needed to hide out his mother and siblings in the mountains when moonshine got the upper hand over Loyd. I had spent many bone-chilling nights in a cove of the mountains with the family, who were trying to escape his moonshine-saturated wrath. A few shots in the air emphasized the importance of mass survival.

I rearranged my criteria for selection: the boy should come from a family who made a genuine attempt to keep their children in school. Was there one family who thought that schooling was basic to a better way of life? There was such a family, and only one. My father used to impress on me the merits of meditating and I had learned my lesson well. Thoughtful consideration became my pattern of behavior but meditation was even more effective. Should I give up the whole idea? Should I consolidate my assumed strengths and venture forth in one more effort to live through the transitional period with a child from the hollow? School attendance cannot be equated with learning, this I knew. After pondering for a few days, I made up my mind to implement my plans. I would take one of the boys from the family who knew the value of education. Their children had to travel farthest to school, but they had the best attendance record of any student in the hollow. The logical choice was Josha Nuratt, a mild-mannered fourteen-year-old with a charming smile and a pleasant personality. Melda and Lester tried to educate their five children on a twenty-one-dollar-a-month partial disability pension they got for Lester's World War II service. My relationship with Melda was the closest woman-to-woman association I had in the entire Branch and Lester was a really fine man. We enjoyed the warm ties of mutual respect and admiration. Early in our friendship, Lester let me know that there weren't too many who were welcomed in his home. I came to appreciate the meaning of those words.

The same slow process was repeated. Josha was willing from the beginning, but my hand was different this time and I intended to play it differently too. I took Melda, Josha, twelve-year-old Kizzie, and eleven-year-old Winn to see my home. The five-hour drive was tiresome for them; none had been farther than fifteen miles away from the hollow. All the way, clocking off the distance at seventy miles an hour, I was assailed with doubts: how can these people place so much trust in one individual? How can faith be so blind? How could I, in so few short years, merit this unquestioning kind of loyalty?

The more unfamiliar sights they saw—expressways, tall buildings, huge apartments—the more uncomfortable I became. I tried to make one-person small talk. Finally my home came into view. I pulled into the concrete driveway beside the white stucco bungalow. "We're here," I announced. "Whar?" asked Josha.

We entered the house and they stood huddled by the kitchen door. I had to prod them on and we inched our way into the living room. I took Melda to the bathroom and explained the stool—how it flushed—the toilet paper. Turning the water on in the lavatory, I said, "This is the pan where you wash your hands. Here are the towels." I showed her how to turn on the light.

When it was time to retire I put the boys in a room with twin beds and Melda and Kizzie in another. I slept on the hide-away in the living room. My house mates stayed with friends. The hall light burned all night. Maybe this would keep them oriented to the unfamiliar surroundings. A night light usually sufficed, but in this instance I was afraid to risk such weak candle power. The back door was left unlocked for the first time in twenty years because I knew how Branchers hate locked doors. Each took his turn, in and out. Eventually I thought all my guests had settled down to sleep. Then I heard Winn ask Josha, "W'en we's headin' out?"

We had planned to go to the zoo the next day. At dawn my bleary-eyed guests, almost in unison, demanded to know, "W'en we's headin' out?" I knew that they were not talking about the zoo. We started back to Duddie's Branch and they were beside themselves with joy. Lester met us at the head of the hollow. He was not surprised to see us so soon. "I 'uz 'spectin' you's back afore sundown." How did he know what his family's reaction would be? How could he so accurately predict when they would be back?

Josha expressed deep apprehension about living in such a "fancy place." Prior to his description I had thought of my home as usual middle-class. I would never have called it "fancy."

I truly worked on Josha after that. If I couldn't win him over with logic, I'd win him over with a snow job. I was the resource person for the American Friends Service Committee family camp. How would he like to come with me? There would be lots of boys his age to play with. The camp was situated in a beautiful forest. Wouldn't he like to see Versailles State Park in Indiana?

Josha agreed to spend a week at a lake in Indiana before making a final commitment about camp. I would sleep in my mobile home and he would sleep outside in a sleeping bag. We would swim every day and fish at night. Our plans were flexible enough to include horseback riding, boating, and any of the various activities available.

With nothing but the clothes on his back we departed one morning at sunup. All his family watched us leave out empty-handed. No one said good-by. They just looked. We walked toward the mouth of the hollow, one mile away. Just as we got there, Josha said that he had to go back home—he'd forgotten something. I wondered whether he would return. Thirty minutes later he came sloshing through the water in the Branch. He was carrying a pocket knife with one blade missing and the other broken off at the halfway point. He said he just figured that he should take something of his along. The knife represented his only possession.

While driving to Indiana, I was deeply touched at times. Josha tried to tell me that after his mother he thought most of me, but he wasn't certain that this would be true outside the hollow.

He had never seen bathing trunks before and did not know how to get into them. There was no one around the men's dressing room to help so I went for the lifeguard. He could not leave his post, and anyway, what fourteen-year-old boy couldn't put on swimming trunks? His expression betrayed the unvoiced question, Whose grandmother are you and where have you been for the past six decades? I went back to the bathhouse and found Josha leaning against the entrance. He eventually managed to get into the trunks with my verbal aid. Never before had he encountered the barrier of a zipper.

We had cold hot dogs and hot Pepsi-Cola for every meal. It was

Josha's favorite menu and it never changed. We swam. We fished. We went for boat rides. Josha learned to row and to put on a life preserver. On nights when it rained he would crawl under the house van and sleep in his bag. That week was remarkably successful in terms of our relationship. Each night I would put my mini television set outside for him. He learned how to turn it on, tune it in, adjust the rabbit ears. I remained inside, thoughtfully reviewing the events of the day.

The time came when I had to report to camp. I offered Josha two alternatives: he could return to the Branch or go on with me to Versailles. He could not make up his mind, yet for days our conversation had centered on the subject. One hour before I had to take off in one direction or the other, he said, "Let's go t' th' camp."

Sid, the director, had been forewarned and he met us as we rolled into the cottage area. He welcomed Josha with open arms. This was Josha's first encounter with a man who was glad to see him. From then on, the two of them were great buddies.

Josha was permitted to choose the cabin he wanted, and he selected the one farthest from the community center dining area. He wanted to be alone. He did not want to share his cabin with another boy.

The following weeks were bittersweet. When he got to my home, there would be no swimming pool. Nor was there any dust in which he could grind the toe of his worn-out gym shoes during morning meditation. He remained aloof from the boys and they from him. The ice was broken in the form of a snake. Conditioned by the hollow, I was more comfortable when seated on a rock. While pandering to my idiosyncrasy one morning, I saw a healthy copperhead slither past my feet. I remained calm. "Josha, why don't you get that snake?" In a flash he had the snake's head under the toe of his gym shoe. He looked at the circle of startled people and then at me. "You's wants me t' kill hit?" "Yes," urged Sid. Josha did the creature in with his half-bladed rusty pocket knife. And so heroes are born. The other boys regarded him with admiration and occupied his time for the remainder of the morning. In the afternoon I conducted an anatomy lesson with the aid of the snake's brain, stomach, and intestines. "Had Josha not been brave enough to kill the snake, all these interesting experiences would not have been possible." Every boy shouted his concurrence.

After evening prayers, I began hiding in the far reaches of the trees where I could see Joshie's cabin. More and more the boys started to congregate there, and Josha himself seemed to be happier. But our relationship did not change. He would knock on the door of my house van at six o'clock every morning without saying a word. I would come out and we would sit on a rock. How did he sleep? Fine. Did he want anything? Nope. Did he need anything? Nope. Was he having fun? Yep. Was he ready to leave? Nope. What had he planned for the day? He hadn't reckoned. Was he hungry for breakfast? Reckon. Together we would go toward the dining hall. As we approached the steps, we could sniff the bacon. "Bet you're really hungry, aren't you, Josha?" "Good grub. Hain't like home."

During benediction I would silently pray for the strength and wisdom to pursue this earthly mystery with compassion and understanding. I could vividly remember the trauma accompanying my entry into the world beyond the hollow. In spite of the preparation, pangs of homesickness swept over me from time to time. My father would say that when one was sick down deep inside it was a hurt that you could not put your finger on. You had all the symptoms of being ill and yet you were not sick. I knew what Josha must be feeling and understood that his active days compensated for his long nights.

Camp was over. On our way to Cincinnati I tried to find out what Josha intended to do.

"You know, Joshie, we can just keep on going straight to the hollow. Is that what you want?"

He was silent.

Two miles from Sunnie-Acre I told him that we were almost at my home. "Shall I drive on to Shade? What shall I do?"

"Stop wastin' gas," he said, meaning that I should stop driving. Josha had made up his mind that he would live with three old maids.

Melda wrote two letters the first week we were back in Cincinnati:

"Aug. 28, 1964
"Pleased you and Josha made your trip to ind safe Josha never

stayed away from home before will be hard for a while Wish I was wity you and Josha think I would enjoy to be away from the branch a while."

"Sept. 2, 1964
"I will write you as I haven't heard from you and Josha in about week how are you both by now . . . his is Josha. does he like away from home any better . . . tell Josha Mother said hi be a good boy his pig and ducks are fine get good care. . . . God knows I want my kids to make good out of life as I have never had a chance in life."

We had a full month in which to buy clothing and prepare for school. Early in September Josha attended clinic for a complete physical checkup. Except for the intestinal parasites he was in fine condition. He also spent many hours with a competent psychologist. She was able to develop an enviable rapport with him in a reasonably short time and there was no mistaking that he was impressed with his visits to her office.

With determination, we attacked the parasites. The school would not admit him until he was worm-free and had a statement from the physician attesting to this. The superintendent at the school was born in a hollow but never made this admission. "Whoever heard of anyone in this day and age in the United States with hookworm?" he ridiculed.

We toured dozens of stores for Josha's wardrobe and bought a few things which were "mod" and many others which were good and substantial. My purse grew thin as the purchases increased. Spending money, though, was the easy part. How do you teach a fourteen-year-old the difference between the right side and the wrong side, whether it be socks, shorts, shirts, or jackets? What is front and what is back? How do you explain underwear to a boy who has never worn any in his life? Why does the hole go in front? " 'At thar hole don't make no sense. Hit's easier jist pullin' down th' pants."

School started, but Josha did not attend the first day. Despite his new wrist watch, I could not teach him to tell time. I left the house at 7:00 A.M. and he was to leave at 8:00 A.M. At noon I called the school. No one had seen Josha. I rushed home. He was sitting on the edge of his bed staring into space, the television blasting away in the background. He couldn't remember how to get to school, which was one block away. After dark I once again showed him the route. We arranged that I would call him from work every morning to tell him to start out for school. I called the next day, but there was no answer. I telephoned a neighbor, and she said that Josha had been sitting on the back porch for quite some time. He had not put his house keys in his pocket, and had locked himself out.

Every day for weeks I was obliged to return home for one reason or another. Josha would start out for school barefooted. He would leave the house wearing a T-shirt. He would ride his bicycle to school, which was not permitted. When he appeared at the door of the school in his pajamas and bathrobe one day, the principal was apoplectic.

Living in an orderly, well-regulated home, however, presented the most difficult adjustments. He could not understand why there were rules and regulations. He was given responsibilities for the first time in his life. He simply could not believe that he had to take a bath every night. He could see no reason why he had to go to school every day or why he had to get there on time. Going to bed at a regular hour was also something new. Going to the circus, Ice Follies, hockey—all these were different. Going out to dinner and the associated ways of behavior was anything but pleasure. His personality had already been formed by an environment hard to imagine. With other kids he had spent most of the time running in and out of the hollow. One simply cannot undo all the previous damage. Children in the hollow know love, but it is a kind that I am unable to identify within the usual frames of reference. Mothers seldom smile at children. Parents never kiss one another or their offspring. Josha was never anxious to please his mother and father. His past behavior had included few instances when pleasing someone was necessary. We constantly reassured him that he was sincerely wanted. He felt he fit at home and did not need reassurance there. Why did we provide it for his existence in a place that was not even home? In the Branch, disputes were settled with fists. Verbal battles left him speechless.

I wrote Melda regarding the various problems we were having.

Her answers were always witten in pencil and she would enclose a letter for Josha in my envelope.

"Sept. 10, 1964
"Will ans your letter was so pleased to here from you and Josha. . . . I don't want Josha to worried you it couldn't be so about you the one Josha dislikes he just a child he will have to learn you are that careing for him . . . every one on the branch has asked about Josha I told them he went to indina."

"Sept. 14, 1964
"Tell Josha to be a good boy his ducks are large ones now his pig is growing pretty . . . all we can do is send our kids to school they have to come with there part Josha don't need to drink so much milk he get to fat Think Louise for helping with Josha"

"Dear son
"How are you fine I hope this leaves the family ok Josha your ducks are fine your pig is a big boy now say hi to Rena We don't have much ice at the present Josha you be a good boy all the family said hi Winn is setting by watchen me writing Josha. from Mother With much love."

I sent one of his grade report sheets to Melda:
Mathematics
  Behavior and Effort: Good effort.
  Academic Work: Average.
  Comments: I think this summer has helped Josha. He asks questions when he does not understand something and this is good. Made improvement in his work.
Band
  Behavior and Effort: OK
  Academic Work: Average.
  Comments: Josha could spend a lot of time going over the first trumpet book. He knows enough that he could pick up what he missed during the year with some practice every day.
Reading

Behavior and Effort: Fair.

Academic Work: Below average.

Comments: Basically I have attempted to work in three areas of reading this summer: word attack, comprehension, and quality reading. Insofar as I am able to evaluate in this short period Josha needs little help with word attack. He knows phonetic principles fairly well, but does not always use them. He needs much help with comprehension. According to the record which he has kept, he has read only 2 books.

Melda responded:

"Sept 16, 1964

"Was sorry to here josha was having such a time with his lessons he all ways had a hard time getting his lessans Isaiah help him some"

I enrolled Josha in the Boy Scouts. On Friday evening each boy in the troop was to have supper at home before meeting at the church with his equipment. As we read the instructions telling each scout what to bring, Josha would check off the list. A ground cloth, a sleeping bag, and sufficient blankets. Warning him that fifty-degree temperatures in late September was cold was like telling him that Venus is surrounded by a cloud layer—he could not understand "fifty degrees." An extra change of clothing, inside to outside, as well as an extra pair of shoes, never ceased to puzzle him. "Inside to outside" he could not understand. Changing his clothes was unnecessary as far as he was concerned. Most of the time he refused to take an extra pair of shoes. He had a complete scout uniform but never wanted to wear it. Upon being bribed and threatened he would sometimes put it on for a meeting. The uniform was not mandatory, but almost all the boys wore one.

The activities at the camp were competitive and this disturbed him because he was slow, did not understand, or just could not do the things required, such as build a fire to cook his food. Each scout was to make a list of camp site errors he observed. Josha never had anything to write. They would do pull-ups, sit-ups, a fifty-yard dash, a six-hundred-yard run-walk, and standing broad jump. He was wrung out when he returned home, always too tired ever to put his things back in place before the next day or so.

We had him write at every opportunity to help him with penmanship and spelling. At breakfast he would make out his list of chores for the day: sweep down basement steps, put cans in trash can, put baskets in back where they belong, water plants, water rosebushes, pick up paper and debris from front lawn, clean rusted shovel he had left out in the rain. Most of the time he would complete only two or three of the jobs on his assignment sheet. He was fairly good at writing or copying words but almost always added an *s*—rainbows, establishments, thrills. In answer to our questions, he said that you could put an *s* anywhere—"hit jist makes hit easier on th' end." All words were usually begun with small letters, but every now and again a capital would creep in—Copper, Been, Pears.

At the beginning of the month the school distributed the lunch menu for each day. Josha took his lunch money daily but just did not like the food, did not like to wait in line to be served, and hated to waste so much play time in the cafeteria. If the lunch was one he did not like or had never eaten, he was permitted to return home to eat.

On Saturday mornings he went to the high school swimming pool for one hour, but he had great difficulty abiding by the safety regulations. He was reported for such things as running around the pool, roughhousing, double bouncing off the diving board, and swimming in front of the diving area.

Josha's reading level was approximately one year below grade level (fifth) at the end of the full year at school. His grade averages for all subjects were as follows: A, 14 per cent; C, 47 per cent; D, 36 per cent; F, 3 per cent. The majority of the A grades were earned in general attitude and physical education. Music, art, and work habits accounted for most of the Cs. Reading, writing, arithmetic, spelling, English, geography, history, science, and health were subjects in which he got the Ds and Fs. Spelling was especially troublesome: be live (believe); practive (practice); seberate (separate); Wes nes day (Wednesday); toking (taking). Words missed in daily practice tests were to be learned by the next day of school, but Joshie continued to spell them incorrectly.

In an effort to help him budget his time, we made a chart with headings: read, television, work, games-sports, study, and horn. Space for days and dates was provided in the left-hand column. Saturday and Sunday averaged two hours each for television. The one hour per day for horn practice always fell short by fifteen to thirty minutes. Work, except for the weekends, amounted to an average of twenty minutes daily. Reading averaged five hours a week; study, four hours; basketball, bowling, etc., eight hours. Whenever he failed to obey, he would have the privilege of naming his punishment. One list ran like this: no television, no candy, no cookies.

Josha became increasingly restless despite any list of activities. We progressed from crisis to crisis and it became nerve-racking for everyone. He was constantly reverting to his old ways and began to feel abandoned and rejected by his parents because they had permitted him to leave the Branch. Melda's letters did not help much in the way of reassurance.

"nov. 13, 1964

"Dear Josha will ans your letters was glad to hear from you. This leaves the family very well you got a nice cat I only have one cat now all the family said hi your Ducks and Pig chickens everything is fine . . . had a nice rain here last night Lishe said hi.

"from Mother an all the family with lots of love write when you can."

"dec. 7 1964

". . . Josha Winn said he would not eat many Duck eggs all the family said hi When will Josha be coming home What time this month Rena I think it getting about time for you to come home again."

"Dec. 9, 1964

". . . can't never know what makes so many lazy people Lester an I sure was pleased with the pitchers of Josha they did look good

Lester said Josha has a nice place to stay . . . any one knoes thiy can't raised a good boy on this Branch."

"Dec. 11, 1964
"Dear Son will write a few lines This leave all the family very well Hope to find you o.k. Josha I have six pigs now. I traded the sow to three. I have to feed them no one likes hogs around but me. I don't mind it. I like to work. Your pig and Ducks are fine. I saw the pitcher you sent ant Pansy looked good of you She was so pleased to have it. All the family said hi say hi to all the girls. I hope them all Merry Xmas happy New years. from Mother with love be good boy."

"Dear Rena . . . I saw the pitcher of Josha he sent Pansy. She was pleased to have it. Said Josha was the pick of the family it all reight for you have the pick of the family Can't get Lester to Write no one. . . . Saw Elzie Hiram the other day she said she missed you so much tell me who don't miss you . . . they han't much change in the branch we just one cat now Lishe is haveing war with the people on the branch. . . . Winn just came home from school he all ways wants write some. he said he was your best friend from Melda an family with love."

One of my friends went to Shade and took Josha for a visit. Melda wrote me about it.

"Dec. 28, 1964
"Dear Rena will write you to let you Josha got here ok ever one was pleased to see him. he was a happy little boy looking at his Ducks and Pig ever thing around. he was said coming back the 3 Jan a sunday We have missed you so much tinks to all that sent gifts sorry I didn't to get all my friends somethin for Xmas. . . ."

"Jan 5, 1965
". . . Lester he sayd he don't care what becomes of the kids as for me I do care I want them all to go to school What will I do if no one helps I think I am the one that makes a mess of ever thin noting

turns out right I try to do things right sure did enjoy being with you as all ways never can think you ennufe for the nice things you have done for me an family I only wish I could do more have Josha to write if hasn't all ready like to know how he made it back hope he behaves himself I don't want you to have so much truble."

After the brief visit in December, Josha was lonelier than ever and yearned to go back to the Branch. Several times he threatened to run away.

"Feb. 3, 1965 Dear Rena

". . . I know you are good to Josha only wish they all had hald good place to stay I can't keep from crying fore Josha to upset you. I enjoyed talken to you on he Phone sorry it had to be like it was if Josha had come home I would have made him catch the next Bus back it is not that I don't love my family, this Branch is not fit for kids to be on no one on the branch wants to work they all want on the lazy aid they are all kinds of people in the world . . . was so up set over Josha when I talked to him . . . it is nothing But right for Josha to work I never did care for work in my life."

"Dear Son will write you this leave the family ok Josha you do what Rena tells you to do. Work won't hurt no one. don't ever try to come hom twill you are let come. You have to go school up there. Josha you know I love you. The girls love you to. Rena loves you to. if not she would never don some maney nice things for you I will take good care of your hog and ducks chickens and you don't have one thing to worry about this one Branch is no good for no one if you would be a good Boy some day I will come up to visit you all . . . how is your cat fine I hope you are haveing a good time playing Ball we are having zero weather here you are having a good time I here Josha be a good boy I no you can from Mother with love"

Her letters seldom contained anything of a different nature.

The first weekend in May I sent Josha back to the Branch to see if his parents would need help with the gardening when school was out.

"May 10, 1965

"Dear Rena . . . was glad to have Josha home he cried when he had to start back I went down to the road with him I have hoed a bout a acre of potatoes to day Josha wanted to know why we planted so many potatoes I was but off the ABC [meaning Aid to Dependent Children] for the kids this mounth The field worker told me he got a report from the VA Doctors. Lester ask his Doctor about it. When he was up friday he said he did not send no report to the field worker. he just lieed. I will Write to frank ford Apeal the case when the man from frank ford come I see if Coon Kelly can show any thing I do hope he is Put out off the Ofice I was Pleased to get the Watch. It is my first Mother day gift . . . hope Josha got back safe"

"May 14, 1965

"Dear Rena will ans your letter. glad to here Josha Got home safe. We do not need Josha to help in the crop. we have all ready worked our potatoes, and hoes some corn We are getting along al right if I get behind any I will get some one here to work. This Branch is no good for Josha to stay on. You can let him come home. with the folks he came with this time when you think he needs to come they said they would be glad for him to come with them any time. This branch is no good for none of us. haft to live some where. I would love so much for Josha to make some thing out of him self. . . . Josha is doing lots of things he did not no about hrere. all the kids on this branch wan't to do hit the road from house to house . . . any one sure don't get no thinks for working like a slave for kids Josha I wan't you to mind Rena. and be a Good Boy you are through well off by a lot of people. . . ."

A visit by Melda that summer proved to be only an opportunity for Josha to plead for permission to return to the Branch for good, but Melda could not be persuaded. She wrote me as follows:

"July 23, 1965

"Dear Rena . . . don't let Josha come home. Tell I get Remus an Isaiah away they both drug back home. They are so sorry they won't work at nothing But few days. Thinks again to you all for being so nice while visiting with you all"

"July 28, 1965
"Dear Rena Josha all was Pleased to get your letter. So sorry Josha got hurt at the letter . . . we will plan out things so he can come home . . . Josha Knows I love him so much. I could'nt keep from crying when I read the letter. I give Josha the last dollar I had if he need it. I have worked so hard for the past 3 years to make ends meet. I was so hurt you had to pay for a motal for a bunch to stay in. They han't nothing to good for me to do for you. Lester said he would bake Josha a cake We have been canning a lot this week Beans Tomatoes Kraut. I didn't think it would be good for Josha to be with Remus and Isaiah. I try to get them away time he gets ready to come home. My bro. took the things up the Branch you all give. me. Thinks to Louise for the dresses they a pretty fit. . . . I am very thinkful I have a Mom yet. Josha don't feel bad I only wan't what I think is best for you. I try my best to take good care of his hog and Sucks. if I ever get the chanct to visit you all again I will come alone on the bus."

There was no containing the boy and nothing would do but that he go back to Duddie's Branch for good. Melda was heartbroken.

Sept. 22 1965
"Dear Rena Got your letter. I have Tried so hard to get Josha to come back. He says he don't wan't to come back. All I can get out of him Sit and cry. I am so up set over what has Happen I can hardly live. I have done all I No to do. Lester could make him come. then he Just be in the way Would not do any thing he was to do. Wish I had knows this Twenty Years Ago. All I ever have got out of raisen a family is heart akes. . . . I know you have tried so hard to help in ever way you can. Thinks so much for ever thing You have done. Please don't be up set over Josha if he don't wan't to make nothing out of him self you have done all you can."

And so the letters continued sending thanks and reassurance

("Josha said he liked all of you. he just didn't like cincinnati"), and news of Josha.

"Oct. 20, 1965

"Josha Goes to school ever day. he is so lazy. I just don't see who They take beeing so sorry after. I enhoyed My visit with you all. thinks to each of you. for your kindness. for the good food. and to Rena for giving me her bed to sleep in. I think all of you girls are Wonderful."

"Sept. 22, 1966

"Josha got up this moring said he was quiting school . . . getting back to Josha. I was to weak to whip him. I called Isaiah Told him Put him out of hear to school he did. time he got thru beating him. he was glad to go. All Josha needs is Lester hold him few times."

"Sept. 28, 1966

". . . Josha is doing all right now. Lester told him not name quitting school again. . . . Josha all ways wan't to know if I get any mail. I told him I had a letter from you. What shc have say. I didn't let him know that you knoed any Things about him. I have not had no more trouble with him going to xchool. They ride out with Lester."

"Sept. 6, 1967

". . . That sorry Josha quit School. Said he didn't make good grades. I have tried to hard To keep them boys in School. He is going to the job corp. I hope he will make good in something."

"Sept. 25, 1967

". . . Josha went to indalouis [Indianapolis]."

"Oct. 9, 1967

". . . Josha is working. he helps make Butter."

"Oct 17, 1967

"Remus was home this week end. Josha all so came home worked out one check. Said he couldn't hardly get it cashed. That was his tail."

My unsuccessful experience with Josha made me realize afresh that there is an almost complete misunderstanding of the people who live in the Appalachian region. Almost from the beginning I found that I really did not know the hollow folks—I unlearned more than I learned. Their culture is much more significant, much stronger than the distortions and adulterations imply. They have nothing to offer except themselves—no crafts, no folk songs, no wood carvings, no needlework to characterize their mountain heritage. We do not understand or tolerate their culture, but they have for such a long time been a law unto themselves that they cannot violate or abandon their way of life.

I took a colleague to the Branch and we stopped in a dozen or more homes so that he could meet the families. In describing his trip, he said, "One very surprising thing to me was how friendly all these people were toward me, a stranger. I introduced myself only by name and by saying that I was a friend of Dr. Gazaway. Their quick acceptance of me is a sign of the very real acceptance that Dr. Gazaway has achieved during her work in the Branch. All of the people spoke very highly of her. They regarded her as one of themselves, and yet, at the same time, as an outside person who is trying to help them. Many of them expressed hope that she would succeed in bringing some sort of financial support or solution to their problems. They all have a feeling that she is working very hard on their behalf. Several expressed the belief and hope that Dr. Gazaway is about to settle permanently in the Branch. I noticed that the majority referred to her as 'Miss Gazaway' and a smaller number as 'Dr. Gazaway' and still fewer as 'Rainy,' their pronunciation of her first name.

"A couple of the men, when asked their occupation, said that they farmed in the Branch. Several others said that they were unable to farm except for vegetable gardens. It was striking that almost nobody claimed to be working full time, and half or more of the men said that they were not working at all. Some of the younger men said that they worked at the coal mines, when work was available, but had not worked for six months or so. Most of the men over thirty said their health did not allow them to work. The most striking feature of the visit was the large number of people who were subsisting without earning a living.

"I reached the conclusion that these people have no desire to work and that they compete with each other to see who gets the most money for not working. The largest number of families are receiving Aid to Dependent Children, a payment made for each child under eighteen, up to a maximum of six children in a family.

"It is apparent that the children are growing up to be just as poor and ignorant as their parents, and will not be supporting themselves by earning a living, but rather trying to get themselves on the public assistance rolls in one way or another. In this way of life, these people are crippling themselves and they are also being a burden to the rest of the people in Kentucky and the United States. The situation is not an isolated one. There are thirty hollows just like this in one county alone. Duddie's Branch is not the worst off, but in the middle of the thirty hollows.

"We can say with certainty that these are people who are not motivated to make effective use of their resources, small as . . . they are. . . . It is my opinion that the majority of the men in the Branch have no physical organic medical condition which prevents them from working; and yet they are not working, and in many cases give medical reasons for not working.

"The most pertinent question seems to be, what motivates these people to prefer to stay in their present squalid way of life, rather than to work toward a better way of life? How can these people be motivated to make an effort to better themselves, and to rise economically? This is a serious problem, basically of motivation. This is a very fascinating problem psychologically, as well as a very important one for practical and economic and political purposes."

Cures cannot be effected without first taking into consideration the social ills of poverty which result in disorders. No one knows what new housing would do for the hollow dweller or what would happen if the physical environment were improved. As yet, no one has come up with a package proposal that might change their lives. I am certain, however, that new housing will not work miracles. It will not remedy undesirable social attitudes among the youths. Adolescents whose fears of the wider society are protected by the subculture of the hollow from which they come are lost and unhappy when removed from the security of their group.

Many of the migrants drifted to the city because they felt that it needed them. Those in this hollow who have had some experience in outer society are firmly convinced that the city not only does not need them, it does not want them. They make little or no effort to move upward into the promised land of America's economic middle-class society. Based on the experience of others, they say, "'Em 'at's tried hain't hankerin' fur 'em fur places." Our society is engrossed in the present and the future, but the deprived find protection in the immediate past, if not in their heritage, and fear the unknown future. The much-publicized flight to the city has not markedly changed the population complex of Duddie's Branch. Purposes and goals are centered in the setting of deprivation in which their parents and kin existed. Whatever their discomfort or their difficulties, they are less traumatic in their own habitat than they would be in the complex outer world. There is a large group of urbanites who see nothing good in the hollowers and they remain apart and uninvolved. But hollow folks don't expect to be universally understood and liked.

One quickly senses a high degree of contentment in Duddie's Branch. The Brancher appreciates his freedom from care. "We lives hard, but you's hain't livin' 't all. Fellers outta th' holler worries 'bout ever'thin'—money mostly, 'r things money buys." Most hollowers are satisfied with their possessions, however poor. Few, if any, would trade places with anyone and they prize their status even though any accompanying prestige is undetectable. For some their only awareness of status is through their family lineage if they belong to the groups who claim kin. While not completely satisfied with every deprivation which must be endured in the Branch, this situation is unquestionably preferable to life elsewhere. Meander assures me, "We'd not make hit outta hyur." He identifies ties and traits or even culture bonds of a past. The hollow group shares one condition in common with those who came before—that of relative isolation and segregation. Duddie's Branchers want to be stranded in the hollow, for they value their escape from crushing, man-made burdens that present false hopes. "We's jist scratch ourself; you's cut yore neck vein."

They have contented themselves with a minimum of material necessities because they are incapable of understanding higher values. Small group interests rank higher in their value pattern than social class interest. The Duddie's Brancher dares to be different. He faces situations which have no parallel in his past, since he is not a part of the past. Groping backward in time to him is "meddlin' in th' dark." Seeking a place for himself in the future elicits the same response—"meddlin' in th' dark." He prizes his life philosophy of postponement. Each tomorrow is dealt with on a daily basis. He values the unchanging routine of his life: today is the sequence of yesterday; tomorrow will be the sequence of today. He values being hidden in the hollow where he is not a part of impersonal statistics—he can elude the plague of charts, graphs, and percentages. He values his feeling that he is fitted for his kind of life in the hollow. He stands up straight and tall when he successfully opposes the forces that would uproot him and his family from their home, friends, and kin to enter a world in which he knows he will never be fully accepted. He can't tell you this, but he really values the main word in his vocabulary—"reckon." "Hain't a yander feller gittin' fur with me reckonin'. He's never talkin' what he's doin'." He values his ability to get paid for not working. Survival without labor is an accomplishment. Remaining unemployed until compensation expires gives him the status of a proud man, while barely keeping his family from starving. He does not know what the word "recipient" means, but his status hinges on his deceptiveness. Outwitting creditors, social workers, physicians—he manages them all. Certain acts that are found to be useful and often repeated take on a symbolic value. It is hard to identify a hierarchy of values but perhaps the most important is his ability to exist with God's help. Meander has often told me that he is like a bloated pig when "fellers hain't heard 'a livin' 'thout movin' fur [exerting any energy in working]."

He cannot see that his present predicament is a consequence of his past behavior. Every difficulty is made more difficult because his values make it so. He has a residue of nothing, which he grandly bequeaths to his heirs.

The child from Duddie's Branch is not awed by the urgency of learning. That he cannot cope with academic pressures or any semblance of regular routine in no way lowers his estimation of himself. He does not know what deprivation means because he is no different from any other hollow child.

Children absorb poverty. They don't know disease from health; they've never enjoyed the latter. They don't know ignorance from intelligence; they've always been exposed to the former. They don't know that people call their way of life destitute; their life is empty, but they don't know how empty it is because they have nothing to compare it with. They are not ashamed of missing teeth or bad teeth because they don't see any others who are different. To them, there is nothing remarkable about the fact that I am well past middle age and have a complete set of my own teeth. Gleaming white teeth as against their mossy-green furry ones mean nothing to them. They trudge in and out of the hollow and it never strikes them that it leads nowhere. The dismal shanties are all that they have learned to know as home. Many grow to adulthood without ever having been inside a house different from theirs.

The child from Duddie's Branch stirs early and climbs over sibling after sibling to land on the floor of a one-room shack. There is no need to get dressed because his custom is to sleep in the wrinkled, soiled clothing he wore the previous day. No line forms to use the bathroom, because there is no bathroom; no one brushes his teeth or washes his face. If a line should form, it would do so across the porch or just outside the door—this is where one urinates and defecates. Sometimes he is pushed off the edge into a fresh mound of feces. That day he misses school because he doesn't have a change of clothing. Time has no value because he isn't going anywhere now. Even if he were, clocks have no value. If someone expresses sympathy or understanding over his soiled clothes, he ignores him because neither expression has value. It is time for breakfast, but breakfast has no value. "Hain't no grub" is the value. "Untidy" has no value connotation. There are no sidewalks and so in that respect he is unlike his urban counterpart. The dark halls and stairways found in the tenements do not exist. The space called a yard is so cluttered all the time that he doesn't notice any additional tidbits of trash. His mother is always there. This is more than an expectation —it is a value. She doesn't work outside the home so he learns to value her presence, maybe not in the house but in the hollow. He knows just where to find her, which he seldom bothers to do, for she will be coming along eventually. Anyway, he doesn't need her— he just needs to know that she is there. There is a man he calls his father, whether he is or not. Most likely he is. Maybe he was conceived before the marriage license was issued but he still has a mother and a father. His father doesn't work so he is always there and the child develops a positive attitude toward him. This establishes a value for him. He has parents.

What a depressing sketch, you think. But he doesn't think so. The ever present, unfailing love of parents and siblings becomes an early value. Love and blind support from those in the home give him status and measure. He does not have to develop ability to cope with the world beyond the hollow. He does not have to work if he does not want to or if this is not a part of the plan he has for himself. He can marry early and marry whomever he chooses. If it is close kin, this is acceptable too. Some logical rationalization will be forthcoming: "She's a Shifter, but hain't kin—even fur."

He doesn't know what patience is, but anyone from the outside who does not possess it returns to the outside quickly. He is not tolerant, either, but woe to anyone else who is not. Value patterns foreign to the outsider, but ingrained in the hollow children by osmosis, become rock-hard and mold behavior.

Aesthetic value, what's that? His values are the values of everyone in the hollow. They never tear down old toilets, even if they are not usable. "Hain't nothin' 'gin leavin' 'em daid." Clearing up riverbanks likewise means nothing. "Hit's jist choppin' fur nothin'."

"Don't you want to amount to something?"

"'Mountin' t' somethin' hain't fur holler folks."

They sit on their heels around the courthouse which some say reflects the general poverty of the area. But the courthouse serving half a million people in an urban county looks little different from others in some respects—like the restrooms, for instance. The courthouse has value, but not as a courthouse. What then? It is a place where they meet other holler fellers. They talk about whatever it is men talk about and the women stay at a distance. They value talk. If their favorite bootlegger's case is called, they may troop into the courthouse for his trial by jury. His name they do not recognize, but names have no value. So the accused had a few bottles of beer in a shack back of his house. So what? Their value pattern cannot begrudge a man a moment of relaxation after a whole day on his knees in a dog hole mine.

They talk about how long they have been out of work. They never admit that they wouldn't work even if a job were available. They feel sorry. They talk about being sorry. But feeling sorrow and being sorry are two different conditions. They expect to be out of work, but they plan to stay in the hollow. Checks might mean that they are on the draw. This is a value. Especially if they are drawing illegally. Value: relief, no: draw, yes. People in town have jobs. But what value does either a town or a job have?

That no one expects anything from the poor has a value. They value the way others ignore them when making decisions about what is to be done with them. They know they won't starve. They may not live high off the hog, but they will live off some part of him.

They value the fact that if they have no voice in those matters which concern them they have no responsibility toward the program devised to save them. They will walk the same way. They will talk the same way. They will go home the same way, over the holes and pits of the Branch. They will sit on their rickety porches. They will look incuriously at the fast-moving pace of the mad outer world. They may be "sorry," but they know that they can in some way be themselves. Not being somebody—that is inconceivable.

Value is identifying a sundog. Their status leaps when they can interpret it as a change in weather. They can't explain or define the sundog, but they can point it out. They don't know the legend of the robin, but they value seeing this harbinger of spring. The cherry-red breast signals the disappearance of snowbanks and the coming of "near plantin' time." Value is a robin. Status is attached to the hollower who sees the first one.

Value is home. They value their roots in the hollow. They never have to worry about being evicted. There is no fear that an express-way will deprive them of their most valued possession. They can continue to live in the place of their choice for as long as they wish.

Against all odds, they value their avoidance of a feeling of hope-lessness. They have never felt a part of the community. They don't accept responsibilities for anything of which they are not a part. But as it was in the beginning, is now, and ever shall be—they have reason for existing. They don't have many problems in the complex world. Why? Because they don't let problems light, much less bore in. Anthropologist, sociologist, psychologist, psychiatrist—let them worry about how to gain true insight into their lives. They value their effortless evasion of social analysis. They defy all the hypotheses. They do not criticize you. They know that you can't solve their problems because there are no problems to solve. But with your presumed knack for doing things, jobs must be found to keep you busy—such as solving a mythical problem.

They won't oppose your intrusion unless the hollow becomes too crowded. Then you move out. They don't intend to move. Their homes will never be substandard, not to them. They like their neigh-borhood. This is their land. Their ancestors lived here. Many of their kin and family are buried right near the hollow.

They value a way of life—contentment. Ignorant? Maybe. Misera-ble? Maybe. But they value sleep uninterrupted by soaring dreams of a life that could be. A depressed region? It is. A highway system, new industry, may be part of the plan for the future, but "they hain't nothin' worth nothin' 'ceptin' bein' mount'in folk fur us'n's 'n' 'em creepers." Barbiturates, amphetamines, the hazards of smoking, mental health, retarded children, marijuana, opiates, the diminishing gold reserve—all these are beyond their ken and they say to me, "Reckon I's hain't got values." As the last sheep falters over the hurdle, I envy their detachment. I must admit, however, that ac-cording to our standards they do not have values.

Value is competition. The first spring vegetables, the biggest po-tatoes, the best squash. The man who digs the most sang (ginseng root), kills the first squirrel, catches the biggest fish, bags the most rabbits. There is no limit to values. What dimensions are embodied in "We'll make hit somehow. We's th' little people"!

They have no established objectives and do not feverishly seek to gain any. They live a life both supreme and valueless at the same time. They value the hollow where life meets death on an equal plane. How could they ever value the soft, prosperous life? They could never see any value in being a creature of the twentieth century, fit only for paper shuffling, patio living, high-rise occupancy, and martini imbibing. They value their instinct for survival, adventure, and challenge.

They value the isolation of their seldom invaded hollow. They take immense pride in their hideaway. They never fear the bulldozer or the destruction of their view. They won't ever wake up and face a huge brick wall that protects an apartment building of sixty-odd units. They value their non-fence phobia of freedom. Observing birds and rabbits in the woods is value not designed by an earthly engineer but by a heavenly One.

They value increased density, for this simply means more kin surrounding them. More of their own who are a part of their daily struggle for survival. More who look to them for advice. More with whom they can share nothing.

The Branchers feel that their children—good, bad, or indifferent —are their greatest assets. Children have real value even though it is hard to get the hollow people to identify why this is true. On the outside parents brag about grade attainment, club membership, participation in sports, and hundreds of other things. But in the hollow the parents don't feel the need to boast about their offspring.

They are unknown as persons, but unique in their own eyes. They can be themselves in the midst of our impersonal bigness. Is this not a value? They have no desire to be a part of or adjust to our democratic autocracy. They feel no pressure to conform and they attempt to impart this value to me. "Hain't knowin', hain't doin'." They cannot be failures in face-to-face situations that can so easily be dismissed. They are important because they are human and not because others view them as part of society. What greater value?

Children learn to value only those things which do not leave their parents behind. Could this be the basic value which is behind their unwillingness to learn new things?

Outsiders say that Branchers are devoid of the personal quality of tenacity. It depends on how one defines tenacity. Dogged, they are. Stubborn, they are. Persistent, they are. Resist, they can. Cling to the past, they do. Persevere, they must. Unyielding to change—they are masters of the technique.

The women value their unchanging role. They know that they will depend completely upon the man they marry. There is an inherent value in attaching oneself to the man of choice. The women value their own accomplishments, even though none may be recognized by the family.

Status is no problem either; they have countless ways in which to reinforce it to dizzying heights.

Heading out shortly after daybreak, with a squirrel's tail in his hand, Meander asked if I was going to town.

"Later," I said, and continued up the hollow. An hour and a half later, I came out. Meander was waiting.

"Reckon I's ridin' with you's."

When we got to town he headed for the courthouse. I completed my chores and saw him thumbing a ride just out of town. I picked him up. He was still carrying the tail.

"That sure is a pretty silvery tail," I admired.

"Yep. 'Em law men din't even know hit war legal shootin' time. Shore s'prized 'em, gittin' th' first squirrel."

"I wish I had a gun and a license. It's been a long time since I've been squirrel hunting."

"You's don't need no license. We's never bother gittin' 'em."

"I'd be afraid that I'd get caught by the law."

"Nope, not less'n you's got th' squirrel. Jist atter 'e falls, I cuts off 'is tail, pulls off 'is dressin' 'n' buries hit."

I remarked about how difficult I'd find hunting to be if I had to carry rubber boots over my shoulder.

"'Em's my hidin'. They's got holes in 'em. They's not so heavy w'en they's got holes."

Status is capturing a four-foot rattlesnake before spectators, growing a seven-pound turnip, drinking a full glass of moonshine with your friends without pausing for a breath, having your pistol cocked by the time you jerk it out of your belt, owning a pocket knife with a three-and-a-half-inch razor-sharp blade, cracking a walnut with your bare heel, chewing a jaw-filling piece of tobacco for an hour without spitting.

Status and values take on different meanings in the hollow.

Television, magazine, and newspaper publicity is offensive, even if it results in money. They regard money from the Welfare Department as something that is theirs and something they have a right to regardless of the irregularities they use to establish their eligibility. Money from publicity is degrading. Beggars lose status among their neighbors and kin. "Gittin' cheatin'" is far more honorable.

Communication is perhaps the basic element in how those in Duddie's Branch look upon others and how others look upon them. I am given a message to deliver to those Branchers who might want to avail themselves of cheap clothing. After conveying the message in detail, I am asked, "Whars 'at secont-handed sellin' place?"

"It's right across the road from the Community Center in Mule Creek."

"Hain't never heerd 'a no center."

Since none in the Branch takes the local paper, or any other paper for that matter, I pass on news in which they might be interested. Once I tried to explain how important it is for people to work together for the success of anything helpful to all, the importance of community effort.

"Thar hain't no 'munity nothin' fur holler fellers. You's al'ays got 'em 'at's fur 'n' 'em 'at's agin. Most fellers hain't fur 'r agin; they's jist plum ornery. They'd be a heap better if'n they's jist usin' years [ears] 'stead 'a eaters [mouths]."

When such money-raising endeavors as the March of Dimes comes along, the hollow folks are missed in the house-to-house canvass. Giving money for anything, however worthy the cause, is something hollow folks will not participate in. They have no meaning for such words as "donation," "participation," "contribution."

Some say that hope has crumbled and wasted away. The eastern Kentucky that I know has not wasted away. Dependency does not produce shame. Dependency produces a kind of warped sense of pride because these people feel independent. They don't talk about a torn land, jobs, roads, etc. They have their place in the hills. Some leave, but they always come back. They don't see their lives as dying out. Far from it. There are more and more and more children coming along all the time to carry on. If you took away what they have they would mourn their loss. They mean to fight for their place in the hollow and fight to keep it as it is, unchanged. Meander doesn't know if he has a long deed. In fact, he doesn't even know if he has a clear deed of any kind but this causes him no concern. He is satisfied that he will be in the hollow on his land long after the exploiters of coal and timber have gone. Anything profitable in timber is generations in the future, if there is indeed any significant growth by then. He knows that he will survive all the programs and workers who, for a while, poured over the hills like "ants, 'ceptin' thar's nary a hole fur 'em." Next to the mountains, the hollowers are the most indestructible. They are scornful of the city folks who struggle to walk up the hollow, sitting down to rest every little while, choking on the smells, grimacing at the sights. They are overjoyed when one of them vomits and they refer to it with regularity. The exact spot of the unfortunate occurrence is known by everyone in the Branch and soon becomes a landmark.

Teenagers, particularly the boys, want to stay in the hills and hollows. They regard their lives and those of their parents as good. They have grown up in a climate where there are few challenges and competition has not demanded extraordinary exertion. Only one boy from the hollow has thus far been accepted into the army. He is proud of this distinction. Now in the thick of the battle in Vietnam, he sends money home to buy him a piece of land in Duddie's Branch, "somethin' I kin come back to."

The simplicity of their lives is too precious to cast aside. Nothing to do in the hollow is different from nothing to do in a small town or a city. Nothing to do in the hollow is a more acceptable nothingness. Furthermore, they are seldom bothered by officials of any kind.

They look on the government with deep skepticism. "Reckon how 'em high fellers comes in hyur with skins t' make work fur us fellers, 'ceptin' they's other high fellers payin' us not t' work 'n' others makin' rulin' 'at keeps us from findin' work." This inconsistency in their mind typifies the gross incompetence of "high fellers." Don says that it is well for hollow folks to shy "'em liken a pisin snake else you's'll end up 'twixt 'n' 'tween with th' whole bottom 'a you's poke gone."

Duddie's Branch is the best place in the whole world. No one hankers to explain his feelings and any questions are resented. A visitor of mine from Washington asked, "Why do you folks stay here in this hollow?" He asked the same question over and over (to an outsider, all hollowers look alike), but he never received a reply. Meander is the town crier and alerts all the families when I bring in a visitor. "Her's totin' somethin'." The visitor asked Meander for the second time, "Why do you stay here in this hollow?" Meander glowered at him and then turned and shuffled off in his tattered, mismatched shoes, both of which were intended for the right foot. After securing the visitor down for the night in the local motel, I returned to the Branch. As I had expected, the headlights of my jeep caught Meander humped on a rock at the mouth of the hollow. I pulled into the weeds just off to the side and walked up to him. He motioned for me to sit on his rock while he squatted on his haunches beside me. " 'At feller hain't bin schoolin'," he assessed, indicating that only the most ignorant would ask the same question twice. "Us'n's hain't thinkin' 'bout leavin'. We likes hit hyur 'n' we hain't axin' fur nothin' no diff'r'nt."

Riot is a word which has no meaning and thus no value to the hollower regardless of how you define it. Mass violence and disorder he abhors. He may settle his feud with another, but "hain't hookin' up with'n nobody t' squar nothin' 'at's b'longin' t' us'n's." I could not get three people together, which is the minimum number prescribed by law, for a public demonstration. Even though he feels very strongly about "broken promises," he is not about to voice his opinion if there is more than one listener about. Broken promises they have lived with for a lifetime and pledges have a reverse or negative value. "If'n you's hain't meanin' hit, mouthin' hit makes you's th' fool." Even if I were to tell them that unless they act they will end up with nothing, I could not incite them to violence. Nothing is their frame of reference for a value—nothing is all they have had ever. "We's hain't had nothin', we's hain't gittin' nothin', 'n' we's hain't 'spectin' nothin'."

The hollowers don't see themselves as underprivileged. Instead, they think of others as belonging to this category. They already have quality in their lives and they are not about to give it up for things they really do not desire. They will never create a disturbance. I doubt whether even the judge, who is their idol, could rouse them to insurrection. The kind of education we propose, which prepares a man for life in a turbulent society, has no value for them.

He cannot express it, but what the hollower aspires to is what the outer society proposes—a guaranteed income. My hollow friends confide that I can "draw if'n you's lettin' 'em quality [qualify] you's. You's ownin' a shack. If'n you's kin turn a jeep feet facin' sky way, you's bound t' be not seein'. You's our'n. You's cain't leave out stayin'." Who says the poor despair and fail to hope?

It is, I think, a mistake to try to assimilate the hollow dweller into the dominant culture of our society. The culture from which he comes is vastly different and if he goes into an urban environment his only means of security is to find a subculture in which he can, at least partially, interact. Even in this subcultural environment he finds, much to his displeasure, that the values of his past do not permit him to interact with the group to his own satisfaction. There are many differences between the hollower and the Negro in an urban setting. Both are poor according to all statistics, but once they attain middle-class status in the outer community each is unwilling to admit his background and far less willing to lend any assistance to the person who wants to come out of the hollows. In one urban school system, 75 per cent or more of the teachers come from Branches or from rural settings of deprivation, but will admit to this only after they know you. They refuse to help salvage those who have any potential to function outside the hollow and they avoid social contact with their kin or former neighbors. "If you think I'm going to lower myself by going into that mess, you can think again. I left there years ago; I made it on my own, and they can do the same. They should have known they couldn't make it. I've worked years for what I have, and I don't intend to share it with worthless kin. If they want to have something, let them work for it like I've worked. If they can't make it, they'll get no help or sympathy from me."

The migrant finds it very difficult to escape the religion of the mountains and the family traditions with which he has become so familiar. He quickly learns that it will be impossible for him to obtain economic and social status because of his poorness, his lack of education, and his inability to enter into a competitive relationship for both recreation and employment opportunities. He soon realizes that his chances of success are quite remote and that those things in the hollow which give him a sense of security now give him a marked sense of failure and inferiority. Subcultures give physiological protection and he does not experience the process of assimilation but continues to function much as he did before except that he is more cognizant of his segregation. The inhabitants of the hollows which form a subsystem within the county as a whole are aware of their status in the value scheme of the larger community. They may be boiling over with feelings about it, but they have no strong, expressive terms to describe the fire that burns inside. Their language does not provide for criticism, so they just walk away.

Any effort directed toward giving the deprived a voice in his own destiny becomes so enmeshed in the non-democratic strategy of non-partisan politics that everyone is confused, particularly the poor. This non-group-oriented populace is not prepared to assume such a responsibility. Who really speaks for the poor? I do not know. I know better who does not: the self-elected, rabble-rousing type bent on stirring up trouble for the local area. Their scheming, designed to help the deprived, results in tragic apathy and public rejection of all programs. Local troublemakers even found their way to Washington. Upon their return many felt that they had scuttled the War on Poverty, having hurt many of the traditional programs already in existence over the years. To accept these noisy meddlers as "leaders" of the poor would be a "doin' not knowin'." Representatives of the poor—never. One man with eighteen children living in a trailer in a nearby hollow went to Washington to represent the poor in the county. What had he accomplished? What had he said? He told those in the meeting that he would first fire the judge and take over the job himself until a poor man could be elected. He really liked the red-carpet treatment. But most of all he just liked the trip to Washington. A collection had been taken among his fellows in poverty to pay the way of those who went to the capital.

They expected something in return. He said he had agreed with everything that had been said by those who arranged the trip. "But you must have said something?"

"Warn't no use; all fellers mouthin' at onc't."

"Guess you told them what was wrong with the poverty program?"

"Yep."

"Guess things will be better now as a result of your trip?"

"Reckon. We's figgerin' trippin' back t' Wash'n'tom. We's got a heap more mouthin' t' do."

He did not go back and neither did any of the other men. Those who had contributed to their "highin'" were disappointed. "He's hain't never mouthin' fur nothin'. Hit's skins wasted. Wind carried 'em plum yander."

After living in the Branch one is haunted with the feeling that they value their "knowin'" and our ignorance, for they have weathered our slow application of time-consuming remedies You get the feeling that they know theirs is a situation for which there are no solutions.

We recognize hard work as the key to achievement, material, intellectual, and spiritual. Not so the Duddie's Brancher with his natural aversion to labor. He avoids the pressures that beset most of us. We link work with self-respect and measure success largely in terms of job status and income. But the Duddie's Brancher achieves status because he does not allow impersonal economic forces to crush him. Maybe it is just as well that he does not know that this rich nation spends only eighty-eight cents weekly per capita for public assistance programs.

Not hankering for material success is a value. It is as if those in the hollow had been struck with a kind of Appalachia of the spirit. Many of the visitors I have taken into the Branch have condemned them. "They are poor because they want to be poor." Is this a value? Elza might say, "You's hyur 'ceptin' you's hain't." Sweeping irresponsible comments are beyond the mountaineer's perception, especially when visitors say, "They accept poverty because it is a status symbol." How can we place a value on an absence of material needs, stunted emotional and intellectual development, none of which we can accurately evaluate in the totality of their impact?

They value knowing their simple needs. They value not having consuming passions that turn to ashes. They are glad that they do not have fanciful dreams which slowly turn into nightmares. Human freedom is the most pervasive element in their existence. I worried about how I could become an insider in the hollow, but I dare say that no one in the hollow ever gives a thought to how he can become an outsider. The core value of the hollow is to remain a Duddie's Brancher—bedbugs, cockroaches, inadequate housing, and all. Dillard's value is recognizing enough self-worth to shed the comments of the outer world—apathetic, hopeless, undeserving—as a duck does the rain. "Hit jist drips off, goin' nowhar."

There is a real value in not having values. You don't despair when you can't attain them. A fancy bathroom has no value when the barest facilities will satisfy your daily habits. There is real value in not having to plan meals. Your appetite dares not reject pinto beans and corn bread because it will receive nothing if it does. There is real value in having a mud lawn. There would never be enough money to buy a lawnmower to cut the grass, if grass grew. There is real value in not owning a thermostat. Then you would have to control the heat. As it is now, the temperature in your shanty remains constant—it never rises above "cold." There is real value in not having several changes of clothing. You have only one set, thereby eliminating the problem of what to wear. There is real value in not using anti-perspirants. Body odor is another means of keeping " 'tuther feller" at a distance—out of the Branch.

VI

Duddie's Branch vs. the Organized World

There must be, not a balance of power, but a community of power; not organized rivalries, but an organized common peace.

Woodrow Wilson
Address to the U. S. Senate (January 22, 1917)

The organized world is a self-contained social entity set apart from the slapdash, unsystematic colony of Duddie's Branch. So unlike are they in cultural and economic climate, they might not exist on the same planet—not even in the same galaxy. The precepts and principles that govern the outer society do not obtain in the ungoverned, guideless hollow. The resultant segregation and stratification that exist between them is a two-sided affair. The Duddie's Brancher thinks of his gloomy gulch as his vital community of geographic and functional identity. He looks upon the outside world as repugnant, restrictive, haughty—one in which his gross inadequacies are magnified. Not for him the competition, the standards, the conformity, the pace. The cars roar through the city streets "liken they's hooked t'gether, makin' noise 'n' smellin' 'n' stoppin' fur nothin'. Hit's good 'em walkin' hain't goin' nowhar." Hollow traffic, moving in low gear on a one-way creek, is ever in the eyes of Argus. "Reckon w'at 'at feller's wantin' in this hyur holler!" His outward vision is negative in every respect.

The other side of the coin looks just about the same. The comparatively opulent outsider is repulsed by and intolerant of a world he has never seen. "We should chase 'em outta those mountains and make 'em work for a living. Will they ever change?" To walk a prudent tightrope between the hollow and the outside world requires a delicate sense of balance; a sure way to suspend relations is to be outspoken in personal conversation and suggest that the double standard damages communality. Why should a certain kind of behavior, which is entirely acceptable in the organized area, be wrong when manifested by the hollower? Herds of people are building subcultures outside their society which they regard as fashionable, yet when the Brancher shows a preference for the hollow, he is ridiculed. The wealthy indulge in gambling as a pleasurable pastime, the middle-income groups routinely engage in this activity, and the deprived are unable to resist its lure. But when this happens, pity the poor! Almost every family in America has at least one television set and thinks of it as a necessity. Still, the outsider does not believe that the Brancher is entitled to one. His inward vision is prejudiced in every respect.

Belief that the hollower is conscious of his lower-class alienation is adulterated by his unquestioning acceptance of the role the outsiders have assigned to him, that of loafer and welfare parasite. Because he betrays no resentment or hostility at being type-cast thus, those that confer the titles interpret his reserve as tacit approval. His preference and preparation for the part are never impugned or explored, but the casting directors are smugly confident with their choice and the audition is concluded. And what of the candidate? Is he happy with the award? Perhaps not, but he says nothing because he is handicapped by his speech. His unique way of expressing himself—"Hain't ever bin t' a tooth doct'r 'r a eyeball doct'r in all m' livin'"—marks him as different and strongly motivates him to remain silent. His deficiencies in and difficulties with the language have prevented him from erecting satisfactory relationships and from participating in civic enterprises. More important, they have disqualified him for jobs in many instances, with the result that he is dependent on some form of welfare aid. He has only a vague understanding of details, and the inability to comprehend explanations adds to his awe, fear, and anxiety. Repetition must be avoided because it distorts his conception of what is "real." The more one repeats something, the more the Brancher doubts his perceptive capabilities. He discards his first impression and tries to form another picture. Verbosity only confuses him, and he will come away not having understood anything. This communication barrier has been a definite factor in earning for him the name of "malingerer" and it is folly to expect that he can become articulate, assuming that he would even want to. Resigned to the circumstances that have seasoned him for the role of sluggard, the Brancher is majestically indifferent to opinions, reactions, and endeavors outside the hollow. It is as if he were chained to his environment, and the limitations of his horizon have enabled him to preserve his dispassionate attitude. Or do the limitations of his interests enable him to preserve his horizon?

People are contemptuous of his sloth and lack of ambition and even the merchants relegate him to a marginal status and ridicule his unwise expenditure of funds. Since money is such a rare commodity to him, he has no experience in management and his spending style corresponds to his chronic poverty state. If he has cash, he spends it—usually on non-essentials or to satisfy a capricious desire: liquor, gambling, women. Savings are not included in his way of life. The young girls reject serviceable footwear in favor of flimsy flats or extremely high-heeled slippers, neither of which is practical in the Branch where they must rock-hop and wade through mud and debris. They never clean their shoes but will sometimes scrape away the collected mud with a stick or a leaf or wait until it is dry enough to crack off. Nor do they buy with foresight. They select the frilliest, most ornamented dress they can afford, unmindful that it will not survive one wash in Branch water and that they will not have the money to have it cleaned.

Most of the Branchers are unable to evaluate the consequences of their bizarre behavior, and the rare one who is intent on making a practical purchase is accorded the same disrespect shown the others. Melda and I went to a department store to buy a pair of socks for her nine-year-old son. She did not know what size he wore, so she opened several pairs in an attempt to approximate size with the visual image of the child's physical proportions.

A young sales clerk came over to us. "You fixing to buy somethin'?" Her manner was insolent.

While Melda was groping for a reply, the girl arrogantly inspected her. "If you ain't, don't dirty up them socks with yore rusty hands,"

Melda finally managed to explain her mission, but neglected to specify that the socks were for a child.

"What kind 'a feet does he have?"

"They's big, I reckon."

On the basis of that sketchy information, the clerk selected a pair of size 11 socks from the men's section and put them into a bag without inquiring about a color preference.

"That's forty-nine cents," she demanded.

Melda paid her and we left.

"Do you think you bought the right size?" I asked.

"They seems a mite big, but they's room in 'is shoes 'at 'is feets hain't needin', so 'e kin stuff th' socks thar. Might 's well fill up th' room 'e hain't usin' fur feets with socks."

The Brancher is radically at odds with the whole tradition of modern culture, with its goals, its standards. He is incapable of a direct appraisal of his situation and is ostracized for not conforming to the rigors of a strange social system. Only roaches, bedbugs, lice, and rodents find him desirable as they compete for space in his bed and on his body and fight for a share of his pitiable food supply and the candle-like warmth of his wretched shelter. The hollower's life touches those in the other society only momentarily—informally and tangentially. When he must venture out, he collides awkwardly with the structure erected by an organization quick to see his deficiencies. He is unable to gauge the depth perception of his relationship with the outsiders and he cannot survive being in over his head any more than the non-swimmer can survive being in deep water. Because he knows this, he has taken measures to protect himself; he sneaks in and retreats before the water covers his head. He has deliberately removed himself from the mainstream of organized society because it has rejected him. If something beneficial is considered for the Brancher, he is not present when it is discussed because he is not invited to the conferences. Even if he were, he would refuse to attend. He feels that the meetings should be held in his home, thereby giving him a sense of worth. "If'n 'em fellers 's wantin' t' git 'pinions, they's knowin' whar I's livin'. They kin mud hit up hyur. I'll breath [tell] 'em, any 'at's hankerin' knowin'."

There is so much distance between him and the outside world that he is not even curious about the economic system which has such control over his life. Fixing prices is an intricate, complicated procedure the merchant resorts to with the Brancher to "protect myself against economic losses I take in permitting credit buying." Paradoxically, those least able to pay high prices are charged the most and the local stores have a captive market. Without cash or transportation to shop in a supermarket, the hollower is forced to buy on credit from a source close to his home. Reconditioned or repossessed furniture is often sold to him for new. Floor samples invariably are sold as new. A cookstove that had no grate was sold for eighty dollars. It had had five previous owners, the first acquiring it "new secondhanded; hit war new, but someun owned hit afore me." The same stove could have been purchased new in any department store for fifty-six dollars. Lola bought a used davenport, priced at a hundred and fifty dollars, with a small cash down payment. She paid more than 100 per cent interest for the privilege of installment buying over a two-year period. Others have paid more than 200 per cent interest for nominally priced television sets and 300 per cent interest for used cars. Those on welfare extend their credit buying beyond all reasonable limits; some eventually pay part of a long-outstanding debt in order to charge more goods.

The local merchant has little difficulty in maintaining contact with those who owe him; he uses his knowledge of kinship ties to elicit information. He also uses the kinship structure as a system of communication to send threatening messages to the debtor. If this proves to be ineffective, he can [and does] threaten the entire kinship group with cutting off their credit if something is not done about the relation who owes money. The situation is somewhat analogous to the company store at the mines. Many older residents can list numerous bills and tell you that they "hain't never bin not owin' somethin'." Their lives have been a cycle of continual indebtedness. But why should the hollow dweller forgo credit buying and live within his means when the majority of the United States' population is guilty of overbuying and overbuilding? Statistics reveal that the average American family is almost $5,000 in debt, blindly following a pattern set at the federal level. We tolerate government overspending and a national debt of billions of dollars, but criticize the man who can not live without credit on less than $500 a year. The brains at the national level are unable to manage financial affairs to the extent that they do not spend more money than they take in, even though it is within their means to increase the sources of revenue as the need arises.

When the Brancher gets into financial difficulties for buying on credit there are no community services to which he can turn for help. Furthermore, he is frightened by human authority. Big buildings are interpreted as authority symbols, too. Government is the law in the county seat. Government in faraway places like Washington, which regulates so many facets of their lives, is remote even for those who wait so patiently month after month for their draw. A sixteen-year-old wife told how a man, who said he was police, came to their apartment at 1:45 A.M. and handcuffed her twenty-year-old husband and drove off with him in a blue car with a Kentucky license plate. She told a neighbor about it and said her husband had never been in trouble with the law. The neighbor called the urban police department and was told that they had no warrant for his arrest and did not send a detective to apprehend him. In the rural areas, the local police usually wear civilian clothing so the appearance of a "law man" out of uniform did not seem unusual to the young couple. The husband was released one week later and they returned to Duddie's Branch. Neither of them could identify a motive for the arrest. The young man lost a good-paying job, and both of them were afraid to cope with the system of the outer world again.

If the hollow stretches only hesitatingly toward contact with outer society, the reverse is also true. A Duddie's Brancher is not included in the numbers and order of the social structure and organization with any consistent success.

The record system of the Health Department was changed in 1960, at which time prenatal and other files were discarded. Information contained on cards, which had been used prior to this, was transferred to individual folders. I made a number of inquiries about the record system and was told in each instance that the decision to convert to the new system was made by state officials who felt that family folders were undesirable. The most obvious disadvantage of the new method is its failure to provide a total picture of the family. Some individual members have no record at all. This is particularly true of the head of the household, unless he happens to have had or has tuberculosis. Many Health Departments are hyperorganized for unimportant purposes and their programs would benefit from a thorough overhauling to bring services in line with current practices and community needs. To say that overemphasis has been placed on outmoded policies and practices is simply to understate the situation.

The child welfare worker for two counties was anxious to cooperate but was somewhat guarded as I approached her. She said that one working under the merit system tended to be cautious because the people responsible for merit-system employees were always vigilant.

As our talk continued we discussed the importance of school attendance. I heard that an acceptable excuse for not sending a child to school was the lack of clothing or lunch money, but many families and parents do not take advantage of this law because they are unfamiliar with it. The consequences of ignorance can be graphically illustrated. About four years ago two families were brought to the court for not sending their children to school. Because they could not furnish a satisfactory reason, not knowing of the poverty law, they were sentenced to one week in jail and served their terms. The punishment produced no results, because upon their release they still could not send their children to school.

This child welfare worker also serves as a probation officer; one of her functions is to compile the social histories of children who are sent to detention homes. In the course of a valuable discussion with the lady, I learned that the county judge handles all juvenile court cases and in each instance holds informal hearings which are closed to the public. Although some feel this is a poor way of dealing with the multiplicity of juvenile problems which were brought to his attention, efforts to change this practice had proved futile. The worker was especially concerned with the delinquent guilty of multiple offenses. One of her charges, a sixteen-year-old boy, was considered to have a low moron range of intelligence. Only in the sixth grade, he scored as a non-reader on the Stanford Achievement Test Form J and it was recommended that he be sent to the

Kentucky Training Home. Her conviction that these tests were not appropriate for Kentucky youngsters from deprived homes was confirmed on the day she saw the boy in a restaurant. He read the selections on a jukebox, chose the ones he wanted to hear, and put in the proper amount of money. After that he ordered a hamburger and a soft drink and counted out the exact amount of money shown on the bill. She described his school attendance as from "time to time." Another seventeen-year-old sixth grader also had a poor school record attendance. On the Stanford Achievement Test Form J he scored 2.8 grades, on the Wechsler Intelligence Scale for Children his IQ tested 80. In both instances the vocabulary used in the tests is completely meaningless to children from a rural Kentucky background and the tests are therefore not a true measure of intelligence. At the age of sixteen, the boy stole some shotguns and was found guilty of his first offense. A year later he was convicted of another burglary and was returned to the juvenile home. The worker referred to his poor school attendance and said that the schools do not meet the needs of some of the children, but that nothing was being done about the truant.

Young men from the hollows are rarely inducted into the armed services for a number of reasons—failure to pass pre-induction mental examinations, physical condition, etc. Although there was a 7 per cent decline in failure to pass army intelligence tests in 1963, the percentage of mental rejects in Kentucky was still above the national average. The Louisville *Courier-Journal* said on July 26, 1963:

". . . A report from the Army Surgeon General's office in Washington shows 29.6 per cent of the 3,849 Kentucky youths called up by draft boards in 1962 weren't smart enough for the army. . . . The 1962 figures for Kentucky show 47.4 per cent of those examined were found acceptable and 52.6 per cent were rejected. For 1961 there were 44.8 per cent accepted and 55.2 per cent rejected. For the country as a whole 45.9 per cent were found acceptable in 1962 compared with 50.9 per cent in 1961. Nationally, 54.1 per cent were rejected in 1962 compared with 49.1 per cent in 1961. Last year 19.3 per cent of the Kentuckians failed the physical examination compared with the national figure of 25.4 per cent. In

1961 the percentage of Kentucky failures was 18.3 per cent compared with the United States percentage of 23.6. In 1962 there were 3.7 per cent of the Kentuckians disqualified for administrative reasons compared with 3.2 per cent nationally. Administrative reasons cover men with significant criminal records and criminal or antisocial tendencies, dishonorably discharged servicemen, aliens ineligible for service, and persons erroneously sent for examination. . . ."

Although hollow parents have deep feelings about their children leaving home, a boy who has been accepted for one of the armed services is a source of pride. They do not know where he is going or what he will be doing, but they do feel that he is important. Alex said, "All 'a my younguns 'uv bin too sorry t' git took. I hain't never had none 'a 'em go fur, but now one's part 'a th' gover'ment. Hit's a heap better'n goin' t' th' mines, even if'n you's git shot. Poundin' 'n' loadin' coal 's almos' worse'n starvin', 'ceptin' we's al'ays had somethin' t' eat." The boys from Duddie's Branch provide slim pickings for selective service. In Shade, the local draft board charters a bus for the boys who have been called up for examination and sends them to Louisville. When William Miller was scheduled to be examined he, along with several other fellows from Earle County, got off the bus in Richmond to buy liquor. They made no attempt to get back on and it left without them. They apparently were unaware of the serious consequences of their actions.

Tom Halt is classified as 4F, Category V, after failing the Armed Forces Qualification Test (AFQT). There are five illiterate categories: I, marginal illiterate; II, illiterate-high mental; III, illiterate-marginal mental; IV, substandard mental and physical, V, administratively unacceptable. Onzie Halt also failed the AFQT and was placed in Category V, but described as illiterate-high mental. Winn Ross is classified as 3A because he is married and has children. Charles Wheeler is 4F because of substandard mentality. Lorin Shifter is currently classified as 3A because he is married and has children. Marshall Wheeler is classified as substandard mentally. Glenn Ross is 3A because he is married and has dependents. Coffee Wheeler has a 3A classification because he is married and has a dependent. The dependent is not his child. Richard Evans was given a 3A classification because he was married and has dependents. The draft board has no record of William Nuratt. Sie Shifter was given a 3A classification because of marriage and dependents. Jesse Shifter has been examined twice. The first time he was declared illiterate. Upon re-examination eighteen months later, he failed the AFQT test. A further notation on his record described him as psychotic with a personality disorder. Gid Shifter has never been examined and has a 3A classification. Herman Shifter failed the AFQT test. Kash has never been examined and was given a 3A classification. Ozzie Wheeler was given a 3A classification. Gene Gilbert has never been examined. Officials have verified that he is living in Indianapolis and have sent letters informing him that he is classified as 1A and giving him the examining date. Nothing happens. Dob Halt is 1A, Category IV; he is married but has no children. Foister Shifter is 4F. He was inducted in September 1952, and separated in November 1954, having only one month and twenty-nine days' service to his credit. His records show 670 days AWOL. He received a dishonorable discharge. Lowell Gilbert also served previously and he too received an undesirable discharge. He enlisted in April 1951 and was separated in December 1953. During that time he was AWOL for 419 days. He was told that his habits made retention in the service undesirable. Andy Gilbert enlisted in the army in August 1956, and was separated in December 1957, because he claimed dependents. He was released to the reserve and was to continue for four years and seven months. By his own admission, he did nothing at all during those four years and seven months to maintain a reserve status. He received credit for one year four months and seven days of active service and was not AWOL during his period of service. He was given credit for other service of two months and eighteen days which is neither explained nor understood by the local draft board. Jeems Smuts was given a 4F classification by the local physician and was not required to take an army examination because of deafness. Ernie has the rather unusual classification of 1D and is supposedly in some reserve unit at this time. He enlisted in the army reserve, had six months of training, and was released to the Kentucky Military District for continued active duty training until June 1964. According to him and his family, he has had no contact whatsoever with the army since completing his six months' training.

Clearly, criminal records are not an important issue in the Branchers' failure to qualify for the armed services, even though they are often in trouble with the authorities. The law enforcement officials in Earle County consist of a constable, a sheriff, deputy sheriffs, a Commonwealth attorney, state police (troopers), and magistrates. The 120 counties in Kentucky are governed by a curious body of magistrates who compose the fiscal court. Historically, their functions can be traced back to the days of squires in England. Each magistrate holds hearings in his own district (Earle County has four) and each represents his section as a member of the fiscal court, which closely parallels the city council in an urban area. The fiscal court must approve all spending by the county and is the sole taxing agency in the county. The magistrate of the district in which Duddie's Branch is located is also a member of the Earle County fiscal court. He is helpful to the Branchers who own their homes by explaining taxes.

Kentucky's constitution provides that all property, unless specifically exempt, shall be subject to property taxation. Classification is provided and now assessments are required to be at full cash value.

Prior to 1965, however, Kentucky courts consistently held that uniformity should take precedence over full value. The state-wide assessment level on real estate and tangible personal property was then slightly under 30 per cent and on intangible personal property was approximately full value.

In 1965 assessments were required to be on a full value basis, forcing most counties to make equalization adjustments. With the change in assessment procedures, it became necessary to lower tax rates although income rose because of the higher assessment ratios.

Each year the Department of Revenue gathers information on real estate sales for the purpose of estimating the ratio of assessment to market values. For each usable sale an assessment ratio was calculated by dividing the assessed value of the property, as shown by the last assessment made prior to the sale, by the estimated market value. The county-wide ratios for all real estate reported were computed by weighting the combined two-year sub-class ratios by their respective 1967 assessed values.

In the 1966–67 year period, Earle County was at the 82.2 per cent assessment ratio as it moved toward full 100 per cent assessment.

The total amount assessed by Earle County Tax Commissioners in 1967 was $31,619,604. This amount resulted from the collection of $1.16 for each one hundred dollars of assessed property. Of the amount collected per $100 of assessable property the city gets 40 cents, the schools 45.3 cents, and the county 30.3 cents. The county portion is divided into general fund (15.1 cents), culture (1.1 cents), health (2.5 cents), library (1. cents), and special bond (10.6 cents).

The land owned by individuals and/or families living in the Duddie's Branch area range from 2 to 63 acres, for a total of approximately 281 acres. Adding to this the 8 acres owned by the non-resident owner, Mr. Green, the total is 289 acres. The real land value is $15,000, but for tax purposes it amounts to a total of $5,000. Including Mr. Green's property, the figures are $15,000 and $5,200 respectively. The actual land value per acre ranges from a low of $19.05 to $174.99. Since improvements are also included in the evaluation of land, its actual value per se is impossible to determine. Tax evaluation of the four possible listings range from $25 to $300, the actual value being $100 to $900. Lester and Melda Nuratt, who own sixty-three acres at the head of the hollow, have the largest individual holdings. The tax value of this land per acre is $6.35 with the actual value per acre of $19.05. The six acres owned by Farmer Wheeler and his wife have a tax value of $350 and the three acres owned by Diza Smuts have a tax value of $175, making these two pieces of land worth the most per acre. For tax purposes, they are worth $58.33 per acre. Letcher and Dana Ross have the least valuable land in terms of per acre value. They own five acres which have been evaluated for tax purposes at $10 per acre; the actual value is $30 per acre. The taxes charged on house and lot and land and improvements in Duddie's Branch range from 1¢ to 20¢ per acre. Taxes charged on house, lot, land, improvements, and car range from 33¢ to $1.05.

The health tax in Duddie's Branch ranges from 4¢ to $2.20, for a total revenue of $6.94 from this neighborhood. The absentee owner pays 32 per cent of this total (or $2.20) and the residents pay the remaining 68 per cent (or $4.74). A total of $3.14 is paid for library tax, 95¢ of it coming from Mr. Green and $2.19 from the Branchers.

There are fourteen motor vehicles in working condition in Duddie's Branch, including passenger cars, pickup and 1½-ton trucks. Almost all of them are old models, 1932 or thereabouts, so that they are high enough to drive over the rocks in the creek. Many of the owners do not have drivers' licenses but drive even though they are not legally permitted or eligible to do so. Some usable cars are not included in the total of fourteen because they carry out-of-state license plates, although the owners are permanent residents of the Branch. It is always interesting to see whether the out-of-state tags are replaced by Kentucky tags when new license plates are due. Kentucky license plates cost $12.50 for all vehicles. Six of the cars have a tax evaluation of $50, two of $60, three of $100, one of $110, one of $150, and one of $540. Taxes on a car only range from 25¢ to $2.70, for a total of $10.40. If Mr. Green's taxes of $14.05 are added (he owns several coal trucks), the total is $24.45.

Fourteen men in Duddie's Branch pay a poll tax in addition to other taxes. Three men pay a poll tax only. Thirty-four Branch families pay no poll tax. The poll tax is still collected in Earle County. In 1967–68, 3,850 paid the tax of $1.50 (the maximum amount allowed by the state). The tax is not for voting, but rather is a head tax levied on all males between the ages of eighteen and sixty-five, except for men honorably discharged from the armed services with a disability. The range on house and lot and land and improvements is from $1.05 to $4.85, for a total of $22.97. The range on house and lot and land and improvements with car is $1.05 to $10.07, for a total of $56.25. The range for a car only is from $1.98 to $5.13, for a total of $14.18. The total amount of county tax as paid by the inhabitants of Duddie's Branch is $93.40; added to this is the $4.50 portion of poll tax, making a total of $97.90; the $31.53 which Mr. Green pays makes a total of $129.43 in county taxes paid. A portion of the poll tax is included in school tax. The largest proportion is $2.00 or 57 per cent. The range on home and lot and land and improvement is from $1.35 to $7.25, for a total of $32.36. The range on house and lot and land and improvements with car is from $5.00 to $14.90, for a total of $82.65. The range on car only is from $2.75 to $8.10, for a total of $20.90. The total amount of poll tax only is $6.00. The total amount of school tax paid by the inhabitants of Duddie's Branch, including the $6.00, is $141.91. Adding to this the $49.25 paid by Mr. Green, the total is $191.16.

In July 1965 the circuit judge ruled that the county had to publish a financial statement for the fiscal year 1964–65 within sixty days. The judge who handed down the ruling on July 1 stated that the report must show "the amount of money paid into the public treasury of the county and the source from which it was paid, the date, amount and what the payment was for, except the total amount paid to each person for wages and salaries may be listed in one item."

Fiscal court pays less than a total of two dollars a day for care of prisoners and the local jail receives criticism from all sides. There are no facilities for isolating prisoners with contagious diseases and no provisions for the inmates who need psychiatric care or counseling. Nor is any thought given to the possibility of a rehabilitative program. During weekends, anywhere from twelve to thirty people are arrested and put into the already crowded jail. To erect a new building, the fiscal court would have to ask for a tax increase. The jail's operating budget is less than two thirds the tax base, the remainder being used to liquidate old debts.

In Earle County local leaders do not lean toward social innovation. The governmental process is anachronistic, but a recent attempt to remodel the constitution of the state failed miserably; interestingly, the overwhelming negative vote did not proceed from the hollow areas. The county seat has a city council, but its meetings are limitedly productive. In one, the councilmen delayed action on beginning an urban development project, placed under study the development of a low-rent housing project, adopted an ordinance to change the fire zones in an attempt to lower insurance rates and restrict the type of housing that could be built in the zones, approved the location of three street lights, refused to take action on the renovation of a burned-out grocery store until insurance settlements were

made, appointed a committee to study a riverbank cleanup project
for eight and a half miles on a local creek, hired a city clerk, and
approved the purchase of eight pairs of trousers for the city police
force.

The Kentucky Court of Appeals is in charge of the circuit court,
each representing three counties. Circuit court convenes twenty-four
days out of every four months. When it is necessary to subpoena
a witness, slated cases may be postponed and rescheduled for a later
session. Most of the cases are dropped, however, because the plain-
tiff dismisses his charges. Many times there is a change in plea from
innocent to guilty and a hearing is unnecessary or set for circuit court.
In some instances the charge may then be heard by the county judge,
who might render a sentence of probation for a period of years. A
number of cases are dismissed by the circuit court judge because
state witnesses fail to appear to testify. Meander was to appear as
a witness, but I saw him in the Branch at the time he was supposed
to be in court.

"You're not planning on going to the courthouse, I reckon?"

"Reckon I's hain't. Any feller kin reckon he's hain't 'xactly sure.
Seein' 'n' hawk-eyin' hain't makin' fur sure. Any feller ought t' be
surin' 'fore he's mouthin'. Skins 'r' a heap more than mouthin' fur
nothin'." Even murder trials are retired from the court docket when
witnesses fail to appear to testify. Meander explained it. " 'Em
fellers, they's licked 'fore they's headin'." Prosecuting witnesses
may request of the Commonwealth attorney that the charges be
dropped.

A 1966 circuit court docket contained 44 criminal cases and 7
civil cases. Nineteen criminal cases were dropped, 12 were continued, and 9 were set for trial. The following indictments and
charges also appeared on the court dockets: cold check (often dismissed when the one holding the check is paid off); forgery; breach
of peace; detaining a female; fraud; damaging personal property by
explosives; selling mortgaged property; carnal knowledge of under-
age female; concealed weapon; fornication; adultery; use of abusive
language; 15 charges against a coal company for polluting water;
selling timber without consent of owner; removal of a boundary for

a tract of land; carrying away an unowned building. The sentences are often ludicrous in view of the crime.

Child desertion (abandoning infant children without proper provision): two-year suspended sentence on agreement to pay $40 a month for support of children. One month later he produced evidence that he was unable to pay monthly support and the charges were dismissed.

Possessing alcoholic beverages: fine $20 and cost with thirty-day suspended sentence.

Manslaughter: three-year suspended sentence on condition the convicted leave the county.

Deserting pregnant wife: charges dismissed after agreement to pay hospital bills and $20 per month child support.

Flourishing a deadly weapon: pistols confiscated, fine $50 and costs.

Drunkenness: $20 and cost, twenty-day suspended jail sentence.

Arson (often called "malicious burning"): seven-year prison sentence.

A charge of knowingly and intentionally receiving stolen property: continued for one year on the condition that the accused remain out of state for twelve months.

Two-year prison sentence for a man charged with cutting and wounding with intent to kill. Suspended for a period of two years on the condition that he leave the state after he pleaded guilty to the charge.

A fine of $20 per month until a total of $200 was paid was levied against a man for failure to surrender for drunken driving.

A fine of $20 and a thirty-day jail sentence levied against a man for possessing alcoholic beverages for purpose of sale. The accused filed bond and was released from the county jail under a $500 local-option bond.

Shooting and wounding and a concealed weapons charge brought a $50 fine and a six-month jail sentence.

A charge of reckless use of firearms: fined $50 and costs and given a thirty-day suspended sentence. His .38-caliber pistol was confiscated.

A fifty-five-year-old mine watchman charged with the pistol

slaying of a woman admitted the shooting, after being awakened from sleep; he thought someone was breaking in on him at the mine, but the incident occurred at the home of the dead woman. The grand jury returned the indictment charging him with willful murder. He was released under a $10,000 bond pending trial. The grand jury had indicted him for willful murder and he received a five-year prison sentence. He was convicted on the charge of voluntary manslaughter. Housed in the county jail pending transfer to the state reformatory, he admitted that he had been dating the victim but said he did not even remember the slaying. Fortunately for him, she lived for six hours and made a dying statement that it was an accident. Authorities indicate that additional action may be taken and that he may receive a probation.

Indictment of deserting pregnant wife and child desertion; charges of deserting his pregnant wife were dismissed when he agreed to pay $10 a week to his wife. The payment was to continue until the birth of the baby.

A two-year prison term was handed down for breaking and entering. The sentence was suspended because the defendant pleaded guilty to the charge and waived trial by jury. He was ordered to pay a fine of $250 to the owner of the store which he had robbed.

Charged with willfully and maliciously setting fire to woods, the accused was sentenced to one year of hard labor. He pleaded guilty to the charge and waived trial by jury. He was transferred from the county jail to prison.

The accused was sentenced to serve a one-year prison term for involuntary manslaughter of an eighty-year-old man and was ordered taken to prison. This was rescinded and he was recommended for confinement to a tuberculosis hospital.

Two city policemen were indicted for shooting the tires on a car they were chasing while attempting to make an arrest for drunken driving. The judge issued a directed verdict of not guilty of charges (shooting into car with intent to kill) after listening to testimony in the case. After a short deliberation, the jury returned a verdict of not guilty.

If a burglar breaks into a car and rifles the glove compartment, he can get up to fifteen years. For stealing the car, he is sentenced to not more than ten years. Dog stealing is punishable by ten years in jail; dog killing by six months and a $500 fine.

Two men were tried in absentia for possessing moonshine whiskey and arrived in court just before the jury returned the verdict of guilty. They were sentenced to sixty days in jail and assessed a $100 fine. A third man charged with the same offense was not tried with permission of the court because of illness in his family. The son of one of these men was fined $20 and given a thirty-day suspended jail sentence after pleading guilty to possessing alcoholic beverages. The circuit court judge suspended jail sentence for him on the condition that he not violate any of the Commonwealth's laws for a period of twelve months.

Charges of shooting on a public highway were dismissed after the prosecuting attorney appeared in court and made a motion to dismiss the charge on grounds that he did not desire to prosecute. Frequently, charges (arson, for instance) are continued if the Commonwealth attorney feels that he is not ready for trial.

A charge of willful murder was changed to voluntary manslaughter against a man and his sister-in-law who shot a state trooper. Each was sentenced to twenty-one years in the state prison.

A woman who lived in the hollow next to Duddie's Branch pleaded guilty to a charge of manslaughter. A sentence of two years in the state reformatory was suspended on the condition that she not return to either of the Branches for a period of three years.

Many break-ins occur in isolated areas. The burglars often are only fifteen to twenty-one years of age and work in groups. Brothers tend to pair off and sometimes one who lives elsewhere will come to assist in the break-in. The loot is usually cigarettes, candy, Cokes, etc., amounting to less than $75. The looters then set fire (usually with coal oil) to the building, which is rarely insured, to eliminate clues. They are often responsible for a loss of $2,000 for a $50 to $75 theft. This practice is becoming a pattern in the county. The owner suffers a complete loss, many times his life's assets, because he cannot get insurance coverage. The companies know the system. Such thefts usually occur around midnight or later when there is seldom a possibility of a witness, particularly one who is brave enough to testify.

Fires present a problem in the county and many acres of timberland are burned during the hunting season. In order to bring the blaze under control the fire fighters burn rings around the area, but if the woods are dry this method may not prove effective. High winds scatter timber fires quickly and extensively. In just one month thousands of acres of timber have been destroyed in this county alone. The answer would seem to be an area well stocked in a natural setting which could be controlled. But the hollower does not seem too concerned about burning timber on land he does not own. Many times I have seen one man bring in the guns and game, while the rest of the hunters go for "fittin' fire if'n they's movin' fur headin' out."

In January a wild, two-mile chase through Shade resulted in the arrest of a sixteen-year-old driver and his nineteen-year-old companion. Both youths were charged with drunkenness and were tried by the magistrate of the district in which they lived. Each was fined $10 and costs. The driver of the car was arraigned before the county judge and after filing bond awaited grand jury action. The arrest was made by the deputy sheriff, who had to blow out the tires on the car with shotgun blasts. In the course of the chase, the driver of the car shot nine times at the deputy. During the same month the Earle County sheriff's office had been making an effort to apprehend persons carrying loaded guns in their cars. The county sheriff said that he had found more guns in cars and on people during this month than at any time since he had come to office some two years before. One man who was arrested on a drunkenness charge had a loaded high-power rifle in his car. Another arrested for drunkenness had a loaded shotgun and a loaded .38 pistol in his car. Both men were jailed until they were sober and each paid a fine of $10 and costs, which did not exceed $15. The guns were returned to them following their release.

Some of the Duddie's Branch boys stole a car and started to paint it a different color, but they ran out of paint. The retail outlet had sold them all it had so they left the back fenders the original color. The boys didn't mind. "Hit might be a right perty car with two fenders hain't lookin' liken they's belongin'." I would agree; light blue front fenders and navy-blue back fenders is not a bad combination.

Corruption appears to be as much a part of Earle County, the Hardstone area in particular, as the weather. And, like the weather, the private citizen has no effective means of determining whether or not widespread corruption exists in local government and/or the various officials elected or appointed.

The Duddie's Brancher substitutes "fur" and "agin" for the party name of Democrat and Republican. Knowledge of and interest in party philosophy, performance, leaders, etc., are absent. He is concerned only with his local precinct, magistrate, and county officials, not exactly sure where political jurisdictions begin or end. The role of elected city officials is unknown to the Branchers because the physical boundaries of Shade mean nothing. If a "bad" official gets into office, the Brancher feels that he was put there by " 'em 'at hain't Branch livin'." He looks upon politics as a form of gambling. "You's bettin' 'im winnin', 'tuther feller's bettin' 'im comin' 'thout nary a dressin' [without his shirt]."

The log cabin symbol of the ballot dates back to 1840, when the state was called Clay's Kentucky. It has been said that the log cabin appeals to the emotions of the voters rather than to the brains. Smoke curling from the chimney is significant and enhances the meaning, particularly for the hollow people. There seems to be evidence that this symbol will stay on indefinitely. The philosophy based on the will of the people is attractive to the hollow voter even though he cannot assess the implementation of his will as indicated on the ballot. The log cabin (Republican) and the rooster (Democrat) appear on the ballot as symbols of the political parties.

Relatively little corruption has been proved. One group contends that the reason is state and local antipathy toward investigations; the other feels that the reformer would be so suspect that he could get nothing helpful in a state with a long history of ballot-box hanky-panky. Elections are tightly governed at the county level but administration at the polling spot is often loosely controlled. The cost of a single vote varies from one to five dollars. Hollow people sometimes vote in several places by using the name of a deceased person or someone who has been out of the county for a long time.

A pay raise up to $9,600 for salaried county officials was approved by the court of appeals but denied by the county judge because there was simply no money available. This did not affect his popularity when he sought re-election; people know his record. He does not believe in responding to charges made against him in the pre-election period because he believes that becoming involved in debate of charges only weakens his position. He is a shrewd politician, knows his enemies, can assess their strength, and can always rely on the hollow people to support him. The judge has been in office for more than a decade and has yet to turn away anyone seeking his help. A large hunk of his $4,000 annual salary goes to the poor who come to him for money. His practice of treating everyone with respect, dignity, and sympathy is a year-round pattern and there is little doubt that this strongly influences the hollow folks at election time.

The Branchers think that many of the candidates are completely unfamiliar with the "workin's in our heads." The disadvantaged lack enough perceptive ability to understand the complex workings of government even at the county level, but they are hesitant to "change fellers in high places afore we knows 'is workin's. How 'r' we gonna keep from gittin' 'em mouthin' fellers? We hain't sure w'at they's gonna give us." They understand that everyone has faults, that not one "is run out 'a 'em" and they feel much more secure and comfortable "knowin' faults."

One would have to be part of life in the county to understand what it is like to be judge. He spends endless hours listening, which is one of the things the disadvantaged most appreciate. Rarely can their problem be solved by the magic sweep of the judge's hand but his reputation as "th' mostest listenin' feller" stands him in good stead with his devoted followers.

After I came to know the Duddie's Branch families and the general neighborhood area a little better, I thought it might profit me to meet the persons who had a direct interest in the welfare of the hollowers. I went to the courthouse at nine o'clock, the time that the fiscal court judge for Earle County usually arrived. I waited for him with many other people, most of whom were poorly dressed and dirty, their preoccupied expressions bespeaking grave problems. After two hours, not knowing how to get into the judge's chamber and finding no secretary, I sought assistance from a person in another office. She interrupted the judge's closed-door conversation and within a short time he ushered me into the courtroom that he uses for his private sessions. The judge received me at first cautiously, and then his reserve melted. "Did you notice the woman who just left?" he asked. "She has been refused welfare, and I don't like it. Her husband has advanced cirrhosis of the liver and he's been tossed back and forth from physician to physician, none of whom is willing to certify that his illness is terminal and that he is unemployable." He went on to say that the unwillingness or delay the physicians exhibited in certifying permanent disability was disturbing.

Upon learning that I was particularly interested in the families from Duddie's Branch he said, "If there is anything that anybody can do to help those people, it will be worth while. Many years ago I tried to build them a road, but they were not interested and you can't build a good road up a stream. Somebody has to give you some land." He then discussed the system of dispensing commodities and explained that magistrates in each of the four Earle County divisions are responsible for determining which families are eligible. Generally, they tended to be too stingy with commodities.

"It frequently happens that the people who have been denied come to me for help," he added.

"What do you do under those circumstances?"

"I put them on. If we can send food abroad by the ton, we certainly aren't going to miss a few cans of peanut butter or a few boxes of cheese over here. Our generous foreign aid program continues, despite the huge number of Americans who are desperately in need of help."

I visited him often thereafter. If I failed to show up for a few days, he would send word for me to come in. Most of the times when I saw him at his request there was nothing special on his mind—he just wanted to know how I was getting on and whether there was anything he could do to assist.

The precinct to which Duddie's Branch belongs has 1,346 log cabin voters and 323 roosters, but the number of constituents whose names appear on the comparative signature book is 564. Criticisms range from unregistered voters to illegible signatures to Xs for signatures. Preshia always votes under her maiden name even though she is now living with a third husband. The number of potential voters in either party in any precinct would never be the same as those who sign the book when they actually cast their ballots. Unofficial returns by precinct in a primary election show the strength of the support for the judge from the poorer areas, primarily hollows. Many of the people don't bother to vote for everyone on the ticket. The judge always gets more votes and, in descending order, the state representative, the county clerk, the county attorney, the tax commissioner, jailer, and coroner. Usually the two offices with the most candidates are the sheriff and the four magistrates. When I asked how they felt about a deputy who was running for sheriff, none seemed to object to him. "Reckon 'e's a good feller 's we's got fur sheriffin'. They hain't none a' 'em 'at's gonna stop moonshinin' 'n' whiskeyin'. I knows fellers 'at's bin 'shinin' fur back's their grandpappy. They gits caught, they pays, they keeps right on 'shinin'. Reckon they al'ays will."

Some of the campaign promises would be impossible to keep. It just doesn't make sense to Seafle that he should forgo his dollar or so at election with the promise that if he votes for the "right" man he can someday get paid ten dollars a day. Seafle catches on slow, but he knows that nobody is going to pay him that much money for not working and he does not plan to work. In his reasoning, the one making such an impossible promise can't by his reckonin' be a right man. The local newspaper always prints victory and defeat speeches. But no one in the hollow gets the paper. They don't read the appreciation of the winners or the rationalization of the losers. Religion often comes to the fore at election time and candidates who claim to be God-fearing encourage voters to consider this when making their choice.

Promises of a road become more emphatic around election time. Candidates for magistrate of District 2 often make this promise central in their vote-seeking effort in Duddie's Branch. The county judge has for years given consideration to its feasibility, but he has had insurmountable financial problems, difficulty in securing rights of way without due process of law (by owner consent), maintenance, etc. Engineers have viewed the hollow under all conditions—high water, ice and snow, vertical hillsides—all challenges. A Branch just across the mountain had a road bulldozed out of the side of the mountain, but when it rains the mud is deep enough to immobilize even a jeep. The Duddie's Branchers decided they would rather have the rocks and water than a muddy road without maintenance. The present magistrate has really been working on the road idea. Every time I go down they tell me that a road is almost an immediate reality. For people who have so little faith in promises, I remain constantly puzzled why this one—made so often before by others—is believed. No other kind of promise elicits the same response. Is it the magistrate and his persuasive powers? The same two landowners at the mouth of the hollow who have on each previous occasion refused to grant space across their land still refused. Finally, however, the magistrate was successful and one landowner gave in. One down and one to go. Melda wrote: "Isiah Gilbert let them make a road thru his land. The magistrate begged Seafle to let the road go thru his land. He had to pay Seafle for the land before he would let it go thru." One of the Branchers told me that Flossie didn't want a road to go through yet. "You got kinfolks 'at lives in th' last house in th' head 'a this hyur holler." Flossie replied, "My kinfolks hain't no more 'n strangers t' me."

Voting machines are an enigma to the hollowers. The ballot is arranged in vertical lines and a small lever is opposite the name of the candidate or the issue. The voter must indicate a "Yes" or a "No" preference for the issue on which he is voting. When he turns the lever of his choice, an X signifies that the vote is expressed. Write-in choices are beyond his ability. On the one hand, he does not know the candidate or the issue; on the other hand, the majority of these people would not know how to fill the appropriate space with a meaningful legible script indicating a choice. Likewise, turning the lever for a person of choice is beyond his ability. If you can't read, how would you know which way to turn the lever? Pulling the lever or pushing the button is a simple procedure once the ballot has been cast by the officials, who of necessity must provide their assistance. Sometimes the illiterate and semi-illiterate play a very limited role. Meander said, "We's goin' 'hind th' winder curtain, me 'n' 'im. 'E's mouthin' 'n' right off 'e grabs a handle 'n' we's headin' out." I said that the procedure would appear to be very simple from his description. "Yep, 'is hagglin's th' hardest. 'E's got nothin' t' haggle fur. I's keepin' 'at feller's promisin'. I's gittin' my pig if'n I's gotta walk 'im up 'at holler leadin' 'im 'hind me." "But, Meander," I answered, "everyone will see that you got a pig for your vote. They'll know that you sold your vote." "None 'ceptin' 'em not hankerin' t' sell their birthright knows you's got choosin' right over w'at you's takin'. 'Em 'at's choosin' money hain't hankerin' fur somethin' bound t' grow into more if'n hit hain't daid afore pullin' time."

The voting machine as a means of assuring an honest election is a myth, and one day of observation at the polls will convince even the most optimistic of how easily the fable can be exploded, whether it be a primary or general election.

On one voting day I saw Seafle trudging up the road again for about the tenth time.

"Seafle, you've voted ten times today. What's bringing you back now?"

"Hain't made up my mind," he told me.

The built-in mechanism allowing for correction of mistakes is seldom used because a change means that the voter must ask for a new ballot. The voting machine is probably accurate, likely to save time in counting the ballots, and I suppose it is as fair as any system can be for those who are unable to read. And for those voters who can perform according to the instructions, the entire process is unaided. The carryings-on of earlier days probably caused the voting machine to emerge as a cure for social ills, but to assume that it thwarts the efforts of the less scrupulous is to exaggerate realism.

Fraudulent registrations, vote buying, and absentee ballot abuses are not monitored by the voting machines. Seafle told how it was with paper ballots. He'd mark his ballot and fold it and the officials would put it in one box, then fold another ballot and put it in "th' countin' box." The one they put in the "countin' box" was marked the way they wanted. After the polls closed, a huge bonfire would consume the ballots that did not get into the "countin' box."

Seafle can remember voting years ago. "Fellers 'uz sellin' their votes then, 'n' hit hain't no diff'r'nt t'day. In 'em days they be bought easier fur less, a drink 'a whiskey 'r twenty-five cents per vote. Now 'em fellers 'n' their wormen up their head at a skin 'n' some 'a 'em stickin' 'round longer wiggle a five, 'at is if'n votin' is skimpy." He says, "Hit din't make no diff'r'nce t' none 'a 'em who teached school 'n' who sheriffed. Still don't."

When I inquired of one of the local officials how the people managed to vote by machine, he assured me that this method was much easier than the old paper ballot system. He explained that the people at the polls enter the booth with the voter and push the levers of choice while the voter is being shown how to operate the machine. One man told me that after each voter left the booth he would slip his hand behind the side curtain and push levers of candidates he wanted elected. When I challenged a deputy at the poll about the possibility of illegal voting, he replied, "If they voted straight I'd be out of a job."

Some hollowers have little respect for the candidates: "Hain't nary a feller worthin' my crossin' [his X signature]." Candidates boast that they will be satisfied to leave the selection to the voters' opinion and judgment. Unsuccessful aspirants are aware of their obligation to thank the voters who supported them even when they lost. After all, most of them have to live in the community after the election and may wish to run again.

Tempers flare between elected officials at the various levels of government. The Commonwealth attorney routinely berates the sheriff and one or more of his deputies and he often addresses the Earle County grand jury and makes serious charges against all of the arresting officers, both county and city. It is generally felt that the Commonwealth attorney takes advantage of his position and uses the protection of the court from which to "venom" law enforcement officers. The interchange often takes place before the circuit court judge, a non-verbal participant. The sheriff calls the county attorney a liar and says he will force him to eat his words. The Commonwealth attorney says that the deputy is lower than a black snake ("lower" and "black" are key words, both degrading to anyone who understands).

Many cases are heard before the local magistrate's court. This always creates hard feelings and in some instances an argument. Magistrates change and keep few records; to avoid such occurrences would present a problem.

Each group accuses the other of letting moonshiners run wild. The commonwealth attorney feels that he and the circuit court rather than the magistrates should try the moonshiners. Trial before the latter is blamed upon the deputies and the state police. The Commonwealth attorney calls all elected officials beneath him "cheap politicians" and says that the people in the county are sick and tired of seeing hard-working miners (a very small minority) fined while the bootleggers are permitted to go scot-free. The circuit court judge in his instructions to the grand jury says that they are to lay aside all personal feelings as they do their job. Each newly impaneled jury is told to use its knowledge of right and wrong as it makes decisions. The main issue is to decide whether the complaint under consideration warrants a trial. The jurors are told that their decision may mean that they will indict a neighbor, a friend, or one of their kin. They listen inattentively as they are told about people who commit crimes like breaking and entering, stealing, forgery, larceny, and bootlegging for the purposes of making a living the easy way—living off hard-working fellows. In an attempt to categorize the suspected guilty and place them in a low strata of society, the jury is told that those who are operating outside the law are unable to read and cannot even sign their own names. The bootlegger is accused of creating more grief and heartache than any other violator in the county.

Violation of the liquor laws, particularly in this dry county, is commonplace. The bootleggers say that the local officials, the law enforcement officials, and the government officials have ways of getting their liquor and it is no more wrong for the Brancher to have something to drink than it is for the others. The officials have often been accused of accepting moonshine in order to prevent arrest. One of the most frequent manifestations of hostility is in relation to moonshine and the law. Few have escaped some encounter with the law during their lifetime and many brag about their ability to get an immediate release and their avoidance of a jail sentence. But even going to jail has its benefits in the group, particularly if the illegal activity in which they were involved cannot be substantiated when they go to trial. It is very difficult in any situation to find a person who will testify against another individual with whom he must live in the hollow even though he saw the illegal activity committed. The fear of the consequences is so great that he is unwilling to elaborate upon the fact even though he knows quite specifically what the facts are. Branchers are inclined to say, "I hain't sure," "Could be," "Don't reckon," or some such comment since most of them wish not to become involved. One man, when asked by the law if he saw a certain man enter another's house and come out with moonshine, said, "I seen a man go in but I hain't sure who hit 'uz." After the trial was over he admitted that he knew exactly who it was. "I seen 'im but I hain't tellin' th' law."

The state of Kentucky is known as the home of bourbon whiskey, yet 86 of its 120 counties are dry, 26 are wet, and 8 are classified as "divided." Local option elections determine the wet or dry status. A retail liquor stamp varies in cost from $100 to $800, depending on the class of cities located in each county, and a beer stamp costs $25. Earle County is legally dry, but moonshining is a way of life in a county dry by choice, as poverty is a way of life—long here and not changing. Distillers just across the county line transporting into Earle County feel that Earle is a heaven on earth for being so kind to their business enterprise. "If'n they's goin' wet, we'd be ruint atter one dark [night]. 'Em fellers in Earle's bin mixin' 'n' notchin' fur too long. Hain't hankerin' fur nothin' diff'r'nt." Moonshine tastes like the liberated furies of Pandora's box and when you take a drink "you's feels liken you's swallerin' a lighted lamp [kerosene]. If'n you's gulp a big 'un, you's stopped daid in you's tracks. Hit 'ud snap both you's suspenders nigh in two."

No one is more interested in the elimination of the moonshiner than those in control of the distilled spirits industry. The illegal operation cuts into their earnings and they are concerned. The industry indicates the profit is in the avoidance of the federal tax of approximately $10.50 a gallon in addition to state and local taxes in amounts from $2.25 to $3.00 per gallon. A pint of liquor costing $2.86 in a legal retail outlet earns $1.57 in taxes. The actual cost of the whiskey is only $1.29.

If you think the dollar profit in moonshine isn't worth the effort and possible "lawin'," you are wrong. A bootlegger who takes his occupation seriously can make a weekly profit of $300 right under your nose. Moonshine is produced at a cost of $1.00 to $1.50 per gallon and sold for $2.50 per quart fruit jar or 25¢ per drink at the bar. Packaging costs are negligible—a quart or half-gallon fruit jar and lid, which can always be used later "fur puttin' by grub from growin'." Meander takes an empty Clorox bottle to his favorite still. The profit for the distiller may be as high as 400 per cent, for the middleman 50 per cent, and for the "skirtin' th' law" retailer as much as 125 per cent. This perhaps explains why moonshiners are willing to pay fines, be seized, and serve jail sentences.

The "feds" have been in hot pursuit of the 'shiners for over forty years, but despite their efforts, profits remain relatively stable for the operator (reported to be a $333,000-a-year business). The purity of the product is important. Seafle says, "If'n 'e's agin drinkin' 'is brewin', hit hain't fittin'." Seafle is a crafty man and offers the distiller, if he is a less well known moonshiner, the first drink from his purchase. If the distiller refuses a drink, Seafle leaves without "payin' nary skin 'r coppers fur nothin' fittin'." Real ingenuity is often required in the proper distilling process. The equipment includes old oil drums as cookers, wooden barrels as fermenters, and some kind of contraption to use for the run-off: old automobile radiators, plumbing pipe, or copper tubing. If the deadly lead from the solder is dissolved into the moonshine, it can be fatal. One of my friends bought a bottle of "rotgut" and demonstrated its dangerous properties. He poured some onto my jeep fender and drop by drop it ate through the paint and left a rough spot in the metal.

The stills operating in Earle County are found in eight locations, in a radius of between eight and twenty miles in all directions from Shade. One, fifteen miles southeast of Shade, makes 50 gallons with 100 gallons of mash. It is the fourth still in two years in this same hollow. Citizens complain that easily available moonshine is contributing to the corruption not only of local families but in particular of teen-age boys who roam the road and commit minor theft and burglary at night. There is also suspicion that some of the nineteen- to twenty-two-year-old boys are acting as dispensers—delivering the moonshine.

The still operator continually battles the wits of the "revenooers" or "feds" and, interestingly, he wins. He has friends while the revenue men have none, not even among the non-drinkers. "Hain't knowin' 'at feller. Hain't knowin' 'em feds, neither, 'ceptin' they's got no right snoopin'." I have seen self-respecting Branchers notify the still owner when federal men begin to inquire. In earlier days all that was required to be a "fed" was a "smellin' nose, seein' eyes, 'n' horse sense," but these assets do not necessarily ensure success today. It is true that the waste product, mash, has a distinctive odor. Arresting officers frequently make use of paths that the operators have created. But the paths are usually circuitous and allow the moonshiner plenty of time to get rid of the evidence. One successful producer boasted that "thirty years I hain't never had no lawin'. I's makin' sure my pathin' takes 'em acrosst 'at mount'in." Every still operator has a lookout and once he fires his gun at anyone approaching, the operator is long gone. One still I often visit has a man posted high in a tree on top of the mountain. There is a non-functional television aerial in the top of the tree; he gently pulls the booster cable and that slight tug tips over a can of water on top of the rock. As soon as the water drips onto the men at the still they leave out in a hurry.

Few federal agents know the system of the hollows. There are many identifying signs other than the permeating smell of the mash. Thin, straight wisps of smoke "headin' skyway" foam in the nearest stream bed, providing there is water in it. However, the old-time moonshiners, often called "shinners," are skilled at hiding evidence. One still I visit regularly siphons off the waste into a pipe which runs into a deserted mine shaft. One operator has mounted a stovepipe hundreds of feet underground from his still. The smoke goes the long route to escape. He has an old fan formerly used for ventilating the shaft of a mine hooked up to a portable generator on the back of an old truck parked a considerable distance away. When it is time, he just starts the fan disseminating the smoke before it can be seen. A lookout stays near the truck and if things look suspicious he shuts off the generator. This is the signal for all at the still to take off. Some still operators carry out bucket upon bucket of mash after dark and slop their hogs with it. These animals are sleek and fat, though they have difficulty walking on occasion. Women and children are often involved, but they too are "fox slyin'." They know that they cannot be charged with possession if officers don't have any evidence. One woman locks the door of her shack while her dozen or so children break the "evidence." The contents from half gallons "hit's runnin' 'twixt floorin' liken hit's Branch floodin'." One's status is always enhanced when the pursuants are all the local sheriff's force, "feds 'n' consibles." This means that one's operation is "worthin'."

It is hard to catch such knowing men. The officers very often know the location but cannot catch anyone operating the still; it is one thing to see backs and hear people running down the mountain but, as the Brancher says, it is taxing catching them. Some of the stills are ready to begin operation when the law finds them. The owner sometimes runs away before the officials destroy it. After the warrant for his arrest is issued they go back to serve it and pick him up. In such cases he is charged with possessing moonshine apparatus. If he pleads guilty, he may be fined $50 and costs. Usually the stills are small and are found in homes. A seven-gallon operation would produce about a gallon of moonshine at a time, most often for the owner's purpose. The number of stills is increasing, but they are becoming smaller and smaller operations. "Pop-up" stills result from what officials call "improved enforcement," but the real reasons are that small stills are just as profitable and are easier to conceal, move, and camouflage. Ray, an old hand at moonshining, said, "Long 's 'at stampin' [federal tax stamps] is a-hangin' on, 'em feds hain't got no say-so 'bout sellin'." The federal agents seem less interested in "red eye" because the tax has been paid. Resale is so prevalent that they devote little time to this, catching the man who sells brewery bottle liquor.

Christmas is a favorite time to raid and it is productive. In 1964, the sheriff's department, the state police, and the local constables confiscated thirty-five pints of whiskey from the grease room of a filling station, thirty-five cans of beer from a private home, and nearly two gallons of moonshine from another private home. There was persistent talk in the community that moonshine was being sold from the Hardstone post office and from the store, both located in the same building. Shortly after Christmas two federal agents, accompanied by two local officials, raided the place. A couple of hours before the raid, the owner of the store and his brother and two friends made several trips from the post office to a house about a mile back from the road where my jeep was parked. Each truckload of material was carefully covered so that the contents of the pickup truck could not be seen. The raiders were surprised to find no moonshine. Neighborhood gossip had it that the store owner had been warned by someone at the local level in enough time to remove the illegal liquor.

Isom and I sat on the side of the hill, having just returned from buying a quart of moonshine. I had provided the transportation and, as in so many instances, arrived at the source of the moonshine without the slightest indication that he did not have enough money to buy a quart. He asked me if I had and I told him that I'd make up the difference between what he had and what it cost, a matter of $1.50. Before getting it, the bootlegger looked at the car I was driving. Isom told him I was a friend and wasn't a "federal." He turned from the remarkably dirt-obscured window and wanted to know if I was the reporting type. I assured him that I was not and the sale was consummated. On the way back, Isom took a few nips to "clear out m' breathin'." When we got to a somewhat secluded place on the hilltop, off he went, leaving the moonshine with me. He came back with a reasonably clean half-gallon jar and poured the contents of the quart into the half gallon. Then he threw the quart jar against a rock on the hill high above our heads. It broke. He saved the two-piece top, putting it in his pocket and saying, "'Em's good fur tradin'." He offered me a swig. I declined, saying I had to go into town later but hoped that he wouldn't drink all that tonight.

"Reckon hit's how fast m' breathin's easier." Then he told me that he planned to offer some of the fellers a drink.

"But why the gallon? It's bigger and heavier."

"I hain't carryin' hit. 'Em fellers be comin' w'en they's seein' me hidin' out. They's thinkin' I's had money fur a big jar. Makin' 'em figger. They knows I's fox sly then."

Moonshining is a problem in urban areas too. The Ohio Liquor Department put a legal form of moonshine whiskey called "Georgia Moon" on the shelves of the liquor stores; its greatest asset was its conversation value, because it certainly had no taste appeal. Perhaps another reason it was rejected was because of price; a good quart of illegal moonshine costs $2.50, while a pint of the legal stuff costs about $2.35. I took my hollow friends some "Georgia Moon" and they spit it out. "Hain't fittin' fur innards liken my guts." They also resented the name. "They's should 'a never left hit outta 'at Georgie place," they'd choke. Furthermore, they resented the abbreviation. "If'n hit's fittin' moonshine, name hit."

In a recent county jail riot in Cincinnati, officials discovered that the inmates who worked at the task of baking two hundred loaves of bread were stealing the yeast and putting it in cans of fruit juice and brewing a finished product which could cause intoxication. That was the end of homemade bread in that jail.

Perhaps the two worlds are not as far apart as they appear.

VII

Of Vertical Fields and Pink Trees

'Tis education forms the common mind:
Just as the twig is bent the tree's inclined.

Alexander Pope
Moral Essays

The cyclical nature of poverty is forcibly demonstrated as the deprived of one generation establish conditions that perpetuate poverty in the next. In the field of education the warning is loud and clear: in the future (if not now), persons with less than an eighth-grade education will be classified as functional illiterates. Their children will likewise inherit this tag, not necessarily because of genetic reasons but because of cultural deprivation; the concept of fixed intelligence is steadily yielding to the concept that experiences are the most crucial determinant of a person's intellect.

Almost all of the Branchers have firmly entrenched attitudes toward education which they have derived from their rural background and experiences in the hollow. They think that the subjects their children are taught in school are not relevant and frequently disapprove of training beyond the compulsory age requirements even though the adult teenager may only have completed the seventh grade. "He's too big t' be with th' little kids," they defensively explain. Once in a while they express concern for a child's earning potential but see no connection between education and financial security. During my early months in the Branch I was misled by their protestations. "I hain't never had no schoolin', but I wants fur m' younguns t' go t' school." Yet day after day several children from one family would not attend. "W'en you's puny, you's hain't hankerin' t' stir. Don't reckon they's larnin' much nohow."

The lack of parental inspiration leads to irregular school attendance and the youngsters occupy their time by purposelessly wandering through the hills. Pupils from Duddie's Branch are absent from school approximately 26 per cent of the time. The child's whole pattern of life contributes to a pattern of educational failure. It is not uncommon for Branch children to be as many as three and a half grades behind more advantaged children of the same age. They may fail to live up to their potential in early grades for any number of reasons, but that very failure often pilots the way to a familiar development: they steadily slide further behind, get tagged as too witless to learn, and lose confidence in their ability to compete. As a result, they drop out of school and either do not cite a reason or supply the most quixotic excuse—one boy said he quit because he missed his hunting dog too much to concentrate.

Educational expectations for Branch children reveal sharp differences of opinion among parents, school personnel, and the pupils themselves. In any event educational expectations are grossly unrealistic. Many hollowers feel that girls particularly are wasting time in school. This opinion is shared by some in the outer community. Sometimes status damage causes them to derogate knowledge. "I cain't read th' first-grade book they gived me. Billy's in the third grade 'n' I axed 'im t' help me, but 'e cain't read, neither. Don't see much point in 'im bein' in th' third grade if'n 'e cain't read." Measurement tools, for whatever purpose, fail to determine the hollow child's potential with any degree of accuracy. The minimal achievement level necessary for hollow children to function in the future remains an enigma.

The low value students from the hollow place on academic achievement is portrayed by the haphazard manner in which they perform. In the "Happy Pappy" work program, Lester is constrained to attend school two nights a week. When he asked me to help him with his studies, I thought it might be useful to ascertain how much fundamental knowledge this middle-aged man possessed. What follows are representative moments.

"Lester, what is the alphabet?"

"Hain't heerd hit."

"Do you know your ABCs?"

"Reckon."

I tried to jog his memory. " 'A' is a letter."

"Reckon."

"What does 'letter' mean to you?"

"Hit's writin'," he answered.

"What is writing?"

"Hit's paper markin'."

I was getting nowhere fast. "Let's say each letter of the alphabet. I'll say the first letter and you say the second, and so on until we have said every letter. When we're finished, we will have said twenty-six letters." I began: "A."

"A," said Lester.

"No, you're supposed to say the letter that follows A."

"Twenty-six," he replied.

"Twenty-six is the total number of all of the letters in the alphabet. You're supposed to say B. Let's start again. The first letter in the alphabet is A."

Lester was alert. "Yep," he agreed.

I was cautious. "B," I proposed.

"B," he responded.

We went through the alphabet in that manner. It occurred to me that a fresh assignment might stimulate him.

"I'm going to write three words. You rewrite them alphabetically." I handed him a paper on which I had written: acorn, aunt, apron.

He wrote for a while and handed me his list. He had written:

A corn

A unt

A pron.

I repeated the instructions and gave him another list: horn, fern, iron. I was baffled when I saw his list:

Bhorn

Bfern

Biron

"Lester, I wanted you to write the words in alphabetical order. Which comes first—*h, f,* or *i?*"

"They all comes secont 'cause I started 'em all with B."

I was up against a logic that I could not defy—I couldn't even understand it. Perhaps, I thought, he is confused because of the different letters. I had better have him alphabetize words beginning with the same letter. I wrote: pear, pair, purse.

He wrote:

cpear

cpair

cpurse

"Okay, Lester, let's move on," I warily suggested, and handed him a list of words for which he was to supply contractions. The results looked like this:

Cannot = Dennot.

Does not = E does Not.

I am = fam.

You are = gyou are.

There is = Hthere is.

They are = I they are.

Do not = J do not.

We are = K We are.

You are = L yu are.

He explained his effort by telling me that he was trying to make the letters follow alphabetically. (Note: D, E, f, g, H, I, J, K, L.)

I told him what synonym and antonym meant, and asked him to supply another word opposite the words I had written. He did:

Synonyms		Antonyms	
Presents	= guive	Rude	= snoty
Group	= gathern	Stale	= spoild
Visitor	= pepel	Graceful	= you ful.

"How do you form the possessive tense for the words on this paper?"

This was how:

> John = passes.
> Man = Walkes.
> Girl = Singes.
> Men = workes.
> Fox = Bunes (bunnies).
> Girls = marry.
> Teachers = teaches.

Sharp pains began to shoot through my head. "Use 'baby's,' 'parents',' and 'Hank's' in a sentence," I rasped.

He complied. "The babey doill is goane. parents' Coming home Hank's Loves to fish."

I still had not had enough. "How about making sentences from these words I have written down?"

"Okay," he answered patiently.

> Rode = He Rade in the car.
> Has ridden = Bfore.
> Eat = Diner.
> Has eaten = to much.
> Ate = candy.
> Let's = have a Dance.
> Wasn't = take Long.
> Jack's = wint fishin to Day.
> Aren't = them piges pretty.

"Write the plural for 'donkey,'" I whispered.

"'At's easin'," he scoffed, and promptly wrote "Donkiles."

I have to get onto something else, I thought. Something simple. Punctuation, that's it. "Now, Lester, I want you to use dots [periods] and dots with tails [commas] in this letter I have written."

"I likes t' make dots," he cheerfully replied.

The results were interesting: "Dec 12:7:67. K.Y. Mrs. Betty· K. Bates is. in. New. York. She is. staying . at. the. St. Regis. Hotel.
,

N Y She. left New. York on Dec. 11 th. She' will. arrive. in. Shade. on. Jan. 2 . 1968,"

I looked for a long time at the periods and commas that were hanging in mid-air. "Lester, when are you supposed to use punctuation and where is it supposed to go?"

"Any time you's hankerin' to you's puts 'em jist anywhar."

"Now, use 'elected,' 'explorer,' 'sly,' 'loyal,' 'president,' 'displease,' 'unhappy,' and 'pledge' in sentences."

He wrote:

> Elected = Mr. John Jones Wase Elixt. I gees.
> Explorer = Jane James Expoled the Kentucky Rifer.
> Sly = Wise Fox Wase sliy.
> Loyal = Frind Kind.
> President = Johson is or present dient.
> Displease = She Wase displease with harse.
> Unhappy = Lost his frind.
> Pledge = Love Truth True.

I asked him to rewrite this paragraph and arrange the sentences in proper order: "Toads and frogs both go to sleep in winter. Then they go to the water again to lay eggs. They find nice beds in the mud. They stay in the mud until soft spring breezes call them out. Soon many little tadpoles can be seen swimming about."

His paragraph read: "The frogs Hiperat on the Winter time The frogs Lae at Sprong times. Tho can be seen Swimming on the ponds and Rifers."

I retreated toward home. The next day I helped him with his homework. The instructions read: "Classify the words given below by putting things that are alike in some way into groups. The words are to be alphabetized in each group: hat, turnips, shoes, rain, lemonade, spinach, hail, cabbage, snow, milk, orange juice."

Lester's reproduction:

Tur nips	below	Spinach	orange
class ify	cabbages	Snow	tangereny
hat hail	carrotes	white	I uses Teas

His reasoning was so simple that it took me awhile to understand what he had done. The word "classify" was not listed, but he used it anyway—he had seen it in the instructions and liked the way it looked. He wrote "hat" and "hail" on the same line because they both began with the letter *h*. "Below" was also taken from the instructions. "Carrotes" was not listed either, but Lester's wife never cooks cabbage without carrots. Nor was "white" listed, but it goes so naturally with "snow" that he could not resist including it. He dropped "juice" from "orange" and added "tangereny"—oranges and tangerines, another natural association. "Orange juice," "milk," and "lemonade" he omitted altogether because, as he explained, "I uses Teas." I wondered whether the teacher would fail him for not alphabetizing.

In the next lesson he was asked to write a story about a picnic. "Mr. Jabe Shifter an I wint on a picnic We went to Wiff cunty and had a Sweel time We seen the Sky Brige an the Natle Brige." Lester has never been to Wolfe County and he has never seen the Natural Bridge which, incidentally, is located in Powell County. But I was impressed with his spelling.

An example of the limitations of the Branchers' vocabulary was graphically demonstrated when the next lesson called for homonyms. To them, a word means one thing and one thing only. An eye, for instance, is always found in the human head, never in a needle. That, of course, is "th' threadin' end."

Show = I shu him my horse, I shu him my puppy.
Have = I hve a right arm, I have nother arm.
Play = I play with my tome cat I. plays with my boys.
View = I got a good view at my house I got. a good view at the plane.
Safe = I wase safe when I wase at home.

"Safe" taxed him—he could not come up with another sentence.

In the next lesson, he was to use "planet," "forecast," "cargo," "voyage," and "concert" in such a way that the sentences would show their meanings. Lester wrote:

Planet = earth.
Forecast = wather.
Cargo = ships.
Voyage = die young.
Concert = band.

"Voyage" mystified me, but I am certain he had a perfectly good reason for writing "die young."

Filling in blanks is not difficult for him because he completely ignores instructions. In the following list, he was to indicate where he would seek information on the topics given:

The capital of your state = Framk ford.
The pronunciation of a word = Sound.
A radio or television schedule = Be casen [Ben Casey].
A weather forecast for today = Snow.
A science story = Race to th Moone.
The movie schedule for this week = D.CK Tracy.
The location of the equator = 400 Derfree South.
A sale on sweaters = he bid hi then I did.

The next lesson: "When *a* is followed by *l* or *w* in a word or a syllable containing only one vowel, the sound of *a* is usually neither long nor short. Make a list of words to show that this statement is true." Lester's proof: "Anony, anothen, anoty, abot, abel, above."

He was then asked to write some words with the sound of hard *g* and the sound of soft *g*. He rubbed his finger across the paper. "They feels th' same t' me."

"Oh, never mind, Lester. Get on with it."

"Okay," he said. And wrote: "fight, group, grape, long, flotting, flage."

He wrote a stanza of a poem he had memorized:

tenty froges Went to school
down be Side the Rushen
poole one day farther frog
cauld out to the Boys to

tell them to qite throing rock
at them hi fun to you But
Dase for us.

When asked what certain words suggested to him, his imagination was hard to stir:

The Star-Spangled Banner = Flag of the V.S.A.
A birthday party = at June 10. [his birthday].
Thanksgiving Day = Mo. 24. 66.
My state flag = V.S.A.
Wild flowers on the hill = Wild flowers on the hill.

Another set of instructions read: "Write the word or words that you might use in the place of the word that is underlined":

The Indian saw the *sly* fox coming = Fox Wase sly.
"Look," said the bear, "I have lost my *beautiful* tail = Wandeful.
Mountain Lady ate something *daily* = Suger.
The *wicked* people made fun of Noah = and godley.
Noah *trusted* in God = yes.
"Let's make a *pledge* of friendship," said Joe = I oned Hanes [joined hands].
Noah built a great *ark* = bot.

Next he was asked to write a sentence telling something the fox did which showed that he was sly. "Plad dead and full the indinans."
After that he was to choose a substitute for the underlined words:

An Indian *brave* was on his way home = School.
A *sly* fox saw the Indian brave = fish.
The fox was *creeping* along over the snow = Woods.
Quick as a flash the fox *darted* into the wood = D.
The fish smelled very *pleasant,* too = the fox.
It was the bear's own *fault* that he lost his tail = yes.

In his own words he wrote these sentences to explain how boys sealed their pledge of friendship, as he understood the story: "the picked blood out of hands and casket tham to gather Mingle the blood to gather frinds for Every."

He was to divide the underlined word in the following sentence into syllables: "The word *especially* means chiefly." Lester wrote, "Fudge."

That jolted me. I stared. I thought. I gave up. "Why, Lester? Why fudge?" I implored.

"I likes lots 'a candies, but I 'specially likes fudge," he illuminated. I sighed.

What is the answer for the hollow child who is reared in such a barren climate? Although the necessity to destroy the poverty cycle has brought the role of education into sharp focus, little progress has been made in identifying potential in culturally deprived children—too much rationalization clouds the issue of selecting and sorting. But if monkeys can be appraised with accuracy, the time will surely arrive when appropriate techniques will be developed for use in humans. How can we justify putting a man on the moon, with its implicit scientific accomplishments, and falter when it comes to devising evaluative guides for our children—particularly when society's expectations toward learning have become so demanding? At the beginning of this century a grade school education was considered adequate for most people. By the 1940s a high school diploma was a necessity. Now, college-level training is the national goal; moreover, a master's degree today has about as much value as a bachelor's degree had a decade ago.

But social expectations to not filter to isolated hollows. What, then, will become of the children from Duddie's Branch?

Unless they avail themselves of the educational facilities at their disposal, they will become grist for the hollow mill that relentlessly grinds out incapacitated adults with proliferated needs for financial aid. No matter how deficient the present school system might be, it is their only means of reversing the trend and it must be fully utilized before its inadequacies can be judged and rectified.

But then come the angry parents who stoutly resist a school

system in which their children are throttled by poorly motivated classmates. And who can fault them? Students with a poor attitude toward learning are incapable of stimulating an appropriate academic atmosphere, no matter how gifted an instructor might be—a remote possibility in Kentucky. In 1967–68, the Earle County school system consisted of 31 schools in which 5,602 pupils were enrolled. Two hundred and two teachers were given the job of educating all who came to school.

What about state-supported schools? Is it unrealistic to expect the state to assume the responsibility of training questionably educable children for independent citizenship? It is. The underfinanced organism, which supplies only $475 per pupil annually (as compared with the national average of $623 in 1967–68), is not equal to this task. Kentucky, which ranks twenty-second among all states in total revenue, spends over $200 million less for education than the average state. A Brancher supplied the explanation: "They's got too many fellers in th' statehouse bein' paid too much fur workin' too little. They took all 'a our gas tax money t' build 'em pay-fur-ridin'-on roads [toll roads], 'n' 'em fellers [from out of state] either hain't ridin' 'r hain't payin', fur I hears they's plum busted."

The Earle County school superintendent is often under fire, but she is an unusually capable administrator. Evidence of her progressive leadership is manifested in the ever increasing number of consolidated school buildings. Her fiscal policies—the primary one, having the school district solvent at all times and funds available to use for expanding development—are often criticized by other counties and by other authorities. She is held in high esteem by the hollower, who admires her ability to resist outside pressures. Her willingness to accept them and to listen are two traits that rate high on the hollow fellow's list of expectations. He doesn't belong to the P.T.A., he knows nothing about the Lunch Room Committee, he cannot evaluate the quality of the school curriculum, but she is "one 'a our'n long's she puts 'em outsiders back a-goin'."

Very few seem to disagree with the view that education is the key to personal fulfillment. How best to provide educational experiences and identify the real educational aspirations, however, provoke much discussion and terminate in disagreement. A great number of parents, teachers, and administrators feel that the complex social problems of today place responsibility upon the schools to provide understanding, competence, and skill. To accomplish this through programs and instruction, all concerned must understand the American way of life—find solutions to challenge all students.

Who really has the answer for all children like those in Duddie's Branch? How do you help these children face an uncertain future? Some say their parents turn their backs on change. How can they when they are so little a part of the community in which they have lived for so long? These parents still face an uncertain future, yet somehow within this rapidly changing world they have managed to find meaning for their lives; they have to the best of their ability attacked their problems. Is there just one American way of life? If an enriched environment is necessary for the preschool children, how is this to be accomplished in Duddie's Branch? These children look and listen to what goes on around them at home in the Branch and they talk too. Unfortunately, their early language growth, measured by outside standards, is not the "mouthin'" which meets the minimum demands to be productive in an organized school program.

We must bear in mind that these children do not know their numbers or letters when they begin their first school experience at whatever age. Is the teacher to blame when there is an absence of a foundation on which to build? Is it fair to blame the school system and say that schools generally are poor? A teacher in a private school said, "Problem solving is a very vital part of our plans for each grade level from the very beginning."

I asked fourteen-year-old Ben, a sixth-grade student, for his views on problem solving. He hung his head and squirmed and twisted the worn-out toe of his shoe in the dust. I waited and squirmed and twisted the toe of my shoe in the dust. At last he spoke. "Reckon I's hain't got no problems t' worry."

If Ben has not, the teachers have. It is not easy to teach students from a poor cultural background with low academic aptitude and little intellectual curiosity, but teachers everywhere have an academic obligation to help all students gain a degree of intellectual life at their own level and on their own terms. Strong protests have been registered against providing individual attention for children who have less than average ability. Resources are limited, it is true, but more time and effort should be centered on stimulating intellectual motivation in the less responsive student who undoubtedly would benefit from special guidance.

I would be the last to subscribe to letting the mediocre student blunder through social promotion until he reaches the age when school is no longer required by law. If we are to adopt this practice, then there is nothing for the poorly educated to do but withdraw to their humble surroundings from which they cannot escape with their limited capabilities. This is indeed a tacit invitation for many schoolteachers to view hollow children with contempt. These children then will be denied the opportunities they deserve.

Students with obviously limited ability, for whatever reasons, are full of disappointments, and learning will be a struggle. Teaching them will be a real accomplishment. Children coming from Duddie's Branch are easily distracted, have few interests, are typically immature, and even crude.

"Why do you teach school?" I asked a teacher who had a number of Branch students in her room. "Same as you—I get paid to do it. I don't intend to spend any extra time with those dirty, ill-mannered, impolite kids, though." "You don't know them," I defended. "I know that they're almost uncivilized," she retorted. "But you are unfamiliar with the life they live and the real difficulties they encounter to get to school at all." "You can't tell me anything I don't know already. I grew up in this county." She had, but her parents were well off as the county goes. She never wanted for anything. "These kids are lazy and indifferent," she continued. "We've got just so many books to read during a school year, and if one of those kids who doesn't know words, or can't say them if he does, gets up to read, all of our time is gone. We'd never get through a book a year."

Dismayed by this teacher's contribution to the continuing enfeeblement of the children from Duddie's Branch, I suggested that she spend a night bedded down in one of the homes and try to sleep. I assured her, on the basis of my own experience, that it was not very comfortable to sleep fully clothed in a crowded bed. I also reminded her that itching and turning to scratch bedbug bites were incompatible with restful sleep. The more I illustrated the realities of the life of these children, the more certain I became that I would only increase the social distance, if this were possible, and in the final analysis would not alter her thinking or behavior toward them. Her attitude is typical of the many who demonstrate ignorance or indifference regarding the effects of life in a poverty setting. Some of the children become discouraged even though their efforts measure up to minimum standards. The teacher asks, "Why are you coming? You aren't learning anything." Few understand or are interested in the problems the child faces in his home, nor do they realize that the results of many of these problems carry over into his efforts as he attempts to participate in school activities. He may be unable to withstand the criticism leveled at him by dropouts because he is going to school. If his parents are motivated to send him to school, he still has to counteract the influence of those who have never attended or who have had a very limited, usually unsuccessful school experience. If a teacher thinks the student is stupid, his classroom performance will be low. He can only respond to teachers who like him, who believe in him.

In defense of the teachers, they have only a certain number of hours a week to work with the children and they must use rigid lesson plans that often do not meet student needs. In addition, teachers are equipped with few instructional materials, and they often fail to receive the support of the principals.

Until we can validate and measure inborn handicaps, children who have been slapped by cultural deprivation cannot be classed as slow learners. Hundreds of school systems have had long experience in educating the physically handicapped, but poverty as a way of life leaves environmental wounds which respond slowly, if at all, to stereotype teaching and cut-and-dried curricula. We know that retardation resulting from a life of poverty creates a wide range of social and economic handicaps. Studies have yet to show the damaging effects of inadequate nutrition, love, shelter, ideas, and experiences. Grade placement with classmates who have greater educational potential creates an almost insurmountable obstacle for hollow children who cannot write their names, who have never seen a picture book, who have never heard a fairy tale. In many of the school settings there is no such thing as catching up with contemporaries. Should we introduce the classroom to these children who do not feel at home with books? who cannot understand or be understood? who cannot express their emotional problems? who cannot even tie their shoelaces? What does a teacher do with thirty children who have similar but different needs when they enter the consolidated school?

Conditions are not much different today from what Sherman and Henry[1] reported more than thirty-five years ago: ". . . The teacher was faced with an obstacle very difficult to surmount—dullness of the senses. Concentration of attention seemed too much of a physical effort for these children who never had known the discipline of this kind. . . . But at first the children sit in school as if asleep or drugged. Their senses have never been trained to pay attention. An effort to do so seems to have a hypnotic effect, until they become adjusted. . . ."

The most dedicated of teachers will be frustrated by the raw material that comes to him from Duddie's Branch, for it is unimaginative, uninspired, uninspiring, and unsophisticated. Asked to draw a field planted with corn, children from Duddie's Branch drew vertical fields. The only gardens they have ever seen are mountainside plots; flat land for horizontal planting and growing is not available. The paucity of experiences is glaringly revealed in their misspelled, ungrammatical, almost illegible narratives.

6th grade, age 11. "STORY OF MY LIFE. I have passed every year since I have been coming to school. I have one sister and 6 brothers. I have five brothers married and one sister married."

In an earlier narrative this child had written: "I did not like school when I first started. I did not get any whippin's the first year I went to school. I got two whippin's the second year I went."

5th grade, age 12. "MY LIFE STORY. One upon a time my brother and I went on a trip on our way we see a Black Cat it took after us we went down the hill run hard as we could and we went on home."

5th grade, age 12. "MY LIFE STORY. Once when I was young. I tried to make a sled. Well I started and I tried to make a good one.

[1] Mandel Sherman and Thomas R. Henry, *Hollow Folk* (New York: Thomas Y. Crowell Company, 1933), p. 114.

My father showed me how to make it and he helped me some. So when we got it finished it looked so good I had to try it once down the hill. I got it up the hill and it went so smooth after that we all rode on it every winter. They said I was good at making sleds. I made some more for my friends and they liked them too."

5th grade, age 11. "AUTOBIOGRAPHICAL STORY OF MY LIFE. I am 11 years old, I have 2 brothers and four sisters and their names are Herman Gilbert, Alex Zeb Gilbert, Eula Gilbert, Flora Gilbert, Gleneva Gilbert, and Retha Gilbert. My parents are Lias and Nicie Gilbert. When I grow up and get out of college I want to be a teacher."

4th grade, age 11. "Once I went to store, I got scaret. One night I walked to hunting, one day I wint to a poke hunting."

4th grade, age 14. "Once my sister and I wanting to go fishing and mother won't let us. We began to cry and mother said if we didn't stop we [she] would patty [paddle] us. Then I told Daddy if we could go he said if mother would let us we could go. Then I told mother again. She said if we would be chreful we could go. We starting and got half way there and asked a friend to go with us. She said that she had to wash the dishing. When we got there we got a pole and put it in the water that [but] we diding catch a fish. When we got home mother asked us did we catch a fish. We said no."

4th grade, age 11. "MY PUPPY. Sometimes me and my friend play ball then the dog run away with the ball. I get the ball from the dog put the home one morning me and the dog went get some boys to play with me and the dog they run away from me we went to get him to play with me I run I see one boy hide behind in a tree they see me and they run away the dog went home and me and my dog went home too."

4th grade, age 11. "MY PUPPY. Once I had a puppy. It followed me everywhere I went. Then one day my aunt and grandma came in. We had some chickens. Daddy tried to kill one for dinner. The dog was right beside the chicken. Daddy shot the dog. I cried because he killed my dog. But he could'nt help it. He said he would get me another one but I didn't want another one. I have a dog right now that follows me everywhere I go. Then one morning I was going to school and I didn't see it following me. When I got down the road where the bus was I never saw it then. When the bus came I started on the bus and I saw it. I whipped it, put it back to the house. It never followed me again after I whipped it."

4th grade, age 13. "TWO PAIRS. Once upon a time there was a man and a woman, a girl and a boy, the girls name was Susan. Her mother sent her to the store to get to [two] pairs [of shoes]. Her mother said she had better have two pairs when she gets back. When the little girl got to the store she met another little girl. She asked the girl to go home with her. The girl said she couldn't go. Susan said if you will go home with me I would give you a pairs. She said she would have to ask her mother. Susan said let's go and ask your mother then. Susan gave the girl a pairs. When she got the little girl to the little girl's house Susan stayed outside til she asked her mother. Susan stayed outside for a long time so she through [thought] she would haller at her. So she hallered and hallered. No body would answer. She throught she would go home. When she got home her mother said I thought I told you to get two pairs. Susan said I did but I gave one away to the girl to come home with me but she wouldn't come. The woman was mean. She told Susan to go get the nife. Susan said no you are going to cut my head off. The woman said I am just going to cut one curl of your hair. Susan said no your going to cut my head off. Mother said I'm just going to cut off one curl. Susan went and got the ax. Susan layed her head down and the woman chopped her head off and threw her head out in the yeard. One day her father went to pick some flowers. He heard the girl say dear daddy dear daddy don't pull my hair. Mother killed me over one single pair. The boy went to pick some flowers the girl said dear brother dear brother don't pull my hair. Mother killed me over a single pair. One single pair. The mother went to pick some flowers the girl said dear deveil dear devil don't pull my hair you killed me over one single pairs."

The instructions for the third-grade narrative read: " 'I Pledge Allegiance' from memory."

3rd grade, age 10. "My cat is pertty. My cat is white. I love my little cat. Rund [ran] down to the house my cat up on the house. I like my little white cat. I love my cat so good. She is pertty as a ball. I love my little cat. My cat is pertty. I like my cat. I love my cat."

3rd grade, age 12. "My dog is Noes is short and scrubby, his ears hang rather low and he always bring the stick back no matter how far you throw. He gets spanked rather oftehn for things he shouldn't do like lieing on beds and barking. And eating up shoes when they are new."

3rd grade, age 11. "Once upon a time there was an old man. He lived in a little house upon a hill. One day he went hunting and found a pet rabbit. He named it Long Ears because it had long ears. One day he said to the rabbit go and get me something to eat. The rabbit went to get something to eat and when he came back the old man was gone and he went to find him. When the rabbit found him he was in a house. The rabbit said to the man now will you give me something to eat. The man gave the rabbit something to eat and he eat it and that be the end of the pet rabbit."

3rd grade, age 8. "Kitten is name Mitten. He is a good kitten. He like mild [milk]. When the [he] eats the mild I give a tring [string] and pull it. Throw the house and he runs aspeer [after] it. I have a borther whose name is Hank. He lays in the baby bed. He jump up and down. He gets the string and shakes and runs after it and Hink laughs and laughs at my mittens. At supper mother has to feed him and at night he cries and mother gives him his bottle."

3rd grade, age 12. "MY FROG. His name is spot. His hat fit him. He can jump and talk. He run, jump and write. He spells words. My frog is pretty. Afternoon my frog play too. The next morning he eat. He cannot play in the back yarn. My frog push the wagon. He word [wore] his little cap."

I met with a group of five urban teachers on a planned basis for a year, trying to help them understand the problems of children who moved to the city setting from all over Appalachia. They were convinced that from the beginning of time all human beings have been involved in the arts—the arts are expressive of hopes and aspirations; the arts are deeply rooted in all human experience; the arts affect and enrich human life; the arts enable the individual to understand himself and his culture.

I took them to Duddie's Branch and they discussed their plans on the way down: they would seek out all the environmental opportunities for cultural enrichment; within two days they would understand the cultural life of the children in this hollow. Two days later our return trip was made in silence.

In my many meetings with the teachers before they went into the hollow, they had all thought that every pupil during his early school life should learn about the history of the United States. He should also learn about its heroes, economy, accomplishments, leadership. With this background the pupil would appreciate his rich heritage as an American, learn and understand his duties and responsibilities as a citizen in a free country, know how to fit into the American way of life and society, and grow in his ability to appreciate and work with other people not of his own "cultural heritage."

When we got back from the Branch, they decided that they would like to think about the experience and that when we met next we would discuss the "field trip." The one planned meeting extended to ten. In the course of the meetings they agreed that the people in the hollow were delightful, friendly, hospitable, and generous; the children had charm; the experience was shocking to the teachers.

In our last session they, as teachers of these children, had no solution for: the school's share of the responsibility with the home; how to help the pupil develop the habits, attitudes, and understandings required to "fit" into the outer world of an urban setting (not even the inner world of a rural setting); expectations based on grade levels; expectations based on various areas of instruction; how a teacher can develop self-reliance, self-discipline, acceptance of the consequences of one's behavior, respect for life and property, judgment in making decisions, wise use of leisure time, learning from parents' good attitudes and good habits, family needs, budgeting for necessities, inspiration, purposeful effort, significance of the Edisons and the Wrights, need to improve and utilize health services, problem-centered education, communication (telephone, radio, television, the "hot line," expressways, air freight). The list they prepared went on and on.

They concluded that they would like to go back again, and asked how much can be expected of teachers who are defeated before they start; how will these pupils discover knowledge; how will these pupils ever understand the world of work; the dynamic force of American culture, fresh concrete, smokestacks, skyscrapers, fine arts, professions, goods and services, ways by which the individual obtains status in a group and at work, ways in which the individual avoids tension, boredom, becoming a "misfit."

One of the teachers said, "When I was in graduate school I learned that the greatest motivating force in any society, including America, was the culture, particularly past and present. Just look at America. Immigrants came into our country; we have the highest standards of living in the world—electronics, automation. All of this is a part of every American today." I waited silently. "How can you unlock the doors at the mouth of the hollows?"

"I don't have the answer. In fact, I don't think I'm even close," I replied. "Our twentieth-century society has virtually eliminated unskilled jobs. New jobs have been created, but these demand academic and technical preparation which result in confusion, frustration, and disappointment to millions who seek employment."

We spent four sessions attempting to define the functional illiterate, basic education, youths and adults without the necessary tools to establish themselves successfully in a rapidly changing economic and social world of today—forgoing tomorrow. Invariably we came back to, "But every single human being *must* have his place in society." Getting beyond the "talking phase" into "solutions," however, was impossible. While some envied the challenge of the rural schoolteacher, none was willing to change places and try her hand at meeting the challenge. Nonetheless, they all concurred that the teacher in the rural area struggling with the children from Duddie's Branch should be able to bring the functional illiterate to a point where he could climb the rungs of the ladder to reach the maximum of his individual potential in technical vocational skills, graduate from high school, and cope with the changing job requirements, even at the first rung of the economic ladder. A young and enthusiastic teacher said, "We can eliminate poverty through education, and give every individual a chance to live in decency and dignity." Yet she could not come up with a 1-2-3-4 plan on how to go about providing a job, human relations skills, and intellectual, emotional, physical, and social development for the child who might aspire to success beyond the hollow. By now it was certainly evident to them that none would be dealing with the college-bound students eligible for advanced placement programs or with pupils whose examinations revealed evidence of superior achievement.

"How can you enrich something which is not there?" they asked. "Instead of devoting my efforts to meet the challenge of change, if I were a teacher in one of those rural schools, I would try to meet the challenge of the present where the mind of the human beings, delightful as they are, have lived a lifetime out of tune with new information, new situations, and basic fundamental skills of communication. Any individual without basic skills will find himself in a world where his personal assets are inadequate for minimum functioning and he will be at the zero minus 40 point in our space age with his inability to meet unknown situations."

Finally I asked, "What would you do if you were, at your age, a hollow dweller?"

"I would stay there and avoid the outer world."

Although some teachers have a little understanding of the nature and type of problems the Duddie's Branch pupils face, we must not expect the impossible of them. If one has not spent a great deal of time with these children in their homes around the clock, one cannot realize the distance between where they are and where they need to go in terms of learning. Even so, the teachers do a remarkable job.

Urban environments have a wealth of resources, interesting and educational. Field trips provide rich, firsthand information. They offer excellent opportunities to broaden the experiences of the pupil and to extend learning beyond the classroom. But the teacher in a rural area has no opportunity for a field trip—a walk in another neighborhood, an excursion to a park, a museum, a local industry, a research laboratory, or a university. Films, which they use in abundance, are poor substitutes for direct observation, feeling, touching, hearing, smelling.

During the long winter evenings in Duddie's Branch, I would engage the children in drawing. In some of the homes even the parents would color; if they did not join us, most would at least watch. After settling ourselves on the floor, I would bring out paper, pictures, and a box of crayons. Each child would color one of every drawing I had made. One of my representations consisted of what I considered to be an unpretentious tree, but it produced a Pavlovian response in the group; whenever I presented the drawing, everyone would automatically reach for a red or orange crayon and promptly render the leafy limbs a sanguine hue. Only Tressie did not conform, and I gradually became indignant.

"Tressie," I finally said, "I have never seen a pink tree. I would be pleasured if you would show me one tomorrow."

The next day we all hiked through the hills, every child in search of a tree that corresponded to the one he had colored. We never found a pink one (or a red or orange one, for that matter).

"I haven't seen that pink tree yet, Tressie," I said smugly.

"Reckon hit's yander."

"Do you mean on that far mountain?"

"Reckon, if'n hit hain't hyur."

I was satisfied that she would now reject the outrageous pink tree-tops for the more conventional orange and red.

This game occupied many long winter evenings over the years. Another of my drawings was a reasonably accurate representation of a dog, howbeit he was endowed with only one leg and no tail, eyes, or ears. Before the children began coloring, I would tell them, "That looks like a dog to me. Your dog." No one protested. Occasionally one of the artists would favor him with another leg, sometimes two, and now and again a four-legged canine emerged. But this was rare. From time to time, someone would add a tail or an ear or an eye; for the most part, however, they ignored details and restricted their activities to just coloring.

I requested Willis to draw a tree. He began with the limbs and started so close to the top edge of the paper that the branches appeared to have a crew cut.

"Why didn't you draw the trunk first?" I wanted to know.

"If'n you's too sorry t' turn over th' paper," he tartly replied, "reckon you's hain't gonna be seein' no tree."

He had continued the picture on the reverse side of the paper.

At first I was equipped with eight shades of crayons, but gradually increased the numbers to twelve and finally to twenty-four. While one child was coloring, the others would be selecting the crayons they wanted. I began by limiting each person to two colors, hoping to go on to three, four, etc. But even though they were instructed to eliminate all colors but two, my arithmetic teaching failed and their color perception in appropriateness never improved.

None of the children was interested in books unless they contained pictures. I sat on a rock with nine-year-old Katchern, who was looking at a book I had given her. She was holding it upside down, carelessly flipping the pages, when she came to a picture of a dog. She peered at it intently.

"'At thar dog's walker's is stickin' sky-way," she advised after five minutes of earnest scrutiny.

I turned the book around without uttering a word.

She re-examined it minutely and, obviously relieved, said, "Reckon he kin take off now."

The tale concerned a lonesome dog who went to visit another dog. After I finished reading the story to her, I said, "Guess he was glad to find his friend at home."

"Reckon," she responded unenthusiastically.

An art class teacher asked Al, a twelve-year-old, to draw a bird. His drawing consisted of a vertical oblong figure superimposed on a horizontal oblong figure.

"Th' teacher gived me low. Said I didn't have no eyes 'r legs on hit. I 'uz drawin' flyin'. Bet she's never seed no eyes 'r feets on flyin'."

"It kind of looks like an airplane to me," I suggested.

"Reckon. Long as hit's sumpun flyin' 'at's all 'at's matterin'."

Schools are designed and administered for the pupil of average ability, average motivation, and average home background. That cancels out the hollow child. Branch parents possess infectious ignorance. Reading and writing are the most they will expect their children to learn, and a little is considered ample. History, geography, literature—none of these has any value. Not even grammar. Most of the hollowers have a regional speech pattern that cannot be understood by their fellow Americans. They speak a kind of English which only vaguely resembles the standard variety we are accustomed to hearing. "Good talk," to them, means that there are no lies in what they are saying. Syntax, usage, pronunciation—these have no frame of reference: satsrite [that is right]; sitshern [it is hers]; tuthertime [at some other time]. "Done gone" has so many meanings that it cannot be taken out of context for definition.

I recorded the conversation of a sixteen-year-old boy on a tape recorder, and we listened to the playback. He was inordinately pleased. " 'At shore 'nuf hain't me mouthin', air hit?"

The hollow student would have to become bilingual if he learned to talk as we do and understand what we are saying because he would still have to retain the old speech patterns in order to communicate with his own kin.

The merits of tranferring ghetto or hollow children to schools in neighborhoods where the student body is primarily from the middle and upper economic strata of society are debatable. The child who has known deprivation from birth and is placed in the mainstream of an educational program which challenges even students from the middle class cannot help but sustain damaging, long-lasting effects as a result of the experience. Even the one-room rural schoolhouse is preferable to abrupt change. Children manifest self-reliance there and are more independent. They not only learn respect for one another, they have a very deep pride in their accomplishments and in their school. Consolidated schools destroy their self-confidence. They look different from their classmates, they smell different, whatever independence they may have had prior to this experience disappears, and any pride in successful accomplishment is hard to maintain in the new setting. They are unable to earn the grades they need to participate in athletic activities; and music, art, and other cultural accomplishments which require skill put them in the outer group.

You wonder how the hollow child knows that he is lacking and what it means to him. He tells you, "Thar's 'em 'n' thar's tuthers." "Tuthers" are the ones always sitting nearest the front. They always do the reading aloud, write on the blackboard, answer questions. Hollow children cannot even volunteer for such simple duties as distributing mimeographed announcements to different rooms, for this involves counting out the number of copies listed on tho guide sheet for each class. Herman, a third-grade student at thirteen years of age, was nonetheless eager to pass out notices. Because of his difficulty in counting beyond ten, I helped him. The first room was to be supplied with thirty copies. Before we collated the sheets, I asked him some elementary arithmetic problems.

"Herman, if you count out ten papers for one pile and then count out ten more papers for another pile, how many papers would you have?"

"Reckon a heap."

"But add ten and ten and what do you have?"

"Reckon two tens."

"Two tens equal how many?"

Silence.

"Add two and two. What do you have?"

"Four," he answered.

"Good. Now add ten and ten. How many do you have?"

"Reckon four."

I surrendered to his logic and began counting the sheets aloud. He echoed each number, one through twenty-nine, as I assembled the stacks. Every so often I would deliberately skip numbers to see whether he was aware of the omission. He never was. Sometimes I would reverse the numerical order: twenty, twenty-five, twenty-three, twenty-two, twenty-four. Herman blissfully repeated each number as I said it, unconscious of the inaccurate sequence. I stopped counting at twenty-nine.

"Herman, do you think we have enough now?"

"Reckon."

"How many did we need?"

"Reckon I's hain't 'memberin'."

"How many did we count out?"

Pointing to the pile, he said, " 'Em thar."

During recess periods Herman plays basketball or the game of the day with the older boys. If a physical fitness program substitutes for recess on bad-weather days, he quietly sits on a pile of mats in the back of the gymnasium. I asked the physical education teacher why he was permitted to remain seated.

"He should be participating," he admitted, "but I haven't the heart to make a boy that's almost a man play with these little kids."

He is absent from school much of the time now because he is too big physically to use third-grade seats and desks and must sit in a regular straight-back chair; he doesn't like to have a different seating arrangement from his classmates. In a school year consisting of 177 days, his record shows 67 days' membership. But this does not mean that he was in school 67 days—he was charged with 42 absences and credited with having attended only 25 days. He is a drop-in instead of a dropout. His twelve-year-old sister, Ollie, also a third-grade student, has a similar record: 67 days' membership, having been absent 51 days and present 16. Another sister Ora is a third-grade student too. Her school membership was 95 days—present 18, absent 77. Their eight-year-old brother Seafle is in the first grade. In a school year of 177 days, his membership was 39 days. He was tardy every single one of those times, which meant that he missed the bus and had to walk all the way to school if his grandfather, who has an old car, did not drive him. His grandparents thought that he was too small to go to school. Age, they told me, meant nothing. "He's jist hain't growed 'nuf fur schoolin'." They frequently intercepted him as he passed their house to give him breakfast, fearful that he had been sent off without having eaten. If the weather were bad, they would keep him at their house all day.

Truancy is a deep-rooted problem reflecting a cultural attitude toward education, and this is difficult to change. The dropout is usually the end result of a pattern of absenteeism, and an accumulation of scattered absences is a real danger sign. However, children from homes such as Herman's are not encouraged to do better in school, or even to attend. Absenteeism is so common that the principal gives a silver dollar to every child who has a perfect attendance for one year, but most hollow parents do not reinforce the school's efforts.

While "sittin' spittin'," Gid and I talked about a high school education.

"Hain't saw but jist one feller head out," he declared. "They jist gived 'im a paper [diploma]. " 'Em younguns goin' ever' day, not

missin' none, gits a dollar. A dollar's better'n paper. If'n I's hankerin' fur a paper, I'd be a-cripplin' t' th' bus fur school."

I silently reflected that it was unnecessary to attend school to prepare for a job if there were no intent to work.

Girls tend to be absent less than the boys. During one school term
of 177 days (counting just those children who were given credit for
a school year) twenty-one girls had an average attendance of 158
days, with average days of absence at 17. Twelve boys had an
average attendance of 138, with average days of absence at 39.

During the year of 177 school days thirty-three children (twenty-
one girls and twelve boys) in the group were given credit for a full
school year. Four girls and one boy had a perfect attendance of 177
days. Three girls and four boys were in school, but were there so
seldom that they were taken off the record as having been in for a
year (these seven are not included in the thirty-three). There were
many children of school age who had not yet started and many had
terminated their educational pursuits before completing the eighth
grade.

No girl missed more than she attended, but two of the boys missed
more than they attended.

	Girls (21)		Boys (12)	
	No. of days	%	No. of days	%
Attended	3,350	57.50	1,655	28.41
Absent	352	6.04	469	8.05
		63.54		36.46

I wondered whether, if the habit of attending school on a more
regular basis were practiced for a while, it would lead to a permanent
routine, so I offered to drive the hollow students to school. I had
previously determined that the number of children who eventually
got to the mouth of the Branch was no more than my jeep station
wagon could carry. But I underestimated the attraction of the jeep
ride. I had to shuttle back and forth several times every morning in
order to accommodate the gang of kids clamoring for a ride. They
did not seem to mind riding the bus home and walking up the hollow
at the end of the day. After a long period of functioning as a trans-

portation agent, I announced that my service would be discontinued. For a few days thereafter I concealed myself in a place where I could check the number of students who came out to meet the bus. Although my experiment had not resulted in a 100 per cent school attendance, fewer than 10 per cent of those who rode with me every day attended school with regularity after I ceased hauling them. I concluded that apparently a stronger inducement than a silver dollar or a jeep ride was necessary to get the kids to school and to keep them there.

The lack of holding power in all grades suggests that we should perhaps concentrate our efforts on the drop-in, who ultimately becomes the dropout. Kentucky's rate of school dropouts is one of the highest in the United States. A survey by the National Education Association places the dropout figure for one group of the school population (ninth grade in 1962–63 to twelfth graders in 1965–66) in Kentucky at 34.9 per cent. This was the third highest figure in the study.

In *Resources and People in East Kentucky,* Bowman and Haynes write: "Kentucky is a laggard at the high school level, as at all others, but the drag of the under educated stands out more sharply than the low rates of high school completion. . . . Over the 40 years from 1910 to 1950 there were advances in virtually all states and the South no longer stood significantly apart from the rest of the country. However, Kentucky lagged, and in 1950 had by far the lowest attendance rate in the nation for children aged 7–13. . . . Unfortunately, the low eighth-grade completion rates were and still are in precisely those counties in which fertility rates continue high; large numbers of children are involved. . . . In Kentucky, and especially in East Kentucky, those who continue through high school are clearly a select group—at least in terms of motivations and parental backgrounds, if not in native ability."[2]

To those who say the dropout is just cheating himself, I say, "Rubbish!" He is cheating me, he is cheating you, he is cheating our children, he is cheating mankind. He becomes a sponge who soaks

[2] Mary Jean Bowman and W. Warren Haynes, *Resources and People in East Kentucky: Problems and Potentials of a Lagging Economy* (Baltimore: The Johns Hopkins Press, 1963), pp. 218, 220, 224, 240.

up welfare funds—a permanent yoke around society's neck. But the inclination to focus on the dropout leaves a huge bulk of elementary school children outside the broad classification. Many have never "dropped in" to school. Others have attended so irregularly that they become eventual push-outs, such as the "tardy-makers." I asked Layuna whether Penny was planning on staying home from school one day.

"Nope. Her's jist makin' tardy."

Penny is good at this; much of her "tardy-makin'" develops into frank absence at the slightest excuse, such as my being in the hollow.

Without sound data on which to base the conclusions, it is unfair to assume that lack of real learning ability is the cause of the dropout. The extent to which this lack of learning ability influences children and their decision to leave school is a missing dimension that needs careful investigation. As in many aspects of the life of the deprived, we cannot ascribe the cause to any one thing. We cannot indict schools and the programs, we cannot evict the children, we cannot point the finger of blame at the parents. The dropout is a symptom of a problem, not the problem itself. We will continue "wastin' shootin'" until we stop fragmenting effort and money by focusing on just one factor, such as dropouts, without doing anything about the ones who have never dropped in or the push-outs. It is absurd to subscribe to the proposition that dropouts are largely the responsibility of the schools and their educational programs. Only 14 per cent of childhood is spent in school. The remaining 86 per cent is spent under the influence of the home and the parents and the environment that patterns their living.

Year-round school training for hollow children, beginning at age four, might be the way to overcome the dropout pattern. Such a schedule would minimize the time for anti-school influences and maximize the learning time. Four- and five-year-old children might, under such circumstances, develop an entirely different attitude toward the building, the teachers, and education itself.

Most of the children have an unusually permissive relationship with their families—they are never driven or pushed into anything against their objections and they learn early to make their own decisions based on their own choices. This selective process and the outcome of their behavior seldom encompass assumption of much responsibility.

Fifteen-year-old Josha dropped out of school a few weeks after he entered the ninth grade.

"Josha, don't you like your teacher?" I asked.

"Hain't got nary teacher. Hit's jist who's standin' fur us. They's a heap standin' [a different instructor for each classroom]." He, like others before him, could not adjust to the variety of teachers, the size of the building, and the complex time schedule directing him to different rooms for each class. Locating the proper classroom was so difficult that he would leave school early if he did not find it within a few minutes. He soon lost all interest in even making an effort and his routine became one of going as far as the school but not reporting for class; he would just roam around where he would not be seen. Without the aid of a watch, though, he managed to get back in time to ride the bus to the mouth of the hollow at the close of the school day.

I was visiting his home the day he announced he was not going to school again. His parents could elicit no explanation from him. Nowadays he sleeps until noon, plays cards with his buddies until 3:00 P.M., and wanders aimlessly about the hollow after supper.

Jess, a fourth-grade dropout, is more voluble about his reasons. "Maw 'uz hankerin' t' draw w'en m' old man got hurt minin'. If'n I 'uzn't goin' t' schoolin' we couldn't git no draw. Figgered I'd not be hurtin' by goin'."

So at the age of ten he dropped into school for the first time. His attendance, needless to say, was irregular, and he could only be persuaded to return when "th' snoopin' feller from th' draw knowed I's layin' out."

He passed from the first grade on to the second, then the third, and finally "graduated" after having spent a few days in the fourth grade.

" 'Em teachers 'ud keep givin' me 'em books. Couldn't never read nary none 'a 'em. Right perty pitchers in 'em, but you's tire out jist lookin' at pitchers."

Now he is working on the "stick weed" gang and has second

thoughts about school. "Lookin' at pitchers hain't tirin' if'n they's payin' you's money fur hit."

Many welfare recipients, when threatened with being taken off the draw, will send their children to school. Their attendance is usually poor, but as long as they make an appearance one day a week they are not removed from the school roster. This drop-in method does little to educate the dropper-in, but it is virtually impossible for school officials to keep book on who is on welfare and who is not. Families who move from house to house in the hollow or who move near the highway during the winter months still utilize the same school system. It is different in the urban-suburban area, however; there you can move from one school district to another—your traces become blurred and you are usually a few steps ahead of the school records.

Edell Marse left Duddie's Branch to live in the Cincinnati slums, moved from there into an incorporated area just outside the city limits for about two months, and then returned to the city and stayed six months without ever having received a request to send her six children to school. She will not concede that the motive behind the moves was to escape "schoolin' 'em younguns," but that was precisely her purpose. Aspirations have decreased with the downward mobility of hollow families, and parents, siblings, kin—even friends— wield a strong detrimental influence on the children. This attitude, particularly among parents, negates any holding power the school may be able to exert.

Edell told me, "I 'uz jist gittin' too many writin's [notes] from 'em school fellers. They 'uz too many 'a 'em door-knockers afore a feller's stirred. Hain't 'spectin' [respectful]."

"Schoolin' younguns" is one thing, but "hawk-eye spyin'" is another. "If'n I's don't send m' younguns to school, I's bound t' git a note from th' principal. 'Bout that time, they's plannin' t' law me. I's leavin', busin' home faster'n a rabbit's runnin'. Hain't used t' 'em fellers hantin' me fur doin' my way." If the school officials back home pushed Edell too far, she could go the county judge; in the urban setting she knows no one who understands her problems, so she flees back to the hollow.

I was at her house in the slums one day when a school official came to check on her children.

"Are your children in school?" he wanted to know.

"I's hain't got no younguns."

He asked her name and she responded with a question: "Buddy, who's you's lookin' fur?"

"The Marse family."

"Reckon I's hain't mouthin' fur 'em."

"But this is the address on Ora's card."

"Hain't nothin' t' me."

Clearly, the man was distracted. "Do you have children?"

"Reckon."

"Are they in school?"

"Reckon."

"Are they at home now?"

"Reckon."

"Did they go to school this morning?"

"Reckon."

For thirty minutes he questioned her, and the only response he ever got was, "Reckon."

As soon as the man left, the children scurried from their hiding places.

"I'll bet he thought the only word you knew was 'reckon,'" I jested.

"Reckon," she replied.

Hollow parents are completely indifferent to the expanding demands for more formal and informal educational experiences. Not one child from Duddie's Branch has ever seen a sandbox. None has played with finger paints, puzzles, or blocks. Their "toys" consist of broken bottles, sharp metal, discarded tin cans. Ask them about Goldilocks, and they will look at you in bewilderment—they have never heard a fairy tale. I made a beanbag from an old rag and asked some of the older boys to catch it. They had difficulty. With an old string ball and a heavy stick, I tried to involve them in batting practice. I was unsuccessful. Not only do games fail to interest them, they are almost completely unable to participate in most activities. They could not be taught to whistle, sing, or even hum a simple tune. I wrote: 1111 2222 3--- --4- -55- on a sheet of paper and asked a number of eight-year-olds who had never been to school to fill in the missing numbers. They could not. Nor were they able to draw a circle, a square, raise their right arms, raise their left arms, extend their fingers, or spell their names. I showed them a series of pictures pasted on cardboard: cat, dog, raccoon, rabbit, otter, rat, squirrel.

"What are they?" I inquired.

"Reckon they's cats," they decided.

Their only learning experience is how to survive, and their instinct for self-preservation apparently blocks out anything they consider superfluous. They have, in their cramped living quarters, witnessed sexual activities, verbal battles, drunkenness and have developed a pattern of not responding to anything they feel is threatening or unrelated to their immediate needs. Surrounded by people with little or no education, they do not hunger for knowledge. They are swathed in a shroud of isolation and ignorance. Upon becoming young adults they are still imprisoned by the tangled threads which were spun around them in infancy.

For every 100 boys and girls in the first grade in Kentucky in 1948, only 32 graduated from high school in 1960; for every 100 in the eighth grade in 1954, only 48 graduated from high school four years later. It is no longer possible for hollow youth who leave school to find a job. This era has passed, and so the problems of employment are largely the problems of education. The post-industrial age calls for people who have a post-high school education—and with each passing year of upgraded requirements, the problems become more acute.

Sadly, educational programs fail to appeal to those most in need of them. These shy, unsmiling children shun school and have no way of relating their future to the amount of knowledge they acquire. They feel displaced and are confused in the academic environment. Each child is terrified of making a mistake, being reprimanded, or inciting laughter. They follow school routine to the best of their ability but are frequently so lost that they do not know when to listen or what kind of help they need or how to ask for it. The road from home to school leads nowhere. Still, it is illogical to recommend remedial education before our current system is utilized to find out what needs to be remedied. How else shall we know what kind of tutoring these children need? Or how much? Or when enrichment experiences should start? How are these to be provided? Who is going to help them with homework? With no light, no space, and no table, where are they to do homework? How are they to learn about other lands and other people when they do not even know about those beyond the mouth of the hollow? Their background is devoid of success experiences, their appetite for knowledge has never been stimulated, they cannot cope with academic pressures, they are restless, they are undisciplined, they are awed by the whole learning process.

Teachers complain that hollow children are always sleepy, that they can't seem to keep their eyes open. It's true—they are always sleepy. They scratch and roll all night long to relieve the itching of bedbug bites and sleep in their clothing for some protection against the bloodsucking insects. But sleeping in their clothing does not protect them against the menace of a barren environment.

VIII

Attitudes Toward Work

Work brings its own relief;
He who most idle is
Has most of grief.

Eugene Fitch Ware
Today

The environmental setting of the hollow not only shapes life day
to day, beginning in early infancy but its effects are broad-based, far-
reaching, and in most cases permanent. A most critical and specific
effect is the hollow's marked influence on chances for employment.
He would not fish if there were no water. He would not look for
honey if there were no trees. He would not look for "sang" in a
marsh. These *are,* however, the characteristic activities of a Duddie's
Brancher. The unique factor for the hollow man is that he must stay
where he grew up, and this limits his occupational learning and the
potential for his participation in the world of work. Only one man
in the entire hollow population ranks above the unskilled labor
category and he, at best, is just one notch elevated. Nobody will
pay the hollower the going minimum wage because he probably
would not get that much in productive work activity for the expenditure.

Incentive toward making a living on steep worn-out land has decreased. Hope diminishes with each year and with each generation.
Indifference toward farming has discouraged the most heroic efforts
for survival subsistence based on what the land will yield for the
effort involved. New land has for years and years been unavailable
in the hollow. Fields for tilling never did exist there. Even the most
energetic of the past generations could not clear enough land to
support a family or supply food and fodder for a family and stock.
The fertility of the soil in the hollow has always been questionable.
Vertical land space even with utilization of the best cultivation

practices is not profitable. Plow power, a couple of willing teen-agers instead of a mule, and tilling mountainsides of steep sterile soil prohibit the Brancher from competing for local market profits, regardless of how industrious he may be.

A number of Branch farmers were interested in a program to grow cucumbers for the market and talked to an agricultural agent about the feasibility of entering the cucumber-growing pool. They were crestfallen to learn that the cost of the seed and the manner in which the planting and tilling were to be handled was beyond them. I insisted that they return to the agent and request some help. They were told that the number of people participating in this venture was so overwhelming that it would be impossible to give them special attention. The agent also informed them that if the cucumbers did not measure up to market expectations they would receive no pay for them. Beyond the obstacles erected by the government, the Branchers had no way of transporting the cucumbers to the center (a fifteen-mile round trip) from which they were to be graded and shipped out daily. There were one or two trucks in the Branch, but the cost of hauling the cucumbers out each morning would eat up any profit the farmer might make.

The people need help, and they need it badly. The land does not lend itself to modernization and there is little opportunity for expansion of the sites the Brancher now uses for crops. If he is fortunate enough to have the weather on his side and can control the bug population, the soil yields only enough for immediate consumption most of the time. In addition to raising food for his table, he must also grow on the same poor land enough corn to fatten one or perhaps two pigs. If he has chickens, they must be fed from his land as well. As a result, surpluses are uncommon. In the unlikely event that there is enough food left over to preserve, his efforts generally fail because he either has no way to keep it from freezing or his canning methods are so unsanitary that the food spoils within a few days.

The labor factor and its cost in terms of sustenance are inestimable. It was time to plant potatoes. Melda gave Winn and Josha two dollars to buy a gunny sack of planting potatoes. The boys were small and thin, but they managed unaided to tug a hundred pounds of potatoes seven miles to the hollow, over the slippery rocks, and to the head of the Branch. Long days of fatiguing work had gone into preparing the soil; before the land could be hoed, the residue of leaves, weeds, and brush had to be cleared away by hand.

We sat on the porch and Melda cut the potatoes for planting; she quartered each, regardless of size. I wanted to find out how much she knew about the vegetable.

"What are those little dents?"

"They jist grows like 'at."

"Are those what they call 'eyes'?" I continued.

"Reckon they hain't," Melda replied.

Winny snickered. " 'Taters cain't see."

I examined one of the quartered potatoes; there were seven eyes in it. Properly cut, the vegetable probably would have returned twice the original amount. As it was, the family would scarcely get more in quantity than what they had purchased.

We went to the garden where something akin to furrows methodically deviated around a reasonably small rock. I told them that when I gardened I picked up the rocks as I went along.

"Hain't no point in stoppin' fur a rock. Hit hain't harmin' nothin'."

Melda dug holes at specific places in each "row." After taking a bite from each piece of potato, the boys put it in a hole and Melda covered it with dirt. The back of the plot, which looked more fertile, was not planted.

"Are you saving that patch for yellow potatoes, Melda?"

"Nope. People's borryin' if'n we's plantin' fur back. We hain't usin' 'at patch fur nary a thing."

If all the Americans who till the soil lived and worked at this low level, the population of our country would be less well fed than that of China.

Farming resources will not produce an income and the income from non-farm activities will be small at best. The most prosperous hollow fellow is the one who either manufactures or sells moonshine. Truck farming is a thing of the past. Cattle raising has been pushed from poorer lands. Neither is the Brancher prepared to "hire out." The vast mechanized practices carried on in modern agriculture are entirely foreign to him. Moreover the occupations of a rural society are unacceptable to him because it is hard work, the pay is low, and the employer is always prodding and complaining about the way in which work is done.

The hollowers have little chance of and even less desire to participate actively in labor's future. Most appear to have lost any ambition they might once have possessed. They are too much a part of the past to function in a system where rough labor jobs are rapidly vanishing and more white-collar skills are needed. Daily they become more outdated because they can neither read nor write English well enough to use it on a job; indeed, they are not literate enough to fill out application forms.

By 1975 the free enterprise system of the United States will have somehow to create over eight million new jobs simply to maintain the current unemployment rate of 4 per cent. The outlook, based on vast supportive data, is not optimistic and the necessary expansion will probably fail to materialize if the present trend persists. The manpower projection for the total civilian labor force is 91.4 million workers in 1975. Farm jobs are fewer than ever. It is obvious that needed jobs will not be found in the coal mines. In 1962 there were 500,000 fewer miners than in 1957. The booming construction industry will help create more employment. It is anticipated that transportation, public utility industries, and factories will increase their employment potential at a slow pace.

Between 1957 and 1962 a total of 3.8 million new workers entered the labor market while 7.5 million were displaced by automation and productivity gains. In order to prevent a serious economic relapse, 11.3 million new jobs had to be provided. However, only 10.2 million persons could be accommodated in this five-year period. Unless dramatic changes ensue, the projected unemployment figure will reach 6 million in the next five years. The job problem is far more acute in certain groups and this circumstance will become increasingly critical. People who have the most trouble are the inexperienced, the unskilled, the overspecialized, the too young, and the too old. The work world is particularly rocky for the less gifted. Many do not even know how to look for work. The rate of unemployment among unskilled workers in general is far higher than the national average of 6 per cent. Since World War II about 1.5 million blue-collar jobs have disappeared in the goods-producing industries —manufacturing, agriculture, mining, and construction. In the overall picture, the increasing use of white-collar workers has replaced the need for merely minimal abilities. Side by side with the surplus occupational groups, the underpopulated occupations exist. There are not enough skilled workers in the metal trades and woodworking, not enough competent stenographers and typists, not enough professional personnel in the health field, thereby creating a few outstanding shortages. These deficiencies are likely to persist despite the general state of the labor market and employers will have to cope with the situation through the usual expedients: overtime work, upgrading less able personnel, hiring people with similar but not precisely the desired work background, and engaging promising beginners. The inadequately qualified will be almost totally useless in this over-all picture; in the 1970s unskilled jobs will be at an alltime low of about 5 per cent and if the disadvantaged find employment, they will be placed on the lowest possible rung.

In Duddie's Branch, unemployment statistics are not valid. If a man has never worked, he cannot join the unemployed. Many of the Branchers are underemployed, never having established a work pattern. Most of them, if they are willing, are not employable even for marginal unskilled jobs. Usually, however, they are so certain that there are no jobs that they seldom bother looking. This is perhaps one of the main reasons why so many escape the statistics.

The demography of any neighborhood and the variables found in this kind of data predetermine the number of individuals who can be expected to join the ranks of the unemployed or to swell the labor force. Age, sex, and family patterns, for example, are a few of the most obvious determinants. Most of the men are orientated to the work world by older members in the family or by close kin. One explanation for the weak impact of the value of work is that no Brancher has been exposed to an energetic, fully employed worker. Another measurable indicator of a worker's potential is academic accomplishment, usually noted statistically as the highest grade completed in school. Other important denominators, some operating insidiously to influence behavior, are real or imagined health problems, personal reasons, and deeply rooted beliefs.

What do the men of Duddie's Branch mean by work? Any similarity between middle-class concepts of work and those of individuals from this mountain hollow is sheer coincidence. The necessity of adhering to a regular schedule, arising at a designated time, working five days a week for a specified number of hours, responsibility, and loyalty are distasteful requirements. Negative aspects of work appear to texture the value patterns and usually outweigh most of the positive factors. Although patriarchy places the man at the pinnacle of the family or kinship structure, it is no exaggeration to say that even this position does little to awaken in him the responsibilities associated with his role. In his mind there is no necessity for a change in his attitude toward employment or other activities which are logically thought of as work. A passionate disbelief in work and any benefits derived therefrom is his only excuse for perennial idleness. The acute pressure of some situation or the desire for some material possession sometimes stimulates just enough ambition to satisfy a specific need. If a family has, by some means, acquired a television set, the husband may labor long enough to earn sufficient money to buy a booster in order to use the appliance. Hungry and ragged children seldom inspire sufficient motivation for a few days' work. Unpaid doctor bills, past-due charge accounts, the approach of a new school year, the impending birth of a baby likewise fail to stimulate or directly influence the behavior of the apathetic male member of the family; that there are no funds to pay for a new mother's hospital care or to compensate a midwife does not alter his distaste for the restrictive factors and expenditure of physical energy associated with employment.

In the selective process, the hollow man would like to continue his dropout philosophy. Work for a while and then drop out. Unregimented work is his idea concept of employment. He would choose a job in which he would not have to contend with authority "bossin'," but even though supervised his performance is not worthy of compensation. The pleasure of loafing on the job and taking off whenever the notion strikes him are the only things that would make work tolerable. Refusal to tell his supervisor that he does not intend to show up for work or that he will be leaving early or that he plans to take a vacation is a pattern of work behavior which employers cannot fathom. But hollow men will not subordinate themselves to an organizational system which they feel is degrading and restrictive of their personal freedom. Teter is a good carpenter, but when he is on the job he wants someone else to do the sawing, lifting, and so forth while he drives the nails. In this way he can assume a partial role of supervision and reject some of the physical labor. Rufus thumbed a ride to Rochester, New York, to visit his brother, who had offered to get him a job. The long process of making application, undergoing physical examination, and the other necessities for securing work were new experiences for him. He was properly indignant when assigned the task of scrubbing floors, to him a woman's job. He voiced his dissatisfaction to the supervisor, who showed little interest in his opinion of that occupational pursuit. Rufus quit after three days.

Hollow men want control over their activities, on and off the job. Their philosophy of work is that what cannot be finished now can always be done on another day if nothing more important occurs to cause additional postponement. Steady work, day after day, week after week, is unacceptable; their entire life shuns routine. When an employment pattern extends sufficiently to become routinized, many will "lay out" a day or more to rest up. Road work as an occupation seems to be something special to Branchers. Many express envy of those fellows getting more pay for not working than for working. There is more truth than poetry in this statement. The average road worker can and often does work as few as 175 days a year.

They are crafty when it comes to receiving an income without working. An unemployed miner will inquire about which mines are operating and which are hiring when fulfilling the requirements to qualify for unemployment compensation. He astutely applies at the mine that is on limited-shift operation and that has a complete complement of men. Upon being told that no jobs are available, he asks the foreman to sign his slip indicating that he has sought work and been refused. When channeled through the proper agency, this "proof" enables him to continue "rockin'" for another month. Through repetition of this procedure he is able to draw unemployment compensation until he has received the maximum allowance.

When he is sincere about working, benefits are computed in cash. A paid vacation, year-round employment, and a job with a definite future are neither desired nor attractive fringe benefits.

Those on public assistance appear to be completely idle. "If'n I's seen stirrin' they's sure t' 'cuse me a' workin'." Unemployment in no way alienates an individual from his friends and neighbors. His freedom from responsibility allows him ample time to exchange stories with the other men, play cards, or just saunter up and down the Branch. He may "mosey" out to the highway and compare news while sitting on his heels. Yet families who have had welfare as a pattern of life, particularly those who have been on various programs for a long period, literally work at getting aid and keeping it. The second generation does not fare so well. Twenty years ago the Brancher could receive aid simply by answering a few questions. Now, because of the increasing complexity of the welfare system, he is required to fill out long applications, return to the agency several times, and be prepared to prove that he is unable to work. Because he has had no previous experience on which to draw, he has less with which to fight the sophisticated system and it is harder for him to beat it.

It is difficult to determine the percentage of men employed because of their "work awhile, rest awhile" pattern. It is equally difficult to count the miners: their work habits are usually no different from the others' and, in addition, mining is irregular and seasonal.

Melda's letters keep me up to date on the work situation in Duddie's Branch:

August 16, 1965: "Tiny Halt. Troy Shifter. Loyd Yancy all went to work Monday."

August 29, 1965: "All the men that wen to work. Troy Shifter Tiny Halt Loyd Yancy got checks today 2 hunder fifth dollars each. Loyd Yancy Bought him a Pistal give sixty dollars for it. five Pints Wine."

September 11, 1965: "I was give a job. when the kinder Garden school Starts."

October 5, 1965: "Sie Shifter drawed a Soical Check for four

Hundard dollars. I don't see how a gowing man like him can just quit work. and Pass on ever thing.

"We had about sixty bushel of irias Potatoes six bushels of sweet Potatoes We have dug about five bushels of Peanuts. I wan't you to get some Pea nuts when you are down again for the squirrels to eat.

"lots of the mens are back on the branch. that worked at indaplaus.

"Lester sold 90 dollars gine Same Roots [ginseng roots].

"I have Put in for a job at the facture that going tup at Shade. they said it would be bout first of Jan. before The Building Would Be Completed.

"I don't Think. I will seel any More of my hogs. I will keep the sows and kill the to Bours. I wan't you to get you a ham. You could have it slices Put it in the freezer It would stay good fresh.

"Ever one that drawed Social Security get checks last month back Pay"

It is important to consider the goals of hollow people. Their main aim in life is clearly not to qualify for a job. They wish to continue living as they are and as their ancestors did for centuries before them, even though they are living much less well and even though they themselves lack real knowledge of how their forebears actually lived or in fact who they were. Most prefer to sit and spit than to work all day for as little as a dollar an hour or sometimes three dollars a day. There is no work opportunity in the Branch, but they are reluctant to go outside to seek it. The experience of failure in society increases rigidity and suspicion. They are allergic to testing programs of any kind or applications which require them to answer questions which are "none 'a 'em fellers' business." When Jude applied for job training and was asked how many children he had, he replied there was no need to say—"I's leavin' 'em home." In talking about work, one hollower said, "I'd druther try shinnyin' up a thorn tree." Some of them have tried their hand at a job in the outside world but, as Tennissee said, "Hit 'uz soon burned." They are returned to the sanctuary of the hollow with bitter memories of their unsuccessful attempts to become part of the System. All complain of the same unremitting chronic illness—yearning for the hollow. "If'n you's hain't in th' holler, somethin's missin'. If'n you's missin' th' holler, hit's grindin' you's innards somethin' fierce." Just getting food after obtaining a job is a complete change. Tennissee confessed that she could not find a single store that would put her food purchases, meager as they were, on the book (credit buying). In the hollow she could get instant credit at any store of her choice within walking distance even though she showed no evidence of being employed. She stated that trust was far more important to her than any job.

The hollow man is constantly suspicious when he gets a job outside the county, for he is faced with all kinds of routine procedures he does not understand. He may be forced to pay union dues and he feels that he is being robbed—paying off someone for the privilege of working. Jobs disappear. Layoffs are frequent. All these help create and reinforce his negative attitude toward work. When he needs money, work is one way to get it. If all else fails he may try to get a job. He is slow about making such a decision, though, if he has parents or kin who are willing to keep his family from starving.

Discrimination is prevalent and the occasional hollower who might be interested in working is not quite aware of what is going on, but he feels the rejection when he attempts to get a legitimate job. One of the first questions he must answer is, "Are you living in the hollow?" The experiences the employer has had with previous hollowers inhibit his willingness to try again with another. Besides the discrimination, the Brancher is helpless to cope with other practices, such as wage garnishment.

Kentucky's antiquated garnishee law, some sections of which date back to 1886, was revised in 1966. Until the revision the law exempted, over and above meager monthly wages, two work beasts or one work beast and one yoke of oxen, two plows and gear, one wagon, cart or dray, two axes, three hoes, one spade, one shovel, two cows and calves, beds, bedding and furniture sufficient for family use, one loom and spinning wheel and pair of cards, all of the spun yarn and manufactured cloth by the family necessary for family use, two saddles, and their appurtenances, and on and on. With the exception of axes, spades, hoes, and shovels, the hollow family has never heard of nor do they own most of the items listed in the old law.

Under the new statute all household furnishings, not to exceed $1,500 in value, are exempt from attachment. Tools, equipment, and livestock up to the same monetary value are excepted providing the owner is engaged in farming. An employed person is permitted to have one motor vehicle and its necessary accessories, including one spare tire exempt from garnishment.

The law now has one section devoted specifically to the amount of income earned by labor which is free from attachment. The range is from 50 per cent to 75 per cent of all earnings in any pay period. Public assistance monies are exempt.

In order to avoid differences of opinion necessities have been listed as articles of food, clothing (including shoes), medicine, medical services, drugs, rent, public utilities, furniture, and household appliances.

Loan companies have been the most persistent users of the garnishee law. Some feel they plan garnishment at the time a loan is made. With the new law, the hollower who falls behind in his payment of debts can avoid claims on his meager assets. It also would make untouchable to creditors wedding or engagement rings, one watch consistent with the claimant's station in life or vocational requirements, and a hundred dollars' worth of books. Cars used in the process of making a living would be exempt from attachment too. A mechanic could not be garnisheed for the first three hundred dollars' worth of tools.

Loan company lobbyists have to date been able to delay initiation of a revised law. Some people voice the opinion that the present garnishment law is absurd, particularly those parts which date back a hundred and forty years. Its antiquity can be judged in terms of what it exempts. More important, the law today encourages extensive credit to the worst possible risks (a family of ten, the father sporadically employed).

When a creditor secures an attachment from the magistrate's court, the employer stops a worker's wages immediately and fires the worker without giving him any of his earned pay. The employer usually stops a worker's wages after a certain number of garnishments—many employers of hollow men fire them after the first notice to avoid the book work. The hollow fellow has no real incentive to negotiate some reasonable payment plan.

Although the small store owner rarely engages in such practice as garnishment, he usually feels that the hollower deserves what he gets. I cannot agree. A functional illiterate is not aware of what his "X" means and he is truly the prey of the smooth-talking loan sharks and easy-credit proposals. The hollow man has no knowledge of the law. He cannot read the fine-print contract which he signs. Why should these easy-credit specialists be permitted by law to victimize the deprived?

Not long ago Kash asked me to drive him and Willis to London to borrow some money. When we got to the loan office, Kash asked for two hundred dollars. After answering a few questions which he did not quite understand and scrawling his signature on the bottom of the long page he got the money. The man then asked Willis if he wanted to borrow some money. He did, and the same procedure was repeated. Then I told the man that I, too, should like to borrow two hundred dollars. I was given a real third degree. Did I have a job? What kind? How much money did I earn? The questions, not one of which had been asked of Kash or Willis, were endless. I was eventually told that since I worked and had an income and was not from the hollow I was ineligible for a loan! Kash and Willis provided character references, but the man suggested that they mind their own business. My friends became incensed and said that if I could not borrow money they would return theirs. The loan man reminded them that they had signed the paper and would have to pay the amount shown whether they returned the money or not. I lost. Kash and Willis offered to share their loan with me, but I told them that I could get by with what I had. The significance of a university appointment in the eyes of a loan-company executive was dramatically brought to my attention.

Garnishment laws, however, apply to every class in the county. A state worker had his $190 plus check taken for a $40 hospital bill which he had paid and did not owe. Wrongful garnishment is a common practice. Kentuckians are not the only ones who go home without pay checks, though. A twenty-seven-year-old man was delinquent with his state tax payment. When his entire pay check was confiscated by the tax collectors, he committed suicide. A previous appeal to his union for help had been unsuccessful. He sought redress from all sources known to him. In a desperate effort to remedy his situation, he asked for vacation pay in his last check, hoping that this would allow him to make payments on his car, but to no avail. The tax officials took $208, leaving him just $30. Not only were his creditors threatening to repossess his car, but he had no money to pay his rent or support himself, his wife, and four-year-old son. How did he get into such a predicament? Why did he owe $300 in state income taxes? For five years he had worked in one state and lived in another just thirty miles from his job. Many other men working for the same company had their pay checks taken for tax purposes too.

Other unfair practices outside the county embitter the Brancher.

Foister, a father of six, is illiterate but he is willing to work at anything to support his family. His service in World War II was terminated by a dishonorable discharge, but to this day he does not know what this means. His record shows that he was AWOL for 611 days of his 670 days in the army. "If'n 'em fellers 'uz mouthin' talk I ketched, I never did nary a thing they's tellin' me," he proudly recalled.

When I first met him he was hired by a well-to-do resident in the local area to clear up an auto junk yard for a dollar an hour. A man whom he did not know would come around on an irregular basis and pay him by check. Foister always showed me the check before cashing it and I found many instances of unpaid hours and inaccurate calculations. One check amounted to $90 for 120 hours of work. At an appropriate time I brought the matter to the attention of a person who knew what was going on.

"Foister seems to think that he isn't getting all of his pay," I told him.

"Sure he is, but if he wasn't he'd be too ignorant to know," the man replied.

I did not tell Foister that he was being cheated because he would have thought that "you's callin' me a dummy."

Not only did Foister never receive payment for his final three weeks of labor, he was saddled with a $300 bill for the acetylene torch he bought to cut up the cars in pieces small enough to be carted away. All the checks had been cashed and Foister did not even know the name of the man who had signed them. I had no trouble in getting

the name of the mountebank from the very people who told Foister
that they did not know his employer.

Foister reflected often about "dog hole" coal mining. He recalled
many of the dangers which he had to ignore if he was to work. He
talked about spending all day in the mine, first on one side of his body
and then on the other, "hand diggin' " out a seam of coal eighteen to
twenty-four inches high. He remembered how he learned the way to
"crawl fast liken a mole" to get back where he was to work. Re-
cently he and a number of other unemployed miners were hired to
work out a thirty-inch seam of coal on a contract basis and were told
that a foreman would be required. None of them was able to understand the contract and each thought that the mineowner would pay
the salary of the foreman, who seldom came around. The men
worked long hours for two weeks. Foister's salary was ninety-five
dollars a week, but on payday each man had to kick back 75 per cent
of his wages to pay the foreman, so Foister actually ended up with
about thirty dollars for two weeks in the mine. In revealing this, he
was a little disturbed and ashamed because he felt that he was made
a fool of. This seemed to bother him more than the fact that all of
his money had been taken away.

Programs currently are being planned to alleviate the suffering of
the underemployed. These are destined to failure, however, if effort
and money are focused on the man who prefers his state of underemployment.

"Regular work" to many miners is a three-day week. "Hit don't
make no sense t' work a full week fur no more money 'n I kin make
in three days." The miner is paid by the carload. If he loads leisurely,
he will have to work five days to accumulate the number of tons he
needs as a minimum. By expending a little more energy, he can meet
his minimum financial requirements in three days.

Seasonal shutdown of mines in the spring and summer causes no
consternation. The diminishing market for coal and the fluctuation
in the demand for the fuel are the problems of the mineowner, not
the worker. Mines become flooded, roads become impassable in bad
weather, and the lack of a sufficient number of trucks and rail cars
are just part of mining. The worker does not relate these factors to

his economic situation. He can always "rock" and enjoy the completely unstructured life he values so highly.

A number of the miners in the Branch calculate how long they will work on the basis of how much they can get by drawing unemployment. The desire to draw this unemployment at times determines the "job hopping" they do. Only a few of them have worked over the years in the same mine. Amon Belph has a long service record in a single mine. His record was exceeded by Lias Gilbert, but within the last few months Lias quit and shopped around for better offers. His demand was a company pickup truck which he would be permitted to drive back and forth to work at his leisure. This was satisfied; he is a skilled miner with some engineering ability and he does not have a difficult time finding a job if work is available.

Work generally means participation in the outside world, and the hollower then assumes a "them 'n' us 'n's'" frame of reference. Some of the men follow the way of their parents and grandparents, who were able, in a sense, to continue their isolation, even in a work situation. They became miners. Meander says, "Hit's liken th' holler. Hain't al'ays seein' even in shinin'. Don't matter hit's dark if'n you's hain't seein' much 'a th' time."

Perhaps the factor which is most appealing, though not often mentioned, is one kind of security that is provided by the underground environment of the mine: there is little need or opportunity for conversation. It is dark, the men work alone and isolated, and supervision is limited. The mine is cool in the summer and warm in the winter. The hostile outside world is as distant from them there as it is in the hollow. They prefer working with their own kind and no strangers enter the mines.

Employment conditions in dog hole mines are quite compatible with the worker's desires and attitudes. In securing employment there, the applicant is not required to take a written examination. No one asks him if he is a high school graduate (in fact, there is no interest whatsoever in whether or not he ever went to school). Grooming and clothes are of no concern to the employer, although the miner's cap, the lamp, and a special type of belt are symbols of his occupation which seem to afford a degree of pride to the miner.

The miners from Duddie's Branch must ride long distances to get to work, thus necessitating an early departure. The wives get up at four in the morning, prepare breakfast, and pack a lunch. Most men prefer an early day because they can avoid the noise and confusion created by the children, who sleep until a later hour. The uninterrupted, individual services of the wife are consistent with the role assignment which the husband feels is his privilege. Commanding her undivided attention is a highly satisfying experience. Upon his return home he doffs his shirt and comfortably relaxes in a chair while his spouse bathes him. Irrespective of the activity in which she may be engaged, it is set aside while she attacks the black, greasy grime that covers the upper portion of her husband's body. She watches for him every day and is uneasy until she sees him trudging up the hollow. He has survived another day in the mine. The wife candidly admits her fear that someone will come with news that her husband has been injured, for the memory of the death of a close relative or of a broken back or a crushed leg is vivid.

The fear of an accident is uppermost in the minds of the miners, most of them aware of the lack of safety devices and proper inspection. Many feel that there is collusion between the mineowner, the mine operator, and the inspectors—particularly when glaring inadequacies are allowed to exist. Stale air, dust, fumes, gas—these are part of the miner's lot. "W'en you's go in th' mine, you's hain't never knowin' if'n you's comin' out agin."

Nonetheless, some of the men apparently are thrilled by the dangerous environment and eagerly relate specific incidents which support the hazards encountered. Each has his version of why a particular miner was killed and what he would have done under similar circumstances. Close calls, such as a cracking roof, are graphically demonstrated and the audience cannot fail to detect the miner's delight in his mastery over the mysterious underground. "Hain't ever' feller who kin git into a dog hole," one miner said with evident personal and perhaps justified satisfaction. A small, strong, skinny stature has its advantages. Those men who are willing to work in dog hole coal mines spend the entire day on their knees mining a low seam of coal and loading it by hand. The tunnels are two to three feet high; the insides are uninspected and the miners gamble their lives against cave-ins and coal dust. They hack away with pick and shovel in these small, non-union truck mines for as little as three dollars a day.

A twenty-three-year-old miner was paralyzed from the waist down when he was struck by falling slate. He had only been hired a few hours before the accident and, according to the foreman, had never worked in a mine before.

A nineteen-year-old youth suffered a broken right leg when it was struck by a 4 × 20-foot rock that fell from the mine roof. He saw the rock slip and tried to leap clear of it, but the heavy boulder caught his leg as he jumped. However, a nearby coal car kept the weight of the rock off his leg. The mineowner stated that the rock, which was so large that it tested the same as solid roof, apparently was held in place by a mud seam.

A fifty-five-year-old miner was crushed between a loading car and the wall of the mine. He was killed instantly.

A bill to bring coal mines employing fewer than fifteen miners under the enforcement provisions of the Federal Mines Safety Act failed to pass the House of Representatives. After studying statistics which revealed that, from 1940 to 1962, 250 accidents in small underground mines killed 94 men and injured 183, the late President Kennedy sought this measure that would have repealed the exemption from the safety act applying to mines employing fewer than fifteen miners. Federal mine inspectors are authorized to inspect the small mines but they are powerless to shut them down if they are guilty of safety violations. Opponents of the bill charged that the real issue was a struggle by big mines to take over little ones.

The uncertainties and risks are financial too, of course. Lack of orders causes the mines to close. As does lack of water. A coal tipple occupies approximately eight acres of land with a side track off the main line and consists of two 75-ton bins with rescreened shakers for loading trucks, one belt conveyor which carries rescreening to the rescreen bin; the screens are four feet wide and can make four grades of coal. The tipples which grade coal and load it into railroad cars also produce washed coal, and, like the mines, they often close, when no water is available. Thus orders which are in cannot be filled.

Mining as an occupational pursuit for those in Duddie's Branch includes a foreman, one cutter, and a combination coupler and driver of the device which brings the coal to the surface. None of the miners has expressed any desire to apply for or be promoted to those jobs which pay better wages. They feel that they lack the pull which would be needed to get them.

Dog hole coal mines are dug by anyone who can get together sufficient money for opening up a pit. I visited a coal company in Dade County. The vein of coal which was being worked was 52 inches. In discussing the amount of salary earned by the various individuals, I learned that a tipple man gets $9.20, jeep drivers make an average of $14 a day, a coal cutter makes $15, a helper $14. A helper may include those persons who are responsible for mine ventilation and other tasks that have to do with cleanliness and general welfare of the workers. A loader will make roughly $12 per day. In some instances the coal company will make a down payment on a station wagon and pay for the insurance for the vehicle. The company will employ a driver and deduct from each worker's pay a transportation fee. The driver of the station wagon also pays a fee and his deduction is usually a little bit more, but he will eventually become the owner when he has had deducted from his weekly earnings enough to pay for the original cost of the station wagon and the insurance, which is carried by the company until he has paid for the car. At this point it then can be turned over to him with a clear title and he becomes the full owner.

Gail described his experiences as a miner. Few of the mines in which he worked provided or adhered to the minimum safety standards required by the state. Most mines pay less than minimum wages. Some days Gail worked all day long and received less than $5.00 for his efforts. He went into the mine when the day was "half done" (the afternoon shift) and came out at "stirrin' time late" (in the morning). Some days he would get $10 for his labor and on other days he got less than $4.00. He said that he did the same amount of "movin' 'n' loadin' coal" each day and did not know why he received a different amount of money. The mineowner explained the variance in salary. If the sale of coal had been good the previous day, he divided half the money with the men who were working that day. If he had been unable to sell the coal, he paid the workers whatever he thought was fair. Truck mine operators often leave the area without paying the men; checks bounce; they refuse to meet union wage scale. But the Branchers work in the mines because their only skill is that of a coal miner and they often ask, "What could I do in a big city?" The United States offers everyone freedom of mobility—to go where there is opportunity. But for the hollower there is no opportunity except in his own environment, and what it offers, primarily, is dog hole coal mining.

The median family income in Earle County is less than $1,900, contrasted with $4,051 for the state. When compared with the average number of welfare recipients in Kentucky counties, Earle County has one and a half times as many people on Old Age Assistance. Two and a half times as many people are on Aid to Dependent Children. Two times as many are on Aid to the Permanently and Totally Disabled. Eight times as many are on Blind Assistance. Earle County ranks 116 out of 120 in welfare dependency.

The young men try to help me understand why they are unemployed. "Minin', 'at's all we's knowin' t' do. Hain't nothin' 'ceptin' minin' 'at pays you's fur workin'." The rise and decline of the economy of this area, the volumes written about it, are now history. Why can't society accept the fact that the coal industry has been sick and dying for fifty years? It will probably never completely disappear, but almost certainly will account for fewer and fewer workers. What is so devastating is that they are not the kind of workers who are apt to be hired for other than menial jobs in the labor markets.

The social system of the hollow has failed to adapt to or feel the pressure from the frightening changes which are vividly painted in discouraging statistics as the phenomenon of automation eliminates the need for workers at a rate of 200,000 a month. Ironically, however, if there is a real desire to increase leisure time, perhaps the lax pattern of work gives the hollow workers an advantage over those who will be adjusting to a decrease in work time and accommodating to more leisure time. We are repeatedly told that one can no longer expect to enjoy pride in work well done. We must change our whole concept of work from one that it is good to work to one that it is better not to work. Any dignity in human labor may disappear in the years ahead as the more efficient machines take over. Have these miners jumped the gun? Have they avoided the emotionally traumatic experience of adapting to an entirely new economic order and associated employment plan almost certain to be part of the completely automated society?

Some say that occupation rather than education accounts for virtually all of the variations in Branch fathers' values, that they are simply not preparing their children for life to come in which working, an occupation, has value.

In the earlier history of this community, children went to work at an early age milking cows, caring for pigs and chickens, helping with garden and small farming activities, carrying water, weeding. They acquired more duties each year—household chores, care of babies, canning, food preservation, and any task which was needed to assure survival at a subsistence level. But family employment no longer exists. Now garden plots are small in comparison, there are only two cows, just a few hogs, and some untended chickens in Duddie's Branch. As a consequence, children have few if any responsibilities. Work is not a pattern of behavior and none has learned to respect its necessity or anticipate engaging in it on a planned basis.

While earning some money to buy a car will probably motivate them to look for work, joblessness does not bother the hollow teenagers. They feel they will not find a job of any kind, would not be able to keep it if they did. None can see any relationship between performance and job security. From the beginning the boy or girl sets the pattern of job mobility: usually unemployed, working only occasionally, getting fired, getting laid off. This pattern perpetuates itself and has deep psychological, sociological, and economic effects.

The youth from this hollow are unequipped for self-support. The demands of the labor market require that the educational background be improved. But it is the rare Brancher who finishes high school and without this he cannot hope for employment as a technician, a skilled craftsman, or a clerical worker. There are limited federal funds for programs to train unemployed primarily in woodworking, metalworking, hospital, and other such skills. The modest salary paid to students while learning has no appeal. Can these young men hope to find work? Only through acquisition of the necessary skills for future employment. We have a need to answer the question, what specific jobs in what places offer the best chance for employment and opportunity for advancement? Just what areas of employment might a youth compete for if he were to become a college graduate? Would he become an engineer, a mathematician, a teacher, a social worker, a scientist, a physician, a physicist, a meteorologist, a dietician, or a lawyer? I doubt it. Young Branchers probably could never prepare for shortages which exist in professional and technical fields because at an early age they become family men with an immediate need to work. They would like to do a man's job, but many of them have become fathers without ever having attained manhood.

If you were to ask the Branchers between seventeen and eighteen years of age what they were interested in, they would invariably answer, "A job." Because they want to work? Because they want to earn money? No. "They's 'xpectin' me t' name workin'." When you attempt to find out what kind of job they would like or feel they can do, the inevitable response is, "Anything." Why don't they itemize specifics, beginning with their first choice? The answer is simple. Their exposure to the world beyond, various work activities, and to job opportunities in their own county and nearby outer community has been so minimal that they do not have the vaguest notion of what kind of work exists.

"Coffee, you can make a car run no matter what's wrong with it. I'll bet you could fix ten cars a day just working half hard."

"Nope. They's not th' kind I's fixin'."

"If you were in a garage with lots of tools, using lifts instead of rocks, you could do a good job."

"Nope. My fixin', 'em drivin'—hain't th' same."

"I can't see why if you can make a car run here you can't make one in Cincinnati run."

Coffee, with considerable pride in his mechanical ability, finally decides—as most of them eventually do—that he will have to give me some explanation and attempt to enlighten me.

"You's got hills. You's got rocks."

"Sure, we have lots of hills in Cincinnati and lots of rocks too."

"Us'ns don't need brakes. We jist pulls up 'em hills, then th' young-uns puts big rocks under each wheel. We's never goin' fur, 'n' we's not hurryin'. We's don't need starters. W'en I's leaving out, th' younguns takes out th' rocks. By th' time I gits t' th' bottom 'a th' hill, I's runnin'. Reckon 'em city fellers don't have 'nuf younguns. Reckon they's not got th' right size hills, neither."

"But you know how to put brake bands on if you had to."

"I could figger, I reckon."

"You have four different-size rims and four different-size tires."

"Yep."

I read off the numbers: 6.70 × 15; 7.50 × 14; 8.00 × 14 . . .

"Yep. Th' younguns names 'em numbers, but I's al'ays buyin' w'at I's needin'."

Any idea about career possibilities is rare. Some who want to be truck or bus drivers don't have any idea of what is involved in getting a driver's license. Those who indicate a preference to be policemen do so because they carry guns. The majority of the fourteen- to sixteen-year-olds say they don't aspire to anything.

"What kind of work would you like to do?"

"None."

The occupations occasionally mentioned by the older boys are postman, factory worker, teacher, and fire fighter. Postman to them means a rural mail carrier. This requires a driver's license, something few of them can attain. When they prefer factory work they are unable to describe a factory and lack any knowledge of job activities. Remus says, "I'd jist work doin' somethin', reckon." Both the boys and girls who say that they would like to be teachers don't know that high school graduation and a successful four-year college course are basic requirements. Many boys indicate mining as a choice because the old man did it. The girls who say that they would like to be nurses are not aware of the need to graduate from high school. Two thirds or more of the hollow girls want to be housewives. There are so few instances of hollow women working that the whole idea is not acceptable to them or their parents. Leaving the hollow, going to a strange environment holds no appeal and receives no parental encouragement.

The difference between young adults from the hollow and the lowest counterpart in the middle-class strata of society is too pronounced to be meaningful. Work as a main goal in life, at least for the male, is non-existent. One night I talked to a group of hollow boys aged fifteen to twenty about occupational desires. Some goals were so incredible that it was difficult to keep the focus of the conversation on work. One said, "I's goin' t' minin' 'n' git myself hurt as soon 's I kin 'n' then draw fur crippled." Another, "I's gonna draw fur blindin'." He referred to others in the hollow, twenty-five years of age on the average, who had successfully qualified for this "occupation." Still another, "I's jist gonna do nothin' 'ceptin' sang diggin'." He admitted that he was willing to "fit fire" if the fire was close by and not "burnin' 'ceptin' this high," and he lowered his hand to within a foot above the ground. Josha complained of the futility of working at a job. He hitched a ride to Indianapolis, about three hundred miles from the hollow, and got a job in a creamery stacking butter into delivery cases. When he got his first check he could not get it cashed without identification and he did not know what that meant. So he kept his first week's check and worked another week. He went through the same experience the second week. Discouraged, he returned home.

"Why did you quit your job?" I asked.

"They's never payin' fur workin'—jist givin' papers."

He showed me the two checks and expressed strong feelings about "cheatin' workin' fellers," and said that one knew who cheated in the hollow but "yander they's hain't nary feller you's kin hawk-eye." Explanations in times like this are futile. I cannot supply the words that match the limited understanding of the hollow people; I am forever in the position of working against years of conditioning.

One boy said that he wanted to be a carpenter.

"Can you drive a nail, Zeb?"

"If'n hit hain't restin' in green [going through green lumber]."

"Can you use a ruler?"

"Yep."

"How much does a ruler measure?"

"Right smart."

"Is a ruler and a yardstick the same length?"

"Reckon."

"How much is a foot?"

He looked at me quizzically and then pointed to his foot. "Reckon a foot's a foot."

"Show me how much a yard is."

"'Twixt me 'n' 'at tree." The distance he indicated was at least four yards.

"That's a long yard."

"Measurin' hain't long 'r short."

A plane, a square, a plumb line, a crosscut or rip saw—an endless list of basic tools he has never heard of. None can saw a two-inch straight line. They have extreme difficulty in even utilizing the saw. And they have no concept of a cutting edge or where the sawing will take place based on how they hold it.

We played a game. Everyone was given ten nails of different lengths but each boy had identical different lengths. The long two-by-four was soft redwood. I timed each one to see how long it took him to drive the ten nails into the board. Many had never held a hammer before. I worked with them. My time was fifteen seconds after I started pounding. The closest any one of them came to that time was twenty minutes and even then all of the nailheads were not flush with the surface of the board. After the demonstration, all who had aspired for the trade still wanted to be carpenters, but not the kind that had to drive nails.

Engaging in fire fighting is one kind of work which has great appeal to the young unemployables who inhabit the Branches. Why? Vance says, "'Em fellers comes clean t' th' head 'a th' holler fur us."

"But fire fighting requires such long hours of work, keeps you gone so long."

"Reckon. Payin' fur ridin' don't give no water knots [blisters]. 'Em fellers gits grub fur 'em 'at's fittin'. Costes fittin' fellers nothin'."

What Vance does not know, however, is that the food he gets does not cost the maximum allowance. The man in charge of the work is authorized to spend up to a dollar per person per meal. The food for each individual will vary from fifty to sixty-five cents per meal. The storekeeper does not keep a record of the actual items purchased but turns in his request for reimbursement on the number of men and lunches. For example, he has provided one hundred lunches. His bill is a hundred dollars. Many times I have heard the man in charge say, "Got twelve fellers." "What you spendin'?" asks the storekeeper. "Give 'em a little more than yesterday. Some of 'em said they was hungry, but keep it low." So on this day each worker eats a sixty-cent lunch. What happens to the extra fifty dollars, the difference between the actual retail cost and the reimbursement? Never having seen this money change hands, I can only relate what others have claimed. Twenty-five dollars goes to the store and twenty-five dollars to the man in charge. Prove it? How could you? The store records only the number of lunches provided. The supervisor records only the number of men and the hours each works. In less than a week after submitting the bill the storekeeper gets his check and so does the supervisor. The Branchers wait and wait and wait.

Early in July Vance received his check totaling $169. His rate of pay for "fittin' fire" is fifty cents an hour. I had heard considerable discussion among the men. The feeling was that the employers were not very accurate about paying the money actually due each man. I talked about this with Vance. "I's figgerin' 'em's payin' a skin fur 'em hours we's fittin'. Reckon if'n they's 'twixt [between fifty cents and a dollar] they's hain't cheatin'. 'Em fellers hain't knowin' numbers no more'n us'ns."

I looked at his check. "You must feel like a rich man."

"Nope. Nothin' 'ceptin' rattle money's left. Owed hit mostly."

All the while I am doing some mental arithmetic. "That much money means you have worked more than three hundred hours. I don't see how you could possibly put that many hours in during the month, especially when you didn't work every day. They paid you for about thirty-four days of work."

"Cain't reckon hit. Reckon nosin' 'bout figgers hit'd destroy a feller." He finally suggested the possibility that the overpayment resulted from a shortage on a previous check.

It would be impossible to know what one should receive. The Brancher cannot keep accurate count of days and hours worked. The few who challenge are told that they will receive the money due them on the next check because the employers have run out of money and cannot pay in full. Each fire fighter knows, however, that the store gets paid "faster'n us fittin' fellers."

How the more fortunate excel in taking advantage! Other people, other times, other places come to life as I live in the hollow. I think often of earlier experiences with migrant workers in Michigan.

We were paid on the basis of the number of baskets turned in. I remembered from pay to pay how many baskets I picked, but my wages were always short. This was my first experience with cheating.

When we were all gathered in the tent one night, I solicited the migrants' cooperation in a plan which would supply accurate data on our productive capacity. Beginning the next week, we were each to put a small pebble in our pockets every time we took in a full basket for credit. Everyone agreed that principle should not be sacrificed— only one pebble to each basket. Before we could implement our scheme, however, every person had to have a pocket and every pocket had to have a bottom. I spent much of that weekend patching, sewing, and improvising and by Monday morning every person had at least one that was functional.

Pebble-crediting became my nightly duty and by the end of the work week I had figures to compare with pay. By this method, we discovered that I received 65 per cent of the amount of money I had actually earned, the other adult migrants got little more than 50 per cent of their actual earnings, and the teenagers received about 40 per cent of the amount due them. We were going to move on in a few days but I was determined to confront the man in charge of receiving and paying even though I knew there would be no evidence to support my charge of cheating.

When I tarried, the owner came over to my car and wanted to know why I hadn't "left out with th' rest 'a th' shiftless?"

I was belligerent. "Why did you cheat me?"

"What are ya talkin' about?" he demanded.

I told him about our records.

"You can't prove nothin', but I'll pay ya what ya think ya got comin'."

He pulled out some money, but I insisted on a check. He refused. I threatened to stay on the highway outside his gate until he met my terms. The next day he came with a check and accused me of having seen the authorities. I did not allay his suspicions.

"Why did you swindle the others?" I asked.

"They're too ignorant t' know they been cheated," he growled.

"Anyway, they won't be back till next year and by then they won't remember."

I glared at him and he uneasily referred to the charges the worker had to bear: basket replacement, hauling to market, housing, water, etc.

"What do you mean by 'housing'?" I questioned. "They brought their own tent. You furnished nothing."

"How about the water?"

"Where? We had to use filthy stream water for everything—bathing, cooking, washing clothes!"

"Well, you igner'nt people should 'a used the hydrant."

"There's not a hydrant in this whole area."

He took me to one.

"Turn it on," I dared.

He did, and nothing came out.

"Must be broken," he alibied.

"Shouldn't you get it fixed?"

A flush slowly crept over his face and his lips were compressed to a thin line.

"Those people never did have no water and they don't expect none," he snarled. "Now get off my property and don't ever let me catch you on it again!"

He wheeled around and stomped away.

That night I slept on the highway outside his house. The next morning he came to the road and asked if I intended to claim squatter's rights.

"What would it take for you to move along?" he wheedled.

"The money due the migrants."

A few days later a local officer pulled up alongside my car.

"How much would it cost to get you out of here?" he wanted to know.

I told him the amount of money which was due the migrants and that same day I received a check in full payment. My friends were. jubilant when I gave it to them.

What does the future employment picture look like for the young people from the hollows?

Earle County is continuously in an economic squeeze. With low productivity and coal reserves that are limited in quantity, it is unlikely that it will expand. Instead it will contract in the next decade or so. The county has always been in a weak position in natural resources, especially coal. In any statistical comparison, its limitations are obvious. It has little to exploit. Earle County is consistently and decidedly at the bottom of the wage scale. Minimal wages have been the pattern for years. High transportation costs have made it almost impossible for coal mine operators to compete favorably with mines in other counties that realize high profits. Manufacturing and industrialization remain mirages. Employment gaps widen, job possibilities decrease. The man from Duddie's Branch is at a disadvantage here. He either has no skills or else possesses skills that will soon become outmoded. He has little to offer an employer. The job potential just is not here, and predicted unemployment rates have little validity. There are not enough local skilled workers for jobs available. Thus most of the money goes to out-of-staters or at least out-of-countians.

With the employment door shut to these seriously undereducated, semi-illiterate boys and girls, they will continue living their completely disorganized day-to-day existence with their families in overcrowded, impoverished homes. The only road open to them seems to be welfare, but it is essential that we break their self-perpetuating cycle of dependency on public assistance. Yet one must learn to walk before he learns to run.

I suggested to a man who anticipated fencing a large acreage that he employ hollow men for the job. I agreed to recruit them and provide transportation. The employer was willing to let the men work if I would meet the payroll and act as supervisor. Not one of the men could use a posthole digger, much less an automatic digger attached to the back of a jeep. None had ever seen a wire stretcher and therefore did not know how to use one. Electronic fence chargers were beyond their ability to visualize. After one month of spending borrowed money, I was willing to concede that the men from the hollow would always be unskilled workers. My error was in assuming that marketable skills could be taught quickly if the men were willing to try—and they were. At 5:00 A.M. I would drive my jeep into the hollow to pick up the six men. Always I wondered how many would be up, ready to go to work. Everyone was always ready, had eaten breakfast (which was a requirement), and was equipped with a packed lunch. They all appeared to be eager for the jeep ride, the prestige of being picked up, or for work—I never knew which. Nor was I able to understand why they accepted me in a role so much in conflict with their feelings of what women were to do. Meander would say, " 'Em thar worman's our'n. You's our'n, too, 'ceptin' you's hain't th' same."

I took my lunch the first day, but before I could take it out of the jeep the men told me that they each had brought something for me. I also shared their "drinkin'." They all brought some kind of container filled with water and we would drink from one jar until we had emptied it before starting on another. I drank from the common containers, tobacco juice and all. My lunch consisted of two pieces of biscuit bread, a piece of corn bread, one slice of pinto beans in hard lard, one piece of rabbit, and one turnip. After expressing my appreciation, I told them that they were not to furnish my lunch again. They were unwilling to accept this and throughout the entire time I shared whatever they had. Meander said that because I hadn't a man I didn't cook so he felt it was perfectly proper for them to have their "wormans" prepare something for me. I was a single female and therefore different from their women.

The lunch break seemed like a good time to bring up the pay proposition and I asked each how he would like to be paid—every day, once a week, by check, or in cash. They decided that they wanted to be paid daily and by check. When the day's work was completed, the men were paid. They could scarcely wait to cash their checks and went right to the store and bought groceries. They always got back some change. There was real pride in cashing a check and getting something besides a box of groceries to take home. They would not accept a ride back home in the evening because they wanted everyone in the hollow to see their purchases: chewing tobacco, Prince Albert tobacco for cigarettes, and some goody for the children. Our lunches never reflected the purchases; the family quickly consumed everything beyond the usual staples of lard, beans, corn meal, etc.

To them, a check is much more honorable than food stamps, which they seem ashamed to convert. Although they strive hard to get the stamps and get on the draw, cashing a welfare check is different from one they think they have earned. Local merchants respond more favorably to a check than to cash. A hollow fellow who comes in every night with cash is questioned. His behavior is consistent with the store owner's reaction. Sie came in with a ten-dollar bill one night and the store owner wanted to know where he got the money. "Wasn't for workin', I'll bet." Sie is noted for thievery, but this money he had earned. He left without spending any of it. I drove him to another store some eight miles away where he could make his purchases without being questioned. When we got to the mouth of the hollow I was going to let him out, but he wanted a ride to his door. The hollow folks would think that he had stolen the groceries. Before he got out of the jeep, he mumbled, "How's a feller gonna make 'at kind 'a money 'thout workin'?" When you have been around these people as long as I have, you begin to feel for them as they meet one degrading experience after another.

The fencing experience was only one of many which brought me to the conclusion that anyone interested in breaking the cycle of work deprivation must be fully informed of the significance of learning. Learning makes people what they are. Where is the point of intervention between the future and the impact of the past?

After one month on the fencing project, I asked the state welfare officials to give me the money the men were receiving in welfare and let me use it in a work-learning experiment. This they would not do because it was not in the rules. All of my arguments failed, but because I had so much faith in my proposal I decided to foot the bill for another month. Again, not one man failed to meet the jeep in the mornings. No one left the job. But performance did not improve dramatically. Apart from the disastrous results of the experiment at a cost to me of several thousand dollars, I sincerely believe that learning is possible for the hollow man, given more time. If learning makes people what they are, it may also tell us what they can be.

You cannot dig a posthole until you have learned to dig a posthole. You cannot use a wire stretcher until you have learned how to use one. You cannot read until you have learned to read. Work-learn programs appear to offer the only solution for these people, but most of the programs are not designed to offer much in the way of learning.

All emergency projects and temporary jobs are unattractive to the hollow people and tend to depress them. Revival from chronic neglect via the project media is not a fruitful approach.

One elderly man, who worked on the WPA, told me, "In 'em days, we's had work t' do 'at warn't 'specially t' we'uns likin', but we's builded perty bridges. They named 'em WPA. I kin take you's t' some nice things I helped built."

"I didn't know you could work with rock."

"I cain't, but I holped shovel 'em outta th' hills."

"What does WPA mean?"

"I warn't ever shore 'bout 'em letters, but I got money fur holpin' hit whatever hit war."

"Would you like for your sons to work on something like that?"

"Well, not 'xactly, but if'n hit 'uz lastin' hit 'ud be somethin' diff'r'nt. 'Em fellers, guessin' 'em t' be pres'dents, cain't seem t' make up they's mind 'bout us poor folk."

About 9,000 Kentuckians have been enrolled in the Happy Pappy program. According to the administrators, the program is structured to provide a better life for the deprived. Best estimates were that approximately 30,000 children will benefit from the results of their fathers' effort in this project, but the only benefit the father will receive is monetary.

The very words used to identify this program, "Happy Pappy," are regarded as derogatory, both in the hollow and in the outer community. One respected citizen told me that he resented the people who go to Washington to testify that we should extend the life of the War on Poverty. "I've been in this county for fifty years, and I will admit that I do not approve of unemployed fathers raising large families, but at the same time I certainly do not agree that 'our troops are in the field fighting a war without ammunition, a war which takes the bravest kind of men.' Outside of you, no one in this county has been fighting anything."

Troy spoke of some of the activities he was required to perform as a recipient of the Happy Pappy program. The most demeaning and embarrassing work was cutting weeds on the side of the road. It is his philosophy that it was a waste of energy because the weeds would only grow again. He told me about one of his sons who had taken the bus "yander." From his story I concluded that he had traveled to one of the Southern states and saw that gangs of convicts also worked at cutting weeds along the highway. The only difference he could detect between these men and the Kentucky workers was that they had chains around their ankles, but this seemed to have little significance for him. The thing that disturbed him most was that the work they were doing was identical. One man told me that there was no disgrace in being poor, but chopping away at brush in plain view of everyone was truly shameful. Another wished those who had thought up the idea of work as hacking at sticks would come and take a day with them: then perhaps they would know how the hollow fellow feels inside. The men deeply resent "make work" jobs. Many of them are put to work hoeing rocks into chug holes in roads, and they think this practice unfair. They did not make the holes in the first place. "We's jist hoein' 'em in fur cars t' toss 'em out." It is not only that they feel this labor is undignified; they regard such exposure as indecent, as "showin' you's welfarin'." If Troy could describe his real feelings he would call himself a puppet, being told to do this and that. He must feel like a slave. If there is one thing they all seem to resent with equally deep feelings, it is being ordered around. With a stick in hand, the supervisor, another Happy Pappy, puts the stick in the hole and says, "Fill 'er up." Troy admits he does not know so very much, but he knows a hole when he sees one. He cannot take much of this and so he takes a day off now and then to go squirrel hunting, dig sang, or spend the day in some way more to his interests and to boost his morale. "Renewin' fur a feller t' streak out in 'em mount'ins." Troy is on and off the Happy Pappy program more times than I can keep track of. He unknowingly disqualifies himself by his absence from the job or from school. But Troy is honest and tells me "hain't hankerin' fur knowin' no rules if'n hit's meanin' I's gonna git told w'en t' spit."

The Happy Pappy program is unpopular in more than one respect. Viewed from the standpoint of one of the hollowers who liked moonshine, it had an adverse effect on the lives of everyone involved. "This hyur Happy Pappy deal has kilt th' moonshine business." I disagreed. "They have more money now to buy moonshine with." But no, I was told, that was not really so, for the best moonshiners had been recruited for the program. When these men had been hard pressed for a few dollars, they would take to the woods and run off some moonshine. Now "hit's so bad 'at a feller cain't find nary a drop t' buy, so we's hain't drinkin'. Hit's a dirty shame."

To qualify as a "Happy Pappy," the candidate must agree to keep his children in school and the father himself must attend classes two nights a week. It would be enlightening to know just how many of the men who participate in the stick weed gangs would go to school if they were not getting paid to go. Lester can give you fifty reasons why he thinks the educational experience is worthless, and invariably sums up with, "Sittin' in 'em feller's chair hain't hard as choppin'. Hain't hard listenin' t' 'em namin' things, fur I hain't knowin' 'em nohow."

Tragically, this plan to eliminate illiteracy among adults is ultimately degrading to them. Two nights each week the Happy Pappy must head for the schoolhouse, while many of the men on the "blind draw" can pursue those things they prefer doing. No school for them. All the way out of the Branch the more fortunate blind drawers make fun of those men who must go to school. Lester tells me that this is more bitter than "swallerin' pure gall. 'N' hit's pure pisin findin' you's younguns cuttin' you's down: 'Don't fergit you's reader, Dad.' "

Sie, twenty-six years old, on the blind now for years, yet driving a fancy car every day and often working in Indianapolis, says, "Cain't you's write nothin' 'ceptin' 'n X?" Gid asks, "You's fellers writin' a'ter all you's trudgin' thar?"

Troy's wife tells how her husband hates to go to school. "Fun makin' hain't 'xactly easin' fur a agin' feller." Troy has attended school intermittently for one year. "He hain't hankerin' fur book larnin', 'ceptin' he's writin' his name right clear 'n' readin' hit. But he's hurtin' schoolin' nights. I's tellin' him schoolin' hain't hurtin' 'ceptin' 'em 'at's sorrier 'n us'ns."

With Lester I can cautiously jest. "Don't you want to be able to sign your name?"

"Nope. Hain't nothin' in hit."

One of the first things Troy did after getting on the Happy Pappy program was to buy a deep freeze. Noticing my utter amazement, he quickly explained. "Hit's fur holdin' a whole hog 'r cow."

"But, Troy, you don't have a pig or a cow."

"Hit don't mean I's hain't never gonna have 'em."

I know better than to say, "Okay, Troy, wait until you have them and storage becomes a problem and then think about a deep freeze." This is not the way you do it if you value your "us'ns" status. Troy has run his deep freeze for months with nothing in it, yet he has no refrigerator. This originally gleaming white elephant cost him $350 on credit. I have also learned not to say, "Why did you buy it?" He tells me without asking. No damage to my esteem that way.

"I 'uz in town 'n' this man tol' me, 'I's got jist w'at you's 'n' you's worman 'n' all 'em younguns needin'. Hit's half price fur Happy Pappies.'"

If Troy knew how to frame the question, he would ask me how that man knew that he was a Happy Pappy. If he were in a jocular mood, I would answer, "How do you know a wolf is a wolf?" His answer would be, "Hit's how you's lookin'."

When the salesman told him that it was half price for a Happy Pappy, Troy took off. He scorns anyone who calls him this. But fortunately for the salesman he recognized his mistake, remembered what Troy looked like, and the next time he saw him he devised another sales pitch. Troy will pay $600 plus before he owns the freezer and, with a family of more than twelve children to feed every meal, he will not have much to store in it.

"I's th' on'y feller in this hyur holler 'at's got a big freezin' box."

This is a fact. That he has to disconnect it when he turns on his television is not an inconvenience. A 120-volt line will carry just so many electrical units. If you are borrowing juice from a high line, then "you's gotta be kerful." Many Branchers have blown a transformer and the repairmen have failed to discover why such an unbelievable thing could occur. One told me that short of lightning this could not happen. But should I be the one to tell him how many non-paying customers he has hooked onto the line? One has to make the decision early in, the game—friend to whom, foe of whom? Once this is decided, one's allegiance is unswerving no matter what the circumstances. Many times the communications system in the Branch warns that "furriners is plannin' comin' in." With that I help the borrowers of electricity pull their lines off the 220-volt lines. I was not sure in the beginning just what this would do to me, but after seeing my friends do it repeatedly I was sure that if they were not hurt I would not be. By the time Troy remembers to plug in his new white elephant, provided he can turn off the television long enough, he has a two- to three-inch layer of water in the bottom of his freezer. I would be willing to guess that Troy has had a maximum of three of something in his deep freeze at any one time in three years.

There is daily evidence of the incorrectness of the name Happy Pappy. The pappies are anything but happy. Maybe times "is easin'" but the federal funds coming in through such an obviously degrading visible means are repulsive to the recipients. The most repulsive factor is that these people do not consider themselves poor. But they do believe that they have a right to food "fittin' fur eatin'." Of the insurmountable obstacles encountered by the poverty warriors, the one which left the most lasting impression was the ability of those who do not consider themselves poor to oppose any semblance of change in their life way; the most insignificant changes are not acceptable. Some warriors agreed it would be easier to tunnel through a mountain barehanded than to effect change against such an impenetrable barrier.

One day Meander asked me to bring my word book when I came into the hollow. This always meant he was hankering for me to see if a word was in the dictionary, and my problem was always the same —trying to understand what word he wanted me to look up and, if I were lucky enough to find it, figuring out how to explain its meaning to him. Many times he would become impatient and accuse me of not being able to read or cipher. Never could figure what the latter had to do with it. But when I was asked to look up what "pappy" meant, it just wasn't there. How could Webster have failed me? But this was grist for Meander's verbal mill. As always, I was frank. "It's not in here."

He smirked, as only he can. "Hit figgers. Cain't come up with nothin' fur holler fellers 'at's fittin'."

"Fittin'" to him means an adequate or appropriate description or explanation.

"Nothin's changin'," he added. "Thar's 'em 'n' thar's holler fellers."

Always concerned about my status with my hollow friends, I asked, "What am I?"

"We's claimin' you us'ns."

I thanked him and told him that I hoped I would always be worthy of being a true "us'ns."

He looked proud and turned his head away. "You's bound t' be 'n us'ns if'n you's hain't changin'."

I tried to assure him that I wasn't "hankerin' fur changin'." Little does he realize how difficult it is for me to shift gears in my thoughts, actions, behavior, dress, and hygiene when I drive those two hundred miles back into middle-class suburbia and a full-time job with an expected standard of appearance and apparel, to say nothing of smell. But few welcome me in the latter, on return from my jaunt to the hollow, with as deep warmth and appreciation as those in the Branch who see so little of me in comparison. When I was growing up on "The Pied Piper of Hamelin," I am sure I never visualized being in a comparable situation myself. Yet comparable indeed was my first entry into the Branch after what I thought was a short absence. The difference was that I was followed by children and adults, coming almost as if out of nowhere, so eager to see me and "us'ns" again. One sees little in their way of life that can be called expressions of joy, but when I come back the adults and the children alike seem to be delighted and instantly everyone is asking, "You's in fur good?"

I must admit that I have to tear myself away from the hollow at 2:00 A.M. on Monday to get back to my job at eight. I have been tempted many times, although this is not a practice with me, to call in sick to delay my return for a day, but to telephone from the hollow into the outer world is so complicated that I have never dared attempt it. Since this is different behavior from theirs, my hollow friends would say, "You's jailed fur shootin' 'thout nary a gun."

At this stage of my life, I would propose an axiom: You can take the people out of the hollow, but you can't take the hollow out of the people. But I would hasten to ask, should we even try? Most of the Branchers have little desire for the material interests of those outside and make no effort to acquire possessions, much less spend for them.

To the contrary, most of those on the Happy Pappy program cling stubbornly to a life way distinctly rural—open country, room for growing vegetables and humans, rustic, unincorporated, without regard for the twentieth-century population living elsewhere.

There are 257 counties in the Appalachian South. Earle County ranks 242nd or just fifteenth from the bottom according to median family income. For median years of school completed by adults twenty-five years and older, the county ranks 252nd, fourth from the bottom. Family income in the 362 counties that make up the Appalachian area range from 10 to 80 per cent below the national average. The national median family income is $5,600 as against an Appalachian maximum below $3,000. Those one would assume to be workers, even though jobless for many weeks of the year, are so inadequately educated that they lack the basic learning experiences upon which to build a retraining program of any kind. Persons interested in promoting the poverty program seem unwilling to accept the fact that the hollowers as well as many others benefiting from assistance programs are not interested in full-time jobs, education, or retraining. Retraining programs are not the answer when there are no jobs after the programs have been completed. Furthermore, for the hollow fellow, it is not retraining. Programs cannot retrain an individual who has never been trained in the first place.

Perhaps success or failure in terms of learning and work participation needs a new frame of reference. Perhaps encouragement is the missing influence; its inclusion might salvage chronic welfare recipients and the young hollow folks who never enter the world of work. Perhaps a large number of the uneducated could be salvaged through school programs if conditions in the classrooms were more advantageous to their particular needs. But the school must make the program to serve the needs of the greatest number. As stated previously, I cannot offer one criticism of the school system as it is now until the hollow children and the adults have exhausted through maximum utilization its full potential. It would be unjust and unfounded in fact to make a blanket indictment of the schools which have the means to provide those from the hollows with opportunities to become producers to the maximum of their capabilities. But if they choose not to utilize the resources at hand it is unreasonable to criticize the schools and expect them to tailor-make programs to meet Branchers' needs when they have not taken advantage of what is currently available.

After the experiment with the six men, I was convinced that at least for the young people an increased productivity ability within the vocational competence of the school system was a real possibility. I doubt that I will ever agree to superimposed solutions from afar. The school system will remain long after those who toy with possible solutions have departed. It is and must be an integral part of an on-going community constellation of services. If our work is to be powered less and less by muscle and more and more by know-how, then the preparation for the latter should be birthed within the educational facilities of this community. Insiders, weak as some critics think they are, can still offer the most acceptable framework to break the cycle of deprivation at any given point of intervention.

In any work activity the hollower needs to achieve. Maybe digging a posthole is not a marketable skill, but few can imagine the personal satisfaction Troy felt when he could use a yardstick to measure depth, increase his speed, and dig more holes in a work day than anyone else. The quality dimension came to light for him when he had a hole and the fence post did not fit. He learned to break a stick the size of the post he was to set and make the hole clean, which would permit the stick to clear the sides and drop to the bottom.

The man with the bull-tongue plow and the man with the grub hoe in any job in the world of work will find it difficult if not impossible to eke out a living in the present decade. The only hope that hollow folks have of securing relief from a life of deprivation is to pattern an escape route, an escape from a non-participating role in the work world to some semblance of self-sufficiency in a setting where the maximum potential is peasant agriculture. Effective production in the labor market may well be the major responsibility or task of the educational resources in this county and those in a similar situation, but such special attention to the educationally deprived should be proposed only after experiments justify the feasibility of human potential development which is practical within the bounds of financial resources, personnel, etc.

In an argument with a so-called authority on hollows, I was told that the hollow parents were irresponsible because they did not have college aspirations for their children. College aspirations, however, depend on grade school aspirations and high school aspirations. We did agree that the future of their work possibility was blighted in proportion to their educational attainment and that the talents and interests of children from the hollows would preclude entry into the world of work in the professions, business and, on the whole, industry. We also agreed that not even a comprehensive high school could be expected to meet the needs of the vast majority of the children from the hollows. Nor was technical educational training for jobs of a semi-professional nature in a two-year post-high school program likely to train technicians for a job. Instead, it might well be a post-sixth grade program in some form within the local school system. Such programs are not now available, but they might become the answer in a restructuring of the school program so frequently called inadequate. The place of education in preparing hollow children for useful and productive work rests with the system already functioning in the county, not some superimposed innovation of unproved worth.

The costs would be high. Patience would be taxed. The problems would be indistinct. The urgency of such an approach is beyond belief. Rural education is more expensive than urban education. Preparing the deprived for a role in the work world is more expensive than preparing others in our society. Education and vocational education is not all there is to training for useful work. Education for marketable skills is not the entirety of a "whole" education. Education for work we agreed upon. Our difference was how to achieve it and when. If a working adult has worth in our society, if his occupation and the quality of his performance are commendable, could he not promote a new philosophy of work among the young adults? Could he not exert a strong motivational influence among young adults to desire to earn a living through some kind of useful, rewarding (beyond monetary) work activity? Uneducated hollow people who lack a marketable skill are destined to underemployment. Should we strive to identify and then maximize the talent, whatever it may be, in the coming generations yet undeveloped? It is conceivable that a part-time job is the beginning, eventually culminating in a better full-time job consistent with the aptitudes, interests, and needs of an individual who just happened to be born in a hollow.

It is evident that those persons who want to participate in the labor market will have to be prepared to do some kind of work. Many changes in living, ideas, attitudes, and behavior will be needed for acceptance in employment. Neither of these necessities seems likely for the mass of those who work only a few days a week in some months of the year.

It would require a cultural upheaval to get the women into a labor force. They fulfill the customary duties of a housewife and mother, in addition to assuming most of the activities involved in daily survival —carrying coal and water, cutting wood, digging gardens, picking up commodities, making necessary contacts with agencies. None of the women is employed. Work outside the home is not only frowned upon by the man of the house, it is emphatically forbidden. Were that not enough, care of children, personal grooming, etc., are other major factors. Extensive dental repair, clothing, ability to communicate in the outer world—these are only a few of the barriers each would need to overcome to hold even the least skilled job. In the history of the hollow, few women have been employed outside the home. But why should they seek a job? Forty-eight of the fifty-five families have a male member as head of the household, although only two are regularly employed. Twelve work occasionally and sixteen are considered unemployable because five claim ill-health, five others declare that they are too old to work, and six claim disability. In other words, one third of the families are supported by some type of employment, one third have no means of support, and one third of the would-be breadwinners are either sick, disabled, or old.

There are jobs in the county that have been unfilled for years. Many of them could be shared with young men willing to prepare and train for the responsibility. One could enumerate an appallingly long list of persons in the county who are employed in good paying jobs: schoolteacher-bus driver, constable-flagman on a construction project, school principal-successful farmer, school principal-coal mine bookkeeper and payroll clerk, to illustrate a few. Inequities in employment opportunity for the better jobs could be corrected if those in the power structure so wished. Being born in the right kinship group or family accounts for much dual employment—yes, even any employment. A husband and wife teach in the same school, one member of a husband-and-wife team teaches in the school and the other is employed by a local agency, for example. There is perhaps less interest in the latter since it could not be remedied without a voting loss to the political hierarchy.

In a county school system in which some of the teachers fail to meet minimum educational requirements and must be carried on a substitute teacher basis, it is outrageous that twenty-five young teachers with degrees cannot obtain employment. This problem is intensified in a system which fails to retire teachers at sixty-five or seventy years of age. Some teachers of considerable wealth are permitted to teach on and on at good salaries. If predictions are accurate and it becomes necessary to share diminished work activities, then barriers to fair employment will need to come down regardless of a local political situation.

Federal trainee programs, at best, can make little more than a dent in the over-all unemployment problem. Often the very mechanics of a program bog down before it can begin. An article in the local paper was written by the county farm agent. The residents were informed that the six Earle County schools and the county agent would be distributing application blanks for persons who wished to apply for job training. The training was to be free and would include several occupations. The Carrie Unemployment Office was responsible for the test counseling and for the selection of workers. I was surprised on one of my regular visits to the home of a county official to see that he was reviewing and "sorting" a four-inch pile of these applications. When I expressed a degree of familiarity, he seemed somewhat uncomfortable and was conscious of the fact that he had no real reason for having the applications. Many of those persons who wished to fill out forms but did not subscribe to the area paper did not know that applications were taken on Thursday and Friday between ten and two. The principal of one of the schools told me that many people came to apply too late. In describing qualifications, the applicant had to be an unemployed or underemployed adult. Members of farm families with less than $1,200 annual net family income were also eligible. There was some question among those interested in Duddie's Branch neighborhood whether or not they could be included as farm families. Persons between sixteen and twenty-two years of age in need of occupational training and further schooling could also apply. A number of boys in this category were successful in making application. The real interest of the prospective trainees was not that they would be prepared for employment but that they would be eligible for allowances, transportation costs, and subsistence allowances which would be paid in cash during the training period. Not once was the question asked, "What will I be prepared to do and how can I secure employment?" Every inquiry was focused on the financial remunerations which would be made available to the trainee.

Hollow men and women could not take advantage of courses for skilled and semi-skilled trades: drafting, printing, business, electronics, and practical nursing. Dropouts are untrainable even in semi-skilled work. Training for training's sake may produce statistics, but it will not produce pay checks. Retraining programs for the underemployed are effective only if they prepare workers to perform satisfactorily in jobs which are available.

In response to inquiries from those who participated in the early formulation of remedial programs and activities, I felt completely inadequate when attempting to explain why these people were not flexible, not versatile. It is difficult if not impossible to create a positive orientation for an individual who is the "boss." Even among their own kind, whether it is "fittin' fires" or "stick weedin'," no one wants to assume the role of a boss. "Me bossin'? Nope. If'n they's workin' 'r layin' out hain't fur me t' name. If'n 'em 'at's restin' mite near all 'a time, I's not namin' hit. Some things hit's better not seein' 'em. I hain't never hankerin' fur no trouble. Ev'n dumb heads hain't fur aimin' trouble at him." A boss may be one who has taken advantage of a man, someone who has cheated, someone who "spies" on some of the men and not on others, but most frequently the one who is "namin' somethin' he cain't do." If dog hole coal mining has one advantage, it is that the boss is too "cowardin' t' snake on his belly fur back as I's diggin'."

For those in the hollows and small towns, their future is closely tied to activity which has some economic return. If we are to continue to spend huge sums of money to support all of the extension personnel, then immediate drastic changes must be initiated so that the disadvantaged can produce his own food if he is to save himself. If we could just get off the new industries bandwagon, it is conceivable that we could develop imaginative plans which have potential for decreasing the huge sums of money we so willingly pour down the rathole. No community receives any benefit from the many fly-by-night industrial developments. Why must there be the plaintive plea for state or federal monies before making a reasonable effort at the local level?

Who are the people who direct and staff a Community Action Commission? How much do they get paid for their work? What do they do? Much could be written about their background. Questions could be raised regarding their qualifications for the work they are supposed to be doing. But one of the most enlightening aspects of the staff members is the salary they receive. The executive director is paid $15,000 a year to run the operation. The assistant director receives $12,000 as his annual salary. Two deputy directors receive $10,000 each. A field director acts as trouble shooter and is responsible for the actual organization work, for which he also receives $10,000. The coordinator of efforts likewise gets $10,000. The salary of one field assistant is $7,500. A second field assistant receives $5,000 for a thirty-hour week. But there are other staff members. The financial secretary is paid $100 per week, the receptionist receives $65 a week, and a student from one of the local colleges works fifteen hours a week, for which he is paid $2.50 an hour. This is a moderate staff when compared with commissions elsewhere. Exclusive of all costs for space, equipment, expendable supplies, etc., this group receives a gross yearly pay of $76,100. Results of the staffs' combined activities, at least to date, fail to justify their high salaries.

During my time in Earle County I attended the dedication of the second largest building, the State Highway Department office building, reported to cost $350,000. (The largest building is the county high school.) Serving eight counties, the building was to be the headquarters for 70 persons who would supervise the activities of 600 employees. The dedication speech was impressive: ". . . This building is a symbol of the desire of the people . . . to go forward. . . . We cannot rest until every boy and girl in our state has a chance for a quality education. We cannot rest until every family in our state lives within reasonable distance of a modern, high-speed highway, until a highway system planned for people rather than politics unlocks every community in our state. . . . We cannot rest until those with whom life has dealt harshly should find compassion and help from a kindly state—the aged, the fatherless, the blind, the mentally ill, the handicapped, and the retarded children."

After the ceremonies were over, a Brancher said, "He's mouthin' but w'en hit comes t' doin' his blood hain't movin' fast 's a hard-back turtle kin run."

Job opportunities are limited and rural hollow isolation continues, as does inadequate utilization of educational facilities. How can skills be upgraded when muscular coordination is non-existent? It is one thing to plan for preparation of the unemployed, but it is quite another thing to plan a job for the unemployable. What would happen if we were to adopt the sheltered workshop pattern in a hollow? The sheltered workshop is designed to give the handicapped a chance. A child who grows up in a hollow has more handicaps than we know how to measure. Is there an analogy between our concern for and help to the blind? Is not the child from the hollow equally as blind?

IX

The Welfare Game

Anticipate charity by preventing poverty; assist the reduced fellowman, either by a considerable gift, or a
sum of money, or by teaching him a trade, or by putting him in the way of business, so that he may earn
an honest livelihood, and not be forced to the dread-
ful alternative of holding out his hand for charity.
This is the highest step and the summit of charity's
golden ladder.

Moses Ben Maimon (Maimonides)
Charity's Eight Degrees

The United States officially declared war on poverty with the Economic Opportunity Act of 1964. Two or three years earlier, other
strategy had been laid: Area Redevelopment Administration (ARA),
Accelerated Public Works Law (APWL), Manpower Development
and Training Act (MDTA), and scores of similar programs. Yet the
success of the various public assistance endeavors is questionable.
ARA, for instance, provides technical and financial help to industrial
development groups in nearly a thousand areas. But new industries
seek communities with capital, good sites, utility services, and a
pleasant environment for its employees; typically depressed areas
cannot offer these advantages. Moreover, the ARA groups must
compete with 40,000 other groups in better-heeled communities who
are also trying to lure industry their way. Nor has the APWL sipped
the intoxicating ambrosia of success. The construction generated by
this slate should be creating thousands of jobs but thus far it has not
reduced unemployment to any noticeable degree. Machines, not men,
are digging ditches for sewer lines and cutting stones for buildings.
Beyond that, it rarely is the source of jobs for natives of the communities. Most construction companies have to bring in their own crews
because the areas in which they are working have few skilled carpenters, electricians, painters, plumbers, masons.

Public assistance payments of every kind in Kentucky more than doubled from about $55 million in 1962 to $135 million in 1968. This, we are told, is a good portent—those eligible for financial aid are getting more money for their essential living expenses and greater numbers of deprived now qualify as a result of new rules. Publicity releases indicate that poor people are getting more, and more poor people are getting. For those who get more, though, "more" averages less per month at a time when the dollar continues to depreciate. The Commodity Price Index, which measures the average change in the prices of goods and services and uses 1957–59 as a base equal to 100.0, shows an over-all jump in the cost of living from 103.1 in 1960 to 121.2 in 1968. When broken down into specific categories, the index reflects an 18 per cent rise in the cost of food, a 16 per cent rise in housing, and a 16 per cent rise in transportation, all within the past decade. Translated into other figures, the rising costs of goods and services mean a continual lowering of the purchasing power of the dollar. The American consumer's dollar, again using 1957–59 as a base equal to 100.0, was worth 97 cents in 1960, 91 cents in 1965, and 82 cents in 1968. At this rate of decline, the dollar will be worth 50 cents in less than twenty years. That's some achievement in the world's most productive country!

The Kentucky state total amount of public assistance payments during 1968 totaled $135,463,795. Of this amount, Earle County received $2,325,738. Still, there are those who contend that the eastern Kentuckians would rather work for a dollar an hour than accept "giveaways." If so, they have access to facts I have not because my observations refute this claim. The majority of the recipients not only accept the "giveaways," they strive to acquire more. Not many hollowers are willing to work for a dollar an hour, eight hours a day, five days a week for two thousand or so dollars at the end of the year. To the illiterate or semi-illiterate, the cash difference between the labor market and the draw "hain't worth stirrin' fur." When he can make a choice between forty hours of self-determined leisure-time activities and forty hours of menial labor, he invariably chooses the former because the monetary reward " 'twixt drawin' 'n' pay fur workin' " is so small. It is not surprising, then, that his children, who are not imbued with intellectual and moral ambition, eventually are cast in deprivation as a way of life. They, too, will find squeaking by on an annual welfare income of $800 preferable to work. And "squeak" they will—welfare provides only 60 to 70 per cent of the minimum needs for food, clothing, shelter, and medical care and the recipient loses all or a portion of his grant if he earns extra money to meet his budget requirements. A forty-four-year-old unemployed laborer who has been on and off welfare rolls since 1955 summarized the unrealistic regulations of assistance programs: "I usually work two or three days a week for ten dollars a day, unloading railroad cars at the lumber yard. The money I earn is deducted from my welfare allowance for the month, so I come out the same whether I work or not." This admission probes a tender area in the welfare program—removal of incentive. A large percentage of the recipients could work, particularly the younger men and women, but the vast networks of federal funds doled out to them in some form of relief have undeniably had an adverse effect on attitude. They resolutely maintain that they have a right to all the draw they can get by whatever means. "If'n Paw got hit, I's reckonin' I's got a right t' git hit too." As long as they continue successfully to exercise this "right," they will continue to shun work.

Any society that supports public assistance programs must somehow prevent welfare from becoming more attractive than work. The poverty cycle cannot be destroyed if dependency breeds dependency —and it does. We are now subsidizing second and third generations of families who have existed almost entirely on relief. Our massive domestic aid program, which took root in the Great Depression of the early thirties, was instituted by President Franklin Delano Roosevelt as a temporary emergency measure. In order to emphasize the harmful nature of his stopgap solution, he said in 1935, "The federal government must and shall quit this business of relief. Continued dependence upon relief induces a spiritual and moral disintegration, fundamentally destructive to the national fiber. To dole out relief in this way is to administer a narcotic, a subtle destroyer of human spirit."[1]

Everyone expected that, as the economy recovered, the programs

[1] WKRC editorial, Cincinnati, Ohio, October 31, 1967.

would be reduced. But the opposite occurred—as times got better, the relief load burgeoned. While Washington boasted of unprecedented prosperity in this decade, direct total federal public assistance doubled in seven years, from $2,033,761 in 1960 to $4,706,738 in 1967. In staving off starvation, we seem to have bred a growing horde of citizens who are unable or unwilling to fend for themselves. And in our anxiety to keep people who don't need relief from getting it, we have engendered conditions that foster dependency and irresponsibility: the welfare recipient will not work to supplement his income because his assistance check is reduced by the amount he earns. If an unemployed, able-bodied father lives with his family, they are not eligible for Aid to Dependent Children; therefore the man either deserts his family or hides when the social worker calls. As a result, slums are becoming matriarchal societies, and we are well on our way toward the third generation of fatherless children who are never exposed to examples of responsibility. Worse, we might be practicing natural selection in reverse. While the state imposes tax burdens that oblige conscientious families who have aspirations for their children to restrict their numbers carefully, it assumes the responsibility of supporting children of incompetents and encourages their production by making breeding profitable.

Although poverty can be "cured" simply by handing out huge sums of money to the poor, how will the hard-working man react to this remedy when his income exceeds the loafer's by only two hundred dollars a year? Perhaps a revival of a WPA type of program is the answer—if a living is a right, then some form of work is a duty. People degenerate if the only bugle call they ever hear is the one that summons them to pick up the welfare check. Many have advocated the abolishment of all government handouts because they have sabotaged spirit, personality, and the true being of the human organism. "The enervating influences of Welfarism have eaten deep into his morale and ambition . . . two decades of uninspired Welfarism have induced the belief that control of his destiny is in other hands . . . The old fierce pride and sensitive spirit of independence have died from the continuing social trauma of a half-century."[2] Opinion

[2] Harry M. Caudill, *Night Comes to the Cumberlands* (Boston: Little, Brown and Company, 1962), pp. 350, 389, 392.

has not inspired the hollower to loftier goals. Some kind of stability in his "drawin'" (whatever the source and consistent with price escalation) and less "pryin' 'n' snoopin'" is the dream of every Brancher. As prices rise and benefits diminish or become insufficient for his desired mode of life, the "more" frame of reference is stressed. Given half a chance, the mendicant would magnify his allotment and reduce his expenditure of energy. Farmer's attitude is representative. "In Paw's day a feller 'ud be might' nigh all day goin' 'n' comin' fur a check. 'At's one thing I's fur 'em fellers now. They's willin' t' pay fur backin' a letter t' let you's git you's check right handy. Saves a feller a heap 'a time thumbin'. Free doct'rs, free pills, free grub fur little 'r nothin'. 'Course, they's still takin' their'n outta mine afore they's sendin' hit, same's they done Paw 'n' 'is paw afore 'im."

"Why should you complain?" I wondered. "You're getting money for nothing."

"Reckon thar's somethin' t' 'at, 'ceptin' I's figgerin' they's gittin' more 'n they's givin'."

But the hollow dweller is not unduly alarmed. He has survived all the proposals: starve him out, move him out, involve him in mass migration, absorb him into the Great Society, ad infinitum et nauseam. "'Em welfare fellers be dyin' on th' vine, fur I's goin' t' draw long's I's breathin'. They's not gittin' fellers liken me 'r th' younguns I's growin' in 'em fur places. We's hain't aimin' fur nothin' diff'r'nt 'n' they's hain't makin' no diff'r'nce t' us fellers."

When President Johnson signed into law the Applachian Regional Commission, he decreed that "the dole is dead," but he also added that the bill would not work miracles overnight. Some years later I am still unable to find anything that even approaches a miracle—just further deterioration and heightened deprivation. The tarpaper shacks still lean in Duddie's Branch. The "dead" cars still rust in the dirt yards and more carcasses accumulate each year. The chuck holes still pit the creek bed and get deeper every year. You can't see any of this from an expressway or even from a paved mountain road; you can't know that only a few miles from the highways rotten shanties with leaky roofs are lurking in the green underbrush of the mountains just as they were before being bypassed by society.

Local officials have for years been trying to cope with their poverty problems, but when the unavailing federal program reared its Medusa head, their long-time efforts were so submerged that it seemed as if they had done nothing. Even state attempts overshadowed local exercises, but they haven't worked either and we have yet to formulate economically feasible approaches to human retrieval.

The hollower has his own answer: to play the game as best he can. He does not understand all the rules, but his philosophy is that "if'n you's shootin' 'n' nothin' drops daid, you's reloadin' 'n' firin' agin." To play the game, he applies each year for some welfare program, is refused, reapplies the next year, and is again refused. This is continued until he has exhausted all the categories. In the meantime, some of the rules change so he begins anew—he reapplies, is refused, and finally gets on some kind of aid.

Webster defines "welfare" as experiencing good fortune, happiness, and prosperity. "Game" is described as a practice for gaining an end, in which the participants are in direct opposition to each other in accordance with the rules. In the process of conflicting personal interests, maximum gains are sought while losses are kept at a minimum. To the Duddie's Brancher, welfare is a practice for gaining an end—good fortune, happiness, and prosperity. The public assistance staff and the applicant-recipient are in direct opposition to one another; those responsible for certifying the applicant must be satisfied that he is eligible and the eager applicant does all he can to convince his adversary that he is qualified. The welfare workers are intent on minimizing expenditures and the applicant is determined to gain as much as he can without working. For generations the Brancher has regarded some form of welfare as his legal right and heritage as an American citizen. Faithful to his doctrine that aid is "somethin' 'at's comin' t' me 'n' I's plannin' t' git hit," he looks upon the rules of the game as "jist mouthin'; hain't meanin' nothin' fur me. Hit's jist talk they's s'posed t' give you's. I's jist as fit fur drawin' 's anybody else."

Letters keep me informed of those who are playing the "game" in Duddie's Branch:

"March 2. 1965
"I findly got a lot of Blanks from frankford saying I was ineligible to draw ABC for Kids. I got with the Blanks all Medical reports. was

on the Blanks of Lester. dr Washbourn report was Lester had chronice brain Syndrome fatty liver said he was Permanently and totally disabled. They still say he is ineligible for social Security lack of severity Told Lester sign up on the Work Program if he could not do light work. Something else Would be done. about all I know left for them to do is to come help dig his grave. I think Lester has been treated bad. He has Worked so hard. do hope he can work seme. he loves to work. wish you would come down get on the aid to Bline This branch are funney art They. Jude as a car now. That Where theire money goes In to junk."

"Dec. 20. 1965
"Some Men that Workes on Work Program are Working on this branch Lester is Working Now He has to go to School to Nights a week"

"May 29 1966
". . . We must be living in the last days. things have changes so much since I was a Kid. ever one worked then for what they eat. Vance Passed on the blind he draws one hundard four dollars a month."

In practice, Aid to the Blind is the most inviting form of assistance. According to Sie, this program has far more advantages than "physically disabled" benefits. "They's likely t' take you's off'n th' draw fur disabled onc't you's gits better, so blind drawin's best." All the while he was extolling the virtues of aid to the blind and deploring his inability to see, his orbs were riveted to the television screen. I set about determining how much he had missed because of his "not seein'."

"What happened to that man on the floor?" I asked.
"Guessin' 'e's blind like me, fallin' over a chair."
An announcement appeared on the screen: "Network difficulty. The trouble is not in your set."
"W'at's 'at writin' readin'?" he inquired.
"It's trouble in the wiring from where the picture comes."
"Reckon I's gonna keep a-watchin' till th' wirin's fixed."

As Sie goes, so goes Squire. The newspaper is dropped in the mail-box across from the Hiram store early every morning and Squire was usually waiting for it. He would gaze wistfully across the street but make no move to go for the paper.

"Guess th' papers 'r' in th' box," he would muse.

"Well, why don't you just stir and fetch one?" I was exasperated.

"I's drawin' fur blind 'n' hain't s'pos'd t' be walkin' along th' high-way, 'at's why."

I got the paper for him and listened in stupefaction as he read the news aloud. He began with the headlines and if he encountered a word he could not pronounce he would spell it. "Reckon 'at's one 'a 'em fur-off places. I figgers thar's nothin' thar I's wantin' t' know about."

A news item concerning Frankfort, Kentucky, captured his attention.

"'At's in Germ'ny. Heerd tell about hit atter th' war."

"Well, this Frankfort happens to be the capital of Kentucky," I corrected.

"Nope, you's wrong. Wash'n'tom's th' capital."

After he read the paper from front to back, I could no longer contain my curiosity.

"How did you manage to get on Aid to the Blind, Squire?"

"Took plannin'. Hain't ever' one w'at's makin' hit."

"You must be smarter than most."

"Smarter'n a fox," he modestly acceded. "You's axes 'round from 'em who's drawin', then you's starts goin' t' doct'rs. Went t' one in London 'n' 'e tol' me t' read th' letterin' on a card in front 'a me. I tol' 'im I warn't no good on letters so 'e tol' me I kin point my finger th' way th' marks 'uz goin'. W'en I tol' 'im I cain't straighten my finger on 'count 'a rheumatiz, 'e sayed fur me jist t' stick m' arm out like th' marks go. If'n 'em marks went 'at a-way, my arm 'ud go this a-way."

"The doctor must have thought you did good," I praised.

"Nope. I 'uz al'ays goin' in tuther way. 'E mouthed 'at 'e c'd give me glasses t' see better with, but I tol' 'im I hain't hankerin' t' see no more—I's wantin' t' draw. 'N' 'e says t' come back in six months 'n' 'e'd check me agin. Then 'e wanted three dollars, but I's tellin' 'im I's payin' 'im w'en I comes back."

Squire never did go back, but neither did he discontinue his search for someone who would declare him eligible for blind assistance. After many unsuccessful months, he went to a doctor more than a hundred miles from Duddie's Branch whose eyesight, he had been told, was so poor that he was unable to see whether the patient pointed in the proper direction. Before being tested, Squire wanted to know "th' charge fur givin' a blind paper" and was told that there was no fee for the examination.

"Th' doct'r axed me t' read from a card. I couldn't see nothin' fur sure 'cause 'e din't have no light on hit."

He was at last accepted for blind assistance. "I don't mind workin', but hain't much use if'n I's gittin' a check 'thout hit." Interestingly, persons whose vision is sufficiently poor to qualify them for Aid to the Blind are never fitted with glasses even if they would benefit from them.

Squire's story is just one of many ways in which the "game" is played. Joanthin's father, an early settler in Duddie's Branch, was on the draw from way back. When he died, her mother continued to receive welfare checks until her death. Joanthin thinks that "workin' is fur 'em 'at cain't draw." Welfare is a way of life for her and even though it is "rough gittin' by, hit's a heap better'n havin' t' stir, 'specially in winter."

At sixteen years of age she married Clem. He was ten years her senior and had lived in a "close-by holler right smart 'a th' time." Their first child was born two years later and she now has nine living children. "'Em 'at's daid 'n' 'em 'at's not breathed I's lost count of." The number of miscarriages and stillbirths she fails to remember, but reckons "they's lots."

Today, 56 per cent of her brood reside in Duddie's Branch and rely on her draw for their existence. Sixty-seven per cent of her children live close enough to have the same post office address. One lives just outside the hollow, one is about two and a half miles away in the next branch, one lives thirty miles away, and another fifty miles distant. Seventy-eight per cent of her children are no more than two and a half miles from her home. Her youngest son is eighteen years of age and is "courtin'," two children are married but have no offspring, and through the others, Joanthin is grandmother to thirty-one children. "Thirty-one 's far 's I's knowin' now. They's bound t' be lots more w'en some 'a 'em gits t' havin' 'em w'at's not birthed yet." One son, his wife, and their children live on one side of Joanthin and another son, his wife, and their two children live just across the Branch. Joanthin meekly justifies their constant presence in her house, especially at mealtime: "Hain't fur fur 'em t' walk fur borryin'." Every day one of her grandchildren will appear with a twig and get a light out of her stove so that his father can start a fire.

Joanthin has the only alarm clock in the family and she feels that "callin' 'em close hain't bad if'n any 'a 'em's aimin' on workin'." This is not often but when they are really pinched they will go to the mines for a few days. A good worker can make as much as fifteen dollars a day loading coal but her youngest son seldom earns more than five, and none makes more than ten at most. Two or three days' work a week is all they ever put in, and this at a time when mine operators frequently work only one shift because there are so few miners available. One man said that he could work every loader who would come regularly five days a week for better than eight months out of the year. He told me that not one loader in fifty worked hard enough to earn fifteen dollars a day; a mine operator cannot make much money with laborers who load only four or five cars a day and work only a couple of days a week.

During the first twelve years of her married life, Joanthin said, her husband was a farmer and a miner. " 'E din't make much money but we had food by grubbin'." From 1933 to 1935, Clem was on PWA (Public Works Administration), working primarily on roads. From 1935 to 1942 he made his "livin' from a job on WPA, mostly buildin' bridges 'n' carryin' rocks." Joanthin was proud of him. " 'E done road work plum through WPA, worked at hit till hit stopped." After that Clem sporadically worked for the railroad until 1946, when Joanthin made application for Aid to Dependent Children. At this time her husband was just past fifty years of age and suffering from an illness which had set in ten years earlier. The medical diagnosis was heart disease, arthritis, and senility. He was considered to have a total permanent disability and, in addition, was found to be markedly undernourished. In 1947 he was diagnosed as having pulmonary tuberculosis.

Joanthin began receiving assistance in the amount of $78 per month as a new applicant in September 1946. Her six children were then aged fifteen, eleven, nine, seven, five, and three months. She received Aid to Dependent Children for twelve years and two months. During those twelve years forty-seven different assistance plans had been worked out for her by the public welfare office in amounts ranging from $50 to $130 a month. The total amount of welfare she received during that period is conservatively estimated at $10,000.

When Clem died in August 1958, his family had received some form of public assistance for twenty-one years and seven months of his thirty-eight years of married life.

As of January 1959, Joanthin had received Old Age and Survivor's Insurance for three and three quarter years. She frequently expressed concern that her draw would be cut off when her youngest son was eighteen. "I's not gonna be sixty-two yet 'n' I's gonna be cut off'n from ever'thing," she wailed. "Th' sixty dollars I's gittin' hain't 'nuf fur two, even with 'modities." She intends to reapply for OAS when she is sixty-two years of age, at which time "you's gittin' more."

"Joanthin, you've fared good so far; you'll figure out something."

"I's gonna git 'em disabled papers somehow," she giggled.

Her financial situation was never critical. In 1961 she received a total of $720 in addition to surplus foods for three, having failed to report the marriage of her daughter a year or so earlier. When her Old Age and Survivor's Insurance benefits stopped in August 1962, she began playing the game for her "disabled papers." Up to that time she had received assistance for almost twenty-six years. Unable to establish total disability, she applied for Aid to the Blind and went to a doctor "who's good 'bout fillin' out papers fur blind" to have her eyes examined. Two of her children led her into the office and her behavior followed established procedure. "I c'dn't see nothin' no matter w'at 'e axed me," she asserted. "Th' doct'r tol' me, 'You's blind fur sure.'" Papers completed, Joanthin was led out of the office and up the street and around the corner.

Via the grapevine communication system I heard that she had

qualified to draw, and went to see her to confirm the rumor. No sooner had I arrived than she showed me two new quilt tops which she had finished piecing. They were expertly assembled with small stitching that few sighted persons could match.

I was impressed, and troubled. "If you're blind, how can you see to do such good stitching?"

"Oh, I's on'y blind in th' doct'r's office 'n' th' welfare office. I likes t' quilt 'n' you's gotta have somethin' t' do. I sells 'em fur five dollars."

Sure enough, less than a year off assistance Joanthin was now drawing Aid to the Needy Blind at fifty-two dollars a month.

Not long afterward I was walking up the Branch in total darkness when I overtook her. I told her that I'd forgotten my flashlight and was having trouble seeing the way.

"Take aholt 'a my arm; I's gonna lead you's."

"This is like the blind leading the blind," I laughed.

"You's may be blind, but I kin see plum good—gooder'n day."

We moved right along up the bank, around a fence post, and down the bank to my destination. I could never have proceeded with such alacrity had she not guided me.

Joanthin's thirty-three-year-old son qualified for Aid to the Needy Blind by putting snuff into his eyes prior to being examined, a common but painful practice. He drives a late-model car down a curving highway at speeds in excess of sixty miles an hour and negotiates each curve with skill. He has been reported several times but his draw has not been discontinued. His wife is also on Aid to the Needy Blind, as is their oldest daughter. Curious about the girl, I visited the school she attends. I was taken aback to see that she did not have a special seating arrangement in the classroom; in fact, she was just one row from the last in the room. The teacher mentioned the child's visual acuity. "They tell me that her sight is poor, but she doesn't have any trouble reading."

There are no limits to the ways in which the game can be played.

Letha, daughter of Jabe and Hede Shifter, met and married her husband, Braker, while both were in a tuberculosis sanitarium. Braker's condition was so serious for the first few months of their marriage that he was never allowed to go home for more than a weekend pass. Letha herself was not exactly the quintessence of good health. While in the sanitarium she underwent surgery twice. The first operation was an upper left lobectomy and the second was a right lobectomy.

In October 1958 she began receiving APTD (Aid to the Partially or Totally Disabled) in the amount of $168 monthly and ADC (Aid to Dependent Children) for one of her two alleged children. The APTD, incidentally, was calculated on the basis of two children, one of whom supposedly was taken care of by a non-existent sister. Soon after the welfare checks started coming in, her husband was released from the sanitarium and he began drawing $55 a month compensation from the Veterans' Administration for a brother who had been killed in service during World War II.

In 1960, Braker deserted his family and Letha told the welfare workers that she lived in a one-room shack she put up next to her parents'. Letha's hutch has four walls and a roof and two LP gas tanks are even fastened to an outside holder. To further the illusion of occupancy, a 110-volt electric line is connected to the house although there is no meter. The entire setup is so well staged that even I was almost deceived and the first time I saw Braker walk out of the Branch I went up to the house and knocked three or four times. When there was no answer, I peeped through a crack in the dusty, frayed curtains that covered the gray window panes. The interior was bare. My Branch friends had been right—neither Letha nor anyone else lived there. She lived with her parents. The house was a sham, erected for the sole purpose of qualifying for assistance, which required that she live alone. The negligible cost of putting up the shack paid handsome returns. Letha could now draw along with her mother, father, and other family members. The hoax was so elaborate, however, that I still could not place credence in what I had seen. At the first opportunity I checked Letha's status with the LP gas company. Their report dispelled any lingering doubts. The gas tanks had never been changed or filled since their original installation years before. The gas people were baffled too.

Although Letha did not have trouble in qualifying for Aid to Dependent Children, most applicants are required to provide a marriage license and birth certificates for children at the time of the initial interview. Bertha applied for ADC by mail: "I am for wording my marage certific and six chillun. I had seven but one died which was babtised on a half shet of paper." Mary also made her overture by mail: "I'm ritin to welfar to say that my baby was born two years old When do I gits my money." Letters and cards are usually brief and to the point. Having been unsuccessful in an attempt to qualify, one written inquiry took this form: "I cant get sick pay. I have six children. Can you tell me why." In addition to the documents, the applicant must testify that her husband is dead or has deserted his family. One bit of testimony read as follows, "Im glad to report that my husband who was reported missin is dead." Another stated, "Please find out for certain if my husband is dead as the man I am now living with cant eat or do nothing until he knows." One woman, questioned about the parentage of her child, replied in writing: "I am very much amazed to find that you have branded my boy as illiterate as this is a dirty lie. I was married to his father a week before he was born."

For some obscure reason, unwed mothers have less difficulty in obtaining Aid to Dependent Children.

Louis was choleric when he discovered that his eighteen-year-old unmarried daughter was pregnant. She had complained for some time of a backache and liniment was applied to the affected area. The backache did not subside, however, and stomach pains developed. Still no one was suspicious because abdominal distress is common in Duddie's Branch where intestinal parasites flourish.

Many months prior to Abbey's labor pains, I had been apprised of her condition by Sie, the father-to-be.

"I's courtin' Abbey 'n' we's playin' 'round."

"What are you saying?" I asked him.

"Bein's you's never married maybe you'd don't know."

"Maybe not," I agreed.

"You's ever court?"

"If you mean date, yes."

"I hain't talkin' 'bout no food. I's talkin' 'bout playin' 'round. Hit's jist th' quar ones who hain't never done hit."

I pressed him for details. His behavior struck me as extraordinary in light of his marriage to Goldie and their three children; my awareness of how little the obligations of a wife and family weigh on some men motivated me to pursue our conversation.

"Hit 'uz this a-way," he continued. "Berley 'uz aimin' t' take Abbey fur a ride in 'is car 'n' I axed t' go. W'en we's endin' up at th' head 'a Coon Holler, I sez t' Berley, I sez, 'W'at you's aimin' on?' "

I could almost hear poor, faltering Berley: "Jist plannin' t' sit a spell." Whereupon Sie recommended that he "hit th' road." As Abbey's condition became more obvious, Berley went around mumbling, "I warn't thar."

Since nothing seemed to relieve Abbey's discomfort, Louis finally decided to take her to a doctor. He owed the two nearest to Duddie's Branch so they went to a physician twenty-two miles away. After the examination the doctor congratulated Louis. "Your daughter is going to have a baby."

"W'at you's sayin'? You's no damn good, 'cusin' my girl 'a sech!!" Louis exploded.

Abbey remained silent. They got into the back of the pickup truck which Louis's son was driving and criticized the medical profession all the way back. Just before they got to the turnoff at the mouth of the Branch, Abbey reckoned that she "might be havin' a baby." Louis was incredulous and demanded that his son drive twenty-five miles to the nearest doctor in the other direction. That physician also confirmed the earlier verdict and against his advice Louis directed his son to head for home once more. Abbey gave birth to her baby en route.

I heard about the new arrival early the next morning and walked up the Branch to see Louis. He was leaning against the house in a chair and a shotgun was balanced across his knees.

"Looking for something to stir?" I tremulously bantered.

"Reckon hit's done stirred," he snarled. "I's plannin' t' shoot 'at skunk soon 's I meets him. Hit happened t' all 'a 'em girls I had, but I warn't 'spectin' nothin' from Abbey."

To resort to reasoning would have been to court disaster and I did not linger. I avoided Louis for some weeks thereafter until he spied me as I was walking by his place at five-thirty one morning. He was a changed man.

"You're stirring early today." It was the most innocuous amenity I could think up.

"Yep," he grinned. "Gotta take Abbey t' town."

"I hope she's not sick," I sympathized, still unwilling to admit that I knew about the baby.

"Nope. Welfare wants t' see her," and with that he produced a rumpled dirty card requesting that Abbey be in the welfare office at nine o'clock. The trip was fruitful; Abbey was told that she would draw $55 a month starting two weeks from that time.

I saw Louis a few days later. He was minus his gun.

"Guess you got that skunk?" I ventured.

"Nope. Abbey's drawin' now so I's savin' my shootin'."

The taxpayer who foots the welfare bill is opposed to any system which has as its primary function the indiscriminate handing out of checks to the "needy" who drain more and more dollars to support their laziness and immorality. Subsidizing immoral behavior that leads to illegitimate children violates the religious beliefs and tenets of human decency and measures have been proposed to take the profit out of welfare. One solution is to remove children from homes receiving relief and rear them in a more stable environment. One state, by a very decisive majority, passed a bill permitting welfare departments to provide contraceptives for mothers receiving assistance payments from ADC. Another possible answer might be to direct county welfare departments to refer ADC mothers for compulsory family planning and birth control instructions consistent with their religious and moral creeds. Yet another recommendation is to limit support payments to one child, requiring the mother to place all subsequent children for adoption. Perhaps none of these proposals is completely satisfactory, but it is evident that something must be done to curb the spiraling costs of ADC.

Paradoxically, the welfare programs very often fail to give assistance to those who are neither dissolute nor slothful but who are in dire need. When Tiny, who is a legitimate applicant, was refused public assistance he incriminated his neighbors, who played the game well.

"Reckon they's scar't they's gonna be 'vestigated 'n' some 'a 'em's tryin' t' do me in."

"Didn't the field worker come to see you?" I asked.

"Yep, but talkin' hain't gittin'. Hain't no need in 'im trudgin' up this hyur holler t' axe th' same questions 'e's already wrote w'en I went t' talk t' 'im in 'is chair. . . ."

"But, Tiny," I interrupted, "it was necessary for him to come. He was supposed to look at your house."

"Oh, I let 'im in. 'E's long on sittin', but reckon my chairs hain't good 'nuf fur 'im." He paused to spit. "Kep' standin', jist questionin' more talk. I'd shore hate hit awful bad if'n I 'uz igner'nt 's 'im 'n' din't have no sense t' boot."

Fifty-four-year-old Tiny has had a stormy on-and-off-the-draw life. He feels that the welfare workers dislike him, as do many of the Branchers, because he is honest.

Every member of his first family, including his wife, died of tuberculosis and he has been in the sanitarium a number of times for the same disease. His second wife is twenty-seven years old and she has borne him four children. This thin, pale man sincerely wants to do anything he can to improve his life and that of his family but fortune has dealt harshly with him. He has not worked for the past ten years, following a severe mine accident for which he did not receive compensation. Nor does he have special skills to sell.

On physical re-examination he is often certified as capable of doing light work and is taken off welfare. But where, near this hollow, can he find "light work"? And what would he earn for light work on a part-time basis, assuming that such a job were available? So, for the sake of his family when they are truly "hurtin'," he applies for readmission to the sanitarium; this is readily granted because his sputum specimens are usually always positive. There is no question but that he actually is disabled and he is justifiably outraged that so many younger people who make no effort to work are dishonestly receiving assistance for mythical disabilities.

A welfare recipient can ask the Department of Economic Security in the state capital for a hearing if he feels that his case has not been judiciously handled, and Tiny has had many hearings. However, the referee's decision has always been unfavorable and Tiny does not know (and neither do I, for that matter) what it takes to be declared incapacitated. When one has almost irreversible health problems, one's physical condition does not improve quickly. It steadily deteriorates. But it is hopeless to fight the system.

During the hearings the judges evaluate the extent of the physical disability in order to determine whether it is serious enough to warrant aid, whether the claimant is able to work at an occupation in which he was previously engaged, or whether he can work at any other job for which he is equipped and which is accessible in the county or community in which he resides. The depth consideration of the latter is disgusting in view of the opportunities in Shade and Earle Counties. There are no available jobs. To complete the farce, Tiny relates facts which are a virtual masterpiece of contradiction. He was discharged from the tuberculosis sanitarium in October 1961 as cured. In April 1963 he was told he had communicable (active) tuberculosis and readmitted to the sanitarium. In October of that same year his case was closed as "inactive tuberculosis since March 1961." Tiny's pulmonary involvement was described as sufficiently grave and of such nature as to contraindicate mining. In the physician's best judgment, although Tiny's condition was gradually worsening, he was capable of gainful employment providing it was "light" and that he remained inactive when not on the job. As a result of the physician's testimony, Tiny was once more adjudged ineligible for welfare. No one thought to ask about the labor it takes just to live in Duddie's Branch—even on welfare. Tiny would still have to carry on his back a ton of coal one gunny sack at a time for three quarters of a mile in the winter. He would still have to spend long hours of toil on his exhausted land in which he attempts a garden plot to supplement his family food provisions. Nonetheless, the decision was irreversible—he would have to get along as best he could.

But the welfare game continues to be played by the administrators and recipients alike. The recipients gobble up the dollars and the administrators enlarge their armies and in the end neither group will be able to declare victory. How can human resources, new growth, and new jobs be developed with task forces? Special programs for special problems never materialize. It's just the same old welfare mumbo-jumbo reheated over and over, but destroy their warehouse of clichés and the entire system might collapse. In Appalachia, for example, they liken the mountaineer to a lawnmower—first you've got to start it and then push it. Maybe that's true of a lawnmower, but pushing the hollower only produces resistance to pressure. It would be more successful to come up with a scheme to separate those who want to help themselves from those who do not, two entirely different breeds of Branchers. Bounty hunting is part of their past and it is natural for some of the hollowers to expect to win by not working. If bounty is two ears from a red fox or a few dollars from the welfare till, what difference?

An important poverty soldier who was a member of the Regional Planning Commission finally agreed to visit Duddie's Branch. On our way out of the hollow, he carefully selected a treasure from his storehouse of stereotypes.

"This is an atypical situation," the erudite gentleman said.

Since he had set aside three free days on his schedule, I offered to take him from one hollow to another until we had toured the more than thirty in Earle County. He declined.

"They're all atypical," he dismissed with a shrug.

"Then I'll take you to another county close by," I urged. "We'll spend all of your time in the hollows."

"This experience has not changed the shape of the problem I have in mind," was his recondite response.

I could not help but wonder what problem his mind was shaping and my expression must have betrayed my perplexity.

"Programs are not intended to do anything for anybody," he patiently explained. "They're just a device to enable people in the depressed areas to do something for themselves."

A great understanding flooded my cranium, and I involuntarily gasped at his cleverness. He was going to give the hollowers a chance to start a stalled economic machine!

The whole welfare system, including its basic philosophy, needs to be overhauled. As it now functions, it seems only to be giving people on relief a designated amount of money rather than coming to grips with the real problem: the circumstances that put the poor where they are today. Welfare recipients in Duddie's Branch are human casualities in no man's land and this status will continue unless their situation is thoroughly explored. Glittering generalities are useless in "meat and muscle" matters. Until the program is revised, though, the literal meat and muscle needs must be met.

The food stamp plan was implemented on an experimental basis in mid-1961 and a county in eastern Kentucky was one of the original eight areas included in the trial run. Administered by the U. S. Department of Agriculture, it was conceived as a method of providing recipient families with a more varied and nutritious diet than was possible with surplus foods. The stamps could be used at any grocery store participating in the program.

In July 1967, the Department of Agriculture announced a reduction in the price of the stamps. Until that time, families had been paying approximately two dollars per person for about twelve dollars' worth of stamps. Under the new arrangement the cost was reduced to fifty cents per person. The local county government is expected to provide the fifty-cent charge for those who cannot pay it, the federal government to find other means to qualify people residing in counties that are unwilling to participate. The plan, once it becomes operational, will include even the poorest families and the less impoverished will also benefit from the reduction in the amount of cash needed to purchase the stamps. Rough estimates indicate that when the program has been extended to more than four million eligible recipients the cost to the government will be in excess of the anticipated $360 million a year.

In order to buy a hundred dollars' worth of food stamps, the recipient must pay six dollars cash. If he does not have it, there is always someone around who will give six dollars for a return of his loan in stamps. Will pays only six cents for each dollar stamp. If he gives twelve dollars' worth of stamps in return for the loan, the lender has made a 100 per cent profit because he can buy twelve dollars' worth of groceries. Will feels that this is a bargain for himself as well; he had to get the six dollars somehow and actually he made money since he only gave away sixty-two cents. Although he cannot figure this, he knows that he is coming out ahead. "They's a heap 'a ways fur money-makin' 'at hain't workin'."

A carefully analyzed pilot project, while it might be impressive, is not always a true index of how families actually spend food stamps. First results showed an increase in meat and poultry consumption, which was encouraging since these animals consumed grain and thus diminished the surplus in the nation's storage bins (and reduced the cost to the taxpayer who pays for the bins). There was likewise a significantly increased consumption of flour; this finding, however, appears to apply more to urban areas than to the hollows.

It is likely that the program has most benefited the small stores which are located in or close to hollows. Even though the stamps enable the purchaser to shop at chain stores, there is still the problem of transportation and most hollow folks prefer to trade at small stores anyway. Supermarket shopping is a bewildering experience for those who are confronted with masses of unfamiliar cans and packages. One small store owner said that the food stamps had improved the economy considerably and that they were the source of the first really hard cash in some time. In spite of the stamps, though, credit buying had not diminished and although the local merchant was getting more cash income than before food stamps were available he still carried a large number of unpaid debts on his books.

After an absence of several weeks, I stopped by a tiny grocery in the bottom of one of the hollows. A new sign over the door read "LBJ Supermarket." When I asked why he had changed the name of his business, the owner explained that the people who received surplus food commodities used his small store as a dumping ground for the supplies they did not want. He understood why the hollowers didn't use everything because he tried to feed his hogs the mountains of commodities that had been left in his place. "When a hog turns it down, it ain't fit for nothin'. 'Em poor fellers are jist like 'em commodities they git. They're surplus. If you git eatin' not fitten fer hogs, I don't blame 'em for not luggin' it no farther than my store." In support of his statement, I have noticed little change in the food pattern in the hollow—the same pinto beans (always short in quantity), white corn meal, etc. We talked at great length about the hollowers' purchases and whether they were following the rules of the food stamp program. The store owner admitted that he did not feel bound to enforce the regulations. "As long as I'm gittin' my's money and I'm sellin' things from my store, I don't care what they buy." He went on to say that most of the families used all their food stamps before the month was half over and that he was required to carry them on credit for the balance of the month. As for any improvement in their conditions, they were living pretty much the same as before—forever in debt and never being able to pay. Some of the small stores give the Branch children lunch money and put it on the books to be paid later with food stamps. The children, instead of using it for hot lunches, spend the cash for candy, soft drinks, and other non-substitutes for solid food.

Many of the items a family needs (soap, toothpaste, bleach, etc.) must be paid for with cash. I was standing in the checkout line directly behind a man from the hollow who would use food stamps to pay for his purchases. The checker removed a big box of laundry powder and said that he could not pay for it with stamps. She checked the remainder of his purchases and accepted the stamps in payment. The man then left his basket at the front of the store and disappeared in the back. In a short while he returned to the checker with a fifth of wine and a carton of cigarettes and paid cash for them. He did not add the laundry powder to the cash purchases.

A few families in the hollow always have a surplus of stamps at the end of the month and loan them to others who run out. Melda knows who will pay them back and who will not, but she lends them nonetheless. "'E hain't borryin'—I's givin' 'em. Walkin' up hyur fur axin' hain't hard; carryin' 'em stamps back, 'at's a mite heavy fur a feller."

Other families are without food or stamps by the middle of the month and many times I have gone to the judge for an emergency order. Another problem is transportation. If I provided the transportation to pick up the commodities in the morning, I was invariably asked to keep them in the jeep until dark, at which time I would return to the Branch to deposit them in the appointed places. The Branchers are sensitive about letting other hollowers see them with emergency rations. Once I went into the hollow at midnight to deliver emergency commodities for twelve families, none of whom was willing to claim the food if "thar 'uz anyone at's seein' 'at hour 'a night." I often made several trips into the hollow in an effort to unload surplus foods, but the recipients would tell me to "bring 'em back later." On several occasions it took me as long as two weeks to distribute the piles of emergency rations I had in the back of my jeep. The hollower is particularly sensitive about the word "donated." Those who are unemployed, who are sick, or whose misfortunes make it necessary to apply for stamps do not go in at the regular time for distribution; they go on an emergency basis so that they do not have to stand in line with the others.

It costs the Branchers who don't own cars anywhere from a dollar fifty to three dollars to transport their commodities. The majority thumb a ride to the distribution center and out again because they don't have the cash to pay for transportation. The drivers who pick them up take the choice food items as their fee.

"Why do you do this?" I've asked them. "You have to go in and out of the Branch anyway, so why charge them for a trip you have to make whether they ride or not?"

"Every time we give these hollowers something for nothin', they get the idea that they have it coming to them."

Resentment smolders in the outer community because some of the Branchers who are on the food stamp programs own cars.

"As long as I'm paying to support them, they don't have no right to a car or a television or anything else beyond their means."

"How will they go about getting their surplus foods?" I inquired.

"It's not going to hurt none of them to walk in and walk back."

"That's a twenty-four-mile round trip on foot carrying fifty or one hundred pounds of food. Could you do it?" I challenged.

"I could if I had lots of time, and they have lots of time."

I wondered whether I could do it, so I told one of the women that I'd walk in with her and her two sons and help them carry the surplus foods. "We'll walk all the way there and back," I said. "We won't thumb a ride." We started out at a quarter past five in the morning; distribution begins at nine. Before many miles, I realized that we would not get there by nine o'clock. When we finally did hobble into the distribution center, most of the "choice" commodities were gone. After a brief rest, we started our twelve-mile walk back; I was carrying almost fifty pounds. The load got heavier with each step I took, but I wasn't about to complain. We still had seven miles to go when the others began discarding commodities they knew they would not use. I did not lighten my load, but by the time we got to the mouth of the hollow I feared that I could not carry my burden much farther. My companions silently relieved me of some of the supplies and I was able to tote the lighter load to the head of the Branch. I would not relish having to repeat that performance every month.

Welfare workers are always complaining that the Branchers just throw surplus commodities away—and they do. I have seen discarded rice and pea beans piled almost three feet high. A common sight on the drive between Earle County and Lexington is that of chickens feeding on yellow corn meal and powdered eggs and milk. Local store owners are truly sympathetic toward the Branchers, but they take a dim view of give-away food programs. They said that for a few days after the commodities have been distributed the water in Duddie's Branch runs white from the powdered eggs and milk that have been dumped into it. The dried milk is not of the instant variety but must be reconstituted with lukewarm water and mixed with an egg beater, which accounts for its unpopularity among the recipients. A store owner said that after hearing the Branchers' complaints about the pea beans which are part of the commodities allotment he asked his wife to cook some to see what the grumbling was all about. "She boiled those beans all day and at suppertime they were almost as hard and inedible as they were before she cooked them."

The commodity foods that are available to the Branchers have never been part of their regular diet. They do not know how to cook rice, for example, nor do they have the necessary ingredients to make it palatable; rice is tasteless, but these families cannot afford butter and very rarely have milk to lend it a little flavor. Shortening is included in commodity foods, but the impoverished use only lard. They also get yellow corn meal but use only white corn meal. Out of their strong dislike for lamb, they shun the canned meat, a combination of beef, pork, and mutton: 95 per cent of it is fed to the dogs in the hollow. Perry said that his dog "has t' be mostly bones and wild hungry, though, afore 'c'll even snoop hit." The misinformed Homemakers, whom I have yet to see in the Branch, are forever praising the "good" foods and talking about how the people should appreciate the program and how much it means to them in terms of proper nutrition. They are also forever saying that the recipients don't use the surplus foods because they do not know how to prepare them. I say that the Homemakers should get up to the hollows and teach residents and use any technique for introducing new staples into their diet in order to check the almost complete waste of surplus commodities. I attended a Homemakers' meeting which dealt only with the policy of the distribution centers and the guidelines they were to use. Someone suggested that posters be prominently displayed, directing the recipients to take only those foods they would use regardless of how much they were entitled to. The recipients, however, feel that if they don't take everything they have coming the employees in the distribution center will take it. For that very reason, they will lug it home—if only to discard it. They always take the peanut butter because it has barter value. Cheese they take, too, because it can be converted into money.

The people who get the shortening and the yellow corn meal and the rest of the commodities that the Branchers reject are in an upper economic group. I have spent many hours at the distribution center and can attest that a lot of people who are ineligible for surplus foods nonetheless get them. Families who fill their larders with the commodities become defensive when questioned. "My tax money paid for this food, and if the hollow people don't want it, there's no point in wasting it. I have a right to it—I've paid for it and I might as well use it."

In April 1964 sensational newspaper articles depicting the plight of the poor resulted in a flood of caravans. Clothing, bedding, food, and other supplies rushed into the hills like a tornado. But the momentum soon faded almost as quickly as the last weak wind left behind by the funnel-shaped cloud.

Local efforts to distribute the clothing, arriving almost daily in the county, all but collapsed. Workers who volunteered to sort and distribute the clothing threatened to quit. Distribution plans were proving to be inadequate to handle the steady arrival of clothing. As a result few of those who requested clothing were receiving any. A feature article in a national magazine and a nation-wide television program on poverty brought response from more persons wanting to contribute to the needy. A company in California donated 1,480 pairs of Levi's. After this shipment of twenty-eight boxes was stacked in the basement storage room in the courthouse accumulated clothing nearly reached the ceiling. A new plan to sort and distribute the clothing was devised. Public health nurses, teachers, preachers, and welfare workers were requested to submit lists of families whom they felt to be most in need of the clothing.

As families learned clothing was available they besieged the courthouse requesting it. They were turned away. Many were evidently in desperate need. Families were told it would do no good to come to the courthouse because clothing would be given only to those families who were recommended and whose names appeared on the lists.

Sorting operations moved at a snail's pace. Excuses for the delay in distribution resulted in mounting criticism. Whole boxes were trucked into isolated hollows. This precipitated a tug-of-war and resulted in a stalemate. Many needy families refused to engage in such dog-eat-dog activities even for clothing.

Some clothing in unopened cartons became unfit for anyone because of mildew and rot. Ultimately much of the clothing went to families not on the lists. Much was discarded and burned. Inequitable distribution kept many poor families from getting any of the clothing. Clothing must be sorted and sized for individual family members if it is to be useful and appropriate. Logistical problems become overwhelming for even the most willing volunteers faced with mountains of clothing.

Door-to-door solicitations in distant communities suggested that the more fortunate adopt a needy family or donate clothing, stoves, washing machines, sewing machines. I am not disposed to criticize the intent of the giver, but what in reality's name can the Branchers do with three washing machines, none of which is in working order, or a gas stove, when all that is available is bottled gas for which they cannot pay in the first place? "Hit's jist 's if'n all hell broke loose," groaned Cully. "Hain't never figgered why 'em fellers haul trash in hyur; we's got nothin' 'ceptin' trash." Reporters periodically play up these gifts in big-city newspapers.

In the hollow an infant who weighs ten pounds at three months of age is not something to write about. It is a way of life—"'E jist hain't fillin' out." Donations of baby foods, cereals, and evaporated milk for the undernourished baby have to be shared with all members of the family. This, too, is a way of life. With seven children under ten years of age all suffering from malnutrition, it is difficult to give preference to the one who has been responsible for the publicity.

When affluent outsiders decided to organize, poverty programs became almost as numerous as the people who needed their benefits. Their banners fluttered in the wind their "mouthin'" created: "The millennium is at hand. The march will commence and we will conquer the ancient enemy." The "enemy" was poverty. Modern armies of social engineers are going to eliminate poverty finally and totally by spending mountains of money, disregarding the fact that previous billions had left the same ills uncured. They maintained that their multifaceted program approach will consume the time and energies of community leaders, volunteers, and even the poor themselves. One warrior predicted, "We are bound to be successful; poverty is already on the run." That's true. As of this writing, at least, it is running ahead of our efforts to catch up to it.

At the time that President Johnson signed the Economic Opportunity Act he said in part, "Today, for the first time in the history of the human race a great nation is willing to make, and able to make, a commitment to eliminate poverty from among our people." So resources were mobilized and the march to liberate the poor began. Loyd was unimpressed. "Promisin' 's somethin' you's years [ears] gits tirin' of. You's cain't feed younguns promisin'; promisin' hain't never put no duds on backs."

We don't hear much any more about the Great Society or the War on Poverty (maybe because it never did amount to more than a light skirmish). Before long it was Strategy Against Poverty and, although it is commendable in theory, its success is minimal in practice. The rural areas are still populated by 45 per cent of the nation's indigent, and the professionals—foreigners in the world of the poor—overestimated the deprived's degree of social sophistication. Jack Weller implied that the mountaineers do not want change. He wrote "Mountain people have a deep feeling of belonging and loyalty. They are unashamedly glad to be mountaineers."[3]

[3] J. Weller, *Yesterday's People*, p. 158.

The parent body for a large number of the programs is the Office of Economic Opportunity, but the ordinary taxpayer is to be pardoned if he finds it impossible to grasp the scope of the current federal poverty agencies. Several of them have been in existence for years, completely new ones have been created, and special departments have been added to both the old and the new. To date the projects have consumed an estimated $6.5 billion in 373 Appalachian counties alone. This figure does not include the breath-taking sums spent by other government agencies for the Area Redevelopment Administration, the Accelerated Public Works Program, etc. In analyzing the ponderous reports, you get the uneasy feeling that costly charges have been listed which are hard to defend as "essential" in a war against poverty (such as the ton of money that was paid out to have mineral right maps drawn up). The Appalachian region, however, is not the only area at which criticism can be leveled. Control of Community Action program monies often leads to savage and prolonged infighting between local politicians, while hordes of patronage hacks are being fattened at the poverty troughs.

The new breed of poverty fighters are shipped to other than their regular agencies wherever feasible. The officials in Earle County objected to this arrangement, which meant that they would not have leadership or guidance on the local level. They also felt that the existing agencies should have the advantage of any additional funds. Both objections, which are worth considering for the good of the present pattern of services, were overruled. The leaders in the county had to step aside and relinquish the reins to a handful of neophytes even though they knew that nothing could possibly be gained by the young lions who were intent on creating conflict and controversy. One "soldier," who had never been outside Detroit prior to his tour of duty in Appalachia, spent his first day among the poor as my guest in Duddie's Branch. He lit into me for not having crushed the county power structure. "I did not see one sign of hope in those people," he accused. "You will never accomplish anything without guts—pure guts. You have to fight! Fight the people who don't want to give up traditional approaches. Fight the politicians who are not aggressive, not imaginative, incapable of getting results. You really do not understand what's going on in the power structure right here under your very nose. Just wait until we get through with them. It'll be like a wrecking crew tearing down a building. The people I saw today will be a lot happier once we have toppled the power structure." Revolution did, indeed, follow his regime—the county power structure toppled him and his co-workers.

The Branchers are disappointed with the way in which aid is being dispensed and administered. Their reaction is not dissimilar to the earlier days of the New Deal when there were also suspicion and mistrust. Jude thinks that the bungling, haphazard approaches and the inestimable waste are "nothin' fur reckonin'. Jist sorry chickens comin' home t' roost. Hain't nothin' changin'. 'Xactly liken hit 'uz, 'xactly liken hit's gonna be. Hain't 'nuf livin' left fur you's fur seein' sorryness endin'. They's winded fur they's hain't sparin' skin, plum tired out from mouthin'. Hain't ever' got nothin' 'ceptin' more sorryness." His eyes twinkled impishly. "Hit's liken pointers on a clock. Thar's lots 'a windin', lots 'a tickin', 'ceptin' 'em pointers goin' nowhar 'ceptin' round 'n' round. If'n windin' stops, tickin's daid; pointers jist stayin' whar they's gived out. Windin' 'n' tickin' hain't lastes [lasting]."

Jude never uses the term "red tape," but he knows what it is and can explain it to me when he wants to furnish one more reason why the "handouts hain't fur nothin' 'ceptin' hurtin'." Red tape to Jude is "footin' 'twixt briars, head highin' [taller than your head]. C'd be you's gittin' in 'ceptin' you's hain't goin', 'n' gittin' out hain't easy even if'n you's backin' in. All you's gits is hurtin' fur scratches."

"What do you think should be done?" questioned a visitor from Washington during the early planning stages of the poverty program.

" 'Em fellers sh'd build us a road."

The politician asked the question over and over. Before visiting the hollows he had boasted that he knew what the people wanted: more jobs, better houses, better schools, etc. None of the responses which he had anticipated was given, nor could he get positive answers to his specific questions. "Would you like to have a better house?" Offended, the Branchers would reply, "Reckon this 'un's fittin' fur livin' long 's I's needin' coverin'." "Hain't hankerin' fur nothin' citified." Regarding a job: "Reckon I'd work if'n drawin' 'uz sappin [requiring too much strength or effort]." " 'Em fellers s'pos'd t' be workin' fur skins. Figger they's gittin' by same 's us fellers. Hain't none 'a 'em sweatin'. Reckon they's no need 'a me sweatin'. Sweatin' saps a feller."

I tried to explain the poverty program initiated in Washington. "If'n 'em guys got poverty thar, how come they kin spare my drawin'?" (Thirty-six dollars a month for a family of seven.)

Most of the Branchers look upon the various programs and the workers with amusement and contempt. " 'Em fellers aimin' on gittin' at us holler fellers; if'n they stays 'round, we's gittin' 'em on th' draw too, easy-like. But don't reckon they'd be hankerin' fur th' hills fur long if'n they's livin' hard."

The Vista workers (Volunteers in Service to America) are to live and work in the hollows, organizing the people to press for road and school improvement. When this happens, if there is any organization, the sparks really start to fly—many of the long-haired workers create dissension among the leaders in the community. There are two contrasting philosophies among these volunteers who attempt to help the hollowers. One is developmental; the other is a depopulate one, which either means decreasing the size of families and some very rigid birth control practices, or moving the residents out of the hollows completely.

The directors are proclaimed as "experts," but some of the projects they endorse fail to support this contention. One Vista volunteer, a man some twenty-odd years beyond the usual retirement age, had been in the program since its inception and had spent his entire time on a reservation teaching the Indians to read blueprints and to acquire home construction knowledge. The administrators apparently felt that these were indispensable skills. Another "expert" confided to me that the solution to poverty in Duddie's Branch was elementary. The women only needed to learn how to use a blender and improve their cooking. Provide each family with a blender and, presto! poverty would vanish.

Often referred to as the domestic Peace Corps, Vista was sold to Congress on the theory that the program would involve thousands of volunteers from all over the United States in improvement activities at the local levels, such as remedial reading programs, centers for youth, home demonstration groups. During election years, poverty administrators try to suppress criticism of this group and paint a rosy picture of accomplishments that have no basis in fact. There were hundreds of Vista workers in the beginning, but many of them—particularly the young—became disillusioned with what they called "the complete absence of preparation and planning." After a few weeks they left the program.

The training period usually lasts about two weeks, one of which is spent on a campus and the other in the field. During the first week the curriculum consists of discussion groups, study of case histories, listening to speakers, etc. The trainee is then sent to live with the residents in the area to which he is assigned. One twenty-nine-year-old volunteer had to live in three rooms with a woman and three children. She had not been there ten days when the rest of the woman's family moved in, bringing the number of residents to fourteen. There were no doors in the house, not even to the toilet. For the lack of a door the cause was lost. The cause also suffered in those homes where everyone slept in one room. Still other volunteers quit because traveling in the rural communities, especially the isolated ones, was too difficult.

Vista workers receive $32.50 per week and return $12.50 of it to the family with whom they stay to cover the cost of the room and board. When the family's set monthly income runs out the workers often have to buy food for the entire household out of the remaining $20. But the problems are not all related to the families. Vista has internal difficulties. Little effort is made to select congenial groups of five or six volunteers to go into one area. One group might be all boys, another all girls, and still another of both sexes. Some of the volunteers are foreigners who speak very little English. The Vista workers assigned to Earle County ran into a special kind of trouble. Three Southern states, including Kentucky, are also served by a federally sponsored agency called the Appalachian Volunteers, Inc. This group is credited with arousing the ire of many officials and, unfortunately, it is easy to confuse one volunteer with another.

The federal cost of each Vista worker in the fiscal year 1966 was $4,684. In June 1967 there were 2,156 workers in the field and 255 in training programs. At the end of the first six months of the fiscal year 1967, almost $22 million had been expended by Vista alone. An expensive way to counteract poverty.

None of the poverty administrators in Washington appears disturbed about the excessive costs and duplication of services. When questioned, they simply retort that their programs must be good since no one has been able to link scandal with them. The purpose of their programs would seem to be to project a Snow White image because all of the things which are identified as causes of poverty—inferior education and training, lack of economic development, few or no job opportunities, poor housing, hostile environment, improper motivation—have thus far eluded their attack, as one sees when he begins to look for concrete results. The general theme of the planners is that the only way poverty can be eliminated is to motivate the youth of the nation and their programs are designed to accomplish this goal. Some hollow children are paid $1.25 an hour to attend school and to work in and around the building for a few hours a week. When questioned, the students frankly admit that they are not attending school because they want an education. No one can deny that these youths have been motivated—if not to learn, at least to earn.

These massive programs are, in large measure, responsible for the continuation of poverty at different levels of our social structure. One of our most urgent problems is that of the multiplicity of agencies, particularly those involved in the care of persons at various stages of illness. Duplication of services is expensive in dollars and personnel and we can no longer afford to finance scattered, isolated ministrations. The program of old age, survivor, disability, and health insurance covered 7,034,000 people in 1966, an increase of 209,000 people covered in 1965.

It is not the purpose of this book to enumerate the endless approaches of the welfare agencies, but some are so absurd as to be worthy of mention. The Sargent Shriver scholarships, to illustrate one instance, provide for a two-month stay overseas as "an experiment in international living." I suggested that the money devoted to these scholarships might be more appropriately spent by sending the national winners into a hollow to work or having them spend a summer with migrant workers or on an Indian reservation. The words were scarcely out of my mouth before I was told that the scholarship programs were primarily designed to acquaint the awardee with the medical, emotional, and social wants of the deprived of some foreign country.

The defenders of proposed welfare schemes engage in "mostly hollerin'." Much of the defense is a stereotype of repetitiveness. Human renewal is not cheap. Human renewal is not easy. Mistakes are inevitable. During one of my early appearances in Washington I tried to convince the planning directors that they should review the capacity of the existing programs to absorb such parts of their proposals as were already included in the activities of federal agencies. I strongly discouraged pilot projects because of their limited effectiveness and because of their fabulous cost. Each time I verbally grappled with a planner I felt like a foiled welfare program abortionist. Poverty fighters wrangle back and forth for hours before deciding on voice vote to defer implementation of a project until it can be studied and presumably revised. Any reference to consolidation of services to increase efficiency and decrease costs brings about angry howls of protest from the experts who feel that their very survival in affluence is threatened by cooperative planning and improved patterning to get more mileage out of the tax dollar and to stretch the steadily diminishing supply of professional help. I ignited a fire of heroic proportions by telling a health commissioner that needs could be more effectively met by full-time nursing services as part of the school system. As I inhaled the smoke of his burning, sputtering, crackling barrage of words, I realized that my survival hinged on early escape from the polluted air.

Not long after that close call I spent the better part of an afternoon with a skilled counselor, listening to his description of an evaluation plan that was going to be put into practice. "We intend to evaluate every boy who has dropped out of school. Our results will then pinpoint which of the several training programs is best suited to each lad's interests and needs. Various training settings and work projects will afford the opportunity for on-the-scene assessment."

He accompanied me to Duddie's Branch the following day. I made a sharp right-angle turn into the Branch stream bed; the water was high but it did not slop in on the floor of the jeep so I drove on. The young man was too frightened to do more than suck in his breath. About halfway up the Branch I took off to the right on a 45-degree angle "pull-in." I got out in mud above my ankles but the counselor hesitated to follow me. I told him that he should talk to Shell and his father and he reluctantly got out of the jeep, choosing what he thought would be the least muddy route. I followed the "walkin' way" I'd learned from the Branchers, gauging the depth of previous footsteps, which is safer than "makin' marks" yourself. He picked up a stick as we neared the porch. I suspected that he might be thinking of removing some of the mud from his shoes and gave him the benefit of my hard-earned knowledge. "What's left after stomping is aiming on sticking." Once inside the house he soon forgot the mud.

I introduced him to the family. "Mr. Patton is one of the men who will be getting jobs for the Branchers," I told Shell.

His father, after a longer than usual period of silence during which Shell sneaked out the back door, asked, "You's aimin' on takin' 'ese hyur young fellers fur?"

The counselor did not answer Frank's question but began talking about giving the boys a chance for more education and finding jobs for them after they had finished the training program. He explained the rationale and mentioned some of the places where the boys might work and some kinds of work they might do. Considerable time had elapsed, some devoted to explanations and some to silence, when Frank repeated, "You's aimin' t' take 'ese hyur young fellers fur?" Still unable to get a satisfactory answer, he continued. "You's named hospitals. 'Udn't let any 'a my younguns do hospital workin'. They'd ketch somethin'. You's namin' paintin'. Paintin's hard on a feller's lung."

I hinted that Shell might like to meet Mr. Patton.

"Reckon hit hain't worth botherin' 'im," Frank said. "'E hain't never bin t' school. 'Im likes home. 'E hain't never bedded down, nary a night, 'ceptin' if'n me 'r my ol' worman's thar."

Mr. Patton was almost beyond his depth by now. "How old is Shell?" he asked.

"'Im's a young feller, mite nigh onto seventeen."

Mr. Patton said that he would appreciate it if he could speak to Shell. A drawn-out pause followed his request. "Reckon b' now 'e's likely t' be two mount'ins gone," Frank finally drawled. "'E's one youngun 'at's never had a hankerin' fur workin'. Reckon you's best give 'is job t' 'nother feller—'at is, if'n you's findin' a workin' feller."

Wading back to the jeep, Mr. Patton looked at his watch and apologized because his time would not permit him to adhere to our original schedule of going to three homes. I explained that it would be impossible for me to turn the jeep around, even with four-wheel drive; the only place where I could turn to go out was at the head of the hollow where Lester had left part of his garden area unplanted so that I could swing around. Riding the side of first one bank and then another at a near 45-degree angle held little appeal for Mr. Patton. I assured him that we would not tip over and turned around and headed out. His only comment after we reached the highway was, "Where did you learn to drive a jeep?"

I never saw Mr. Patton again, but the next time I met up with Shell I said, "You should have hung around and talked with Mr. Patton."

"Don't reckon, long 's I's hain't aimin' on workin' nohow."

"Shell, don't you want all the things that the War on Poverty is trying to do for you?"

"Don't reckon. If'n they's promisin' things they's gonna be takin' 'em first afore hit gits t' me."

Wise Shell. The high cost of publicizing the War on Poverty and the funds it takes to meet the "army" payroll and support money-devouring projects leave very little for the poor. Extravagant salaries are paid to the executives of some of the programs to administer impotent operations. Woefully, a sizable part of the multimillion-dollar welfare kitty has been diverted from its original objective. For example, upon the recommendation of a $22,500-a-year Poverty Operations Board director, three consultants were appointed to assist her. One of them, whose salary was $100 a day, was also a consultant to the U. S. Labor Department and the National Institute of Mental Health at a fee of $75 a day. In addition, two private foundations paid $250 a day for her services. The second assistant, wife of a civil court judge, was paid $65 a day. The third appointee, a consultant on small business problems, received $60 a day.

The House Education and Labor Committee paid ten investigators $200,000 to conduct a five-month study of the anti-poverty programs. Their 32-page summary did not disclose anything which had not been previously reported in newspapers.

A $359,638 grant was awarded to four Ohio counties to investigate the causes of poverty over a nine-month period. It was administered by a staff of ten, headed by a director at $1,000 a month and two assistants at $722 a month each. In yet another county, several poverty fighters were paid $1,500 each for every unit of a thousand families in their poverty group. For what? To teach the poor how to spend their money!

In one city, three hundred salaried executives and employees of a Mobilization for Youth program used eight million tax dollars to find work for a few hundred kids. Apparently dazed by their wild spending spree, the staff hadn't the foggiest notion of what percentage (if any) of the youngsters were placed in steady jobs. Preliminary data estimated the cost of this program to average out to about $10,000 per trainee and none of the administrators even knew whether one of their boys had secured permanent employment.

The government proposed giving a group of underprivileged Kentucky teenagers $50 a month "pocket money." One mother of four boys said, "Why should my tax money go to support that kind of luxury when it is all I can do to scrape enough together to pay for haircuts for my sons? When will the taxpayer be given a voice in the ridiculous practices that are initiated year after year?" When, indeed?

One welfare agency, whose alleged purpose is to help the poor, uses $5,130 of its poverty budget annually just to park its cars.

But these are the ways in which we fight poverty in the twentieth century. We fashion countless costly programs, appropriate prodigious sums of money, and organize an army. We set the poverty director up in headquarters thirty times the size of the National Security Council, pay 52 per cent of his staff annual salaries of $14,000 each, and hire writers at $7,500 a crack to oversell the public with press releases, speeches, and staff reports.

Already a number of years devoted to "lick poverty forever" have gone by, and what has been accomplished? Our vocabulary has been enriched by such slogans and terms as "Stamp out Deprivation," "battle plan," "the War on Poverty," "the poverty program," "Community Action," "self-help projects," "crash programs." This collection of words was strung together by the people who are spending your money and mine.

That just about summarizes the positive results. Now for a review of the negative aspects of the operation.

The self-help projects and emergency measures cannot offer economic development activity for the future. Crash programs inevitably fail to sift down to the needy and should more appropriately be called "trash" programs.

The conflict of opinion about what to do with the people in the hollows has resulted in many programs that are at cross-purposes with each other. The same confusion reigns when an accounting is sought of how much money is being poured into the educational programs in deprived counties. Literally millions of dollars have been pumped into the hollows in recent years, but the environmental and human decay process becomes more invasive every day.

Recent federal and state court decisions uphold the philosophy that the needy have a legal right to funds that no longer are thought of as charitable handouts. There is a wide variation in the interpretation of the regulations, however. In most instances the federal government pays in excess of half of the welfare costs, yet the states have the authority and the responsibility to determine eligibility of the recipients. Some states prohibit granting of funds beyond the stated maximum allowance, no matter how many children there may be in a family. Other states have stringent residency rules which all too often cause the disadvantaged to migrate in search of work. Even though a Supreme Court decision some twenty-five years ago granted the indigent the privilege of admittance into any state, the mechanics on the local scene are not this simple. A number of states require one year of residency without aid from any tax-supported agency before becoming eligible to apply for welfare funds. The most disruptive influence is felt at the local level where each welfare worker establishes his own arbitrary standards as to which applicants should get aid and how much. Infinite examples of inequitable administration of specific rules and regulations can be cited.

What does it all mean? It means that the War on Poverty has not improved the lives of the poor. "A war 'thout shootin' 'n' bloodin' hain't winnin' nary nothin'. 'Sides, we's hain't hankerin' fur no fightin', but they's al'ays mouthin' 'bout 'battle plans.' War is war, 'n' we's hain't hankerin' fur any war hyur." Nonetheless, if the War on Poverty turns out to be merely a token effort, impoverished and depressed millions will have been deluded and the millions of American taxpayers who accepted public welfare as their financial responsibility will have been swindled. We did not think of our obligation as an interim measure but as a duty that we were willing to assume for however long it took to accomplish the intended aims. General progress in the direction of the public goals, though, has been less than rapid. In Appalachia it has been next to nil. Attempts at planning designed to alleviate the poverty in the mountains failed in the decision stage. Dealing with the deprived in an urban setting is far different from dealing with the deprived in the rural setting. In cities, the emphasis has been placed on playgrounds, swimming pools, basketball and tennis courts, and carefully organized recreational opportunities of a wide variety. For the deprived rural families, the food stamp program seems to be the approach. Although maintenance of the physical being is essential for life, welfare of the spirit is essential for hope. These people need complete help—housekeeping, home management, health and assistance services, recreational facilities, educational opportunities and, most of all, jobs. But retraining is not enough. Where can they find work within a reasonable commuting distance of the hollows?

The current programs are devoted almost exclusively to remedial measures whereas research into the causes of poverty should constitute the main focus of attention. Upon completion of such investigation, a parallel prevention and remedy tactic could outmaneuver the poverty foe. The formats are all second-step considerations, however. The first is to examine the sharpshooters of the war. A lot of them are eminently qualified on paper but glaringly short on dedication. Too many got into the action only for the opportunity to dip their fingers into the federal spoils. One girl was asked, "How much of the two billion dollars has gotten down to you?" "Jist 's much 's I's bin t' Wash'n'tom—'n' I hain't never bin thar yet," she replied. A young man observed that "th' on'y fellers who're makin' money outta th' poverty racket is th' ones w'at already have money aplenty." Jude's prediction was gloomiest of all. "WPA wastin's gonna look like somethin' good afore all this hyur money gits played out 'n' I's reckonin' hit hain't gonna take 'em long afore hit's all plum missin'."

X

What Lies Ahead?

Stars may be seen from the bottom of a deep well, when they cannot be discerned from the top of a mountain. So are many things learned in adversity which the prosperous man dreams not of.

Charles Haddon Spurgeon,
English clergyman, 1834–92

At this point in time, it appears that the first major assault on deprivation is to be scuttled before the hurly-burly has begun. Merely to label this cowardice an "unfinished task" is to affront those who live on the ragged edge of survival. The poverty program not only failed the hollowers, it never really reached them. Once again, in the lifetime of many, they have been short-changed, double-crossed, trapped in poverty because the unrelated and uncoordinated task forces perished. If these people are deserving of a chance, then they are entitled to more than the few preliminary backfirings that signaled the beginning of the war. Otherwise, why tamper with the practice that the spoils of democracy belong only to the fortunate?

The trends of today and the uncertainties of tomorrow hover like menacing clouds above the crusader brave enough to submit fresh approaches to the troubles of a hollow that moves in a reverse direction. He would have to dispatch his emissaries into a background of unsuccessful federal projects and he would have to restore the shaken confidence of the public. He would be obliged to slay the money-devouring dragon and would be vilified for creating its equally avaricious counterpart. He would have need of miracles, but they have been wondrously rare for the past two thousand years. He would be the intolerable martyr, yet we will not enjoy the best of all possible worlds until he has made a breakthrough to the netherland of the deprived. Nor can he use the mythical Great

Society as his launch pad; our society will not be great until the lot of the impoverished is improved.

The reader may have his own thoughts concerning what should or should not be done for the hollow dweller. Perhaps he would suggest that more expensive pilot projects be undertaken, even though previous investigations have already yielded more information than has been analyzed and evaluated. He may advocate helping only those who help themselves. He may be more acutely conscious of the existence and effects of deprivation, or he may conclude that Duddie's Branch is, after all, not so bad. Then again, he may feel that the only answer is to whip up dissatisfaction in the hollows in the expectation that the resultant discord would hurl the Brancher into the mainstream of twentieth-century life. His proposals may be sound or absurd or old or original, but would any of them work? How can we destroy a culture based on the dole and sittin' 'n' spittin'? What will it take to inspire the hollower to chart his own destiny? Who can design the key that will unlock a door which has thus far remained sealed? What is our first step?

No matter how noble our motives, can we in all good conscience impose our will on the hollowers and arrange their lives according to our blueprint? If so, then let us proceed slowly. Let us not rip them from the familiarity of their hills only to trample them into oblivion in the concrete deserts of our cities. Let us not regard them as resources, but rather as people whose most urgent need is to be understood and to know that someone cares.

What are the realities of the present? It would seem that only money is more prevalent than the controversy over what should be done. Why? Because the taxpayer will be forced to continue to foot a high bill for the deprived, who really do not benefit from our sacrifices. Poverty, as a good business for those involved in the programs, is simply too attractive. In any case, the hollower is unable to provide for himself. There is no industry in the near vicinity to employ or train him, and none is anticipated in the near future. The Appalachian Regional Commission, which spent millions of dollars on a cause lost almost from its inception, is finally giving up the idea of attracting industry to small towns. As predicted by so many from the very beginning, industry located in small communities does not create as many jobs as it would if it were in or near a city where plant payroll money keeps turning over. In order to survive, the Commission changed its tactics to encouraging rural people to move to the cities and to providing vocational training. There really is little need for this agency, since anything connected with vocational training should be done by the school system. Unfortunately, it is not and there are few jobs available for the unskilled anywhere but particularly in the mountains where welfare is the only big business. Instead of abolishing poverty, however, welfare has encouraged a mentality geared to permanent dependence on society. The hollower has become psychologically unemployable because he has neither the incentive nor the personal habits to get a job. He lacks the self-discipline to be on time, perform conscientiously, accept authority, or work regularly. Being available for work and being willing to work are two different conditions, the former not indicative of the latter. But if the Age of Leisure is indeed just around the corner, if labor is to be outmoded, there's not much point in becoming excited over the unemployed Brancher.

Left to their own resources, however, their attitudes and aspirations are not likely to change in the future. Each generation will follow the last victims into the ever widening gap with the outer world. The many complexities and perplexities of their situation are interrelated. Deprivation will not be eliminated by a single cure because it does not issue from a single cause. The hollow is a miniature world beset with colossal problems. Its people live in an extremely limited life space with a stimulus-poor climate. The only passport that will permit them to move about freely in the outer world is one of education or skill. They are without either, and the obvious hostility of the general community pervades their entire existence and influences their every action. Just to achieve a language communication, which is necessary in the world beyond the hollow in order to take advantage of job programs and vocational education, may be impossible for most of them. Without help, they will be unable to tackle the enormous difficulties they face. They have no clear-cut sense of purpose, they cannot conceive of a future, they personify superstition, distrust, and paranoia.

Appalachia has come to symbolize the poor, but emphasis has

now shifted to the urban poor whose problems, concentrated in city slums, are most difficult and costly to solve. There is a real possibility that government sympathy and, to some extent, private enterprise will focus almost entirely on the Negro ghettos in the city. While this is laudable, it is inequitable. Must there be a Selma march of hollow folks to lure political sycophants back to their side? If this is the case, they will continue to be overlooked—because they refuse to protest publicly. They even refuse to complain, and will continue to permit you to believe that their needs are not dire. They will continue to suffer with ineffectual representation at every level of our government structure when, in fact, they are a hopeless society. No one yet knows how to come to grips with their problems in an efficient and acceptable way. The War on Poverty definitely was not the answer. It has scarcely bothered to identify the basis of their troubles, much less touch them.

The slow evolutionary development of unrelieved deprivation, the interlocking complexities of the system, have eluded the multitudinous programs designed to provide escape hatches. The difference which exists in welfare benefits among various states may encourage population migrations from rural areas where the benefits are generally poor, but it does not entice hollow people to urban areas where the benefits are usually higher. Strong anti-poverty legislation may be a moral victory in the books, but entrenched poverty continues to be a way of life in Appalachia. In the final analysis, we are a two-society nation: one in which belong those who prepare for life and the other in to which the dropouts drop.

We cannot fight poverty in the hollows until we have cleared away the structures that have grown out of different problems and originated with different generations. If the Branchers are to have a different future, they must arrange it themselves and on their own terms. No one can predict what the cost will be beyond money. The most fundamental problem is that of human development. What can be done with people who are completely disconnected from a fast-moving world? The answers lie in a new focus on the Branchers, not on the financing mechanisms. The truth is that most programs would collapse without the huge sums of money they need for their own existence and not for the good they do.

Nonetheless, new programs which duplicate already existing efforts are being considered despite ever mounting deficits and endless debt-ceiling increases. The only change they represent is in slogans—reveal, renew, revitalize, re-energize. The themes continue to grow: New Deal, Fair Deal, New Frontier, Great Society. Others will be added to the list. When are we going to demand that our tax money stop being spent on slogans and themes? When are we going to insist upon tangible results for the money that is squeezed from our pay checks? When are we going to complain because the government paid 5,789 farmers $333 million to let their fields lie fallow at the same time that welfare recipients fed each of their children on twenty-seven cents a day? When?

Suppose the present plans for the guaranteed minimum annual income materialize? How much would this cost in Duddie's Branch alone? These people already receive welfare benefits, education allowances, Social Security, Medicare, and Medicaid. The handouts to welfare cases can be labeled guaranteed wages or negative income tax or anything else, but one thing will not be changed: we will be stuck with the tab. If the purpose of welfare is to care for those who cannot earn a livelihood, then there seems to be no solution other than to keep pouring money into the poverty coffers. If we really believe that all Americans have a right to the essentials of life, decent housing, food, clothing, then we have no alternative but to provide those things to all who qualify, whether they are on welfare or not. The question is, how? Many needy people are deprived of aid because they do not fit into any of the special programs. The cost of deprivation in dollars and cents will be appalling no matter what methods are applied to relieve it.

If the present giveaway system were replaced by one paying a family of four $3,200 a year plus $500 for each additional child, some families would have to take a cut because they are currently getting more on welfare. Many hard thinkers oppose (to no avail) our system which inhibits human development and promotes increasing dependency. Who wants to invest his labor for $3,000 a year when he can get at least $3,200 for not working at all? Such a proposal is not calculated to develop independence.

The negative income tax would provide impoverished families

with whatever amount their income falls below a certain level. Most of the hollow families pay no income tax, have more than four children, and earn less than $3,000 a year. They would receive payments equal to the exemptions and deductions they could declare if they were taxpaying units. A family with no income at all would receive a basic allowance related to its size. This is tantamount to guaranteeing an income to people who refuse to get a job, although the negative income tax is supposed to preserve some incentive to work. One can seriously doubt the claims made by the strong proponents that such a plan would eliminate poverty. True welfare fails to reach many of those who most need help, while multitudes receive help without meriting it.

Each newspaper and periodical suggest new approaches, revision, consolidation, or discontinuation of existing programs. Readers are perplexed. Some are surprised, others are bewildered, many question. Almost everyone seems to have his own idea about success and failure in approaches and results. Heated discussions of the pros and cons seem to emerge from nowhere like the fog at dusk. Some sincerely seek answers to the problems; others argue for an accounting of expenditures; still others want supporting evidence of measurable results based on cost and commitment. The success-fail frame of reference constantly crops up.

After all the promises in the New Deal, the Fair Deal, the New Frontier, and the Great Society where do we go? What programs will continue? How much money will be made available? What priorities will be used for allocation of public funds? The old cliche, the rich get richer and the poor get poorer, still seems to be a truism.

It seems unrealistic to anticipate sweeping changes in the bureaucracy at the federal level. Implementation of any program at the state level will lack the kind of flexibility necessary to meet basic needs of deprived human beings. How can programs, once implemented, become meaningful dimensions in the life of hollow dwellers?

An initial effort should begin to explore the potential in the Integrated Counterbalanced Measure of Intelligence for Appalachia (ICMIA) test. Cultural deprivation is recognized as a real hardship for those who wish to secure employment, particularly a job outside the hollow. If, as indicated, the test can be used as a predictive tool, it should be put into use in the hollows, thoroughly evaluated, then continued in a broader area if preliminary results are encouraging.

Present indications are that the substance of the poverty effort will continue almost as is for another year. It will be much the same as it was during the Johnson Administration.

Today Kentucky occupies the forty-fourth spot in the constellation of fifty states in per capita income even though expressways crisscross the state almost like a well-designed spider web. Many brag that by 1970 not one of the 120 counties in Kentucky will be more than one county away from an expressway. Glowing statistics give evidence of increased employment along the Parkways yet it has been difficult to find Duddie's Branchers who have benefited from the highway extension into the vast hinterlands of the state.

No one can really predict with any degree of accuracy how much taxpayers' money is being squandered or spent uselessly. Why? Because spending practices aimlessly approach objectives with varying degrees of effectiveness and impartiality. In many instances promising alternatives have been selected with little data to support decisions. One Representative after an eight-month effort recognized that slightly over one thousand programs were acting as vehicles through which federal monies were channeled, free or on loan, to individuals, institutions, cities, counties, or states.

In 1969 HEW will spend eight million dollars to prevent smoking. Simultaneously the Department of Agriculture will spend thirty million dollars to support tobacco growing. If there are really fifteen agencies dispensing federal monies through two hundred different programs to meet one need, that of higher education, then do we need more clues for revision and remodeling of current programs?

Recommendations strongly suggest the dismantling of the Office of Economic Opportunity with the transfer of its major functions to other agencies. It is really too early to evaluate changes which may be adopted and implemented at the federal level. Some changes in the welfare system seem a certainty; for better or for worse, we must wait for the details.

For several months now an opinion poll has been going on in Earle County. It is difficult to attach appropriate significance to the answers since there seems to be no way to determine who responded to the questions. Percentages without the number of respondents can be very misleading.

	PERCENT		
	Yes	No	Undecided
Are schools properly educating the students of today for the society of tomorrow?	36	39	25
Do the poor need a stronger voice in the management of current welfare and other assistance programs?	37	63	
Should people who completely depend on public assistance be required to adopt birth control measures?	79	18	3
Should people who cannot read or write be allowed to vote in county elections?	63	37	
Are the laws to keep children in school adequately enforced?	11	89	
Are current medical aid programs of the federal government too expensive?	84	0	16
Are OEO leaders misusing the influence of their office?	100		
Should the federal government encourage local factories as a step in reducing welfare programs?	100		

I would be inclined to guess that few of the poor were asked to contribute to the many questions in the poll.

Although widespread outside interest in the Appalachian area is relatively new many concerned citizens from within the region have been actively involved in its development for a long time.

The Council of the Southern Mountains, for example, has been serving the Appalachian South for more than fifty years. It was organized in 1913 in Atlanta, Georgia, by a group of religious, educational, and health leaders who shared common problems in their work in the mountains. They hoped to devise a continuing forum for the exchange of ideas and to help overcome the isolation of the mountain people. An annual conference attended by all those with a special interest in the region was the principal means of accomplishing the goal. This conference is still held today along with an enlarged communications program including a monthly magazine, newsletters, and workshops.

While the council acts as a clearing house for information in the region, it is also involved in action projects financed largely through federal funds to help in the development of the area. These include manpower development, enterprise development, the Talent Bank, Planned Parenthood, and others. A full-time staff of professional experts work with interested members and community people to help those who live in Appalachia.

The chief governmental agency involved with the development of the mountain areas is the Appalachian Regional Commission. This Commission was created to administer the provisions of the Appalachian Regional Development Act of 1965.

The Act authorized over one billion dollars for developmental programs in the twelve-state area. An amount of $840 million was earmarked for highways and local access roads. In 1967, Congress authorized an additional $175 million for highways and $170 million for non-highway programs during fiscal years 1968–69.

Whereas the Council of the Southern Mountains is concerned with human resources in the area, the Appalachian Commission is responsible for public works projects which will help the region to create a self-sustaining economy.

The Commission membership consists of the Governors of each of the Appalachian states, a federal Co-chairman appointed by the President, and a professional staff which provides technical assistance and advice.

The Act authorized a wide variety of economic development programs each designed to contribute to the growth of the region. These development programs include highway construction, land restoration, multicounty health projects, vocational educational facilities, and others.

The Commission was to concentrate funds in areas which have significant potential for growth and where the return of public dollars will be greatest. There were to be eighty potential growth centers, each center a network of new cities. Effort was concentrated primarily on access as the key to depressed populations and as a means to attract industry. The first necessity was the transportation network, the relocation of people not necessarily out of the area. Proposals for projects must come from the states.

Kentucky has just submitted requests for $17.3 million in health service and construction project funds to the Appalachian Regional Commission. In 1968 the Commission provided roughly $8 million for thirty-three such projects in Kentucky.

There is a bill under consideration at the moment which would extend for two more years the Appalachian Regional Development Act. It is proposed in the extension that up to $225 million be appropriated for non-highway programs.

Appalachian Regional Development provides the framework for the establishment of local development districts which call for multi-county planning and development of economic resources. Those involved in the development program say the impact of projects funded in 1965 and 1967 is just beginning to show.

In late 1968 boys and girls were still being encouraged to file applications for the Job Corps at the county courthouse. This continuing surge was billed as their "big chance to train for a job." Enrollees could get an education, earn while they learned. Those who might be interested had certain requirements to meet: they had to be out of school, unemployed, and between sixteen and twenty-one years of age. Some gave the impression of interest but few sought applications.

What is happening to the Job Corps program? There are approximately 106 Job Corps centers in the United States with eighty-two in conservation areas and twenty-four in cities. Half of the rural conservation areas are to be closed. There have been about fourteen thousand young persons, mostly high school dropouts, enrolled in the rural areas. Eight urban centers will be closed.

Almost everyone has his own ideas of the merit of the Job Corps programs depending on one's place of residence. Some feel that closing the centers will add to the disillusionment among the poor, others believe closure will result in boys and girls "going to the dogs." Many think the effort was no more than limitedly successful. Others deny any identifiable benefit and cite long lists of data to support their positions.

The Job Corps budget has been cut by $100 million and authority for the program has been transferred from OEO to the Department of Labor.

Time will tell us of the Job Corps and its fate in the future.

Many have felt the short summer programs in Head Start have been too expensive, for the benefit derived by those children who attend. In spite of criticism Head Start seems to be the one program which emerged from the original poverty package with the greatest support at the local level.

Shifting funds to full-year programs may become a reality. Transfer to the Department of Health, Education, and Welfare may assure survival and bring about imaginative changes to include more children under the age of five years.

Many say good luck to Head Start Year-Round!

We hear many statements regarding welfare. Slash the welfare rolls. State costs in welfare field continue to soar. Boost welfare payments. Suggest alternatives for welfare families. Welfare misses most of the poor. Welfare recipients cannot even live a minimally decent life. Welfare payments will be substantially increased as the federal government pumps in more monies. The federal government will attempt to remove the freeze on families with dependent children (AFDC) scheduled to go into effect July 1969. The federal government should do more. Federal funds for welfare should be increased. Welfare rolls continue to grow even with low unemployment rates and a flourishing economy. What can be done?

States have been asked for their ideas for removing recipients from welfare rolls. How do the states suggest teaching recipients to perform a job in order to become fully independent economically or at least partially so? Top priority seems to be public assistance rehabilitation through which it is hoped to decrease the number of recipients.

Federal and state governments in the calendar year of 1968 spent $5.7 billion in four programs: Aid to Dependent Children, Aid to the Disabled, Blind, and Aged. Just over 50 per cent of the amount was federal money. Assuming economies and successful rehabilitation efforts government must add $1.5 billion each year to meet the demands for welfare and Medicaid programs. The two major phases of the welfare program, Aid for Dependent Children and health care, seem to be contributing most significantly to the total increase in costs.

There is a proposal to double the present budget of under $500 million for Aid to Needy Children. But chances for an increase in Aid to Dependent Children seem slim. In Ohio, for example, ADC payments are $38 a month per child and parent, $22 from the federal government, and $16 from the state. The most important question which needs an answer prior to an increase is, are parents who are receiving such funds actually using the money to care for their children? There are many problems on the fringes. For instance, children from welfare families who do not attend school cannot have free lunches but no way has yet been found to feed these hungry children. Effective organization to coordinate public and private programs is still to be worked out. The inadequately fed are awaiting the first real breakthrough in finding a way to feed hungry needy children.

Equalizing welfare payments may have considerable appeal particularly in urban areas. It is thought such a plan would be one way of decreasing the steady migration of the poor seeking to live where welfare payments are higher. Regardless of revisions and final outcomes, welfare payments have not really solved any of the basic problems. Can they ever?

Currently there seems to be evidence that the food programs will not be shifted from the Department of Agriculture to the Department of Health, Education and Welfare. Some critics feel the outlook on malnutrition would benefit from the firmer thrust if HEW were to supervise the health and welfare package. The question is which agency should really control the major food program at the federal level. At the moment, the decision seems to indicate that the Department of Agriculture will control the food programs and presently the Department is conducting studies intent upon expanding the war on hunger. As of now, both the food stamp program and commodity distribution will remain in the Department of Agriculture.

The fate of proposals left behind by the previous administration seems to be questionable. Will the present federal administration be willing to spend more money to make provisions for lunches and breakfasts for needy school-age children? Government food programs for the needy will reach only those persons who live in counties that participate in federal programs. Best estimates now indicate there are between two and three million who are denied in counties which do not participate.

The food stamp program will probably continue. Administered at the local level this program enables poor families to purchase food at lower than retail prices because the stamps are bought for so many cents on the dollar. Hunger and malnutrition will be decreased only if the stamps are used for food purchases. If the Food Stamp Reform Act of 1969 passes Congress its provisions will lower the purchase price of stamps for families whose incomes range from $20 to $60 per week. Many congressmen seem to favor free food stamps to all families whose earnings are under $20 a week. This Act will cost an estimated $1.8 billion for the fiscal year beginning July 1, 1969. Tax money going to support people who do not work is very unpalatable for the average citizen.

In January 1969 low income families in Earle County received food stamp program benefits approximating $114,681. Food stamps were sold to 5,461 persons during the month. Earle County has the sixth largest number of persons in Kentucky on the food stamp program. In Kentucky during the month of January low-income families exchanged $952,384 of their own money for $1,824,750 of United States Department of Agriculture food stamps. In other words, the low-income families benefited from $872,366 in free food stamps. These free stamps do increase the family buying capability in local groceries of their choice.

The General Accounting Office was given the task of a massive study of the war on poverty. This investigation has taken over a year and has cost a half million dollars. The GAO report to the Congress and the Administration may contain some astonishing surprises Perhaps we will have the number of poor who have been extricated. The dollar cost is bound to be fantastically high. For example it is estimated that the cost of women Job Corps enrollees who graduate after one year in the OEO program is almost $40,000 per person.

More persons in the middle economic strata of society may have benefited from the cash outlays intended to help the poor whom it never reached. Just two years ago there were at least a thousand poverty positions in the OEO budget paying $10,000 or more a year.

Early indications are that present federal efforts to help the poor are in such disorder that much coordination and control will be needed if they are to derive beneficial results.

A decision from the new administration is yet to come on a guaranteed annual income plan, sometimes referred to as a negative income tax. This plan is to establish for all families of the nation a minimum income of $3200 a year for a family of four. Major features of such a plan besides the guaranteed income base would be the elimination of a means test, built-in incentives to work, allowance for family size, and comparatively low operating costs. These packages have price tags from a low of $3 billion to a high of $15 billion a year. Such a plan, by whatever name and in whatever form, would have to be federally funded.

Theoretically at least, if a family of four earns less than $3,200 the United States Treasury would make up the difference. The built-in work incentive feature would permit families included in the plan to keep 50 per cent of amounts earned over the admissible base. Guaranteed work for the employable is another part of most of the proposals. Enough work would be guaranteed to assure workers, paid at standard rates, to bring home about $60 per week or an economic base of $3,200.

Limited information now available suggests that in fiscal 1970 experimentation with the guaranteed annual income under HEW will begin in several model cities neighborhoods. Rough estimates are that eight hundred families may be involved in the trial. It would be unfortunate if this were not tried in a rural area. I would welcome a chance to try it in Duddie's Branch. I seriously doubt that such a plan would really end poverty in the hollow. Many of us who have been in the hollows for so long already know how many of the families spend the money they receive. Added dollars have had little impact on their way of life or their employment. Nonetheless, it should be very exciting and revealing to try such a plan in Duddie's Branch.

As a child, I was always being reprimanded for woolgathering, and especially for cogitating on what I would do if I were king. While Father was opposed to building air castles, he did not regard them as harmful so long as they did not strain the budget or encroach on one's daily livelihood. Years later, I still dream of what I would do if I were king. But the outgrowth of dreaming big at the level of pure fantasy should be tempered with realism. Those who would blaze a trail in helping the Brancher help himself toward slow recovery from the past must have the necessary inner resources to sustain them in their efforts. Perhaps something can be done, especially for the children, but only a fool would be entirely optimistic. Still, it would be a worth-while endeavor if for no other reason than to obtain irrefutable data for use in future plans and programs. Defeat need not be total; the clay will remain and we will at least know how *not* to mold it. Above all, we should not continue to deny the undeniable. A lifetime of deprivation may well have administered the coup de grâce to the future of the hollow folks. How would I determine this if I were king of the hollows? Where would I begin?

I would first decide on the goal, estimate the cost, and set a reasonable time limit before initiating programs to eradicate poverty in the hollows. I would not refer to the deprived in a single frame of reference applicable alike to the urban poor, the poor in the deep South, and the poor in the hollows. The problems and the solutions are different. Each nucleus, large or small, requires individual analysis and a tailor-made plan of action to combat social poverty, economic poverty, spiritual poverty, intellectual poverty, etc. My escape route would consist of stairs. The Brancher would be permitted to ascend step by step and when he could no longer climb he could claim a spot in the social structure at the level of his maximum potential. The factory-made approach emanating from Washington would be abolished.

The steps would include those things that would improve the quality of their life, with or without their help. All welfare recipients would be thoroughly re-evaluated by strangers representing a wide variety of disciplines. After that, the administration of funds would be the responsibility of an impartial group with no political connections and removed from patronage influence. Once physical status was determined, recipients would be required to engage in some useful activity for at least four hours a day, five days a week. The aged, for example, could take walks every day for improvement of their general health if nothing more. Or they could bathe and dress their grandchildren, thus permitting the mothers to engage in other pursuits.

Those families with the largest number of children under six years of age and with the greatest number of childbearing years ahead would receive prior attention. Every actual or potential mother would be eligible for injections of a new drug which, when taken every three months, induces infertility. A non-monetary item of value would be offered as a reward for every childless year, and I would strive to stabilize the family size of young parents at two children.

Other steps are as follows:

I would accept the fact that their life style does not fit outside the hollow and their values would come first in anything I did.

I would avoid rupturing family ties.

I would respect the wholeness of the individual as a human being; money alone is just not enough.

I would provide a one-to-one type of service, in the beginning operating independently of organized community services and gradually including appropriate use of agency help.

I would document exactly how money was currently being used by each welfare family. Instead of issuing a check, I would have them bring in their bills for payment; only statements for certain things would be honored. I would try to find something to replace money for such essentials as shoes, clothing, food, fuel, etc.; perhaps a credit card, indicating exactly what could be purchased and requesting a receipt.

I would encourage officials to activate a quasi-armed forces type of program for all the boys and girls who dropped out of school or failed to attend regularly, with work, discipline, education, and health improvement as the goal. Compulsory service in the regular army is for two years. I would double this for hollow children on the justification that it would take them four years to attain the same level of achievement. It is a rare hollow child who is still in school at age fourteen. He or she could go into the program from fourteen to eighteen years of age. If he chose, he could spend three months during four summers and decrease the time starting at age eight. He would have one year completed by the time he was twelve. Compulsory entry into the program would begin at the point of school dropout. Retired army personnel would be in charge of the program. Pay would be accumulated with a small amount, a dollar or so a week, allocated for spending money. All necessary clothing, etc., would be furnished by the corps but deducted from earnings. Eventually, every hollower who lies around until he has "rocked out" his unemployment insurance would have a choice: he could go back to work or enter the service corps. This should apply to all, but specifically to those who plan their lives the hollow way.

I would erect a hollow services center, a kind of child-parent facility. It would operate on a modest scale in the beginning. The building would be located near the center of population density in the hollow, and its purpose would be for learning. Learning could be as simple as how to get clean in a shower.

There are many questions which will remain unanswered until something is done in the hollow to provide the answers. What would happen if a washer-dryer machine were available? A central facility which could be shared by all would be cheaper than a washing machine for every family. Soap powders, bleaches, and a dryer would probably provide incentive for many of the mothers to use the washer. A dryer would eliminate the necessity of hanging laundry all over the house during the winter and during rainy weather.

It might be expedient to hire a man to keep the equipment in repair and a woman to supervise its use. Or perhaps it would be better to have the Branchers bring their laundry and have someone else sort and then wash it. Two young boys who have dropped out of school are possibilities for training. They would be paid a salary.

How well would a learn-as-they-go approach do? There is no reason why some of the women could not be taught to do mangle ironing. They might even be willing to learn how to fold laundry and sort it for various children. Many mothers do not iron clothes now because they do not have an ironing board and they can't keep an iron in repair. I feel quite sure that the young girls, and even some of the boys, would use an iron.

Would the mothers be willing to follow a schedule and come on a designated day to use the facilities? Would they stay to iron? Could it be required that every mother using the washer stay until she had dried and ironed whatever she brought?

The center would make yard goods available for the mothers who wanted to sew and mend. Three or four sewing machines would furnish answers to whether they would repair their clothing. If sewing lessons were offered to the mothers, would they avail themselves of the opportunity? Right now we do not know whether hollow folks would participate in any learning endeavor. Those willing to care for their clothing would be provided with replacements for worn garments. Does the reward of personal satisfaction have any value for them?

Facilities for personal cleanliness such as showers, toilets, and lavatories would be available. If they are willing to wash their clothing, would they be willing to bathe? Hot water, soap, washcloths, and towels should appeal to mothers who have many small children and no way of keeping them clean. Children might stop in to brush their teeth before going to school. Would locker space with one change of clothing for each of her children induce a mother to bathe them and dress them in clean clothing? Storage space in most of the homes is simply not available and it would not further the cause if they had to pile clean clothes on the bed during the day and on the floor during the night.

Would the miners stop at the center for a shower and clean clothing before going home? Or would they continue their old habits of being washed to the waist at home by their wives?

Would children on their way home from school stop at the center to change into play clothes?

One of the hollow men might want to be trained as a barber for the center. Likewise, one of the women might be willing to train as a beauty operator if facilities were made available for her use in shampooing and setting hair. How many of the hollow women, both young and old, would get their hair washed? A beauty shop could provide employment for one person and the potential for a job elsewhere.

If families did use the center, it could be expanded to include stoves, sinks, refrigerators, deep freezes, utensils, and dishes. Meals could be prepared at the center and fruits and vegetables could be preserved there. Would this prompt them to enlarge their gardens? Food for a well-balanced diet would be made available to those mothers who wished to cook for their families. It could be eaten there or taken home. A central dining room with family tables might be preferable. Children who plan to use the recreational facilities at the center would be required to stop in for breakfast before going to school. Mothers could prepare breakfast, serve it, and clean up on a rotation basis. Would any of the men come into the center for a sturdy breakfast before they left for work? Would they carry to work with them a lunch prepared in the center? Lunch is provided by the school for the children, but many do not eat it. I would hope that the school would permit them to bring a lunch of those things they would eat so that their nutritional status might be improved. Gradual introduction of new foods would be part of the center plan. Milk in unlimited quantities would be available to all. Children not old enough to go to school could come in for food any time. Each child would be taught to check off his name for a daily vitamin capsule; small children would be given vitamin drops. The Branchers eat reasonably well on food stamps for the first couple of weeks during the month, but unwise buying and their inclination to consume all they can hold when it is available results in the same old diet of pinto beans, corn bread and gravy by the middle of the month. How much food would children eat if it could be had every day of the month? Scales and competition for the most weight gained should appeal to them. Would good food eventually become more important than soft drinks and snacks? Some families of from six to eight members spend about twenty dollars a month on cigarettes and a similar amount on colas. Since they cannot have these things and food too, the latter becomes second choice. Better nutrition for the children is vital. How to achieve it will require experimentation.

Initially the center would probably be a women's and children's world, but I am certain that the men would join them before long. Perhaps a center is the way in which to get the hollow people group-oriented.

How much pride would a man take in raising hogs for a hollow larder? Who could learn to raise chickens in pens in order to provide a sufficient number of eggs for the center and chickens to fry and roast? Who could raise rabbits, a meat they all like? Production beyond a prescribed need could be marketed, with the producer keeping the money.

Some of the hollowers could be trained to order and dispense groceries, soaps, etc., from the central supply. If some welfare money were made available to the center, wholesale buying would furnish them with more for less and might decrease expenditures on non-essential edibles.

If there were enough chores to be done in the center, would some of the Branchers develop pride in accomplishment? A community facility could be more meaningful than a welfare existence.

Would mothers cook at the center under supervision? Would they prepare food for their families if it were available? Would they bring their children to the center if there were toys and games for them? What kind of planned experiences would the children accept? How many families would eventually use the center, and would it be those who are most in need of such services?

I would devise a system of credits for families and for individuals commensurate with contributions whereby trips and certain recreational activities could be earned. This may or may not work or have appeal. Some way to purchase goods and services without money would seem to offer the assurance of greater good.

Would the mothers accept any kind of educational program, and if so, what? Many of the men enjoy playing pool. If there were facilities at the center, how many would come in to play? Are there other activities in which they might be interested? The men are expert at bartering. If they were encouraged to barter for things beneficial to all in the hollow, would they be willing to make this kind of contribution or would they do it only for personal reward? Barter might just be a way for some to contribute.

Programs aimed at children and teenagers could be arranged. Would a hollow version of 4-H and home economics interest them? They could grow roses from cuttings, sew, make dresses, equip a sewing box, prepare different dishes. How can we enrich their spare time? Youth programs, clubs, dances, singing, games, holiday parties, chartered bus trips, and picnics work in urban areas. Would any of these be attractive to hollow children? Would adults be willing to assume at least some of the responsibility for their leisure-time activities? I would employ a very flexible strategy, changing often enough to concentrate on those things which maximize children's participation.

Camping trips, a specially adapted scout troup for girls and one for boys, after-school study periods, tutoring services, day-care services—would any of these have appeal? Hopefully, there would be activities to cover every age group and a wide range of interests. We need to find out what kind of early learning experiences are suitable for their needs. I would like to duplicate functionally the one-room country schoolhouse in an attempt to find a new way to organize and administer preschool and early elementary education for them. No one seems sure where to begin in order to make school experiences meaningful enough so that they will attend regularly.

What kind of educational program would inspire the children when they enter the county school system? A Head Start program of a sort would be initiated for the three-year-olds. A follow-through program would place them in school when they start at the level of their attainment potential. They would be bathed at the center, given breakfast, participate in planned activities, have lunch, rest, and return to their homes in the late afternoon. Mothers would be given guidance in their work with the group and would take turns in supervising them. Head Start has been hailed as the new direction in early childhood education. We need to know whether these early experiences do make a difference in the development of the hollow children and in their school achievement. Language is probably their most pressing need. We know that they are deficient in key experiences. The goals of such a program would include health and nutrition.

I would take them on trips to note their reaction. Playing games and picnic lunches have thus far not been successful ventures. At the present time, "explore" means nothing to them; once they get used to the idea of new involvements, they might respond.

Transportation for those who need medical and agency services would be available. One or two men could be taught to drive and eventually qualify for chauffeur duties. I would plan and supervise utilization of community health facilities. This would permit some continuity and result in measurable impact on multiple health problems. Their present practice of shopping around for services is costly and precludes any real benefit.

I would seek ideas that really work. Any solutions, if there are any, may be the "little drops of water, little grains of sand" approach. Money alone will not do the trick. I would attempt to teach them how to spend and save their money, what and how to buy. For those willing to stop credit buying, I would pay off their debts so that they could start from scratch again.

I would seek answers to such questions as:

What would families do if they were provided with sheets and pillowcases? What would they do if they had pajamas and nightgowns?

What would happen if every household were provided with an adequate number of garbage cans? Would they really use them for disposal of all of their debris? With the center, there would be no need to use the cans as bathtubs.

I would take the 1970 census of all the hollows, either by myself or with the aid of competent, reliable assistants closely supervised, in order to get an accurate count of the population for the first time. I should like to discover all the heretofore missing persons. I would not omit those who, for one reason or another, did not want to be counted. I would develop a special form which would include all of the required information for the federal government, but also much needed data to make an accurate appraisal of life at their level of living.

Jointly with the community leaders, we would formulate an acceptable plan for my work in the hollow since anyone's effort must fit into the ongoing life of the county.

I would not become involved in party politics. I would hope that those in command could see the desirability of changes which could be supported by documented evidence. For those situations which they chose to ignore I would hope that they would be willing to share their reasons for inaction in an honest and forthright interchange.

I would work with those officials who are elected by the voters. I would not strive to remodel a way of life on a county-wide basis. I am optimistic enough to believe that one person can tackle the basic problems of the hollow within existing county government.

Many of the people in the county do avail themselves of education, use services intelligently, abide by the laws, pay taxes, secure drivers' licenses, and so forth. True, some operate in the gray areas, as in every community. But unless and until someone is willing to make an effort in just one area of deprivation, without complete social upheaval, we shall not have any answers. Neither can we place blame with any accuracy.

County administrators may well continue operating on limited money resources, this is their decision. They can scarcely expect the hollow people to report new buildings and improvements unless this is a county-wide requirement.

Impartial law enforcement with no escape, for those who fail to comply or who violate the law must be enforced for all county citizens. Those in the hollow employ less costly and sophisticated ways of avoiding compliance with the laws. Realistically the outer community should make it unprofitable for all who use fraudulent methods for individual-family benefit, otherwise expectations for the hollow will remain unchanged.

The burden of proof that they really want anything different from their present way of life rests with those who live in the hollow. It is conceivable that the current appraisal of hollow potential is more accurate than we are willing to admit.

I would hope to show that it can be profitable to take a firmer attitude toward the lazy who refuse to work. Actually, every single family in the county should be objectively re-evaluated for welfare eligibility, particularly the young who are able to work but yet refuse and those who pretend to be blind.

I am not sure that we are really committed to remedy situations like poverty. Society can choose to be a neutral onlooker or become committed deeply and sincerely. If we are really a committed society, why has it taken so long to do so little for the deprived? Maybe there is no way to manage the preposterous system which we have permitted to grow beyond any reasonable hope of economic feasibility. Social Security cash benefits for the month of February 1968 in Earle County amounted to almost $120,000 for slightly over 2,000 recipients. This was a 17 per cent increase over the payments received just one year earlier. Residents in Earle County received almost $900,000 in food stamp coupons during the fiscal year of 1968. Almost $500,000 of this amount was taxpayers' money. Families in 52 of Kentucky's 120 counties received almost $10 million in so-called free food stamp coupons and this was almost $4 million more than they received during the 1967 fiscal year. This is a lot of money for just one very small part of the total welfare program in the United States.

There appear to be two ways to work within the existing framework. Should I be unsuccessful in getting full cooperation, I would strive for at least passive acceptance on the local level. One can choose to win within the county framework or lose in an isolated hollow.

I would ask the county to develop a dump regularly supervised by appropriate personnel. It would be impossible to clean up all the debris in the hollow without some place to dump it. Some of the hollowers could be taught how to make land fill and to use the necessary equipment. Everything done under the local governmental structure would be acknowledged as such and county officials would have to run county programs. Working with them in some plan they too can accept will be the only possible way to achieve any results. This county is their responsibility and they perform to the best of their ability and resources. They are not always happy with the results, but they do try. However, it should be the aim of every welfare worker and every agency that is dispensing funds to obey the rules of the law objectively and not base its application on an individual notion of what is good for the recipient and who should receive the benefit of the programs. The abuse of constitutional and statutory rights of the recipient, which so vividly expose inequities, can be explained in no way other than personal prejudice.

I would hope that the county school system would assign a teacher and other necessary personnel to work in the hollow to determine the degree of retardation and potential basic learning abilities. Children with IQs between the 60 to 90 range are considered to be retarded. Are there two kinds of learning—academic minimums for successful school attainment and a kind necessary to participate in society?

These children do not look like the usual retardates, regardless of their IQs. At this point it seems reasonably accurate to assume that they lack basic learning ability. The theorists feel that hollow children have been disabled by their economic and cultural background. Tests are admittedly culture-bound. Maybe hollow youngsters are at a dull level, but this kind of determination is really the responsibility of the school system. They should work out the necessary remedial programs and provide them. IQ testing has its limitations for the deprived child, but then most of the teachers in the schools know this. These teachers in the hollow are the most appropriate persons to set up a system which will permit determination of the kind of educational experiences deprived children need to function in organized school experiences and eventually in the outer world. They can utilize mental tests already developed to determine basic ability and learning potential. If none seems appropriate, they can devise and validate some of their own. If there is merit in challenge for hollow people, then the teacher should experiment with motivation until she finds the most effective means. This rural hollow setting would be the teacher's living laboratory in which to reach the retrievable and help correct some of their learning problems. The teachers could decide whether the needs of the children are really being met. And if hollow children are unteachable, it is the teacher's responsibility to judge this. The hollow is a prime beachhead for the combined efforts of the doers.

The teacher in the hollow could utilize all available educational materials, and there are excellent ones for enrichment programs for all ages. Preschoolers, ages three to six, would seem to be the logical group with which to begin. Materials are designed to provide learning skills in sense perception, manual coordination, reading readiness, number concepts, rhythms and rhymes, abstract relationships, and environmental awareness. For the older children, the teacher would find out skill potential. She could identify those who can avoid becoming welfare recipients and help them chart their course for continuing education.

Hollow children, particularly the boys, would receive driver training, in order to pass the test for a driver's license. Those who did not avail themselves of this opportunity should be picked up by the law. If just a few instances were used as examples it would be helpful in determining responses and willingness to conform with rules and regulations.

Graduate students from a university could survey the land and establish ownership. Graduate students in a law college could unravel the accumulated maze of deeds to permit sale of land and determine from whom the purchases would be made. I would buy up all the land (of the roughly 126 acres, mostly vertical) and unoccupied houses available. The purchase price would be around $5,000. There would be eight houses on the land, six of which are uninhabitable and would be torn down. There is a good possibility that others would wish to sell all or at least part of what they own.

Control of the land and future building would be one means of avoiding an influx of people from other hollows who would want to be part of the new life. Interventive activities would be hard enough with the 238 people now living in the hollow without complications from hollow people who might wish to move in from other areas. The land could be put in some kind of trust to prevent resale until the experiment had been terminated. The use of the land would be determined by those helping in the effort. At the appropriate time, selected hollow people could participate in this and other decision-making policies.

Land for sale close to the hollow would be bought from a land fund set aside to secure out-of-the-hollow space for those who could move just beyond the hollow and make a go of it on their own in due time.

Ownership of the land with no houses available would prevent the constant in-and-out migration of so many families. The population in the summer almost doubles. With the first snow, the families move out to avoid the hard living during the winter. One could decrease the potential population and give some stability to the families left in the hollow. In other words, there would be a nucleus of families with which to work and find the leaders if indeed there are any among them.

Planned utilization of the land would make more available space, limited at first, for specific use. Once boundaries were legally established, all would know who owned what and the constant bickering over lines could be a least minimized.

Some kind of year-round all-weather road is a necessity. Men from the hollow could be assigned to road work—maintenance primarily. Keeping brush out and holes filled up, grading, debris collection, and disposal, plus myriad other necessary tasks, would keep a number of them busy. Getting in and out of the hollow is vital to any effort one wishes to make. If a road were available, some of the Branchers might try raising marketable produce.

The most critical problem is water. Solving the water crisis should have early priority. After determining minimum necessity per family, the next step would be to supply it. Tank trucks could be filled and distributed at strategic places to meet the needs of a group of families. One or two young men could be given the job of getting the water from the nearest source, driving the truck, and keeping the water supply at a certain level. This would provide an opportunity to see who used how much water and for what purposes.

If the availability of water improved general cleanliness and health, a water system could be provided by creating a dam at the head of the hollow. Pipe could be laid and areas in which houses were concentrated could get water from a spigot in the yard. With a little planning, the supply could be made available in the winter as well.

If purification of the water were necessary, it could be done at the source—at the dam site. The community water supply could have fluoride added to minimize dental caries.

In the beginning the availability of water seems quite sufficient.

There might come a time when some would like to have it in their houses, but this could be something for them to work toward.

I would make decent housing available in the hollow. Since "decent housing" is defined differently by everyone, I would settle for a working definition which would probably be far short of current acceptable, extremely unrealistic standards.

Housing is a problem, indeed. The present definition of "low"-cost housing for those who live in the hollow is not low. A $4,500 house for each of 55 families would be almost $250,000. I would move them out into vacant homes and get them to tear down their present dwellings, salvage all the lumber they could, and then use native rock for much of the construction. Cement floors would be cold in the winter, but they would be rodentproof. House building could involve all members of a family. The materials needed for construction should cost no more than $2,000 per home if little or no outside labor were involved. As for the elderly or those adults living alone who do not have labor to contribute, a small secondhand trailer for each would provide convenient and comfortable living arrangements.

Families moving into empty quarters on a temporary basis would go back to their homes as soon as construction was finished. This would encourage some to put in more time and effort.

Certainly in the hollow adequate housing would not comply with present standards as prescribed by the government, such as two children of the same sex per bedroom. For Layuna, who now has twenty-one in her home most of the time, eleven bedrooms would be needed. Bunk beds for no more than six children per room would give each child his own bed.

Some companies specialize in low-cost housing. They might be interested in scientific experimentation with one type of construction. One on the market is continuously extruded from a truck-mounted framing device, on the site, with minimum labor and time at extremely low cost. Using this technique, a 100-square-foot shell can be erected in six hours at a cost of $2,800. Maybe the self-help could begin by completing the interior of the shell to fit individual family needs. These houses need no foundation and the walls have built-in insulation with decorative surfaces. Duddie's Branch would be very appropriate for testing such innovations in housing. There are dozens of other kinds of prefabricated houses of every conceivable type of material.

Electricity for each house would be a must, with wiring safely installed and sufficient to avoid use for all purposes from one socket.

Homes utilizing funds from the improvement project could not be sold until the youngest child came of age. At present there is a tendency to sell their present dwelling, move into a much less desirable one, and then in time move back to the hollow into a still more dilapidated dwelling. My efforts over the years to encourage home repair and building have been complete failures. Older children might be enlisted to help but at the moment I am not the least bit enthusiastic about long lines of eager volunteers, not even for work on their own family homes. This might come in time.

Can the hollow be conceived as a halfway house for the children twelve years of age and under? Or is it the children under ten years of age? Where is the upper chronological limit for effective intervention? In the year 2000 these children will be entering the period which is considered to be the prime of life. The underlying motive of a concentrated effort in the hollow should be to increase the chances for effective and creative lives for the children. Maybe some improvement in life in the hollow would at least give the youngsters a better chance. It is the young, maybe even the yet unborn, who appear to offer the only hope of breaking the vicious cycle of deprivation.

Hollow folks value personal face-to-face relationships, especially the children. If I had as many arms as a centipede has legs, I would still not have enough to hold hands with all the children who want to walk with their hands in mine. We really do not know what kind of approach would make a difference in their lives.

Starting with a once-a-month schedule, all children properly groomed and dressed would be taken on a trip. Mothers and fathers also, if they wished to go, and they could chaperone the group. The children could choose where they wanted to spend the weekend and what they would like to see. We would read and talk about places which offered exciting possibilities. Chartered buses would transport them. If this operation proved worth while, whole summers could be planned for selected age groups.

Since the women do most of the work, I would provide some employment opportunities at first in the Branch. Their earnings would supplement the income of the family, and this is something the husbands view favorably. Would at least some of the women become first members of a Branch work force, then move on into the outer community?

Is there a tough line one can take with malingerers who prefer life on welfare to work? Can we really cut the hard-core unemployed off welfare funds? I say we can. I would require full participation in work projects for individuals or families as prerequisite to qualifying for *any* welfare benefits. This system should really be established on a county-wide basis with all loopholes removed. Any salary payment, particularly welfare, would be made only after the work had been performed and pay would be calculated on the amount actually done. Now a designated amount of money is paid monthly whether any work is done or not. I would find some kind of job for everyone who was able and then deal with those who were unwilling to work. Those who could not work, the aging and genuinely disabled, would receive essentials for maintenance.

What about men who do not really want regular jobs, even for a few days each week? Young men and fathers of families, who spend four to eight hours after dark carousing around, find it difficult to get out of bed before noon the next day. Such a pattern of living is not conducive to full employment. Would some of the men actually become employable as mechanics, for instance, if they had a building in which to work and the proper tools?

I should like to try the following work possibilities:

Get bulldozers and let young hollow men level strip mining areas. With mechanical equipment, they could plant forests for future timber development.

Have them plant the hills of the hollow with pine trees.

Form work crews to clean up the indiscriminate roadside and stream-bed dumping.

Give them an opportunity to learn how to use heavy equipment.

These, then, are proposals and questions, programs and dreams.

Henry Thoreau, in 1847, wrote: "If a man does not keep pace with his companions, perhaps it is because he hears a different drummer. Let him step to the music which he hears, however distant or far away." The music I hear may indeed grate the ears of others, but if improvements resulted and if we could identify the processes which brought the improvements about, it would be worth the din. If I should be out of step with the music, the hollow would be no worse off.

Suggestions for Further Reading

POVERTY IN THE UNITED STATES

Bagdikian, Ben H., *In the Midst of Plenty*. Boston: Beacon Press, 1964.

Fishman, Leo, ed., *Poverty Amid Affluence*. New Haven: Yale University Press, 1966.

Gans, Herbert, *The Urban Villagers*. New York: Free Press, 1962.

Harrington, Michael, *The Other America*. New York: Macmillan, 1962.

Moynihan, Daniel P., *Maximum Feasible Misunderstanding: Community Action in the War on Poverty*. New York: Free Press, 1969.

National Conference on Law and Poverty, *Conference Proceedings*. Washington, D.C., 1965.

Theobald, Robert, *The Challenge of Abundance*. New York: New American Library of World Literature, Inc., 1961.

HISTORY OF THE SOUTHERN MOUNTAINS

Arnow, Harriette, *Flowering of the Cumberland*. New York: Macmillan, 1963.

———, *Seedtime on the Cumberland*. New York: Macmillan, 1960.

Caruso, John A., *The Appalachian Frontier: America's First Surge Westward*. New York: Bobbs-Merrill Company, Inc., 1959.

Clark, Thomas D., *Kentucky: A Land of Contrast*. New York: Harper and Row, 1968.

Frome, Michael, *Strangers in High Places: The Story of the Great Smoky Mountains*. New York: Doubleday, 1966.

Moore, Arthur K., *The Frontier Mind: A Cultural Analysis of The Kentucky Frontiersman*. Lexington: University of Kentucky Press, 1957.

GENERAL WORKS ON THE APPALACHIAN REGION

Appalachian Regional Commission, *Annual Report*. Washington, D.C., yearly.

——, *Appalachia: A Report.* Washington, D.C., 1964.

Campbell, John C., *The Southern Highlander and His Homeland.* New York: Russell Sage Foundation, 1921.

Ford, Thomas, ed., *The Southern Appalachian Region: A Survey.* Lexington: University of Kentucky Press, 1962.

Kephart, Horace, *Our Southern Highlanders.* New York: Macmillan, 1926.

McKinney, John C., and Edgar T. Thompson, eds., *The South in Continuity and Change.* Durham, N.C.: Duke University Press, 1965.

Odum, Howard, *Southern Regions of the United States.* Chapel Hill: University of North Carolina Press, 1936.

Ohio University, College of Business Administration, Center for Economic Opportunity, *Appalachia: A Case Study for Regional Business Development.* Athens: Ohio University Press, 1966.

Weatherford, W. D., and Earl D. C. Brewer, *Life and Religion in Southern Appalachia.* New York: Friendship Press, 1962.

Weller, Jack, *Yesterday's People.* Lexington: University of Kentucky Press, 1965.

SPECIALIZED WORKS ON APPALACHIA

Bowman, Mary Jane, and W. Warren Haynes, *Resources and People in East Kentucky: Problems and Potentials of a Lagging Economy.* Baltimore: Johns Hopkins Press, 1963.

Caudill, Harry M., *Night Comes to the Cumberlands.* Boston: Little, Brown, 1963.

Caudill, Rebecca, *My Appalachia: A Reminiscence.* New York: Holt, Rinehart & Winston, 1966.

Fetterman, John, *Stinking Creek.* New York: E. P. Dutton and Co., Inc., 1967.

Ford, Thomas, *Health and Demography in Kentucky.* Lexington: University of Kentucky Press, 1964.

La Barre, Weston, *They Shall Take Up Serpents.* Minneapolis: University of Minnesota Press, 1962.

Matthews, Elmora Messer, *Neighbor and Kin: Life in a Tennessee Ridge Community.* Nashville: Vanderbilt University Press, 1965.

Pearsall, Marion, *Little Smoky Ridge: The Natural History of a Southern Appalachian Neighborhood.* University of Alabama Press, 1959.

Reed, Louis, *Warning in Appalachia: A Study of Wirt County West Virginia.* Morgantown: West Virginia University Library, 1967.

Sherman, Mandel, and Thomas K. Henry, *Hollow Folk.* New York: Crowell, 1933.

Stephenson, John, *Shiloh: A Mountain Community*. Lexington: University of Kentucky Press, 1968.

MOUNTAIN LIFE AND CUSTOMS

One of the best sources of information about mountain life and customs is the vast body of literature written by and about people living in the Appalachian region. Authors such as Jesse Stuart, John Fox, Wilma Dykeman, and Harriette Arnow have captured the unique flavor of life in the Southern mountains in their works. A comprehensive survey of such literature can be found in:

Boyer, Louise C., *The Southern Mountaineer in Literature*. Morgantown: West Virginia University Library, 1963.
Munn, Robert F., *The Southern Appalachians: A Bibliography and Guide to Studies*. Morgantown: West Virginia University Library, 1961.

PERIODICALS

There are two magazines which deal with various aspects of life in the Appalachian states. These are:

Appalachian Review. Published quarterly by West Virginia University, 307 Armstrong Hall, Morgantown, West Virginia 26506. Each issue contains a bibliography of new material on the area.
Mountain Life and Work. Published monthly by the Council of the Southern Mountains, Inc., College Box 2307, Berea, Kentucky, 40403.

K

LANE PUBLIC LIBRARY

HAMILTON, OHIO

Books may be kept for four weeks. Pamphlets and other materials may be borrowed for two weeks. A charge is made for library materials kept overtime.

BRANCHES:

Lindenwald—2531 Pleasant Ave.
Community Center—1140 S. Front St.
Fairfield—Pleasant Ave. & Wessel Dr.
Oxford—E. Park Place

HOURS: MON.-FRI. 9 to 9-SAT. 9 to 5:00

Telephone 894-7157 and 58